Hi, Johnbug.

Christmas '74

Discriminations

Dwight Macdonald

DISCRIMINATIONS
Essays & Afterthoughts
1938-1974

GROSSMAN PUBLISHERS
A Division of The Viking Press / New York   1974

ACKNOWLEDGMENTS

Bantam Books, Inc.: From *The Tales of Hoffman*, edited from the official transcript by Mark L. Levine, George C. McNamee, and Daniel Greenberg. Copyright © 1970 by Bantam Books, Inc. All rights reserved.

Chicago Sun-Times: "Incomplete Nonsense: The McLuhan Message," June 7, 1964 *Chicago Sun-Times Book World* review. Reprinted with permission from the *Chicago Sun-Times*.

The Columbia Forum: Letters from the winter 1972 *Forum*, Vol. II, No. 1, reprinted by permission from *The Columbia Forum*.

New York Review of Books: Letters from Ivan Morris, July 18 and August 27, 1968, Copyright © 1968 by Nyrev, Inc.; letter from Arthur Schlesinger, Issue #2, 1963, Copyright © 1963 by Nyrev, Inc. Reprinted by permission.

The New York Times: "Luce and His Empire," October 1, 1972. Copyright © 1972 by The New York Times Co. Reprinted by permission.

The Observer: "Deponent Sayeth Not," June 2, 1957.

Washington Star Syndicate, Inc.: William F. Buckley's column of December 5, 1967

These essays originally appeared, in somewhat different form, in *The Antioch Review, Chicago Sun Times, Columbia Forum, Commentary, Dissent, Encounter, Esquire, The New Yorker, The New York Review of Books* and *Partisan Review*.

For dearest Gloria

Foreword

I.

Some of the pieces reprinted here are rather elderly ("Kronstadt Revisited" is a ripe thirty-six) like their author, but most are in their teens or younger—a couple are still in diapers—having been born after my two earlier collections, *Memoirs of a Revolutionist* (1957, reissued in 1970 as *Politics Past*) and *Against the American Grain: Essays on the Effects of Mass Culture* (1962).

I have added footnotes and afterwords whenever later events struck me as worth comment for reasons of history, my own included.

II.

The selection is my own, but I am grateful to Carol Weiland and Dick Grossman of The Viking Press for their discriminatory suggestions as to omissions. For the truth is I'm no judge of my own stuff. I tend to admire (almost) everything once the embryonic typescript—swollen by inserts, crippled with deletions, pocked with revisions—somehow gets reborn into clean, orderly print. Then it looks to my paternal eye as inevitable and comely as a newborn baby must appear to a mother after her messy travail. I remember the long struggle to work the amorphous, recalcitrant material into coherence—all those rewritings and rethinkings, those myriad stylistic decisions, as individually trivial as they are collectively important—and it seems a miracle the result makes any sense at all.* A struggle, by the way, that becomes no easier with age and experience. On the contrary, I was much surer at thirty what I wanted to say and how to say it than I am now, pushing seventy. About all I've learned is that Paul Goodman was right when he objected "Dwight thinks with his typewriter," and that my *riposte* was also right: granted, but every writer's thought has to start somewhere and that's where mine does. It's in the actual process of composition that I discover, gradually, by trial and error, hit or miss, what I really think about the subject. Embarrassing but there it is—and it doesn't make writing, or thinking, any easier, either.

III.

The title, *Discriminations*—for which I'm grateful to Thelma Henner —perhaps needs a little justification. The word has been reduced, in modern usage, to a synonym for social injustice: "2. To make a difference in treatment or favor (of one as compared with others); as to *discriminate* . . . against a special class" (*Webster's New International*, unabridged, second ed., 1934). But its primary meaning, historically, is not pejorative. On the contrary, it describes just what I've always tried to do as a critic. Thus Webster's Second (the reliable one):

> DISCRIMINATE (L. *discriminare*, to divide, separate, fr. *discrimmen*, division, distinction, decision) . . . *v. Intransitive*: 1. to . . . distinguish accurately; as to *discriminate* between fact and fancy [my life work].
> DISCRIMINATION, n. (LL. *discriminatio*, the contrasting of opposite thoughts). . . . 3. The faculty of nicely distinguishing; acute discernment. . . . 5. The perception of a difference [Ah!]

---

* The analogy with child-birth breaks down here. For the natural processes the mother has merely to cooperate with to produce her baby, the writer or artist must substitute mind and will. With chancier results: most babies do get finally born as recognizable babies, but most literary or artistic works, even modest journalistic articles like the ones here, notoriously don't. Abortions and stillbirths are the statistical norm in this sort of creation. And the effort takes a lot more out of us than it does out of those mothers.

A lexicographical summary of my career. Nor does the Oxford English Dictionary fail to strike some equally sympathetic chords:

> DISCRIMINATE. . . . 2. To distinguish with the mind or intellect; to perceive, observe or note the difference in between . . . . 1677 BARROW *Wks.* I, xx, 283 We take upon us . . . to discriminate the goats from the sheep. 1836 J. GILBERT, *Chr. Atonem* v. (1852) 139 . . . that we discriminate a mean from a noble transaction.
>
> DISCRIMINATION 1. . . . making a distinction or difference between things . . . with the mind or in action. . . . 1889 *Spectator* 9 Nov. Life is a constant series of discriminations between what it is well to attempt and what it is not well to attempt. [How true! Just what I kept telling LBJ—see Part 4 below.] . . . 3. The power of observing differences accurately, or of making exact distinctions. . . . 1866 GEO. ELIOT *F. Holt* II, xvi, 15 It was essential . . . that his waistcoat should imply much discrimination.

And finally: "DISCRIMINOUS, *a. obs. rare.* . . . Critical, hazardous." Two *a.*'s that sum up what I hope are the main qualities of this collection.

Contents

xi

3 / Politicking

4 / A Political Chronicle

1

COSA NOSTRA

Stop-Press Foreword

Revisiting de Tocqueville's *Democracy in America,* the *I Ching* cum Madame Sostoris prophetic book of our time, for professional reasons last week, I ran across a passage that I can't resist shoehorning in as a premature footnote to my Amendments XXVI and XXVII:

> On entering the House of Representatives at Washington, one is struck by the vulgar demeanor of that great assembly. Often there is not a distinguished man in the whole number. Its members are almost all obscure individuals whose names bring no associations to mind. . . .
>
> At a few yards distance is the door of the Senate, which contains within a small space a large proportion of the celebrated men of America. . . .
>
> How comes this strange contrast and why are the ablest citizens found in one assembly rather than the other? Why is the former body remarkable for its vulgar elements, while the latter seems to enjoy a monopoly of intelligence and talent? . . . The only reason which appears to me adequately to account for it is that the House of Representatives is elected by the people directly, while the Senate is elected by elected bodies. . . . The Senators are elected by an indirect application of the popular vote. . . . This transmission of the popular authority through an assembly of [popularly] chosen men makes an important change [in the Senate] by refining its discretion and improving its choice. Men who are chosen in this manner accurately represent the majority of the nation which governs them. . . .
>
> The time must come when the American republics will be obliged more frequently to introduce the plan of election by an elected body into their system of representation or run the risk of perishing miserably among the shoals of democracy.
> —Alexis de Tocqueville, *Democracy in America,*
> Vol. I, chap. 13

Updating the Constitution: Ten Modest Amendments

The editors of *Esquire* have asked me to bring the Constitution up to date. One attraction of the subject for the political journalist is that it probably won't "date" before publication—the Constitution will still be around when this appears, I assume.* Weightier ones are that I have long admired it as a political document—and have longer thought it could be, for present uses, improved.

Wise in its compromises, sagacious in its vagueness, far-seeing in its resistance to the abstract and the doctrinaire, our Constitution is one of the most impressive intellectual productions of that great age of American politics in which a few provincial colonies gave the lead to the world, first in revolutionary action and then in the working out of that action in democratic—or, as it was then confusingly called, republican—theory.

---

* (1973) It's still around but more by luck and pluck than by good management. The Milhouse Demolition Corp. had made considerable progress on the Constitution, as we've been learning daily, until an *ad hoc* Preservation Committee began to crystallize around such disparate nodes as a conscientious night watchman, two persistent city reporters (and their editors on the *Washington Post* who printed their "unfounded"—i.e., anonymously attributed—findings), a feisty Senate committee, a tough federal judge, a repentant burglar, and two Harvard Law School *cum* Boston Brahmin types.

The Constitution was worked out in four months during the summer of 1787 by a convention, in Philadelphia, of fifty-five delegates from twelve of the thirteen colonies. (Rhode Island refused to participate.) George Washington was chairman and the delegates included Madison, Hamilton, Franklin, Edmund Randolph of Virginia, Roger Sherman and Oliver Ellsworth of Connecticut, and two unrelated Morrises—Robert and Gouverneur—from Pennsylvania. The immediate problem was how to make one nation out of thirteen hitherto-autonomous states without undue subordination of the smaller to the larger. The Articles of Confederation had avoided the issue by giving a minority of states veto power, the result being that Congress, in theory empowered to raise money, conduct foreign affairs, and mediate disputes between the states, in practice lacked authority to such an extent that civil war was a possibility and presenting a common defense against the Indians was a problem.

The solution to the big-state-versus-small-state conflict—typical of others devised by the prudent, cautious, reasonable Founding Fathers—was Mr. Sherman's "Connecticut Compromise" (they were always compromising): a Senate to which each state elects two representatives—this is the only provision not subject to amendment—and a House in which the states are represented in proportion to their populations. The more general problem of a central government which would be strong but not too strong was solved by the "checks and balances" system, which distributed authority among three branches—executive, legislative, and judicial—each independent of the other two in some ways and subject to interference by the other two in other ways.

Their aim was to establish a republic which would be difficult to subvert in either a democratic or an aristocratic direction, to prevent a popular majority voting a Caesar into dictatorship or an elite minority installing a king. The Federalist papers Hamilton, Madison, and Jay wrote to persuade the states to adopt the Constitution—another impressive product of that golden age of our political thinking—devoted some space to reassuring the plebs that a monarchy was not to be feared. On the other side there was the "Bill of Rights" drawn up by Madison and Jefferson and others of the democratic faction: i.e., the first ten amendments, which were really part of the Constitution since they were shortly incorporated *en bloc* and were offered as an inducement to ratification by New York and other reluctant states.*

A remarkable achievement, all in all. De Tocqueville thought that our supreme historical moment was not fighting the Revolution but drafting the Constitution:

> If America ever approached (for however brief a time) that lofty pinnacle of glory to which the proud imagination of its inhabitants is wont to point, it was at this solemn moment, when national power abdicated, as it were, its authority. All ages have furnished the spectacle of a people struggling with energy to win its independence; and the efforts of the Americans in throwing off the English yoke have been considerably exaggerated. Separated from their enemies by three thousand miles of ocean and backed by a powerful ally [i.e., France], the United States owed their victory much more to their geographical position than to the valor of their armies or the patriotism of their citizens. It would be ridiculous to compare the American war to the wars of the French Revolution, or the efforts of the Americans to those of the French when France, attacked by the whole of Europe, without money, without credit, without allies, threw forward a twentieth part of her population to meet her enemies. . . . But it is new in the history of society to see a great people turn a calm and scrutinizing eye upon itself when apprized by the legislature that the wheels of its government are stopped, to see it carefully examine the extent of the evil, and patiently wait two whole years until a remedy is discovered, to which it voluntarily submitted without its costing a tear or a drop of blood from mankind.† . . .

---

* In our democratic century, the Bill of Rights has served mostly as a deterrent to majorities who would deny to unpopular minorities their rights as citizens; demagogic populism rather than oligarchy has become the chief threat to civil liberties. It is ironic that the first ten amendments, originally designed to protect the many against the tyranny of the few, now serve the opposite purpose. It is also an instance of the even-handed temper of the Constitution and its consequent adaptability to new purposes.

† (1973) A sour bicentennial note. "The United States owed their victory more to their geographical position than to . . . valor . . . or patriotism" indeed! But the Count, as usual, had a point. Maybe we should celebrate not the Revolution of 1776 but the Constitution of 1787. That would also give us an eleven-year breathing space in which to recover our democratic composure.

The assembly which accepted the task of composing the second Constitution was small; but George Washington was its President, and it contained the finest minds and noblest characters that had ever appeared in the New World.

The document whose genesis is thus celebrated by de Tocqueville—enthusiasm was not one of his foibles—has survived: we now possess the world's oldest written constitution. It has endured partly because of the soundness of its architecture: the tripartite division of power, the balancing act between autocracy and democracy. More important was the fact that the Founding Fathers left many blank spaces to be filled in by the future. Their silence may be assumed to have been from prudence rather than from lack of ideas, of which they had plenty.*

In the following ten amendments, I have tried to keep within the bounds of what is possible in some foreseeable future. While all my amendments are, I think, practical—given a few years for ripening— some are more practical than others, as for example, XXVII (extending the term of representatives to four years), XXVIII (putting the armed forces on a volunteer basis),† XXIX (giving every American a guaranteed minimum income), and XXIV (postponing our Space program until our Earth program gets going). But some may take a little time, as the first (abolishing the presidency) and the last (abolishing the states). They're all modest and reasonable enough, however, once you begin to think big—i.e. on the scale of our problems today.‡

---

* (1973) Historically prudent though the Founding Fathers were, some of their blank spaces have proved a little *too* blank, as in the matter of the President's war powers in the last two administrations. And in the current one, the President's legal mouthpieces have made great play with "executive privilege," a blank they tried to convert into a loophole. One concludes that the Rules of the Game were more generally agreed on, within the Establishment (which then meant between gentlemen), in 1787 than they are in 1973.
† (1973) This has now been achieved by simple Act of Congress—as many, perhaps most, of my amendments could be. I cast my proposals in the form of amendments because my journalistic assignment was to update the Constitution—and because Constitutional legalese was more fun to parody.
‡ (1973) The scale has not diminished.

Amendment XXVI: Section (1) The office of President of the United States of America shall be Abolished and the Functions of the President described in Article II shall be assumed by a Chief Executive who shall be known as the Chairman.

Section (2) The Chairman shall be elected by a caucus of the Members of Congress belonging to that Party which shall have at the Time more Members in Congress than any other Party. Each Senator in this Caucus shall have three votes and each Representative one.

Section (3) The Chairman shall hold office until his Party loses a Major Vote in Congress; by "Major" is meant a Vote for which at least three days' advance Notice is given by a caucus of either of the two most numerous Parties. After such a Defeat, the Chairman shall resign and national elections for both Houses of Congress shall be held.

Section (4) The office of Vice-President of the United States of America is forever, eternally, and for all time abolished.

The proposal is that we shift from our peculiar system, in which the chief executive is elected by popular vote and holds office for four years, to the parliamentary system commonly used in other Western democracies, in which the legislative representatives are elected by popular vote and then select their own executive leader who holds office as long as his party commands a majority in the assembly or parliament. The advantages of this proposal are that it responds more flexibly to changes in public opinion and that it reduces the prestige our president now commands because he is directly elected by the whole country. It also limits his power by integrating the executive more closely with the legislative branch. This integration is carried far in Britain where the prime minister and his cabinet members sit in the House of Commons and can be questioned, argued with, and chivvied about by the members.

The dominance that the president has come to assume in this century is understandable: a complex mass-industrial society can be more easily (though not necessarily better) run if power is concentrated at the top. Five hundred and thirty-five members of Congress are an unwieldy, inefficient instrument of control compared to one president and a dozen cabinet members he has chosen to work with, and under, him. So the executive branch has gained initiative and vigor at the expense of the legislative. This has had its advantages, of course, notably Roosevelt's New Deal reforms, which originated in the White House with its "brain trust." But, as scarcely needs to be labored after President Johnson's military exploits in the Dominican Republic and Vietnam, initiated without benefit of congressional debate or approval, it can have serious disadvantages.*

The inflexibility of the presidential system is perhaps even more dangerous today than the concentration of power. Senator McCarthy's victory in the New Hampshire primary showed that the President, his methods, and his policies had become far more unpopular than any of the existing indicators of political feeling had shown. So unpopular that the late Senator Kennedy was emboldened to become a candidate for the Democratic nomination and, a few weeks later, the President himself announced he was "stopping the bombing" of North Vietnam and also that he was not going to run for reelection. An underground of opposition to the war, and to the President who had escalated it for three years, was suddenly revealed after New Hampshire. It now appears that this underground sentiment may have included a majority of the American people. When one man concentrates in his person the power and the charisma of the president of the United States, it takes too long for popular discontent to make itself felt. De Gaulle is the only Western head of state comparable in this respect to our president, and he has lately had his New Hampshire, one that came close to revolution.†

And suppose Senator McCarthy had not made his lonely decision in the fall of 1967 to challenge his party leader for the nomination?‡ And suppose President Johnson had not had the impulse to take out of his pocket the sensational coda to his March 31 speech —so literally a last-minute decision that it wasn't in the text given in advance to the press? The fate of the Republic shouldn't depend on such accidents of individual psychology. There should be some

---

* (1973) As to the present incumbent, on this point, words don't fail me but space does.

† (1973) I.e., the student strikes and riots of 1968 which almost toppled him—and would have if the trade unions had joined in.

‡ He was publicly supported, before New Hampshire, by no important Democratic political boss, by no Democratic governor or mayor, by none of his fellow Democratic senators, and by just four Democratic congressmen, Brown and Edwards of California, Reuss of Wisconsin, and Ryan of New York.

way of public opinion expressing itself continually on an administration's policies, and not only in a quadrennial convulsion. Our politics should move to a more organic rhythm, our history shouldn't be chopped up like salami, in arbitrarily equal chronological pieces. Dissident members of Congress should be encouraged to press their opposition by the prospect of an appeal to the electorate at any time. They should also have, as in Britain, the chance of public, personal debate with the executive branch and on terms of more equality than at present—one recalls the years it took for Senator Fulbright to get Secretary Rusk to submit to questioning by the Senate Foreign Relations Committee.*

At certain historical moments, four years is a long time. We should be able to free ourselves from the death grip of some presidential Old-Man-of-the-Sea without waiting for him or his term of office to expire. Our present president is a sobering example.† There is also the not-so-distant presidency of Herbert Hoover, who was conked by the 1929 stock-market crash a few months after he took office as the businessman's businessman and who never fully recovered consciousness for the remaining three and a half years of his term, reeling from disaster to disaster as the Great Depression ran its course despite every standard remedy in the Republican pharmacopoeia—or perhaps because of them. It was the best butter, but it didn't suit the works. The Mad Hatter could have told him. Unfortunately, Hoover took the advice of such *luftmenschen* as Ogden Mills, Andrew Mellon, and the National Association of Manufacturers. So by the time he was removed from the White House by automatic

---

* (1973) Or cf. the later inability of Senator Fulbright's committee to pry loose the Pentagon Papers from the Nixon administration until Daniel Ellsberg disobeyed the letter of bureaucratic regulations and obeyed the spirit of the Constitution. Also the frustrations experienced by Senator Ervin's committee and Professor Cox's "task force" in the Justice Department when they uncovered evidence of criminal acts and tried to get a look at White House records to settle this horrid possibility one way or the other.

† (1973) His successor is enough to make one take the pledge for life. Had some Cassandra croaked in 1968 that I'd look back not in anger but in nostalgia at LBJ, I'd have been as contemptuously incredulous as had I been told, in the fifties, the day would come when I'd like Ike. Relatively, you understand: Ike's great virtue in foreign affairs was that for eight years, like Kutuzov in *War and Peace*, he didn't do anything.

chronology—the 1932 election was just a formality—our rate of unemployment was almost the highest in the world, just below the German rate which gave Hitler his chance. The banks were closing like sea anemones; and a Democratic empiricist had to improvise the saving of American capitalism with unsound measures dreamed up by academic types who had never met a payroll. Can even so rich a nation afford that kind of theater? Vietnam may be the last indulgence granted us in presidential dramatics.* A parliamentary system might not have worked either, but the legislature, and the populace, would not have masochistically endured almost four years of Mr. Hoover without it occurring to some of them that something could be done about it before 1932.

There are other advantages to Amendment XXVI:

The electoral college would be eliminated. This strange device made sense when it was put into the Constitution because the electors then really elected the president, no nonsense about a popular vote. But for a century and a half it has been as useful an organ of the body politic as the vermiform appendix, and sometimes as dangerous. Choosing the chief executive by popular vote is unwise, but choosing him by finagling in the electoral college is silly—all

---

* (1974) I underestimated the patience of the deity. His mills may grind exceedingly fine but they're sure slow. . . . We've just reeled through the first year of Nixon's presidency ("toughing it out," you might say) and today's (January 4, 1974) *Times* reports the results of a special "in depth" Roper poll on how the citizenry now feel about the President they chose last year in the biggest electoral landslide in our history. Four out of five (79 percent) "believe one or more of the most serious charges against the President are justified." A bare, indeed nude, majority (45 percent *vs.* 44 percent) are against impeaching him but for their sake ("fear of the destructive effect an impeachment would have") rather than his: only 11 percent of those against impeachment "believed the charges against him unjustified." A Gallup poll at the same time shows that, asked "Do you approve or disapprove of the way Nixon is handling his Presidency?," 29 percent approved and 60 percent disapproved (11 percent actually had "no opinion"). Better than the 27 percent pro, 63 percent contra early last November—the Nixon White House is Cold Comfort Farm—but still a sickening chute-the-chutes decline in one year (how have the petty fallen!) from the 68 percent pro that Nixon racked up last January after his front-man, Kissinger, returned from the Vietnam negotiations with a "peace in our time" as solid as the one Neville Chamberlain brought back from Munich. Apologies to the Nobel Committee and sorry about that. But, after all, *I* didn't give him the 1973 peace prize.

the disadvantages of both systems. And there is the current possibility that if Wallace gets enough electoral votes to prevent either major party from getting a majority in the electoral college, the election will be thrown into the House of Representatives, also as per Constitution, with a possibility of a low demagogue like Wallace playing a major part in the selection of our next president.*

The vice-presidency would also be eliminated. Inventing this office was one of the few big *gaffes* of the Founding Fathers. It is an insoluble contradiction. The vice-president—or "veep" as he is nicknamed; it's significant that the president is never called "prexy"—has no Constitutional function except presiding over the Senate; whatever else he does, or doesn't, is up to the president. Not a job to attract men of ability or ambition: four years of monkish renunciation of worldly political pleasures. As Tom Marshall, Wilson's monk, put it: "The Vice-President is like a man in a state of catalepsy: he can see and hear everything that's going on around him but he cannot speak or act." But this official nonentity becomes the president when and if the real president dies. The gamble is too extreme: *either* four years of political oblivion *or* supreme power. Like that terrible choice in fairy stories: the princess or death. Most who have accepted a veepship have been modest types, like Marshall, who asked only for his country a good five-cent cigar: par for the course. Granted that some who have had greatness thrust upon them haven't done badly: Chester A. Arthur, the first Roosevelt, and Truman come to mind. But some have not—the first Johnson and Coolidge—and in any case there's no need for such an Arabian Nights rags-to-riches atmosphere. The second Johnson is a special case: a man of ability and ambition, who reluctantly accepted the offer from Kennedy and who went into a severe, almost catatonic, depression when he discovered the powerlessness of veepship, and who then recovered his native energies, too much so in fact, when Dallas gave him the prize. He might have won the presidency on his own in 1964 without benefit of the impetus from succeeding the elected president, but he also might not. As for the current veep, the demoralizing effects of the

---

* (1973) He only got 13.5 percent of the vote in 1968 and so was defanged in the electoral college—it's really a kindergarten—and a kooky bullet saved us from a possibly kooky electoral-college mess in 1972.

office, with potential power always in view but actual power always denied and with the added pressure of a master who is adept at corrupting good men with the baits of power,* have made Hubert Horatio Humphrey into something very different from his former liberal-humanitarian persona.†

The presidential primaries and the national conventions would also be eliminated. Every four years on the dot the Republic is convulsed with labor pains and brings forth a president who is usually no more distinguished than millions of his fellow citizens but who is invested with an automatic charisma because he is the people's choice. An odd effect of mass psychology: a deity revered because his worshipers have created Him. A great waste of time, energy, and money: all those endless columns of newsprint, those interviews and newscasts and opinions by highly paid experts on TV and radio, plus the enormous expense for the candidates of buying time on the networks and advertising space in the newspapers, and all to "sell" one or the other presidential "personality." The parliamentary system is better because voting for geographically limited representatives means a closer connection between the special, individual interests of the voters and the candidates they elect: voting on issues rather than personalities. Nobody can be president of two hundred million people.

Because he is elected by everybody, the president has too much prestige and therefore too much freedom of action. When President

---

* (1973) His successor has made a profession out of what with LBJ was just a hobby.

† (1971) Up to last year's congressional elections, Agnew appeared to be an exception to the monkish impotence of veepship because of the novel way his president used him for ultraright forays he was too sly to venture himself: a cachinnating caterwauling cat's-paw clawing conservative chestnuts—sorry, cabobs—from the conflagration. The 1970 elections showed, however, that Agnew wowed only the already wowed and unwowed the rest of the voters so effectively that the candidates he helped might have done better without his aid. (Thus Wisconsin, despite, or because of, Agnew's efforts—plus three barnstorming trips by his master—went more heavily Democratic than it had in years.) Agnew has been under wraps of late though his tricky controller may still use him in 1972 as a misguided missile. . . . (1973) He didn't. Maybe Nixon smelled the rat—it takes one to smell one—that has now emerged with Agnew's resignation after being indicted on charges of bribery, extortion, etc. In short, our veep was on the take. Another first for the Guiness Record Book from the presidency of Richard the Ready.

Johnson conferred with Premier Kosygin in Glassboro, N.J., I'm told, he proposed they make a "deal," man to man. The Soviet Premier was taken aback: "But I can't, Mr. President, I'll have to consult the Politburo." With the possible exceptions of Mao and Castro, the American president has more individual power than the head of any other major government today. Like other potentates, our presidents develop a caste feeling: the two surviving ex-presidents, Truman and Eisenhower, have both gone all out for their colleague's Vietnam war, despite considerable differences in political style when they were in office. "The club with only three members," Hugh Sidey called it in the May 17, 1968, *Life*. "While club members have unanimous scorn for unwashed dissenters and draft-card burners . . . they almost never have a harsh word for other Presidents. . . . Lyndon Johnson, for instance, has become a defender of Herbert Hoover. 'Hoover didn't want people to starve,' L.B.J. protested the other day. 'He tried to do the best he could.' If the President's club had a slogan, that would be it." I'm reminded of the sympathy Stalin showed for his fellow club member Ivan the Terrible.*

The undemocratic prestige of our presidents has its reverse side, for them, in the style of Greek tragedy, *hubris* bringing on the retribution of the Furies. If our chief executive were not one man representing everybody, he would not be so tempting a target for assassination. His very eminence attracts the hatred and envy of underdog crackpots like Booth, Guiteau, Czolgosz, and Oswald—also cf. the unsuccessful attempts on the lives of the two Roosevelts and Truman. In the last century not one British prime minister has been assassinated. Four American presidents have. And now there is the murder of Robert Kennedy, which extends the peril to candidates for the presidency. "Maybe we should do it a different way," Senator

---

* (1973) Cf. Nixon's clubbily prolonging Johnson's war from 1968 to 1972 for no discernible advantage to the American people, and much discernible disadvantage to the Vietnamese people. Also his clubman's fury when Ellsberg leaked the Pentagon Papers. A cool, unclubbed head might have thought they were to his political advantage since the beans they spilled were from the Democratic, not the Republican pot. But our virtuously masochistic leader never does "the easy thing." Also that old-school presidential tie is above politics. So burglary and attempted corruption of a federal judge were clearly indicated as the hard, lonely path of rectitude in dealing with an uppitty outsider like Ellsberg.

McCarthy reflected after this most ghastly and, in terms of American politics, irrelevant of our political assassinations. "Maybe we should have the English system of having the Cabinet choose the President. There must be some other way."*

Amendment XXVII: The House of Representatives shall be composed of Members chosen every Fourth Year by the People of the several States.

Congressmen now have a two-year term, which hardly gives a new member time to find the men's room† before he has to begin campaigning for the next election. This is not enough time for new members to learn their business, and it distracts all members from their legislative duties. It also makes them oversensitive to their constituents. Democracy can be too direct. The kind of representative government outlined in the Constitution—which is accepted here, otherwise no point proposing amendments—requires a nice balance between the individual judgment (and conscience) of the representative and the wishes of those he represents. Their wishes must, of course, guide him in general and in the long run, but he should be able to resist them, if he has his own ideas, long enough to reflect and, if he thinks it necessary, try to persuade his constituents to reflect also. Sometimes the pressures come from informed minorities with special interests that may conflict with the public interest—the "gun lobby" of the United Rifle Association is a current example—sometimes they are the uninformed expressions of mass moods and prejudices, as in matters having to do with unpopular minorities. A two-year term doesn't give a congressman much of a base for asserting independent judgment. That senators are elected for six years may be one reason the Senate has reacted to the problems of our time more intelligently than the House, which has produced such grotesqueries as the ancient, but not venerable, House Committee on Un-American Activities. The level of the House was

---

* (1973) Long before the Senator, my wife suggested this at a little conspiratorial meeting in our apartment (we're in the Manhattan phone book) to plot, unsuccessfully, the impeachment of President Johnson. "Who *needs* a White House?" Gloria cried. "Why can't we just have a prime minister? There's something wrong with our system." We ruled her out of order.

† (1973) Or women's.

demonstrated by last summer's [1968] jocosities about the poor during the debate about appropriating a few millions for a modest, and inadequate, rat-control program in the urban ghettos. (It was defeated.)* Doubling the term to four years would be a first step toward raising the House to the not impossible level of the Senate. President Johnson has recommended it but I still think it is a good idea.†

---

* (1973) The vote was 207 to 176. The proposal was to appropriate $40 million for the "Rat Extermination Act of 1967" to be administered by the Housing and Urban Development (HUD) department. There was much hilarity or, as the Congressional Record puts it, "(Laughter)" during the "(Debate)." "The gentleman spoke of city rats. What of country rats?" (Rep. Gross, R., Iowa) "Mr. Speaker, I wonder if some of our distinguished committees that bring before us a monstrosity such as this would take into consideration the fact that we have a lot of cat-lovers in the nation. Why not just buy some cats and turn them loose on the rats?" (Rep. Haley, D., Fla.) Rep. Broyhill (R., Va.) warned about "a bunch of new bureaucrats on rats" and "a great demand for rat patronage" and concluded punningly amid (Laughter): "I think the rat smart thing for us to do now is to vote down this rat bill rat now." "The bill discriminates against persons suffering from bites from other animals," cautioned Rep. Latta (R., O.) adding a plea for sufferers from snake-bites. Rep. Bray (R., Ind.) bravely met the issue: "We who vote against this bill are well aware that we will be accused of being for rats and against people. [The idea did cross my mind.—D.M.] However, we are willing to face that baseless charge in order to keep our government from being financially ruined." ($40 million looks rat big sometimes.) The (Laughter) must have been Homeric when he perorated: "Perhaps HUD turned against those rats when they started biting rioters. If they had bitten policemen, nothing would have happened." This (Debate) in the House was just after the Newark riot and just before the more extensive one in Detroit. Perhaps because the latter penetrated even the congressional hide, perhaps because public reaction was unfavorable, two months later the House reversed itself and did vote the money despite Rep. Jones' (D., Mo.) warning against "pouring money down a rat-hole." . . . That same summer, the House Judiciary Committee reported out a bill, in mindless-symbolic reaction to certain youthful hotheads' mindless-symbolic burning of American flags (it's just a colored piece of cloth, fellas), that provided a year in jail or $10,000 fine or both for such m.-s. desecration. It was passed by the House, 385 to 16, after five hours of superheated oratory in which the Hon. L. Mendel Rivers (D., S.C.) sounded the bugle-cry: "Let's deal with these buzzards!" The Hon. James Haley (D., Fla.) again distinguished himself: "Load a boat full of them, take them five hundred miles out into the ocean, handcuff them, chain the anchor around their necks and throw them overboard." Even the House thought that might be Unconstitutional.

† (1973) Eisenhower and Kennedy also favored it. So does our present, or pro tem., president. He's only human—you can't be wrong all the time.

Amendment XXVIII: Every male Citizen between the ages' of eighteen and thirty shall be Conscripted, except for present exempt categories and any others that Congress may wish to establish, for a Period not to exceed two years of Service either in the Armed Forces or in nonmilitary Work of Social Value. Each Draftee shall be allowed to choose whichever alternative suits his Conscience, or his Fancy. This shall apply at all times, during War and during Peace; also during "War" and during "Peace."

Hardly need to labor the civic principle: wrong for a nation to force citizens to violate their consciences by taking part in a war they feel is immoral and have some reason to believe is also illegal—cf. the Spock trial for current arguments and the Nuremberg trials for general principles. The practical objection to giving draftees such a choice is, of course, that not enough would now choose military service to provide the manpower needed for victory in Vietnam. This is the kind of risk Constitution amenders must take, and take it I must. But there is a way out, a little sordid, but respectably bourgeois: raise military pay enough to compete with the going wages offered in civilian life for the same skills. (That special attraction of government jobs—retirement on pension after not too long a period—should be taken into account: don't let's overpay our boys, business is business.) The reenlistment rate of blacks, now more than twice that of whites, is significant even allowing for the fact that the army has become the most successfully integrated American institution—compare, for example, the percentage of black sergeants with that of black foremen. (What this reveals about our society is a non-Constitutional matter.) Americans will volunteer for any job if the pay is right. Where do all those policemen come from, after all?

What my amendment proposes is a free market in jobs, Manchester Liberalism. Not very elevated: one knows the economic status of the young men who will be attracted into the army by increased pay, and that of those who won't be. But it will be superior, practically and ethically, to our present arrangements: the velvet

---

* *(1973)* This amendment is now moot since the draft has been abolished—or, more accurately, suspended—by an Act of Congress unvetoed by Nixon. I've left it in because the argumentation—or, if you like, speculations—may come in handy in some later, unsuspended period.

caress of personal gain is preferable to the iron fist of State compulsion, the system of Adam Smith is more benign than that of General Hershey—or Chairman Mao. And as a Constitution amender, one must be content with the lesser evil.*

Two other objections are: (1) that it will cost so much that the size of our armed forces will have to be reduced; (2) that it will create a professional army, and that this may bring into being, for the first time in our history, a military caste which may intervene in American political life with the same disastrous results as in the cases of France and Germany between the Franco-Prussian War and World War II.

To (1) I would say that a reduction in our military establishment is the price you have to pay for progress—and that I'm glad to pay it.

As for (2), one of the positive features of our inchoate, irreverent, and generally mixed-up national character is that Americans aren't disciplined enough to take military leaders seriously in politics. We've had lots of presidents who were generals, from Jackson through Grant—even Garfield was a general—to Eisenhower. But once in office they didn't act like generals. (Teddy Roosevelt, the only one who did, never got beyond colonel.) Americans find something intrinsically comic about a general when he tries to impose his martial style on real, that is civilian, life. They are awe-inspiring, like the late General MacArthur, or the biologically still extant General Westmoreland. But also faintly absurd. When the ultra-civilian Truman (he was a major but it didn't take) fired General MacArthur as unceremoniously as a board chairman might get rid of a vice-president who got out of line, the general's Caesarian rhetoric and Wellingtonian profile availed him naught. Our old soldiers do fade away when they leave their native element, as the colors of certain game fish fade when exposed to air.

General Westmoreland has succeeded the late General Patton as My Favorite General, the kind that gives the trade a bad name and makes civilians proud of their round shoulders and baggy tweeds,

---

* A wholly volunteer army is advocated by Barry Goldwater and Norman Thomas; by Dr. Milton Friedman of the University of Chicago, who was for Goldwater in 1964, and Dr. J. K. Galbraith of Harvard, who is for McCarthy in 1968; by Senator Edward Brooke, who supports the administration on Vietnam, and by James Farmer, who doesn't.

the Generally kind of general who always stand up straight just like my mother told me to, who stick out their prognathous chins (mine is receding, index of a weak character; can hardly bear to think how strong Westy's character must be), and who wear all those ribbons (plus a brace of pearl-handled revolvers in Patton's case for executing Italian mules convicted, doubtless after a drumhead court-martial, of obstructing his staff car) and always have immaculate, knife-edge pants and tunics that seem to have been painted onto their virile torsos.*

I recall with nostalgia—actuality and one's prejudices don't often coincide so beautifully—My Favorite General's address to a joint session of Congress in those long-departed days—could it have been only last year?—when Westy wasn't the only Pangloss on the beach. He delivered his tidings of good cheer in full martial fig, more ribbons than a Victorian belle, chest out, head up, physically in top condition, the very model of a modern major general. And that great moment at the end when he acknowledged the thunderous applause of the assembled legislators with a snappy three-way salute—left, FACE, hup!, right FACE, hup!, as you WERE, hup! It was magnificent, but it wasn't politics. For a ghastly moment, Westy was teetering on the brink of unintentional comedy. A snicker might have set off an epidemic of giggling, like a girls' school. Fortunately there was no triggering snicker and the general kept his aplomb and his ribbons untarnished. But I can't see any political threat, if we do professionalize our armed forces, from the likes of him. That goes for the Joint Chiefs of Staff too. How can they push us around when they couldn't cope with McNamara? Eisenhower, the civilian's general, is more in the American grain—as a soldier he was a good account executive. Also, it occurs to me that before a military caste can break out of the barracks onto the stage of History it would

---

* Must be a lot of dry-cleaning and pressing activity at G.H.Q., Saigon. Military stuff, too, of course—planning the next blitz to liberate the capital (code name: "Sunnybrook Farm"), working out logistics for defense of "friendly" villages (code name: "Valley Forge"), keeping the wall maps up to date (sextuplicate Requisition Form 5D678XX; subject: shortage of colored pins), mimeographing press releases, laying on a plane to fly Joseph Alsop and Bob Hope to inspect their war and the front-line-of-the-day, cooking the body counts to keep up Lyndon's and Walt's spirits.

have to impress the populace with some victories. The present crop of American generals is not very threatening in that direction either.

Amendment XXIX: Section (1) Every citizen whose income is below the Minimum Health & Decency Standard as established annually by the Bureau of Labor Statistics of the U.S. Department of Labor shall be paid a Supplementary Grant from the Federal Treasury sufficient to bring his income up to the above Standard.

Section (2) These Supplementary Grants shall be solely Determined by Need. They are to be considered neither Charity nor a Privilege but a Right of American Citizenship. They shall therefore be paid without regard to Work, Moral Character, or any other Consideration except Need.

Our chief domestic problem is the persistence of a hard core of poverty despite the longest period of prosperity in our history (1940 to date).* Also the most widely distributed prosperity. Roosevelt's famous 1936 phrase, "one-third of a Nation ill-housed, ill-clad, ill-nourished," was a gross understatement: two-thirds of the nation were then below the poverty level. Today only 15.4 percent of the nation are poor; great progress, but still 29,731,000 of them. Unlike the temporarily poor of previous generations, the contemporary poor are tending to form a static, chronic caste of poverty because they are almost all unemployable: the over-sixty old, the under-fifteen young, mothers with small children and no wage-earning husband, the physically or mentally handicapped. The very fact that poverty has been so much reduced makes it easier for the 84.6 percent who have escaped to ignore those that haven't. The poor have become, politically and culturally, invisible. Michael Harrington's *The Other America* (1962) first made the general public aware of the persistence of this mass poverty in the middle of postwar plenty. Taking off from his book, I wrote "Our Invisible Poor" (see below in this book) which ended:

---

* (1973) Written before Nixon and his practical hard-headed Republican business administration had begun to manage our economy with the same expertise Herbert Hoover and *his* practical (etc.) Republicans displayed from 1928 to 1932. So much attention has lately been given to Nixon's moral failings, which are indeed spectacular, that it is often forgotten that while he is certainly a scoundrel on a heroic scale, he is also, in his own quiet way, a sensational bungler in running our economy.

To do something about this hard core [of poverty], direct intervention to help the poor [is necessary]. We have had this since the New Deal, but it has always been grudging and miserly, and we have never accepted the principle that every citizen should be provided, at state expense, with a reasonable minimum standard of living. . . . [This] should be taken as much for granted as free public schools have always been in our history.*

Others at the time, notably Robert Theobald, who was actually an economist, proposed the idea independently of me or Harrington, but only lately has it become respectable. The currently most favored technique is the "negative income tax"—those below the poverty level, according to income-tax returns, would receive enough from the Treasury to bring their incomes above that level. The conservative Dr. Milton Friedman was one of its first advocates, which shows you never can tell. On April 29, 1968, a committee of national business leaders, headed by the chairman of the Xerox Corporation and appointed by Governor Rockefeller to suggest "new approaches to welfare problems," came out for the negative income tax. And on May 27 more than a thousand academic economists—headed by Samuelson of M.I.T., Galbraith of Harvard, Tobin of Yale, and Walls and Lampman of Wisconsin—endorsed a "national system of income guarantees and supplements." It was significant that their statement referred specifically to the Poor People's Campaign and the recent report of the President's Commission on Civil Disorders.

For much the greatest threat from the poor to the survival, or at least the stability, of American capitalist democracy comes from the blacks. They are only one-third of the poor, contrary to the common belief—most people I've asked put them at a half or more—but the

---

* (1973) "The Government is about to mail out the first checks providing, in effect, a guaranteed minimum income to 3,200,000 aged, blind and disabled Americans early in January. . . . The number of eligible needy recipients is expected to reach 6,200,000 persons in 1974." So, a UPI dispatch of November 23, 1973—the first modest, but concrete, step by the federal government towards implementing the theory which looked so visionary ten years ago: that free subsistence from public funds should now be taken for granted in our society as much as free education was in the last century.

poverty rate is more than twice as high among blacks as among whites, and they are the most alienated, bitter, and vengeful, for good reason. Poverty and racial injustice are intertwined today and, leaving aside the moral arguments for a rich society not leaving almost thirty millions of its citizens to stagnate in squalor, a guaranteed minimum income would be a first step toward bringing the poor, black and white, back into the American community. The alternative is repression by the police and troops of the majority, which might mean an authoritarian society—and the end of the Constitution.

Amendment XXX: Section (1) A Tribune of the People shall be appointed for each Congressional District. He shall live in the District and shall receive and consider Complaints or Suggestions from Anybody about Anything. "Anything" includes the Actions of Mayors, Governors, Judges, Police Officers, Regulatory Commissions, School Boards, Building Inspectors, Welfare Workers, the President and his Cabinet Members, General Hershey, J. Edgar Hoover, and the Army Corps of Engineers. It also includes the Actions of Business Corporations, Churches, Small-Loan Agencies, Hospitals, Mail-Order Houses, Banks, City Planners, Philanthropic Foundations, etc.

Section (2) With the aid of an appropriate staff, the Tribune shall investigate such Complaints or Suggestions as seem to him (a) Serious, (b) outside the Scope of existing Institutions, such as Courts, or unlikely to be effectively acted on by them, and (c) to offer some chance of Remedy by him and his Staff. He shall Communicate his Findings first to the appropriate existing Officials or Institutions and then, if no Action results, to the Public.

Section (3) Each Tribune shall be appointed by majority vote of the Faculties and Student Bodies of the three largest Universities in the State in which the Congressional District represented by his office is Located.

What I have in mind here is a multiplication of Ralph Nader by 435—one Tribune per congressional district. It is an extension of the scope of the "ombudsman" invented by the Scandinavian countries and recently adopted in Britain: an official who receives miscellaneous complaints from citizens, and acts on those he thinks reasonable—and that he can do something about—by negotiations with the governmental departments concerned. He has no power to enforce his recommendations except persuasion: presenting his findings to the officials involved and appealing to their conscience and/or reason.

My amendment adds an appeal to public opinion, which, as Mr. Nader has demonstrated, like Lincoln Steffens, Upton Sinclair, and other "muckrakers" in an earlier period, is perhaps the most effective weapon in the arsenal of reform. (I apologize to some of my New Left friends for using this dirty word—I mean "reform," not "arsenal," which is a clean, upstanding militant term—but plead compulsion: my mandate is to amend an old Constitution, not to write a new one.) One of the weaknesses of a mass democracy—a contradiction in terms but the briefest way to describe the political cameleopard we've evolved—is the justified feeling of the Common Man in the Street that the machinery of government is on too gigantic a scale to respond to, or even hear, his own little personal reactions—which are sometimes not so little. Tribunes of the People would be useful here. They might also be called, less resonantly, Professional Troublemakers, Licensed Busybodies, Official Buttinskys, or, more classical, Gadflies of the Republic. Their salaries should be large enough to attract able men—using the term generically, not sexually: Jane Jacobs would make an excellent Ombudswoman—but not so large as to attract hack politicians. Say around $20,000, which would come to about $11 million total for the 435 salaries. Add another $60 million for offices and staff and it would still come to considerably less than the cost of one day abroad in Vietnam, an expensive country for American military tourists.

Amendment XXXI: Section (1) There shall be established a National Memory Commission whose functions shall be wholly Negative: to slow down the Progress of Progress. This Commission shall be divided into two autonomous Councils: the History Preservers and the Nature Preservers.

Section (2) The History Preservers shall consist of the Chairman of the North American Union [see Amendments XXVI and XXXV], or his deputy; three members selected by the National Arts Council; five members selected by Congress; the Directors of the five largest Art Museums and of the five largest Libraries; the

President of the American branch of the Victorian Society plus five more persons the Society will select; and six Artists and/or Architects to be chosen by the members enumerated above. The History Preservers shall be empowered to Forbid the Alteration or Destruction of any Building or other Man-made Object they decide, by majority vote, is of Artistic or Historical Importance; also to pay the Owner thereof a fair price, by its determination not subject to review by the Courts, out of the Federal treasury.

Section (3) The Nature Preservers shall have the same Powers applied to Lakes, Marshes, Forests, Canyons, Mountains, Valleys, Plains, Seashores, and all other natural phenomena including Fauna & Flora. They shall consist of the Chairman of the North American Union, or his deputy; the Secretary of the Interior; the National Park Commissioner; the head of the Bureau of Indian Affairs; five members selected by Congress; the directors of the seven largest zoos and/or botanical gardens; the President of the Sierra Club, plus five more persons he and his Club will select; the President of the Audubon Society, plus five more persons he and his Society will select.*

Section (4) The History and the Nature Councils shall each Receive an Annual Subsidy of Five Hundred Million Dollars OR one-sixteenth of one percent of the Gross National Product, whichever is larger. This shall be Automatic and not Dependent on Congressional Appropriation. They shall use not more than ten percent of this Subsidy for staff operating expenses; the rest shall be devoted to Compensations for Property Owners.

Section (5) On petition of Five Thousand† or more Citizens whose Homes or Places of Business or of Rural Recreation are threatened with Extinction by Urban Renewal, Highway Projects, or other Alleged Improvements, the two Councils, sitting jointly, shall be empowered to proclaim a Progress Armistice of up to five years during which NOTHING WILL BE DONE. In this period, the Councils and their staffs shall seek some Compromise, by way of

---

* (1973) I would now add the President and five delegates from The Nature Conservancy.

† (1973) Hereby amended to "Five Hundred" as more realistic, considering our communal lethargy.

*compensation, new geographical proposals, etc., between the Improvers and the Resisters. If this fails, either Party may submit the matter to the Federal courts, whose Decision shall be Final.**

That about covers it, I think. The problem this amendment tries to meet is the preservation of some of our connections with the past. I assume (a) that a people cannot live in health and ease and pleasure in an environment in which such connections are destroyed beyond a certain point; (b) that if this cutting of roots goes too far, a people, like an individual, will become disoriented and neurotic (as happened to the Russians between 1929 and 1953, when the Stalin regime systematically wiped out their past history and culture—the modest recovery since then is evidence both of the resilience of the forces for life and, in the slowness of their recovery and their vulnerability still so many years later, of their fragility); and (c) that in this country the destruction of the past is going on largely unchecked, through a casual surrender to the demands of private gain. The British Empire is said to have been founded in a fit of absent-mindedness; the American landscape is being unfounded in the same way. Although our history is short, compared to Europe, we are bulldozing its physical traces with a lavishness comparable to theirs. But they can afford it better than we can: an early-eighteenth-century building in London is equivalent to an early-twentieth-century one in New York, and much less rare. We have still considerable remnants of our natural past—even Americans couldn't devastate thoroughly in two centuries so vast a terrain—but that's going too: the West Coast redwoods, the Florida Everglades, and now even much of the Grand Canyon are all threatened. Not to mention the steady bulldozing of populated areas dear at least to their current inhabitants. One-sixteenth of one percent of our gross national product—now about $800 billion a year—seems not an exorbitant price to pay for controlling the erosion.

Amendment XXXII: The Number of Military Employees outside the Boundaries of the United States of America shall not Exceed one-fourth of one percent of the Population of the United States of

---

* In style and content—can they be separated?—this is my own favorite amendment.

America EXCEPT THAT *a larger Number may be Authorized, as a Temporary Exception, by a four-fifths vote of both the Senate and the House of Representatives. This Exception must be renewed Annually by the same Majority in both Houses, else it shall Lapse and the extra Troops authorized by it shall be Recalled.*

At our present population of close to two hundred millions, this would limit the maximum armed forces abroad to 500,000. Considerably less than half the current number overseas? True. Hard to see where to cut except Vietnam? Yes. Regression toward isolationism? Granted. Abdication from our commitment to defend against Communist Aggression the Peace-Loving Peoples of the World—sorry, wrong side of record—the Democracy-Loving Peoples of the World? Precisely.

Amendment XXXIII: The Military Budget of the United States of America shall not Exceed three percent of the Gross National Product of the United States of America in any year.

The current military budget is 10 percent of GNP, or about $80 billion. Cutting it by two-thirds may seem extreme, but I assume by the time two-thirds of Congress and three-quarters of the state legislatures get around to enacting Amendment XXXIII—let's be realistic, it will take at least two years—Vietnam will have been decently or indecently buried, saving $30 billion a year, plus a few lives.* So the proposal is merely to cut the normal or un-Vietnamized military budget in half, from $50 billion to $24 billion. A few less Polaris submarines, spy ships (so expensive electronically and diplomatically), and those around-the-clock, around-the-globe plane patrols with live nuclear warheads that are so reassuring to the Spaniards and the Icelanders we are defending against communism, especially when they crash in their countries—these cutbacks plus firing half the civilian employees of the Department of Defense, as it is quaintly called, and many of its expensive higher military

---

* (1973) Vietnam has been indecently buried, but I was naïve to expect $30 billion—or indeed anything—to be thereby "saved" from the military budget. Pentagon math is to the civilian, or CPA, variety as Hare Krishna is to Euclid. A lot more variables. The chief one being that the Joint Chiefs of Staff aim their budgetary planning at that open-ended goal Sam Gompers once defined as the program of his A F of L "business unionism": More.

employees above the rank of (chicken) colonel—*et voilà!* There may also have to be some scientific losses. The CBW (chemical and biological warfare) researchers at Fort Detrick, Maryland, may have to retrench some promising programs: an improved nerve gas that will kill in seconds, not minutes; a new strain of bubonic plague of a virulence unknown in the Middle Ages—sometimes called "the Dark Ages," before Fort Detrick; a mutation of the anopheles mosquito which may restore malaria to the proud place it once had in human ecology; crop blights, rusts, and insect infestations of an efficiency undreamed of in the worst nightmares of another part of our schizoid government, the Department of Agriculture.*

Still and all, $24 billion will finance quite a lot of warfare, CBW or otherwise. My effort is, as always, to be reasonable and to avoid extreme proposals that General Westmoreland and Walt Whitman Rostow might be able to dismiss as Visionary & Impractical.

Amendment XXXIV: Until the Bureau of Labor Statistics shall Certify that the Number of Citizens with Incomes below the Health & Decency Level (see Amendment XXIX) is less than One Percent of the Population, it shall be Forbidden to Spend any Governmental Revenue, Federal, State or Local, in the Transportation of any Matter, Animate or Inanimate, more than ten miles above the Surface of the United States of America.

---

* The examples are invented but true to life as lived in the Frankenstein laboratories of CBW. See Seymour Hersh's definitive survey, *Chemical and Biological Warfare: America's Hidden Arsenal* (Bobbs-Merrill, 1968, $7.50). Rice blast and stem rust are now "receiving special study." . . . Insects are being coordinated with germs: "The Fort Detrick insect inventory in 1959 included 'mosquitoes infected with yellow fever, malaria and dengue; fleas infected with plague; ticks with tularemia, relapsing fever and Colorado fever; houseflies with cholera, anthrax and dysentery.' " Quite a troupe of performers, and their repertoire is being extended: "There is some evidence that the goal now is to develop insects that will deliver anti-crop agents." . . . And the CBW Frankensteins nurse their dreams. Mr. Hersh quotes from one of their papers: "Therefore it was concluded that a germ-warfare attack using bubonic plague in infected fleas or rats would have a great chance of spreading the disease beyond all possible control." He adds that pneumonic plague—which in the mirror-world of CBW has the advantages of superlative infectivity: "untreated [it] kills ninety to one hundred percent of its victims"—is being worked on at Fort Detrick.

This amendment is sensible to the point of boredom and I expect it will be ratified sooner than any of the others, with the possible exceptions of XXVII and XXVIII. First things first. I'm sure the Founding Fathers would have included this veto in their Constitution, along with those against patents of nobility and bills of attainder, had it occurred to them that federal monies might some day be diverted from the problems of human society they assumed were the primary concern of government in order to satisfy the curiosity of a small minority of scientists about the behavior of distant bodies in the sky which have never had any discernible effects, for good or ill, on the fortunes of the Republic. The Fathers were prescient but not omniscient. (I find the Space Program hard to believe myself.)

Had the question been raised during those great days in Constitution Hall, I venture that Hamilton would have declared such use of revenue unsound, Jefferson undemocratic,* Madison imprudent, Franklin extravagant, and Washington, the Eisenhower of his time, postponable. "Whether the moon be made of green cheese or whether it be composed of other materials," I hear Gouverneur Morris replying, had some anachronistic delegate (a Yankee from Connecticut, say) proposed an Early American space probe, "is doubtless of lively interest to scientifical projectors but not, I submit, to this convention. We are met to resolve not celestial problems but terrestrial ones. [Applause, cries of "Hear! Hear!"] Our concern is not with remote speculations about the nature of God's universe but with the immediate survival of God's country. [Renewed applause at this last happy new coinage.] I appeal to our learned friend and colleague, Dr. Franklin, whose physikal experimentations are as celebrated as his common sense." Whereupon Dr. Franklin—played by George Arliss in my scenario—totters impressively to his feet and after some stage business with a snuffbox gets off one or two Poor Richard apothegms, notes that the total cost of his most famous space probe was three shillings (one kite @ 2 s., one ball of twine @ 1 s., one superannuated key that had lost its lock @ zero) and comes down heavily for common sense and economy.

---

* (1973) Had he been there, which he wasn't.

We've lost ground in two centuries. First things first. It's encouraging that the Space Program will probably be reduced more drastically than other nonmilitary programs in the current budget cuts: it is expected to lose $700 million, which would mean indefinite postponements of manned lunar landings, also of "probes" of Mars once scheduled for 1971 and 1973. I can wait.*

Amendment XXXV: Section (1) The present States shall be Abolished and shall be Replaced by new Governmental Units, which shall have the same Powers and Functions as the former States.

Section (2) These new Units shall be determined by a Map Revision Committee appointed by the Chairman with the Advice and Consent of Congress and the Supreme Court. The Duty of this Committee shall be to redivide the United States of America—which shall henceforth be known as The North American Union—into such Governmental Units as the Committee determines Correspond best to the present Economic, Social, and Political Geography of the North American Union.

When the thirteen colonies made their revolution, they were distinct political entities, each defined by its own economics, geography, traditions, and style of life. They were, in the thinking of their inhabitants, really thirteen countries and the problem the Constitution solved, after the Articles of Federation had failed to, was to subordinate them to a central authority and so make a nation of them. To get their agreement, the Constitution-makers had to make considerable concessions to "states' rights." But these original countries lost more and more of their distinctiveness as the nation enlarged and as changes took place—industrialization, the growth of cities and of a working class, universal education, etc. The cities were separated, in interests and in psychology, from the nonurban

---

* (1973) The lunar landings did take place, to increasing popular apathy, but Mars is still unprobed and the Space Program has been drastically cut back. The "Skylab" caper is about all one has to skip in the news today. I make an honorable exception for that gutsy little projectile ("Mercury," I think?) which has survived Pluto's radiation belt and is now gamely headed into outer space, sending back messages like a faithful retriever. Long may its tail wag back to us! Another decade, its masters estimate. Great thing about "Mercury" (or is it "Rover"?) is that it's unmanned. Nobody aboard to pollute the air waves with our first Saturnian intimacy: "Hey, look at those great *rings!* Outta sight!" Man's best friend.

parts of the states they were in. States with commercial and manufacturing development like New York, Pennsylvania, and Massachusetts came to have more in common than not, especially as
against the agrarian states of the South and, later, of the West. Even
conservative New England changed—Vermont was split off from
New York, Maine was invented. And as the country expanded
westward, Congress divided the new territories into states that were,
in Constitutional fiction, assumed to be of the same kind as the
original thirteen but which in fact were often as arbitrary exercises
in map-drawing as some of the postwar African countries.

In less than a century, the real divisions had become regional,
with a subdivision between urban and rural inside the regions. But
the state system continued to be imposed for no better reason than
we had begun that way: biological rather than political genesis, like
an organism reproducing its cell pattern. Because the original cells
had been small (compared to the enormous new areas) the size of
the new states was held down to a scale comparable to the old one.
It had to be bigger—so much land out there—but an effort was
made to keep the scale in some balance. They gave up on Texas.*
And when national expansion crossed the Mississippi, geometry took
over from history and from human ecology (not much of either out
there at the time, after all). Cf. the huge quadrangle formed by
Colorado, New Mexico, Arizona, and Utah, rectangles of about
equal size that meet at the center in four neat right angles; or the
five slightly more irregular but still satisfyingly rectangular states
just to the east of them marching down a thousand miles from
Canada to Texas, like giant children's building blocks: North
Dakota, South Dakota, Nebraska, Kansas, Oklahoma. Plus Wyo-
ming to their west, which shares with Colorado the distinction of
being utterly square.

Just what new political divisions would make more sense than
the present fifty states is a difficult question, requiring a rethinking
of our national Gestalt in functional terms, like a man having to
revise his body and decide whether an extra arm might be a good

---

* For a reason interesting in this context: because, of all the new states—with
the exception of Mormon Utah—it had the most definite historical identity:
like the original thirteen, its people had freed themselves from a foreign ruler
and had set up a republic of their own. Nobody dared to carve up the Lone
Star State.

idea, or maybe the nose no longer serves a useful purpose, and *are* two heads better than one, let's give it a try. Perhaps that's the way it would look to the present American population, and if so, nothing can be done. My hunch, however, is that most Americans don't have strong emotional state ties, for the reasons just indicated, and that they would therefore accept a revision of the map which would promise functional improvements. However, it is a complicated matter and I'll leave it to the Map Revision Committee, suggesting only two general principles: the regrouping of the states into larger regions, and the dissecting out from these regions of autonomous urban areas with their own separate national representation. The two latest states, Alaska and Hawaii, are so isolated and so homogeneously distinctive in other ways that they are ready-made regions, and so should be left alone.*

The regional superstates I'd suggest, just to get the discussion started, are:

New England (everything east of New York)
Atlantica (N.Y., N.J., Pa., Md., Del., D.C.)
Appalachia (West Va., Ky., Tenn.)
Southron (Va., N.C., S.C., Ga., Fla., Ala., Miss., La.)
Midland (O., Ind., Ill., Mich., Iowa, Wisc., Minn.)
The Prairies (N.D., S.D., Neb., Kan., Okla.)
Texas (Texas)
The West (Wyo., U., Col., N.M., Ariz., Nev.)
Pacifica (Wash., Ore., Calif.)

Before somebody writes in to complain that four states are omitted from the above, let me admit they are. I couldn't figure out where to put them. Should Mo. and Ark. be filed under Midland, Southron, or Prairies? Arguments for each; can't decide. And would Mont. and Id. (or is it I.?, either way an interesting abbreviation) fit better into Pacifica or The West? Well, let the Map Revision Committee do some work.

---

* It is a sign of progress that nobody proposed dividing Alaska up into four or five states, on the Western pattern, although it is even more out of scale than Texas. On regions I might add that "states' rights" might more accurately be called "regional rights." Historically, the issue has been raised mostly by the South, the one region which has been sharply separated in its style of life, its economics, and its "peculiar institution" from the rest of the country.

While the regions would be merely the present states writ large, the urban areas present more complex difficulties. The intention is to recognize the long-obvious fact of life that the interests of their inhabitants are strikingly discordant to those of the nonurban populations of the states in which they are now uncomfortably imbedded: New York City vs. upstate New York; Los Angeles and San Francisco vs. the California hinterland; Chicago vs. downstate Illinois; Dallas–Fort Worth, Houston, and San Antonio are very different from the rest of Texas—and what about Austin? Some planners now consider the whole Atlantic coastal area from Boston to Washington one "megalopolis." Should that be one of the region-states? How far should Chicagoland stretch? To Milwaukee one way? To Toledo, Detroit, perhaps even Cleveland the other? My notion would be to limit each urban area to its immediate satellite hinterland, so as to avoid that forcing of disparate electorates into unsuitable marriages that is precisely the objection to the present state boundaries. Thus New York City would include the industrial New Jersey cities across the Hudson as far inland as Newark, plus the "dormitory suburbs" in Westchester, Long Island, and Connecticut—one rule of thumb would be commuting distance; Chicago would include Gary, Indiana, and the North Shore suburbs, but not Milwaukee or Toledo; Minneapolis and Saint Paul would be a unit, but Saint Louis and Kansas City would be separate, etc. A series of twenty or thirty "city-states," each autonomous, each with its own representatives in Congress who can both express its special interests and also join with other city-states on urban-versus-rural matters, or with the representatives of its own region on other matters.

Each of the regions—eleven by my redrawing of the map, including Alaska and Hawaii—and each of the twenty or more "city-states" would get two senators apiece, as the states do now. The House of Representatives would be elected, as now, on the basis of districts that are numerically equal. The one-man, one-vote reform recently decreed by the Supreme Court would be followed. This rule, plus the Map Revision, would end the present domination by nonurban minorities that makes Congress unresponsive to racial ghettos and other problems of the cities—and besides, it isn't fair. It would also make unnecessary a XXXVI Amendment to appropriate funds and set up a commission to deal with these urban traumas. There are enough amendments and commissions already in these proposals and

I'd just as soon not have to think up any more. The new regional-urban Congress should do some work, too.

As the compulsive type of reader who noticed the omission of four states above has doubtless observed by now—I can see him inserting his letter-to-the-editor into his portable with a tight smile—my XXXV Amendment cops out on implementation, leaving it up to a committee "appointed by the Chairman with the Advice and Consent of the Congress and the Supreme Court." This is vague even by the Founders' standards. Actually, I didn't mean to give the federal government a centralized authority Alexander Hamilton himself might have drawn back from: the power to carve up our electoral map without democratic controls. A caesarian operation, one might say. Trouble was I ran into difficulties whenever I tried to think concretely how the people might vote on which region, or city-state, they wanted to become part of—if indeed they wanted to change their boundaries at all. The possibilities so numerous, each affecting each other and also all the rest, the permutations and combinations endless. Suppose the citizens of one or more states clung to their old topographical Gestalt the way Rhode Island held out against the Constitution—and here are four times as many chances for a R.I., or several R.I.s, to gum up the works? Or suppose some sizable population groups—two or three would be serious, more might be fatal—preferred one of the dozens, scores, hundreds of different ways to redraw the map from that suggested by the commission? And suppose they stuck to it? Who or what could decide? Even in our etiolated American democracy of 1968* could the citizens of, say, Minnesota, be compelled to merge themselves into Midland if every nerve of their civic psyches craved to be united to Prairies? And suppose the majority of the Prairies electorate—a hypothetical political division that could only become real after all the other states, including Minnesota, had been fitted into place on the new map; but let's assume this difficulty has been somehow surmounted, perhaps by some John Marshall or Daniel Webster of our time, then suppose the inhabitants of Prairies—N.D., S.D., Neb., Kan., and

---

* (1973) The plant (*popularia aspiranta*) has revived of late more from presidential pruning (often stimulating to growth) than from horticultural vigor. Also, as Honest Abe—was he only a century before Tricky Dick?—put it: "You can fool some of the people [etc.] and all of the people [etc.] but you can't [etc.]"

Okla. if you've forgotten—suppose they voted, in democratic plebiscite, that their interests would be damaged by the addition of Minnesota, or perhaps just that they would feel more comfortable without all those alien Minnesotan infiltrations, nothing personal of course. Just a Different Way of Looking at Things.

So I decided to define merely the first step in Amendment XXXV, hoping that the joint proposals of the three independent, and Constitutionally fairly well-balanced branches of our federal government—executive, legislative, and judicial—could provide a basis for a popular discussion and, finally, some consensus. But after the Map Revision Committee has made its proposals, I confess I can't see anything clearly. We'll just have to play it by ear. Like the Founding Fathers.

—*Esquire*, October, 1968

Appendix:
Some Historical
Background

Author's Note: These historical notes were intended as an introduction to the above article but they got out of hand and it became obvious even to the author that few readers would last to the main event if they had to sit through such extensive preliminaries. But it seemed a pity to waste them, and so, at the suggestion of the then editor, Harold Hayes, they were run in the same issue but separately, as an installment of my political column. (The fans didn't sit through the main event anyway—see Afterword below.)

Our peculiar custom of popular election of the chief executive is not only unusual among Western democracies* but was also unforeseen by the Founding Fathers.

---

* When it has been used in France, for example, it has been exceptional and antidemocratic, as the plebiscites that made Louis Napoleon Emperor in 1852 and de Gaulle something or other a century later.

Their admirable Constitution says little about the way the President should be selected except: "Each State shall appoint, in such manner as the Legislature thereof may direct, a number of Electors" —i.e., that Electoral College which has given us so much trouble. Nor did they specify just *how* the legislatures were to "direct" the process. In practice, what happened was that the first seven presidents (through Jackson, in his first term) were chosen by party caucuses, as in the parliamentary system. By 1830, George Stimpson writes in *A Book about American Politics*, a useful collection of historical data, "King Caucus was dead, but as yet no satisfactory substitute had been devised. Finally the Anti-Mason Party showed the way. . . . On September 26, 1831, it held [a] national convention in Baltimore and nominated William Wirt for President and Amos Ellmaker for Vice-President. This was the first national convention composed of delegates representing the people and called to nominate candidates for the highest Federal offices." The National Republicans followed with a convention in Baltimore in December, 1831, nominating Henry Clay for president, and the Democrats a few months later convened, also in Baltimore, to nominate Jackson for a second term. "In the early days of the republic," Mr. Stimpson notes, "it was considered undignified to solicit support openly for the Presidency, and Presidential candidates did not make campaign speeches. . . . In 1836, when Harrison ran for President against Van Buren . . . he departed from the time-honored custom that a Presidential candidate should not electioneer." Alas.

Nor did the Fathers define the president's functions, in important ways, beyond "shall be Commander in Chief of the Army and Navy," "shall have power, by and with the advice and consent of the Senate, to make Treaties" (we've seen what *that* means) and "shall from time to time give to the Congress Information of the State of the Union, and Recommend to their Consideration such Measures as he shall judge necessary and expedient." They were rather elliptical, even for them, about the presidency, perhaps because they realized it was an office with novel powers and so didn't want to tie down future generations too closely. "[Hamilton] is careful to distinguish between the office of the President and that held by the King of Great Britain," Professor Wright observes in his introduction to *The Federalist*. "He does not compare the President with the

Prime Minister. The system of cabinet government, or ministerial responsibility, in Britain was as little understood by Americans, even Hamilton, in 1788, as it was unknown to the laws of Britain." Hamilton was optimistic about the Electoral College system: "The process of election affords a moral certainty that the office will never fall to the lot of any man who is not in an eminent degree endowed with the requisite qualifications." Poor Hamilton: Polk, Fillmore, Tyler, Pierce, Buchanan, Johnson I, Grant, the two Harrisons, McKinley, Harding, Coolidge, Hoover, and—let's stop there. Demos crossed him up—"Your people, sir, is a great *beast!*"—after popular conventions became the rule.

But even before that, when the Electoral College was a gentlemen's club, there was that narrow squeak in 1800 when, because the "process of election" didn't specify separate ballots for president and vice-president, loosely providing that the candidate with the most votes was to be president and the one with the next most votes was to become the vice-president—that awful moment in our history when Thomas Jefferson and Aaron Burr, the candidates of the new Democratic-Republican Party for president and vice-president, respectively, got the same number of votes in the Electoral College since every one of their followers had voted for *both* of them. Anybody but Burr would have solved the dilemma by withdrawing. But not Burr; he was in control of Tammany Hall—he had a genius for doing the wrong thing—and he was quite ready to take advantage of the situation. The election was thrown into the House of Representatives, which was controlled by the other party, the Federalists of Adams and Hamilton. After thirty-five ballots failed to resolve the tie, Hamilton intervened and broke the deadlock in favor of his greatest political enemy, Jefferson. He was an ardent Federalist—and the 1800 election was the beginning of the end of that party—but he was also a man of sense and a patriot. The prospect of Burr as president alarmed him.* So he threw his support to Jefferson.

---

* As well it might have: Aaron Burr was the son of the second president of Princeton, the grandson of Jonathan Edwards, a creditable commander in the Revolutionary armies, a man of charm and brilliance; but his character was bad to the point of absurdity. Like Johnson (II), Burr was a man of parts, but

They were political men in those days, not sectarians, not true
believers, not liberal or Marxian ideologues (nor conservative ones
either), not even loyal party members as we understand the term
today. Jefferson called the Federalist papers, mostly written by Hamilton, "the best commentary on the principles of government, which
ever was written." The other principal author was James Madison,
"the Father of the Constitution," the wisest head in that age when
our political thinkers commanded the respect of the world: Madison,
who joined Hamilton and other conservatives in working out the
Constitution during those months at Convention Hall in Philadelphia (as Charles A. Beard and others have pointed out, it was a most
retrograde, property-minded document: none of the prominent democratic leaders were there—Jefferson was ambassador in Paris, Sam
Adams and Tom Paine were not invited, Patrick Henry was, but
refused, saying "he smelled a rat"); Madison, who kept a daily
record of the discussions that is our most important historical source
on the writing of the Constitution; Madison, who played a major
part in persuading the country to accept this conservative Constitution—and then joined Jefferson in drafting and pushing through the
Bill of Rights; Madison, who became Jefferson's ally in their successful campaign to destroy the reactionary Federalist Party of Hamilton,
Adams, and Washington and to supplant it with their own liberal-
democratic party, which survived and gave him two terms as president.

---

neither judgment nor integrity was among them. A few years later he challenged Hamilton to a duel and killed him. After that he got involved in his
own Vietnam: a harebrained filibustering expedition on the lower Mississippi
aimed at splitting off part of the country which, aside from making poor
Philip Nolan "The Man Without a Country," resulted in Burr's being tried
for high treason before Chief Justice Marshall, who acquitted him on what
to me seems a strained interpretation of the Constitution. . . . My disorderly
files have thrown up an invitation from "The Aaron Burr Association" (Dr.
Samuel Engle Burr, Jr., President-General) to a dinner to celebrate the two-
hundredth anniversary of Colonel Burr's birth. Date: February 6, 1956; $5
("includes tax and gratuities") black tie or business suits for the gentlemen;
street dresses, afternoon or evening dresses for the ladies." . . . Well, if Lyndon
Johnson can get the University of Texas to build a library to house his presidential papers, and can also look forward to occupying in his sunset years—if
one can imagine the sun ever setting on Lyndon—the same elevated academic
rank I myself once held there, Distinguished Visiting Professor, then why not
an Aaron Burr Association?

A man like Madison is impossible to fit into any political category of our time.

The Burr-Jefferson impasse of 1800 stimulated the XII Amendment (1804) which spelled it out, at last: "The Electors . . . shall name in their ballots the person voted for as President, and in distinct ballots the person voted for as Vice-President." The Fathers were more specific about the powers of Congress, which they list in detail, including "To declare war." (We've seen what *that* means too, although Congress doubtless still retains the authority next mentioned: to "grant Letters of Marque and Reprisal.") They were also definite about the election of senators: "two . . . from each State, chosen by the Legislature thereof." Too definite indeed; as the electorate widened and "We the People" slowly became *really* we the people (because of property restrictions on the franchise, not more than a quarter of the adult males voted for delegates to the Convention and not more than one-sixth voted to ratify the Constitution), it finally became necessary to pass the XVII Amendment in 1913 providing that senators be elected not by the legislatures of the states but "by the people thereof." The rules for the election of congressmen, however, were vague enough to allow them to be chosen first by the state legislatures and then by popular vote, without the necessity of an amendment.

Vagueness is the most striking characteristic of the Constitution, in fact. Article III, which defines the third branch of the federal government, begins bravely, "The judicial power of the United States shall be vested in one supreme Court," but then tails off to "and in such inferior Courts as the Congress may from time to time ordain and establish." Had Congress not ordained the inferior, or U.S. District, courts, the Supreme Court—and why did the Fathers, so lavish with eighteenth-century capitals, deny one to "supreme"?—would have been left a head without a body. Section (2) of Article III, which minutely details the functions of the supreme, or Supreme, Court, says nothing of any authority to review legislation in the light of the Constitution and to strike down such laws as it believed to be "Unconstitutional." This blank space was filled in promptly, and fully, by the fourth chief justice, John Marshall, who became a belated Founding Father, adding to the Constitution one of its most important features, a uniquely American invention: judicial repeal of laws. Cf. *Marbury* vs. *Madison* (1803): "We must never forget it is a Constitution we are expounding" and "The question respecting the extent of the powers actually granted [by the states to the federal government] is perpetually arising and will probably continue to arise, so long as our system shall exist." That the Constitution gave his court no right to expound it nor to decide on "the powers actually granted" didn't bother John Marshall. He simply asserted the right and he got away with it because there was nothing in the Constitution that said no—except for the Bill of Rights amendments, it's a most permissive document—and because it seemed a reasonable, necessary function. Also because Americans at all times have had a passion for settling things by legal procedures, law being our national substitute for philosophy—and sometimes, it seems, for politics, as in the first McCarthy's "point-of-order," district-attorney-style operations and the second Johnson's finagling with the Tonkin Gulf Resolution.

Whether Marshall's addition was a good or bad idea depends on one's politics—mostly bad, I'd say, up to the Warren Court—but it has kept the Constitution alive by providing a major way that change, or resistance to change, can be expressed without altering the basic text. The brevity of that document (it can be read in half an hour) and its silence on so many major questions—on minor technical matters it is often pedantically explicit—has made it possible for the White House, the federal executive departments, the state legislatures, and Congress, as well as the courts, to constantly revise the game to meet new problems without having to make formal changes in the rule book.*

In almost two centuries, there have been only twenty-five formal changes, or amendments—only fifteen, if one excludes the first ten ("Bill of Rights"), all ratified by 1791 and, in effect, part of the

---

* (*1973*) The Nixon presidency, most subversive in our history, has shown the dangers of this looseness by stretching the baggy fabric of the Constitution into novel (and sinister) forms. But vagueness has its advantages, too: arguments can always be found on the other, or conservative, side, as represented by Chairman Sam Ervin of the Senate committee investigating Watergate and other White House Horrors.

original document. Of the fifteen between 1791 and the present only four seem to me of much importance: the three post-Civil War amendments, XIII, XIV, and XV (1865–1870), which abolished slavery and were intended to protect the newly freed blacks against a reimposition of white domination by (slightly) subtler methods,* and the XVI (1913), which established the income tax that has become the chief means of raising federal revenue.

The XIX Amendment ("The right of citizens . . . to vote shall not be denied or abridged by the United States or by any State on account of sex") is formally important but in practice doesn't seem to have made much difference. The first three presidents elected after the ladies got the vote were Harding, Coolidge, and Hoover; we men could have done that on our own. The only gain from the XIX I can think of is the League of Women Voters, an admirable outfit but hardly worth all the trouble of an amendment. The XVIII, or Prohibition, Amendment certainly did make a difference: more drinking, bootleggers, Al Capone; never has a law been so enthusiastically violated, even by this lawless people. Talk about civil disobedience! It was such nonsense—a sumptuary law that, like most

---

* By the end of the century, they had been emasculated by the whites, Northern as well as Southern, with the Supreme Court providing the American-style sanction by a series of decisions that amounted to judicial nullification, all perfectly legal and in order. Thus the late-nineteenth-century Court reduced the mighty strophes of XIV—"nor shall any State deprive any person of life, liberty or property without due process of law; nor deny to any person within its jurisdiction the equal protection of the laws"—from a shield over the new black citizens in the South to a buckler protecting the new business corporations (in legal fiction, they were persons too, just like the freedmen) from state regulations as to minimum wages and child labor. Except for the heroic John Marshall Harlan (grandfather of the later Justice Harlan, though the blood seems to have run thin) who sat on the Court from 1877 to 1911 and was for most of that time the lone dissenter on civil rights cases: cf., his great dissent in *Plessy* vs. *Ferguson* (1896), a classic refutation of the sophistry the Court adopted, namely that racial segregation is not in itself discrimination—the "separate but equal" doctrine. Except for Harlan, who was later joined by Holmes and followed by Brandeis (Harlan was more courageous and consistent on civil rights than they were, though for some reason they have always had top billing) the post-Civil War Supreme Court was a disgrace. It was not until the Warren Court reversed seventy years of precedents in *Brown* vs. *Board of Education* (1954), that the Supreme Court began to interpret the XIII, XIV, and XV Amendments in the way Congress had intended.

sumptuary laws, made for corruption more than for civic virtue—
that it had to be repealed in 1933 by the XXI Amendment.*

The other amendments have been mostly minor reforms like the
XXIII (1961), which enfranchised the District of Columbia, and
the XXIV (1964), which made the right to vote in national elections independent of poll or other taxes. Or housekeeping changes—
rearrangement of the living-room furniture—mostly about that trou-
blesome presidency business from the XII (1804), already described,
to the XXII (1951): "No person shall be elected to the office of
President more than twice." We know the ghost that one was aimed
at. I suppose "Some persons shall not be elected to the office of the
President once" might be Unconstitutional, a Bill of Attainder
maybe, and we can hardly expect the overburdened Supreme Court
to take on the job of deciding who *isn't* fit to Preside over us. But I
can think of lots of candidates at the moment.†

—*Esquire*, October, 1968

---

* President Johnson has now proposed *his* XXVI Amendment: to lower the
voting age from twenty-one to eighteen. Excellent idea—why didn't *I* think
of it?—and it will probably make more of a difference, and a beneficial one,
than the XIX did, since age differences in America now are more important
than sex differences, the latter becoming less obvious every year, the former
more so. That is, if the young aren't too alienated to vote at all—after four
years of him. The President's supporting arguments are sound enough, though
I'd have borne down more heavily on his brief aside: "At the age of eighteen,
young Americans are called upon to bear arms." And I'd have gone light on
the corn: "The ballot box is the great anvil of democracy, where government
is shaped by the will of the people." Leaving aside the difficulty of visualizing
a ballot box as an anvil, I would say that this opening sentence is just the
way *not* to begin. It suggests something up the sleeve. However, the President
can't help it if his most useful and innocent proposals have the greasy slick of
the con man. . . . (1973) This was written five years ago. Today, what with
Women's Lib on the one hand and the senile decay of the youth movement
on the other, the point should be reversed. A volatile culture, ours. . . . In
1971, the voting age was in fact lowered by Congress—no amendment needed
—as, I dare say, most of my ten proposals could just be enacted by Congress—
if the Supreme Court went along, of course. I called them all "amendments,"
however, for reasons more journalistic than legalistic.

† (1973) A large majority of my fellow citizens, according to the polls, can
think of just one at this point in time.

Afterword

If "Our Invisible Poor" (see below pp. 75–98) was my most effective political article, the above was by far my least. Although *Esquire* has a circulation close to a million and although its publicity department lavishly distributed advance proofs "for comment"—every member of Congress received a set—there was no comment. Reader response came as close to zero as possible, namely, exactly one letter (and that from one of the magazine's editors, a very nice, perceptive letter but still . . .). In his campaign a year later for the Democratic nomination for mayor of New York City, Norman Mailer got a lot of mileage out of his proposal that the city become the fifty-first state, and Congresswoman Bella Abzug is still talking up the idea, but neither seems to have been aware of my Amendment XXXV, at least they've never referred to it. Nor has anybody else. I've never published a major (in subject and intent anyway) piece with so little resonance, in fact none. I can't explain it. True, it appeared in *Esquire*, which has twice the circulation of *The New Yorker* but, from my long experience writing for both, I'd say stimulates a tenth as many letters. Even so, I always got *some* reaction to long pieces in *Esquire*.

Why this total lack of response, I wondered at the time. Aren't Americans concerned about their Constitutional system? Have they given up all hope? Or are they hopelessly complacent? . . . Or—a more unsettling line of thought—was the trouble literary? Did the piece seem overwritten, too exuberant—a stylistic *tour de force* the readers wished had never been forced? Were they turned off by my inversion of standard American journalistic practice, my substituting the (medieval) inductive for the (modern) deductive mode of discourse? That is, reducing The Facts to mere illustrations of my theses, or Amendments, rather than the usual method of laying out the information first—let the Facts Speak for themselves, if only they ever did!—so that the ideas, if any, at least *appear* to follow from, rather than precede, the data? Or was the piece just too long? too speculative? Or, though it seems to step along briskly enough to my inspection, to a less paternal eye simply, let's face it, boring?

The present reader may judge the above matters for himself/herself. But I hope it's not copping a plea to suggest the historical timing of the piece was unfortunate. It came out just before the 1968 presidential election, which was centered not—as the 1976 one will be—on large questions of the validity of our democratic system including the Constitution, but rather on such trivia (on a hind view) as whether HHH was LBJ's man or Nixon was Ike's man. How Hubert Horatio would have turned out I don't know, which way the jelly would have jelled, and probably I should have voted for him as a lesser evil but somehow I couldn't pull down his lever. It soon became clear that Nixon, with his unerring instinct for total disaster, was programed straight toward the greater evil: Ike's man on domestic reform and Johnson's man on Vietnam. Then in 1972 he was re-elected by practically everybody except anybody one knows—this time it was easy to pull down McGovern's lever—and now my Constitutional meanderings have become more to the point, or points, especially the first (XXVI: "The Office of President of the US shall be Abolished . . .").

When I proposed substituting for our peculiar presidential arrangement—the one major *gaffe* of the Founding Fathers—a more flexible, and normal, one of parliamentary, or congressional, responsibility, it was on the basis of experience merely with Hoover and Lyndon Johnson. Now that we are faced with a choice between impeachment (and Gerald Ford) or three more years of slow strangulation under Tricky Dick—now, in this winter of our discontent, my pages of argumentation for Amendment XXVI look as obviously commonsensical as they did wackily far-out five years ago.*

A dramatic current instance of tide-turning, I won't say coat-turning, is my old friendly enemy, Arthur Schlesinger's latest tract for the times, *The Imperial Presidency*, in which he argues with his usual verve, conviction, and amplitude of historical reference precisely

---

* The present editors of *Esquire*, aware of the article's current topicality (and also of its journalistic failure five years ago), have had the happy, and bold, idea of reprinting it *in toto* this spring with updating side comments by me. After all, nobody seems to have read it at the time.

the opposite thesis he so gushingly (and incautiously) expressed in the title of his 1960 essay, "On Heroic Leadership and the Dilemma of Strong Men and Weak Peoples." (There's always been a Walter Mitty side to Arthur's historiography.) Then, as in his earlier hagiographical celebrations of such heroic leaders as Andrew Jackson and FDR, he was for a strong presidency, full speed ahead and damn the Constitutional torpedoes! A cynic might explain the shift from "heroic" to "imperial" by noting that Kennedy lived in the White House in 1960 and Nixon in 1973, but Schlesinger insists, "Nixon's presidency was not an aberration but a culmination." If so—myself I think it's a bit of both, like Stalin's relation to Lenin-Trotsky—it's taken him a long time to culminate: *The Age of Jackson* won the Pulitzer Prize in 1945. He was far from culmination ten years ago when I reviewed *The Politics of Hope*. See "Mr. Schlesinger's *Realpolitik*" later in this volume, especially the sentence I quote from the "Heroic Leadership" v. "Weak Peoples" dithyramb: "While the Executive should wield all his powers under the Constitution with energy, he should not be able to abrogate the Constitution except in face of war, revolution or economic chaos." I complained the exceptions took in a lot of misty ground that no actual president, with the partial exception of Lincoln (and he did his abrogating reluctantly, not heroically), had yet ventured to invade, and wondered why liberal ideologues were often quicker to cut Constitutional corners, in a good cause of course, than practical politicians. Arthur's reply was loftily dismissive of the "lamentations" of "old Dwight," but that was in the last year of Camelot heroism. I'm glad that Sir Launcelot —he's no Galahad for sure—has finally come around to my viewpoint about the presidency. Culminatively.

America!
America!

When I came back to New York
in the fall of 1957, after a year in London and two months in
Tuscany, I felt I had crossed a boundary wider than the Atlantic.
We are an unhappy people (I felt), a people without style, without
a sense of what is humanly satisfying. Our values are not anchored
securely, not in the past (tradition) and not in the present (community). There is a terrible *shapelessness* about American life.
These prosperous Americans look more tense and joyless than the
people in the poorest quarters of Florence. Even the English seem
to have more *joie de vivre*.

No nation in history has been richer or has had a more equal
distribution of wealth, and since 1940 there has been a fantastic
increase in the wealth and a considerable decrease in economic differences. If socialism be the equal sharing of plenty, then we are far
along the road. We have more of everything a human being can
conceivably, and inconceivably, want than Fourier, Proudhon, or
Marx could have imagined possible. According to *Fortune* (June,
1954), we spend over $30 billion a year on pleasure ("The Great
Fun Market"): sports, travel, hunting and fishing, books and magazines, liquor, gardening, home workshops, movies and television, etc.
Yet we are, I insist, not happy. Why not?

(1) The British and the Italians know how to live together, we
don't. Each does it differently, the British with all sorts of formal,

moral, legalistic inhibitions against interfering with the "rights" of
The Other, the Italians with a vivacious pleasure in the human other-
ness of The Other; but each people in its own way has very good
manners. Our manners are either bad or nonexistent. (I'm referring
to public, not private, manners; Americans are generous, kindly, and
hospitable to people they've been introduced to, but their "street
manners" are atrocious, as are the manners of those whose jobs
bring them into contact with strangers—taxi drivers, bus conductors,
sales clerks, waiters, policemen, porters, etc.) This is not as trivial as
it might seem. When manners are defective, ego clashes nakedly
against ego, the I collides with The Other, and the results are distressing and sometimes fatal. In our frontier West, differences of
opinion were settled with six-shooters.

(2) I think the lack of manners is connected with the sense of
violence one has in this country. The Italians are excitable and
passionate, they shout, curse, and gesture broadly; yet one feels far
more secure, physically, in Italy than here. In a single recent issue of
the *New York Times* there is a report of a twelve-year-old girl being
raped in a Brooklyn public school by a fifteen-year-old fellow student; of a traffic argument terminated by one driver shooting the
other and then later killing himself; of two teen-age girls being
stabbed in the back at noon outside a subway station by some teen-
age boys who had tried to get money from them; of the principal of
a city school who killed himself because he was being questioned by
a grand jury about violent episodes among students (another rape,
several assaults on teachers and one on a policeman *inside* the
school).* It's true I live in New York, where there are many Negroes
and Puerto Ricans whose crime rate, for understandable reasons, is
exceptionally high. But there are lots of Irish, Italian, and even
"good Anglo-Saxon" names in our daily crime reports. Nor is the
hinterland exactly pacific. About the same time as the above, the

---

* A friend who chances to have a thirteen-year-old girl cousin in this school
says her response to the rape and the newspaper publicity was: "My, aren't
we getting *popular!*" This is a very American reaction. Since the real community is too feeble to confer status, the individual looks to the synthetic mass-
community of newspaper readers. Like the boy recently arrested for robbing
a bank who said to his weeping mother, "Say, look at those headlines. Mom,
I'm famous!"

Nebraska National Guard was called out to protect the people of
Lincoln, the state capital, against a nineteen-year-old boy. Young
Charles Starkweather killed eleven people in three days, for various
reasons: because they disapproved of his "dating" their daughter,
because they had cars or other possessions he wanted, or because
they happened to be around. "Here was a totally defeated ego which
had no satisfactory anchorage in social life," explained Dr. James
Reinhardt of the University of Nebraska. (No American crime story
is complete without the psychiatrist's report, which is seldom as
perceptive as Dr. Reinhardt's.) "Socially, he was an empty man. The
only way he could become important was by killing."*

---

* (1970) The most egregious expression of this American underdog syndrome
was "Mother Oswald's" exultant *cri de coeur* after her son had been arrested
on suspicion of having killed the President of the United States: "They can't
push us around any more! We're in the history books now!" After failing in
everything from defecting to the Soviet Union to holding a job, or a wife, Lee
Harvey Oswald's daydreams came true: he was at last a success. For six
seconds in Dallas—enough to sneak into History by the servants' entrance. The
two days he survived in that surrealist jail—before he was gunned down by
Jack Ruby, another lifetime loser out to make a rep—these were, I venture,
not the least happy days of his life. Nor was his tearless widow, Marina,
unappreciative of her sudden rise in status (or "visibility," which has become
a synonym in this cockeyed country) due to what she grandly called "Lee
Harvey's fateful rifle." A trueborn naturalized American, Marina knew her
rights, including first serial.

It's gotten worse since 1957: the symbiosis between the violent clowns
and the mass media which put them on the front page and in prime TV time
(with whatever moralistic cluck-cluckings) because that's what the customers
want. Instant nationwide attention is guaranteed every wretch arrested for
some peculiarly atrocious murder—or better, murders: the one in Chicago who
cut the throats, seriatim, of half a dozen helpless young nurses; the demented
graduate student whose "fateful rifle" killed fifteen passersby on the University
of Texas campus in two hours, from his sniper post at the top of the university's skyscraper library (America!); the Manson "family" (America!) and
the "Boston Strangler" whose exploits are celebrated in drama, cinema, and
the press, underground as well as above.

Notoriety becomes fame in the case of murderers whose victims are
celebrated. Every quirky dullard who pulls a trigger to "equalize" himself
with a King or a Kennedy becomes immediately fascinating to millions of
fellow citizens who wouldn't have looked twice at him before he blasted his
way into History. In our mass psychology, the mana of the famous victim
spills over onto the obscure killer. A nobody couldn't bring down a somebody,
could he?

Or could he? My view is he could, and often has. But in either case,
there's no doubt that the American public, via its symbiotic parasites of the

(3) The American landscape is lovely save where American man has touched it, and since by now he has touched it almost everywhere one is likely to go—and torn down the structures of earlier American men who had more sense of fitness—we live in ugliness. There is the great American roadside, lined with motels and diners and hot-dog stands, paved with the best quality concrete (and the worst quality intentions) that writhes through the land like a tapeworm. And there are the cities, vast deserts of the present that sometimes look spectacular from a distance, like the Grand Canyon—and are as pleasant to live in. By comparison, in London or in Tuscany one lives embedded in the past, a state of being I, personally, like.*

(4) *There:* a community, each person differentiated by status and function but each a part of an orderly social structure. *Here:* everybody "equal" in the sense that nobody respects anybody else unless he has to, by *force majeure;* the national motto should be not "E Pluribus Unum," not "In God We Trust," but "I got mine and screw you, Jack!" (or better, "Brother"—"friend" and "brother" being used by Americans to express extreme hostility and contempt). *There:* continuity with the past, so that some level is taken for granted: there is a bottom, some things aren't done; the bottom may be broken through—as in the London mass newspapers—but at least there is a sense of something being violated. *Here:* no bottom, no continuity, no level: a jungle in which anything can happen without anybody's thinking it out of the ordinary. Each individual makes his

---

mass media, is willing and eager to pay attention, plus sizable cash sums, to mediocrities like Oswald and Ray, nuts like Manson and Sirhan—it's a nice question which type is duller—whose one achievement in a lifetime of obscure frustration is the orgasmic moment when they shed the blood of their, putting it mildly, betters. Orgasm is one of the last unalienable rights left to the common man: it costs nothing, takes little talent whether a trigger or a penis is squeezed, and it can't be controlled by the authorities. And when one adds the prospect of Publicity, one sees why violence has been spreading. The more unimaginative New Left Radicals like the Weathermen have begun to go in for it, a perversion of frustrated idealism not without parallels in nineteenth-century Europe—cf. Dostoevsky's *The Possessed.* Individual violence is the last American frontier, the one remaining career open to nontalent. Look, mom, I'm famous! . . . (1973) Add Bremer.

* I have just returned (September 15, 1958) from my first visit to Los Angeles, which is to New York, so far as attractiveness, sense of the past, and human scale, as New York is to London.

own culture, his own morality, and sometimes very well—our individual saints and savants don't compare unfavorably with those abroad —but it's "all on his lonesome," as we say—a significant American idiom. The same *tendencies* exist in Europe—the same destruction of the order of the past, physical and social, by the cancerous growth of mass society—but they are much less advanced. When one hears Europeans complaining about the Americanization of Europe, one wishes they could spend a few weeks over here and get a load of the real thing. Or rather a few years—most European tourists, except for Madame de Beauvoir, seem to like America. For them, the customs and the landscape are as strange as if it were Java or Tibet, and they find it all "stimulating" and "fascinating," as I dare say it is if you don't have to live here. The tourist's exotic is the native's poison.*

(5) Our Cult of Youth. Old people bore us, and we send them to nice rest homes if we can afford it. In London and Tuscany, where the idea of a community persists, the old are a normal part of life; they are considered interesting because they know about the past. But we think of them as has-beens, forgetting that what has been is the root of what will be. Americans think of the ideal age as somewhere around twenty. In the next two decades, this will become crucial because both Old and Young will increase much faster than the rest of us. The teen-age population will grow fantastically by some 70 percent, because of the post-1945 was babies.† The over-fifty population will grow next fastest. So far, the social workers are

---

* Friends have suggested that perhaps the same applies to me, that if I spent not one year but five in London my admiration for the British way of life might be considerably moderated. I doubt it; but in any case, I'm sure my criticism would be directed to quite different defects than the ones I'm conscious of over here. Different, and, I think, less serious.

† Our teen-agers in the last fifteen years have become a new social group, a pressure bloc like labor or the farmers, complete with their own subculture (rock 'n' roll, hot-rod cars, horror movies). They have been able to free themselves from parental control because they have their own money (our post-1940 prosperity means bigger allowances for teen-agers and also bigger earnings from spare-time jobs) and because the parents, like other ruling classes in history, have lost confidence in their right to rule—in this case because of progressive education and of Freudian theories. See my two-part profile of Eugene Gilbert, the Dr. Gallup of teen-age market surveys, in *The New Yorker* of November 22 and 29, 1958.

worrying about the old folks, but everyone else is fascinated with the teen-agers.

(6) When we come into contact with other peoples, as our post-1945 imperial role has forced us to do—never has a world power taken up the insignia of *imperium* so reluctantly—we don't impress them. The British and the French weren't popular with their wards, but they weren't laughed at. Even the Soviet Russians, for all their ruthlessness, barely covered by the fig of ideology, seem to speak a more common language with other peoples than we do. I think the difference is that Americans appear to other nations to be at once gross and sentimental, immature and tough, uncultivated and hypocritical, shrewd about small things and stupid about big things. In these antinomies fatally appears our lack of style. John Foster Dulles, the pious Artful Dodger, is our prototype in world affairs. A London journalist once complained to me, apropos Henry Luce's organization: "I can deal with gangsters or with Boy Scouts, but I must admit I'm at a loss with Boy Scouts who act like gangsters."

The point was illustrated during Mr. Nixon's recent agony in Latin America. On the one hand, Nixon getting himself chronically mobbed while attempting to spread "goodwill" and let's-talk-it-over-boys reason in those dark regions—"Don't you want to hear *facts?*" he cried desperately to the students of Lima amidst the jeers and stones. On the other hand, Eisenhower's instant explosion of anger when he learned of the violence in Caracas, and his instant reflex: send in the marines! "The President of the United States," spoke the Secretary of State to the Venezuelan ambassador, "expects the authorities in Venezuela to take every possible measure to protect the Vice-President. . . . And if there is any lack of will or capacity to give that, we would like to know about it quickly." Eisenhower expects every Venezuelan to do his duty by the mother country. This was backed up by airmailing four companies of marines and paratroopers to our military bases in the Caribbean, lest the Communists have trouble keeping green the memory of Haiti and Nicaragua. Thus a goodwill tour ended up with the marines. It was all very American. American in the notion that a big smile, a firm handshake, and a sincere willingness to Talk It Over will soothe the most savage breast—our old faith in democratic discussion and our new faith in public relations—and also American in the mindless resort to force when this naïve illusion collapses.

Eisenhower's handling of the Little Rock school-integration crisis is curiously parallel, and not only because the 101st Airborne Division was involved both times. Racial integration is as explosive an issue in the South as anti-Yanquism is in Latin America, and with as deep roots; the Supreme Court since 1954 has been dealing with it admirably, with a combination of firmness and patience. Eisenhower first tried to "talk it over" with Governor Faubus, a goodwill tour of an intractable issue, and then, when Faubus, a demagogue with a perfect cause, expectably made trouble, at once went to the other extreme and sent in the troops. It has so far cost us over four million dollars to keep eight Negro children in Little Rock High School, nor does the wound show signs of healing. Indeed, the use of troops, objectionable in principle as a violation of states' rights (since other means of enforcing the law had by no means been exhausted) has inflamed and prolonged the infection. There are some issues that yield *neither* to the public-relations smile nor to the paratroopers. Most puzzling.

Since I've been away, the March of Progress has been progressing. Out of every ten American houses, eight (81 percent) now have television sets, almost nine (87 percent) have washing machines, and practically all (96 percent) have electric refrigerators. Everybody but me has a new car. The Negro janitor of my apartment building has a bigger, sleeker one than I have ever been able to afford. I can't say I entirely envy him. The new cars are hideous beyond the imagination of a Dante (or a Steinberg), mobile juke boxes that violate every principle of taste and functionalism, longer and lower and more insanely powerful than ever, lathered with chrome in fantastic zigs and zags and rhomboids, their behinds elongated and streamlined until one can't tell if they're coming or going, with upswept fins and quadruple taillights winking and gleaming like a moon rocket about to take off. (Anal eroticism? Protecting the rear lest a certain backward country "catch up with and overtake" us in the March of Progress? Or both? A traveler back from New Guinea says the natives sum it up: "This fella Sputnik him bugger-up Uncle Sam.") We are contemptuous of Victorian taste, or used to be until we entered the fluorescent age, but what, oh, what will they say about these cars in 2058, assuming there is a 2058?

The March of Labor has continued. For a long time now—in America this means about ten years—unionism has been part of the normal American Way of Life. While this is on the whole good, it also means that another disruptive force in our society—which I think could do with a little more disrupting—has been neutralized. . . . The average worker has now completed twelve years of schooling, that is, he has gone through high school; as recently as 1940, it was only nine years. . . . One Leo Perlis, Director of Community Service Activities for the AFL-CIO (that such a post exists is a sign of labor's maturity, if not, indeed, its senility), has revealed that his department is about to train bartenders in social-work techniques. "Bartenders," he explained, "see more people with social problems than social workers do. Instead of just listening to a customer with a problem, these trained bartenders would be able to refer them to the proper community agency." . . . The Welfare and Retirement Fund of the United Mine Workers announces, for the year ended June 30, 1957, receipts of $157 million, of which $138 million was spent on pensions ($100 a month), medical benefits (the UMW now has a string of ultramodern hospitals and clinics that give its members better medical services than all but the wealthiest nonminers can afford), and payments to widows and orphans. When one remembers Ludlow, Harlan, and other mineworkers' battles in this century, one is again impressed by the phenomenon of John L. Lewis, the Winston Churchill of our labor movement, a leader of large, courageous, and retrograde views who in 1946 bullied the mineowners into financing the Fund. "No pen can write, no tongue can tell, no vocabulary of language is large enough to express the many benefits that will come to the American coal-miner and his family through the establishment of the Welfare and Retirement Fund," Mr. Lewis observed at the time. Like Churchill, he exaggerated, but not much.* There has even developed a union of union organizers,

* (1970) Later developments in the UMW have revealed the Lewis machine, which functions along the old lines long after his death, to be a less benign dictatorship than I thought in 1958: collaborationist with the industry against the union rank and file under the guise of being "practical" and "responsible" (the term for this kind of sell-out used to be "labor statesmanship"); even the health-welfare program has dubious, retrograde aspects not visible to me twelve years ago. The murder of Mike Yablonsky, his wife, and his daughter

the Field Representatives' Federation, which for many months has
been demanding from the AFL-CIO recognition as the collective-
bargaining agent for its 225 organizers, as well as grievance procedures, a better pension plan, and higher dismissal pay. The employer
has not only refused to bargain, but also has fired almost half of its
organizers.*

One of the hardest things for an expatriate to get used to is our
advertising. Not only that it's blatant and vulgar; it's that, too, but
not so much as Europeans think, and often it's more sophisticated
than *their* advertising. After all, we've been at it longer. In fact,
judging by its ads, American capitalism is mature to the point of
decadence. For several generations, our economy has been organized
around consumption rather than production. The consumer has
manfully, doggedly done his best. (*Life* once reported that the average American family has accumulated in its closets and on its shelves
about ten thousand separate possessions; these constitute "a major
problem of family life"—our national symbol is not the overflowing
cornucopia but rather the overflowing wastebasket.) But by now the
poor fellow is just picking at his plate. His appetite must be stimulated by outré refinements: A left-handed checkbook. An under-
water scooter that motorizes lazy skin-divers ($350). The Executone,
an interoffice communication system with "built-in courtesy"—about
the only kind you get around an American office—that announces
calls by "soft chime and signal light." A fountain pen that fills itself
by capillary attraction. A toothpaste that is shot out by compressed

---

last year—like the Moscow Trials in Soviet Russia—suddenly revealed the rot
and corruption in the UMW establishment. Mr. Yablonsky had been rash
enough to challenge, effectively, the Lewis-machine incumbent in an election
for the presidency. . . . (1973) Several high officials of the UMW are
going to jail for this murder.

* I ran across one recently, a veteran New Dealer I have known and respected
for years. He told me that the AFL-CIO disregarded seniority in cutting down
its field staff, selecting for immediate discharge those who belonged to the
union. Also that the most insistent on thus punishing members of the Field
Representatives' Federation were the "liberals," notably David Dubinsky and
Walter Reuther. I asked him why. He shrugged. "They're so damned
virtuous. With them, it's a noble cause, and we're betraying the workers when
we organize."

air at the touch of a button (no more of that laborious squeezing), and another that comes out in red and white stripes. Parallel-O-Plate, a new window glass that "keeps buildings from looking wrinkled." A heart-shaped electrical anti-snoring device called "Turn Over, Darling" that buzzes under the pillow of the party of the first part when the party of the second part presses a button ($10). A new girdle with the perhaps unfortunate name "Open Sesame." An Esso lubricant that makes pop bottles shiny: "Oil research adds a bright note to your moments of pleasure. Take the clean, glistening bottle that lets the sparkle of a soft drink shine through. . . ." Etc., etc., etc.

In the balmy pre-Goldfine days, Sherman Adams, the "Assistant President," revealed that the actual president had asked "some able people" to work up "a world-wide cultural conference" on ways and means of Using Scientific Progress for Peace not War. (This is presumably a supplement to the guided-missile program.) "Who is there who can say," asked Mr. Adams in one of the longest rhetorical questions since Demosthenes, "Who is there who can say that a convocation in this country of scholars, historians, artisans [sic], theologians, educators, sociologists, philosophers, artists, and musicians —representatives of the cultural pursuits of all the human race— meeting each other in their respective groups, could not suggest new and better ways for human beings to exist peaceably together and to reap the greatest rewards from man's scientific discoveries?" Well, I am one who can say they could not. And I can also tell the Research Society for Creative Altruism (founded by Professor Pitirim A. Sorokin of Harvard in 1949), which lately convened at the Massachusetts Institute of Technology to work out "a scientific approach to man's moral problems," that its efforts will come to naught. Unfortunately, space doesn't permit giving the reasons for these predictions except to observe that science and morals are parallel lines that have never, so far, met. But of their accuracy there is, also unfortunately, no doubt whatsoever.

Last fall the New York Board of Education removed *Huckleberry Finn* from its approved textbook list for public schools because Negro groups had objected to its use of the term "nigger," as in "Miss Watson's big nigger named Jim." That the book is (in part)

a protest against the indignity of slavery, that Jim is its moral hero—
these trivia didn't weigh in the scale against "nigger." Doubtless
Mark Twain should have had his backwoodsmen refer to "Miss
Watson's big Negro named Jim."* After this *putsch* against *Huckleberry Finn*, another news item appeared. In 1942, the National
Association for the Advancement of Colored People met with the
Motion Picture Producers Association to protest against "the stereo-
typed representation in films of Negroes as bumbling, comical
characters." The protest was effective and fewer "undignified" roles
were offered to Negro actors. In fact, fewer roles of any kind were
offered to them: between 1945 and 1957 the number of Negro movie
performers declined from 500 to 125. Last fall, the NAACP was
therefore constrained to hold a second conference with the MPPA.
"At the meeting," reports the *New York Times*, "Mr. Wilkins,
executive secretary of the NAACP, said 'misconceptions' had arisen
[and] disavowed any intention on the part of the Association to act
as a 'censor.' . . . He said there was no objection to Negro actors
playing 'menial' characters, such as maids, butlers, or janitors, or
being cast in comedy roles. He stressed that the Association wanted
to dispel the notion that it insisted on a 'one-for-one policy,' whereby
if a Negro were shown in a menial role there must also be a dignified
representation of another Negro." In short, Mr. Wilkins climbed
down. The arts are a chancy field for pressure groups, even ones with
aims as admirable as those of the NAACP. Censorship has what our
ad writers would call a Built-In, Automatic Kick-Back.

The New Yorker for October 26, 1957, contained some extremely
important (and extremely disturbing) data on the American Way of
Life: a lengthy article by Eugene Kinkead summarizing the findings
of a team of army experts, mostly psychiatrists, who have completed
a man-by-man study of the 4,428 American soldiers who came back
from Communist prison camps after the Korean war. The army
made the study to find out what lay behind two shocking statistics:
(1) "roughly one out of every three American prisoners in Korea was

---

* (1973): Now would have to be: "Miss Watson's big black named Jim." Or
should it be "Black"?

guilty of some sort of collaboration with the enemy"; and (2) over one-third of our war prisoners—2,730 out of 7,190—died in captivity. It was not starvation or hardship that caused the high American death rate—the army report shows the Communists fed their prisoners fairly well.

> "It is a sad fact, but it is a fact [said Major Anderson] that the men who were captured in large groups early in the war often became unmanageable. They refused to obey orders, and they cursed and sometimes struck officers who tried to enforce orders. Naturally, the chaos was encouraged by the Communists, who told the captives . . . rank no longer existed [and] they were all equal as simple prisoners of war released from capitalist bondage. At first, the badly wounded suffered most. On the marches back from the line . . . casualties on litters were often callously abandoned beside the road. Able-bodied prisoners refused to carry them, even when their officers commanded them to do so. If a Communist guard ordered a litter shouldered, our men obeyed; otherwise, the wounded were left to die. . . . The strong regularly took food from the weak. . . . Many men were sick, and these men . . . were ignored, or worse. Dysentery was common in the camps and . . . on winter nights, helpless men with dysentery were rolled outside the huts by their comrades and left to die in the cold."

Many of the 2,730 prisoners who died died because they just lay down and gave up. It was partly that no one washed them, fed them, kept them on their feet—"I got mine—screw you, Jack!"—but it was also that they had lived too long in the land of plenty:

> What struck Major Anderson most forcibly was the almost universal inability of the prisoners to adjust to a primitive situation. "They lacked the old Yankee resourcefulness. This was partly . . . the result of some new failure in the childhood and adolescent training of our young men—a new softness." For months . . . most prisoners displayed signs of shock, remaining within little shells they had created to protect them from reality. There was practically no communication among the men, and . . . very few seemed to be interested even in providing themselves with the basic necessities of food, warmth, and

shelter. . . . "An American soldier goes into the field with comforts that the majority of the world's population doesn't have even at home," said Anderson. "The average prisoner seemed lost without a bottle of pills and a toilet that flushed."

So, too, with collaboration. The army researchers found there had been "a fantastic amount of fraternizing with the enemy." The majority of American prisoners "yielded in some degree to Communist pressure." Quite a large majority—87 percent, in fact. The basic reason was the same as that which had caused the high death rate, a lack of solidarity:

> Major Segal told me that most of the repatriates came home thinking of themselves not as a part of a group, bound by common loyalties, but as isolated individuals. This emerged in their response to questions about what their service unit had been. Where the Turks proudly gave their regiment and brigade the Americans were likely to respond with the number of their prison camp.

Thus the latest effective authority (as with the Americans obeying their Communist guards but not their own officers) is the one the isolated, rootless American obeys. This is not individualism but "floating collectivism," as in "floating kidney."*

—*Dissent*, Autumn, 1958

---

* (*1971*) In Vietnam some of our soldiers have reacted very differently to the same Asiatic-Communist enemy; cf. My Lai and other atrocities the media are getting around to informing us about now that guilt-ridden veterans are beginning to speak out on what they saw—and did. But it's merely the other side of the same coin: submission to the powerful, brutality to the weak, and always a proper respect for authority. The "GIs" ("Government Issue," originally an ironical term for the nonofficer underdogs, coined by themselves, that has lost its irony in our Asiatic wars) who betrayed their comrades in the North Korean prison camps under pressure from the effective authority, which happened to be Communist, were blood brothers to the GIs in Vietnam who betrayed their humanity by torturing and massacring prisoners and civilians because they were encouraged to do so by *their* effective authority, from Lieutenant Calley down to sergeants and up to generals, which happened to be anti-Communist. Like a pilot-fish attaching itself to the nearest shark, our free-swimming conformism instinctively gloms onto the nearest authority. It is an accident of time and place whether this is represented by Chinese prison guards or American field officers.

Afterword

When the above article was published in *Dissent*, I prefaced it with the following note:

"America! America!" was originally written as a New York Letter to Encounter, *the Anglo-American London monthly, of which I was an advisory editor for a year. Before I returned to the States in the fall of 1957, I suggested to the editors, Stephen Spender and Irving Kristol, friends with whom I'd worked pleasurably, that I might write up my first impressions of the old country after a year abroad in England and Italy. They thought it a good idea and I did so. They accepted it, then a month or so later rejected it, then almost immediately re-accepted it, and finally after another six weeks definitively rejected it. These shifts reflected the attitude of* Encounter's *"front office," the Congress for Cultural Freedom in Paris, which publishes the magazine with funds supplied by several American foundations. The people in Paris felt the Letter was exaggerated, one-sided, unfounded, and in bad taste, and they feared it might cause American foundations to cut off supplies. The editors did what they could—hence the shifting—but ultimately yielded. Perhaps they felt that Paris (and its moneyed foundations) was worth a mass. Or a mess. I'm sorry to feel obliged to make all this public, because I like* Encounter's *editors (and even its front-office Metternichs) and because I very much enjoyed the year I spent in London on* Encounter. *But I think readers have a right to know when a magazine makes an editorial decision for extraneous reasons, especially this kind of reason. But I must also state that (a) the Paris office is not ordinarily consulted about manuscripts (mine apparently was shown to one of the Paris boys merely as a matter of interest—the editor thought he'd enjoy it!) and also that (b) such intervention is extremely rare. I can recall no such pressure from Paris while I was there.*

The above took on a more sinister meaning ten years later when *Ramparts* revealed that the CIA had been the secret angel (via one of its "conduit" foundations, the Farfield) of the Congress for Cultural Freedom, and so of *Encounter*. My puzzlement at *Encounter*'s long havering over, and final rejection of, my piece was because it seemed journalistically not inferior to others I had written for the magazine which had been accepted without hesitation or palaver. It was in fact printed twice: by *Dissent* and also in the October, 1958, number of *The Twentieth Century*, a London political-literary magazine like *Encounter*—except that it was not financed by the CIA.

So now the mystery is explained. I'm convinced that Spender and Kristol didn't know about the CIA financing, for reasons too long to explain here, including my one year's close editorial association with them plus letters and talks, both before and after the *Ramparts* bombshell exploded. The Paris office of the Congress was, of course, in the know. It does seem odd that they should have felt so strongly about my little un-American raspberry: one would have thought the CIA more sophisticated. Couldn't they see that for *Encounter* to publish it would weaken the rumors even then going around that the magazine was financed by the U.S. government? And could they have thought I would shut up about it and drop the matter?

I devoted my "Politics" column in the June, 1967, *Esquire* to what might be called "Confessions of an Unwitty CIA Agent." It's too long to reprint here, but a note I had in the September, 1967, column gives the ethical gist:

> What the London press calls The *Encounter* Affair has ripened since my Confessions appeared here last June I offer as an updating footnote a letter I wrote to the *New York Times* on May 10. (They didn't print it—the *Times* never prints my letters—and they didn't even send me their usual printed letter explaining it's nothing personal, just lack of space.) I wrote the letter after the *Times* had reported that Stephen Spender and Frank Kermode—the two English editors—had resigned over the CIA-financing issue, leaving Melvin Lasky, the American editor, as sole occupant of the burning deck whence all but he had fled; also that, unlike the junior Casabianca, he felt quite comfortable there, thank you, hardly even warm; he

implied his two colleagues were oversensitive and were making a fuss about trivia.

The latest installment of My Secret Life with the Editor of the *New York Times* reads:

Sir:

As a former editor of *Encounter* in 1956–7, may I express my distaste for Melvin Lasky's flippant dismissal of Stephen Spender's statement of resignation as "a storm in a teapot"? And may I make two observations?

(1) Secret financing infects the good faith of a magazine, and all the more so when it comes from an espionage agency of a government. I should myself not have accepted the job with *Encounter*, nor would I have written for it, had I known about the CIA funding. I was made an "unwitting" accomplice of the CIA's dirty work. I was played for a sucker, and I resent Lasky's sneer at Spender's quite proper anguish over the magazine's dirtied past.

(2) "What is really involved is our own past," Spender stated. "Therefore I think the magazine should have a new start. A new start involves new editors." When *Ramparts* exposed the CIA link, I privately urged in letters to some of my former associates connected with the magazine and the Congress for Cultural Freedom (which was used to transmit the secret funds to *Encounter*) that the solution which would do *Encounter* the least damage would be for the old editors to resign and be replaced by new ones. In resigning, Spender acted with a sobriety and a sense of responsibility Lasky has not shown either in his comments or in his behavior. That Frank Kermode, the other English editor, has also resigned—and done so because he feels Lasky was not straightforward with him about the CIA subsidy—makes Lasky's position all the more embarrassing.*

—Unpublished letter to the *New York Times*, May 10, 1967.

---

* *(1971–1973) Encounter* still appears, Lasky is still its editor. Embarrassment is a painful but not fatal editorial complaint, it seems. No worse than a bad cold, really.

The 1960 Campaign:
An Anarchist View

I have been reading a book called *Candidates 1960* edited by Eric Sevareid and published by Basic Books, and it has activated two old prejudices: against newspaper journalism and against voting.

To take the more important one first: I have long been puzzled by the mystique that surrounds newspaper writing. People—especially newspapermen or, even more especially, ex-newspapermen—talk as if it were a craft practiced by a glamorous few who happen to be endowed with arcane skills. But in fact, anyone of normal intelligence can write a news story—I often wonder what they teach in those journalism schools, must be like learning to tie one's shoelaces. No special literary or mental qualities are required, since the point is not in the writing but in the mere presentation of brute facts which, since they are new, are of interest in themselves. The citizens of Athens probably didn't worry much about the diction or the profundity of thought of the messenger who brought them news of Marathon.

Speaking as a magazine journalist, I find the by-line stories in our leading dailies full of clichés, badly organized, wordy, superficial, and, in general, child's play compared to the simplest task I undertake. I have never been on a newspaper, but for a few weeks during my first year on *Fortune* I got some sense of what it is like. The editor of *Time*'s Business & Finance department was sick and I was put into his place. It was a delightful vacation; compared to the labor of organizing and writing even a short (three thousand words) *Fortune* piece, knocking out a half dozen little news stories a week was nothing; and yet *Time* must be harder to write for than a daily newspaper, since each *Time* story is the distillation of many news clips, which takes some thought and some writing skill. I concluded that the labor and talent involved in writing a magazine article is to that of writing a newspaper story as playing a Brahms sonata is to playing chopsticks.

Candidates 1960 has not changed my mind. The book consists of nine articles on Nixon, Kennedy, Symington, and other leading presidential "hopefuls," as we newspapermen say. They were written by "top-flight Washington correspondents." But except for a sensitive sketch of Stevenson by Mary McGrory of the Washington *Star*, they are all badly written and even worse organized, slinging a great many Facts at the reader with only the most primitive effort to put them into a coherent pattern. (Mr. Sevareid's introduction, "The Ideal Candidate," is thoughtful and well written, but he doesn't count since he is a CBS news analyst rather than a newspaperman.) The first article begins: "Two slabs of honeydew melon, one patently green, the other lusciously ripe, were among the many odd links in the chain that pulled Nelson Aldrich Rockefeller to his smashing victory in New York's gubernatorial election." Leaving aside the awkwardness of melons being links in a chain, one feels that this sort of writing cannot get at the truth. Another begins: "Just before midnight on December 1, 1958, an American traveler burst into his room in Moscow's National Hotel and startled his dozing wife with an excited account of an interview he had conducted a few minutes earlier." A third: "On a gray January day in 1952, after an excellent lunch with a group of important Democrats at the St. Louis Noonday Club. . . ." One can hear the instructor at the Columbia School of Journalism: Be Specific ("gray January day," "just before midnight on December 1, 1958"), The Lead Must Arouse Interest (those two slices of melon, now what could they *possibly* have to do with Rockefeller's career?), Get Color Into Your Copy (that "dozing wife"). Now these are all professional writers, at least newspaper writers, and this is the degraded language they have become habitu-

ated to using. The lack of thought or elementary organization cannot
be demonstrated without tedium. Apparently when a newspaperman
tries to write anything over a thousand words that is not a simple
reprise of yesterday's Facts, his higher faculties, long disused, are
stunned.

As for my prejudice against voting—reading *Candidates 1960*, or trying to read it, has set me again to wondering why one is always
considered irresponsible if one shows no interest in presidential
elections. I recall voting in four: for Al Smith in 1928, for Roosevelt
in 1932, for either Roosevelt or Norman Thomas in 1936 (can't
recall which), and for Stevenson in 1952. The first three may be
set down to youthful inexperience, but the last needs some explaining. My excuse is that Stevenson appealed to me personally. He got
me with his televised speeches on the night of his nomination: that
moving, spontaneous and *real* let-this-cup-pass-from-me talk on the
lawn when he first got the news; and his formal acceptance speech a
few hours later at the convention, which struck me as intellectually
clear and morally serious, in short, as noble. How hollow, fat-headed,
and "official" his predecessors sounded that night, even Harry
Truman! The quality of the man came through even more positively
than Roosevelt's in his "fireside talks," for Roosevelt was instinctively a demagogue, a gentlemanly demagogue, a decent and sensible
demagogue, but still a demagogue, craftily keeping himself on the
level of his hearers. But Stevenson in 1952 was an actual person. I
liked his campaign; he was decisive and courageous; I liked especially
his humor, which the Republicans claimed showed he was not
serious but which I thought showed just the opposite. Well. We
know what happened that time. By 1956 Stevenson was behaving
like a politician or even, God help us, a statesman. He was avoiding
"the tough ones," was generalizing as much as possible, and was
severely repressing his alleged frivolity. So I didn't vote.

　　　Nor do I expect to vote for any of the Candidates 1960. My
chief objection to them is, I'm afraid, personal. Each of them seems
to me to have allowed his handlers to "build him up" into a candidate by rubbing off all the rough edges that make a Somebody out of
Anybody. As E. E. Cummings writes: "a politician is an arse upon /
which everyone has sat except a man." It might be called building

up by tearing down. The trouble is they've all been built up (or torn down) to the same level, so that there's not enough to choose between them, to justify standing in line and making the muscular effort to pull down this or that lever. And what's it to me, really?

If I were threatened with a gun (or a fine of, say, over $100), I should probably "throw away my vote" with a write-in for Stevenson, who still remains, after eight years, not only the most distinguished, honest, and intelligent candidate on either side but also the *only* distinguished, etc.

There are several possible criticisms of the above position from the Good Citizenship standpoint. One is that it is frivolous to vote for a candidate merely because he appeals to one as a person. Another is that it is immoral to put a price on one's vote, even a negative price of minus $100. A third is that the victory of one or the other candidate "makes a difference" and so it is one's duty to pull down that lever. All assume (a) that there are important issues before the country and (b) that one has at least some vague idea as to which candidate, or at least which party, will do best, from one's point of view, on these issues.

What are the issues this time? The only important domestic one is racial equality, that is, it is the only issue on which there is any serious disagreement as to the need for a change in the *status quo*. We are not threatened with the loss of our traditional freedoms; McCarthyism is quiescent and no major candidate is on record against civil liberties. Quite the contrary—civil liberties are definitely chic. Nor are there any important economic issues, as there were in 1932 and 1936. Since 1940, the country is rich beyond the dreams of Midas (or Karl Marx); the rich are richer, as is their disgusting habit, but the poor are doing far better than they ever have before.* It is true there still are disgracefully many millions of them. It is also true that the classic proletariat of Marx—the miners, the steel and auto workers, the truckdrivers, etc.—have made disproportionate

---

* (1970) True, especially the next sentence, but a half truth, and the half ignored has proved to be the more important. See next piece, "Our Invisible Poor," for this dark side of the moon to which in 1960 I was as blind as you, *hypocrite lecteur, mon semblable, mon frère.*

gains while the white-collar workers, the clerks and librarians and teachers, are being paid much less than the social value of their work. But the proletarians are organized into powerful unions—the farmers aren't doing badly either—and I see no candidate or party that is dedicated to redressing this balance.

So we are left with the race "question"—though why it is a Question, or a Problem, I don't see, since the Negroes have all the right on their side—and even this is not a political issue except in the South. Both parties are for desegregation. Perhaps the Republicans are more reliable here, for obvious reasons. (And we shouldn't forget that the present splendid attack on the ancient *mores* of the South was initiated and has been kept in being largely by the U.S. Supreme Court under the leadership of Eisenhower's appointee, Chief Justice Earl Warren.) But even the Democratic floor leader in the Senate, Johnson of Texas, a most accomplished politician by all reports, felt it wise to push through twenty-four-hour sessions to defeat a Southern filibuster on the latest civil rights bill. One might also note, as explaining perhaps Senator Johnson's concern for Negro voting rights, the curious behavior of certain Southern police forces when race riots threatened to develop as a result of the equally curious insistence of Negro students on being served sitting down at lunch counters. (It was okay for them to get their food standing up, it seems, one of those fine distinctions which will always baffle us Northerners, who don't understand the real, the existential nature of the nigras.) The cops actually upheld law & order, turning fire hoses on the rioters and arresting *both* races. This history-making advance in civilization, like Senator Johnson's behavior, was of course due only partly to the Supreme Court. It was primarily a recognition of the political and social strength which the Negroes have built up since 1945. They have done it themselves to a large extent, but they have been able to do it only because of a swing of the political balance in their direction which is the most hopeful postwar development in these states.

Foreign policy is the other area where it might theoretically make a difference which candidate or which party one voted for. The crucial area, in fact, since it involves the survival of humanity. But it is just here that (a) the amateur voter cannot be expected to have any sensible opinion, and (b) there is no detectable difference between the parties.

(a) I assume that everyone except perhaps James Burnham and William Buckley, Jr., who have other fish to fry, are (1) worried about the effects of radiation on the human species and are therefore (2) anxious to avoid a war with the Soviet Union. (1) involves the matter of bomb tests, but I have personally been unable to decide what dangers exactly may be expected from continuing such tests; one eminent scientist issues an alarmist statement and another claims it is no worse than a bad cold; how in the world is an amateur to decide? Obviously it would be best to run no risks and stop all the tests, but then the political issue arises—if We stop and They don't, then will We lag so far behind Them that We become an inviting target? (There is a moratorium on tests at the moment, but God knows how or why it was arrived at.) (2) involves our general policy toward the Soviet bloc—should it be tough, soft, or in between? Containment or Coexistence? Is a tough policy more likely to avoid war than a soft one? I would say so, but this is merely because of my intensive study of the Soviet phenomenon when I was a Trotskyist twenty years ago, and I really wouldn't want our government to commit itself on this basis; also, Khrushchev is quite a different proposition from Stalin. And what is "tough" and what is "soft"? Can an electorate, most of whom are probably even less equipped than I to judge these matters (at least I read the New York Times), be expected to have a sensible judgment?*

(b) Even if some of the electorate do have such a judgment, what is the difference between the parties? One would expect the Democrats to be "softer" but they don't seem to be. They are the ones who press for bigger "defense" appropriations—I put the word in quotes because in this age of push-button wars the concept of Attack or Defense seems to be either casuistic or accidental—while the Republicans, for budget-balancing reasons unconnected with foreign policy, are on the other side. One would also expect the Dem-

---

* (1970) I now favor abandoning all bomb tests, including New Left ones; also the softest approach toward "the Soviet bloc," a much-battered hat that has long needed reblocking. Things have changed, information has surfaced since I wrote this ten years ago—it seems a century.

ocrats to be more sensitive to (a), but, except for Stevenson, they aren't. I'm not aware of any ringing statements by Humphrey, Kennedy, Johnson, or Symington on the horrors of atomic radiation (or is it, by now, hydrogenic?—that I don't know shows how specialized the whole subject has become). But I do remember that Truman came out *against* stopping bomb tests several years ago. And I also recall, when I was a Hoyt Fellow for a week at Yale two years ago, sitting in on a class conducted by Dean Acheson, another temporary Fellow, and discovering that he was not only of the opinion of Truman (who was also a Fellow that week—the groves of Academe are right on the main line these days) but had apparently not even heard there was any other. Stevenson had come out against the tests—maybe one should, really, write him in this time—but Acheson, the Republicans' *bête noire*, the non-back-turner on Alger Hiss, was blandly, genuinely perplexed when I raised the point. Finally, the Republicans used to be sincere isolationists; one could depend on them to be wrong on principle. But now their leading contender, Mr. Nixon, has for years been throwing his weight on the side of foreign aid, worrying about underdeveloped countries, and in general behaving in this area like Henry Luce or Max Lerner. It's all very confusing.

I suggest that our national elections—local ones sometimes present issues on which, since they are circumscribed, the voter may have some sensible opinion as to which side will advance his interests—I suggest they are perhaps elaborate techniques for avoiding, rather than resolving, political issues. In a country of almost two hundred million inhabitants, the scale is so large that nobody really knows what will be the effect of any political action.* All this excitement about presidential elections, this enormous expenditure of space in the press, these ridiculous conventions so thoroughly "covered" by

---

* Tolstoy's lengthy remarks in *War and Peace* on the absurdity of even a genius like Napoleon—and I see no genius among the Candidates 1960—pretending to foresee or control events involving millions of people each of whom, for such is the marvelous unpredictability of the human condition, may act in a way which throws out the larger calculation; I say Tolstoy's observations, while an artistic blemish on his great work, seem to me sensible per se.

highly paid technicians, all this is mere escapism, since whoever is elected will do roughly what he must and in any case cannot do very much, as compared to the changes that a newly elected mayor of a smallish city can, if he will, make. The bigger the job, the slighter the chances of effective action. I see national politics as mere busy-work to divert the civic-minded from the real political questions, which are local, practical matters that (a) make a real difference in the lives of the voters, and (b) can be decided one way or the other.

Granted that in certain historical turning points it does make a difference—Roosevelt's victory over Hoover in 1932 is an example, also Churchill's replacing Chamberlain in 1940—my opinion is that Armageddon happens rarely and that most times, this year for instance, the effect of one as against another built-up-torn-down candidate is in the realm of metaphysics and so of little interest to sensible people.

I realize this view is not universally shared. One of my fellow citizens has given a touching picture of his reactions to a presidential campaign:

> So that day in 1952 somebody said: "But you can't have a heart attack *now*. You've got to vote tomorrow if we have to take you there on a stretcher." As I walked away from the polling-place in that same autumn sunlight, I was struck down. . . . Later, I clawed my way through drugs and made out foggily a small bare room and a little nurse, sitting in one corner. When I stirred, she jumped up and asked if there was anything she could do for me. I said: "Tell me how the election turned out." She hesitated, disappeared, reappeared almost at once and said: "A landslide for Eisenhower." I stopped fighting the sedative and fell almost peacefully asleep.

This is Whittaker Chambers writing in the *National Review*. But it might have been Murray Kempton, also a master of politically emo-tive prose, who works the other side of the street. For in general the liberals get more hopped up about elections than the reactionaries do. For them, Armageddon is a quadrennial festival—already I'm being exhorted to use my vote to Keep Nixon Out of the White House.

But the odd thing is that, while one is made to feel like a lonely pariah if one says one is not going to vote, almost half the qualified voters in even the most hotly contested presidential election are in the same boat. That is, they simply don't bother to vote. Since the process takes only an hour or two, about as much as to see a movie or to drink a few beers in congenial company, one must conclude that almost half the electorate of this country couldn't care less who is to be the next president. I salute them. They have the root of the matter in them, they are politically mature, even if most of them don't know why they don't vote. They probably think they are just too lazy or ignorant or selfish or drunk to do so, but these excuses, adequate for a social worker, don't go down with me. They don't vote because they don't want to vote, of their own free will, and they don't want to because they feel it won't make any difference and that none of the candidates represents them and their interests. It's also discouraging, in a country this size, to think that one's vote is only about 1/70,000,000 of the total.

One thing is sure, however and unfortunately: almost none of the 45 percent of the electorate that never vote—the dark side of the political moon—are abstaining because of anarchist principle. They would probably be shocked to read Proudhon's famous indictment of elections, written a century ago but still to the point:

> What do all these elections matter to me? . . .
>
> It is said that it is necessary to do something, but I do not see the necessity of doing anything at such a price. Neither election nor voting, even if unanimous, solves anything. . . . I understand that one may submit to an arbitrary decision upon questions that are of no personal importance to one. . . . But upon principles, upon civil liberties and social tendencies, upon my labor, my subsistence, my life, upon this very question of Government—on all these vital matters, I reject all presumptive authority, all indirect solutions. *Here* I see universal suffrage as simply a lottery. . . .
>
> On the tenth of December, 1848, the People were consulted upon the choice of their first magistrate and they named Louis Napoleon by 5½ million out of 7 million voters. . . . From the standpoint of universal suffrage, I ought to accept his policy as the policy of the People. . . .
>
> Do you still talk of the People? I mean the People as it

shows itself in mass meetings and at the ballot box, the People which they did not dare consult about the Republic in February, the People which during the June Days overwhelmingly declared itself against socialism, the People which elected Louis Bonaparte because it adored Napoleon Bonaparte, the People which did not rise on June 13 and did not protest on May 31. Is this the People which will be enlightened from above when it comes to choosing capable and virtuous representatives and deciding upon the organization of Labor, Credit, Property and Power itself? . . .

Enough! Let us be frank. Universal suffrage, the popular mandate, the whole elective system is but child's play. I will not trust them with my labor, my peace of mind, my fortune. I will not risk a hair of my head to defend them.

Anarchist theory is almost as forgotten today as Gnosticism was after the third century, when Christianity had exterminated it as heretical. Yet anarchism has more to tell us today, I think, than does Marxism both about what's wrong with our overcentralized and overorganized society and about what steps might be taken to improve matters.

"Bakunin has a peculiar theory," Engels wrote in 1872. "The chief point is that he does not regard capital . . . as the main evil to be abolished. Instead, he thinks it is above all the State which must be done away with, and then capitalism will go to hell of itself. We, on the contrary, say: Do away with capital, the appropriation of the whole means of production in the hands of the few, and the State will fall away of itself. The difference is an essential one." It is, indeed, and in Bakunin's favor. Capitalism was abolished in Russia, but the more industry and agriculture were collectivized the more powerful grew the State. It is anarchism that shows a way out from the central problem of our time, the submerging of the individual in mass industrial society and in the centralized super-State. Marxism is revolutionary about private property, but this is no longer a central issue, and it is reactionary on the State, which it glorifies so long as it is that contradiction in terms, a "Workers' Socialist State." The only hope is some kind of anarchist decentralization which will break up mass society into communities small enough so that the individual can make himself felt, can express and defend *his own special interests*. The horrors of collectivization in China, which recently disturbed even Khrushchev, show what happens when the revolution goes according to Marx. Anarchism leads back to the individual and the community. It substitutes for coercion voluntary cooperation and it dares to think that people can help themselves better than Robert Moses, the U.S. Senate, and the cops can help them. This approach to politics is revolutionary: i.e., it is both impractical and necessary.

There is quite a lot of anarchism going on now in this country. The bourgeois free market, insofar as it still exists, is an admirably anarchist device for distributing goods—even the Russians have been forced to edge back toward it lately, the effects of state control on the economy being what they are. Our national talent for voluntary groups—from taxpayers' leagues to parent-teacher associations, garden clubs, farm cooperatives, charity organizations, and alumni associations—is in the anarchist tradition of free cooperation. The lunch counter sit-downs in the South have anarchist features: they were started spontaneously by Negro student groups, and they have been using a Gandhian technique of nonviolent resistance that has been worked out by one of my favorite cause groups, CORE, or the Congress of Racial Equality. What I like, as an anarchist, about CORE is that its members use nonviolent direct action on small, local, immediate problems, going in groups to segregated restaurants, soda fountains, swimming pools, barber shops (they got a nonsegregated barber shop in State College, Pennsylvania, by offering an initial stake of $1,800 to a Philadelphia barber to open a shop there), parks, beaches, and lunch counters.

Local issues these, but really much more important than whether Nixon or Kennedy gets that job. The Montgomery bus strike was also a small, local action, but the capacity for spontaneous organization and self-restraint shown by its participants was inspiriting to all of us and must have enormously raised the morale of the participants. They were doing something for themselves, which is the first quality of a good citizen. Compare the mess that Eisenhower made of the Little Rock situation by rushing in the troops; it is only the Supreme Court's tenacity in insisting that the Fourteenth Amendment means what it says, plus the equally cool tenacity of the colored population of the South in fighting for its rights, that has prevented Little Rock from being a national disaster.

Last summer John Bowles, the president of Rexall Drugstores, during a visit to Moscow was bothered when a Soviet girl guide asked him why, if the United States was so democratic and the Soviet Union so not so, only 60 percent of the former's electorate voted in the 1956 elections, while 98 percent of the latter's turned out for every election. Mr. Bowles was all the more irritated because her figures were right: "This burned me up, but I also came back as something of a dedicated man." His dedication, according to the *New York Times* of February 24, took the form of a great get-out-the-vote campaign which now involves not only the ten thousand Rexall drugstores but also the American Legion, the League of Women Voters, the American Heritage Foundation, the Coca-Cola company, and, more or less *ex officio*, the chairmen of the Democratic and of the Republican parties. (Politically active types always seem to prefer that one vote against their party rather than not vote at all. Nonvoting tends to throw doubt on the whole business, like not bothering to answer back in an argument.) It sounds like very big stuff, but when one gets down to reading the fine print, one finds that the combined political imaginations of Mr. Bowles, the American Legion, and the rest of his colleagues, including Coca-Cola, have, after their patriotic labors, come up with a very small mouse indeed: those ten thousand drugstores will be used "as centers of information on where, when and how citizens may register to vote and [in the stately prose of the *Times*] subsequently may cast their ballots." Coca-Cola will cooperate by "providing display boards, posters and signs to be erected in the drugstores," perhaps with a Norman Rockwell painting of Coke-drinkers lining up before some sleeve-gartered, bespectacled, kindly old Vermont registrar—The Pause That Refreshes. In some of the more wacky states like California, it will be legally possible to deputize the drug clerks as registration officers. And that's about all there is to Operation Rexall.

So many things don't seem to have occurred to him. For instance, that the 98 percent turnout in Soviet elections is a symptom not of democracy but of totalitarianism: Hitler also got 90 percent plus in his "elections." And that it really isn't because people can't find the polls that they don't vote. That a free-born American citizen, even after being completely informed as to "where, when and how" he could vote (not to mention those convenient drug clerks—let's hope an order for a cherry phosphate doesn't get converted into a

Republican registration); that he even then might choose *not* to vote, this is beyond the imagination of Mr. Bowles and the American Heritage Foundation.

One more thing that didn't occur to Mr. Bowles (a native of Monroe, North Carolina) is that the only part of America where such a get-out-the-vote campaign is necessary is the South. He was asked "what his Southern retail outlets would do when Negroes sought information in areas where registration of Negroes was discouraged if not prevented." (The "if not" phrase may be recommended to all journalism-school students who want to get a job on the *Times*.) His reply was forthright and definite: "Our clerks will offer no advice. They'll simply point to the blackboard containing all the information." One looks forward to a massive Negro registration in the South.

Mr. Bowles and his impressive supporters are typical ·of the sober, serious, and civic-minded citizens who have had a good educa tion and have a stake in the country. But their stake and their education have perhaps made them obtuse as to what elections really mean to the actual living breathing individual American citizen. It is this individual interest which is the only serious political point; I agree with the young Marx when he insisted, against Hegel, that the State is made for Man and not the other way round. The State, our euphemism for free democratic elections, has become a fetish with our educated classes, especially in contrast to the horrors, and they are horrors, of Soviet totalitarianism. Certainly it is good for citizens, all other things being equal, to have a chance to vote freely on Candidates 1960. But this is a minor good compared to the real political issues, which, except in some local elections, are not touched at all; I mean issues like sitting down at lunch counters or, in New York, the successful efforts of that great planner and public servant, Robert Moses, to destroy such slight remnants of community life as remain in this urban wasteland.

The trouble is also that all other things are not usually equal in historical crises, where it counts. The majority may be swayed, against their own interests, by some demagogue like Louis Napoleon, or they may be euchred, in a semilegal way, as they were by the Bolsheviks in 1917 and by Hitler in 1933. Do you still talk of The People? Let us rather talk about ourselves.

—*Commentary*, April, 1960

Afterword

I must confess that in 1964, only four years after this article was written, I voted for Johnson, stampeded by Goldwater's neanderthal bellicosity into believing his opponent's rhetoric about not sending American boys to do the job Asiatic boys ought to do. (It now seems neither can do the job.) Abandoning my time-tested anarchist principles, I whored after strange gods of Responsible Citizenship. I should have remembered the Wilson campaign slogan in 1916, "He Kept Us Out of War," also FDR's similar promises in 1940. But in the fall of 1964 Vietnam was—and in fact, still is—one of the smaller pebbles on the global Communist beaches we have been trying to police, ineffectually, for a quarter century. ("They wept like anything to see / Such quantities of sand. / 'If this were only cleaned away,' / They said, 'it would be grand!' / 'If seven maids with seven mops / Swept it for half a year, / Do you suppose,' the Walrus said, / 'That they could get it clear?' / 'I doubt it,' said the Carpenter / And shed a bitter tear.") Who could have foreseen in 1964 that this pebble would soon become a boulder? That five months after his election on a peace·platform, Johnson would be bombing North Vietnam and escalating into an open-ended war engulfing half a million American troops who would be dying—and killing the natives, more copiously —to crochet this antimacassar of Kiplingesque imperialism? "Take up the White Man's burden— / Send forth the best ye breed— / Go bind your sons to exile / To serve your captives' need. . . . Take up the White Man's burden / And reap his old reward: / The blame of those ye better / The hate of those ye guard. . . . By all ye cry or whisper / By all ye leave or do / The silent, sullen peoples / Shall weigh your Gods and you."

Who could have possibly foreseen it? Not me. I was habituated to the more plausible overseas military interventions of Woodrow, Franklin, and Harry—situations where American interests of some kind were involved—imperialist interests but still interests, a rationale that made sense from a nationalist viewpoint. So I was unprepared for the lunatic *Weltanshauung* of Hitler cropping up in the White House. Downright un-American. Still, I'm ashamed to have yielded, in a moment of weakness, to civic virtue. And if the compulsion to pull down a voting lever was overmastering, at least I could have kept my anarchist cool enough to pull down the one opposite Goldwater, who couldn't have done worse in Vietnam than Johnson (could he?) and who, as a minority-party president lacking control of Congress would have met more opposition to his war games (wouldn't he?). . . . I must also confess that in 1972 I voted for McGovern and proud of it as of 1973. Principles, even anarchist ones, must sometimes yield, or bend slightly, before brute reality—and the presidential choice in 1972 looks more brutal every day.

Our
Invisible Poor

In his significantly titled *The Affluent Society* (1958) Professor J. K. Galbraith states that poverty in this country is no longer "a massive affliction [but] more nearly an afterthought." Dr. Galbraith is a humane critic of the American capitalist system, and he is generously indignant about the continued existence of even this nonmassive and afterthoughtish poverty. But the interesting thing about his pronouncement, aside from the fact that it was inaccurate, is that it was generally accepted as obvious. For a long time now, almost everybody has assumed that, because of the New Deal's social legislation and—more important—the prosperity we have enjoyed since 1940, mass poverty no longer exists in this country.

Dr. Galbraith states that our poor have dwindled to two hardcore categories. One is the "insular poverty" of those who live in the rural South or in depressed areas like West Virginia. The other category is "case poverty," which he says is "commonly and properly related to [such] characteristics of the individuals so afflicted [as] mental deficiency, bad health, inability to adapt to the discipline of modern economic life, excessive procreation, alcohol, insufficient education." He reasons that such poverty must be due to individual defects, since "nearly everyone else has mastered his environment; this proves that it is not intractable." Without pressing the similarity of this concept to the "Social Darwinism" whose fallacies Dr. Gal-

75

braith easily disposes of elsewhere in his book, one may observe that most of these characteristics are as much the result of poverty as its cause.

Dr. Galbraith's error is understandable, and common. Last April [1962] the newspapers reported some exhilarating statistics in a Department of Commerce study: the average family income increased from $2,340 in 1929 to $7,020 in 1961. (These figures are calculated in current dollars, as are all the others I shall cite.) But the papers did not report the fine type, so to speak, which showed that almost all the recent gain was made by families with incomes of over $7,500, and that the rate at which poverty is being eliminated has slowed down alarmingly since 1953. Only the specialists and the statisticians read the fine type, which is why illusions continue to exist about American poverty.

Now Michael Harrington, an alumnus of the *Catholic Worker* and the Fund for the Republic who is at present a contributing editor of *Dissent* and the chief editor of the Socialist Party biweekly, *New America*, has written *The Other America: Poverty in the United States* (Macmillan, 1962). In the admirably short space of two hundred pages, he outlines the problem, describes in imaginative detail what it means to be poor in this country today, summarizes the findings of recent studies by economists and sociologists, and analyzes the reasons for the persistence of mass poverty in the midst of general prosperity. It is an important book.

The rich are almost as rich as ever and the poor are even poorer, in the percentage of the national income they receive. Yet, as will become apparent later, there have been major changes in the distribution of wealth, and there has been a general improvement in living standards, so that the poor are much fewer today than they were in 1939. "Most low-income groups live substantially better today," Dr. Gabriel Kolko admits, in his *Wealth and Poverty in America* (Praeger). "But even though their real wages have mounted, their percentage of the national income has not changed." That in the last half century the rich have kept their riches and the poor their poverty is indeed a scandal. But it is theoretically possible, assuming enough general increase in wealth, that the relatively poor might by now have achieved a decent standard of living, no matter how inferior to that of the rich. This theoretical possibility has not been realized, however.

Inequality of wealth is not necessarily a major social problem per se. Poverty is. Charles Péguy remarks, in his classic essay on poverty, "The duty of tearing the destitute from their destitution and the duty of distributing goods equitably are not of the same order. The first is an urgent duty, the second is a duty of convenience. . . . When all men are provided with the necessities . . . what do we care about the distribution of luxury?" What indeed? Envy and emulation are the motives—and not very good ones—for the equalization of wealth. The problem of poverty goes much deeper.

What is "poverty"? It is a historically relative concept, first of all. "There are new definitions [in America] of what man can achieve, of what a human standard of life should be," Mr. Harrington writes. "Those who suffer levels of life well below those that are possible, even though they live better than medieval knights or Asian peasants, are poor. . . . Poverty should be defined in terms of those who are denied the minimal levels of health, housing, food, and education that our present stage of scientific knowledge specifies as necessary for life as it is now lived in the United States." His dividing line follows that proposed in recent studies by the United States Bureau of Labor Statistics: $4,000 a year for a family of four and $2,000 for an individual living alone. (All kinds of income are included, such as food grown and consumed on farms.) This is the cutoff line generally drawn today.

Mr. Harrington estimates that between forty and fifty million Americans, or about a fourth of the population, are now living in poverty. Not just below the level of comfortable living, but real poverty, in the old-fashioned sense of the word—that they are hard put to it to get the mere necessities, beginning with enough to eat. This is difficult to believe in the United States of 1963, but one has to make the effort, and it is now being made. The extent of our poverty has suddenly become visible. The same thing has happened in England, where working-class gains as a result of the Labour Party's post-1945 welfare state blinded almost everybody to the continued existence of mass poverty. It was not until Professor Richard M. Titmuss, of the London School of Economics, published a series of articles in the *New Statesman* last fall, based on his new book, *Income Distribution and Social Change*, that even the liberal public in England became aware that the problem still persists on a scale that is "statistically significant," as the economists put it.

Statistics on poverty are even trickier than most. For example, age and geography make a difference. There is a distinction, which cannot be rendered arithmetically, between poverty and low income. A childless young couple with $3,000 a year is not poor in the way an elderly couple might be with the same income. The young couple's statistical poverty may be a temporary inconvenience; if the husband is a graduate student or a skilled worker, there are prospects of later affluence or at least comfort. But the old couple can look forward only to diminishing earnings and increasing medical expenses. So also geographically: A family of four in a small town with $4,000 a year may be better off than a like family in a city—lower rent, no bus fares to get to work, fewer occasions (or temptations) to spend money. Even more so with a rural family. Although allowance is made for the value of the vegetables they may raise to feed themselves, it is impossible to calculate how much money they *don't* spend on clothes, say, or furniture, because they don't have to keep up with the Joneses. Lurking in the crevices of a city, like piranha fish in a Brazilian stream, are numerous tempting opportunities for expenditure, small but voracious, which can strip a budget to its bones in a surprisingly short time.

It is not, therefore, surprising to find that there is some disagreement about just how many millions of Americans are poor. The point is that all the recent studies* agree that American poverty is still a mass phenomenon.

The reason Dr. Galbraith was able to see poverty as no longer "a massive affliction" is that he used a cutoff of $1,000, which even in 1949, when it was adopted in a congressional study, was probably too low (the CIO argued for $2,000) and in 1958, when *The Affluent Society* appeared, was simply fantastic.

---

* (1973) I.e., *Income and Welfare in the United States* (McGraw-Hill) by Dr. James N. Morgan and others, *Wealth and Poverty in America* by Dr. Gabriel Kolko, and *Poverty and Deprivation*, a bulky and important pamphlet issued by the Conference on Economic Progress in Washington—its chief author is said to be Leon Keyserling.

The model postwar budgets drawn up in 1951 by the Bureau of Labor Statistics to "maintain a level of adequate living" give a concrete idea of what poverty means in this country—or would mean if poor families lived within their income and spent it wisely, which they don't. Dr. Kolko memorably summarizes the kind of living these budgets provide:

> Three members of the family see a movie once every three weeks, and one member sees a movie once every two weeks. There is no telephone in the house, but the family makes three pay calls a week. They buy one book a year and write one letter a week.
>
> The father buys one heavy wool suit every two years and a light wool suit every three years; the wife, one suit every ten years or one skirt every five years. Every three or four years, depending on the distance and time involved, the family takes a vacation outside their own city. In 1950, the family spent a total of $80 to $90 on all types of home furnishings, electrical appliances, and laundry equipment. . . . The family eats cheaper cuts of meat several times a week, but has more expensive cuts on holidays. The entire family consumes a total of two five-cent ice cream cones, one five-cent candy bar, two bottles of soda, and one bottle of beer a week. The family owes no money, but has no savings except for a small insurance policy.

One other item is included in the B.L.S. "maintenance" budget: a new car every twelve to eighteen years.

This is an ideal picture, drawn up by social workers, of how a poor family *should* spend its money. But the poor are much less provident—installment debts take up a lot of their cash, and only a statistician could expect an actual live woman, however poor, to buy new clothes at intervals of five or ten years. Also, one suspects that a lot more movies are seen and ice-cream cones and bottles of beer are consumed than in the Spartan ideal. But these necessary luxuries are had only at the cost of displacing other items—necessary necessities, so to speak—in the B.L.S. budget.

The Conference on Economic Progress pamphlet, *Poverty and Deprivation*, deals not only with the poor but also with another large section of the "underprivileged," which is an American euphemism almost as good as "senior citizen"; the authors define "deprivation" as "above poverty but short of minimum requirements for a modestly comfortable level of living." They claim that 77 million Americans, or *almost half the population*, live in poverty or deprivation. One recalls the furor Roosevelt aroused with his "one-third of a nation—ill-housed, ill-clad, ill-nourished." But the political climate was different then.

The distinction between a family income of $3,500 ("poverty") and $4,500 ("deprivation") is not vivid to those who run things: the 31 percent whose incomes are between $7,500 and $14,999 and the 7 percent of the topmost top dogs, who get $15,000 or more. These two minorities, sizable enough to feel they *are* the nation, have been as unaware of the continued existence of mass poverty as this reviewer was until he read Mr. Harrington's book. They are businessmen, congressmen, judges, government officials, politicians, lawyers, doctors, engineers, scientists, editors, journalists, and administrators in colleges, churches, and foundations. Since their education, income, and social status are superior, they, if anybody, might be expected to accept responsibility for what the Constitution calls "the general welfare." They have not done so in the case of the poor. And they have a good excuse. It is becoming harder and harder simply to *see* the one-fourth of our fellow citizens who live below the poverty line.

> The poor are increasingly slipping out of the very experience and consciousness of the nation [Mr. Harrington writes]. If the middle class never did like ugliness and poverty, it was at least aware of them. "Across the tracks" was not a very long way to go. . . . Now the American city has been transformed. The poor still inhabit the miserable housing in the central area, but they are increasingly isolated from contact with, or sight of, anybody else. . . . Living out in the suburbs, it is easy to assume that ours is, indeed, an affluent society. . . .
>
> Clothes make the poor invisible too: America has the best-dressed poverty the world has ever known. . . . It is much easier in the United States to be decently dressed than it is to be decently housed, fed, or doctored. . . .
>
> Many of the poor are the wrong age to be seen. A good number of them are sixty-five years of age or better; an even larger number are under eighteen. . . .
>
> And finally, the poor are politically invisible. . . . They are

without lobbies of their own; they put forward no legislative program. As a group, they are atomized. They have no face; they have no voice. . . . Only the social agencies have a really direct involvement with the other America, and they are without any great political power. . . .

Forty to fifty million people are becoming increasingly invisible.

These invisible people fall mostly into the following categories, some of them overlapping: poor farmers, who operate 40 percent of the farms and get 7 percent of the farm cash income; migratory farm workers; unskilled, unorganized workers in offices, hotels, restaurants, hospitals, laundries, and other service jobs; inhabitants of areas where poverty is either endemic ("peculiar to a people or district"), as in the rural South, or epidemic ("prevalent among a community at a special time and produced by some special cases"), as in West Virginia, where the special cause was the closing of coal mines and steel plants; Negroes and Puerto Ricans, who are a fourth of the total poor; the alcoholic derelicts in the big-city skid rows; the hillbillies from Kentucky, Tennessee, and Oklahoma who have migrated to Midwestern cities in search of better jobs. And, finally, almost half our "senior citizens."*

The most obvious citizens of The Other America are those whose skins are the wrong color. The folk slogans are realistic: "Last to be hired, first to be fired" and "If you're black, stay back." There has been some progress. In 1939, the nonwhite worker's wage averaged 41.4 percent of the white worker's; by 1958 it had climbed to 58 percent. A famous victory, but the nonwhites still average only slightly more than half as much as the whites. Even this modest gain was due not to any Rooseveltian or Trumanian social reform but merely to the fact that for some years there was a war on and workers were in demand, whether black, white, or violet. By 1947, the nonwhites had achieved most of their advance—to 54 percent of white earnings, which means they have gained, in the last fifteen years, just 4 percent.

---

* (1971) I left out a major category which was apparently less "visible" then than it has become since: families—largely black—in which the mother is the sole support of the children since the father/fathers have vamoosed.

The least obvious poverty affects our "senior citizens"—those over sixty-five. Harrington estimates that half of them—eight million—live in poverty, and he thinks they are even more atomized and politically helpless than the rest of The Other America. He estimates that one-fourth of the "unrelated individuals" among them, or a million persons, have less than $580 a year, which is about what is allotted *for food alone* in the Department of Agriculture's minimum-subsistence budget. (The average American family now spends only 20 percent of its income for food—an indication of the remarkable prosperity we are all enjoying, except for one-quarter of us.) One can imagine, or perhaps one can't, what it would be like to live on $580 a year, or $11 a week. It is only fair to note that most of our senior citizens do better: The average per capita income of those over sixty-five is now estimated to be slightly over $20 a week. That is, about $1,000 a year.

The aged poor have two sources of income besides their earnings or savings. One is contributions by relatives. A 1961 White House Conference Report put this at 10 percent of income, which works out to $8 a week for an income of $4,000—and the 8,000,000 aged poor all have less than that. The other is Social Security, whose benefits in 1959 averaged $18 a week. Even this modest sum is more than any of the under-$4,000 got, since payments are proportionate to earnings and the poor, of course, earned less than the rest. A quarter of them, and those in general the neediest, are not covered by Social Security. The last resort is relief, and Harrington describes most vividly the humiliations the poor often have to put up with to get that.

The problem of the aged poor is aggravated by the fact that, unlike the Italians or the English, we seem to have little respect for or interest in our "senior citizens," beyond giving them that honorific title, and we don't include them in family life. If we can afford it, we are likely to send them to nursing homes—"a storage-bin philosophy," a Senate report calls it—and if we can't, which is the case with the poor, they must make do with the resources noted above. *Income and Welfare in the United States* (McGraw-Hill), a study from the Survey Research Center of the University of Michigan's Institute for Social Research compiled under the direction of Dr. James N. Morgan, has a depressing chapter on "The Economics of Living with Relatives." Nearly two-thirds of the heads of families queried were opposed to having their aged parents live with their children. "The old do not understand the young, and the young do not understand the old or the young," observed one respondent, who must have had a sense of humor. Other replies were "Old people are pretty hard to get along with" and "The parents and the children try to boss each other and when they live with you there's always fighting." The minority in favor gave practical reasons, like "It's a good thing to have them with you so you can see after them" and "The old folks might get a pension or something, so they could help you out." Hardly anyone expressed any particular respect for the old, or a feeling that their experience might enrich family life. The most depressing finding was "People most able to provide support for relatives are most opposed to it. Older people with some college education are eleven to one against it." The most favorable toward including older people in the home were Negroes, and even they were mostly against it.

The whole problem of poverty and the aged is especially serious today because Americans are living longer. In the first half of this century, life expectancy increased 17.6 years for men and 20.3 years for women. And between 1950 and 1960 the over-sixty-five group increased twice as fast as the population as a whole.

The worst part of being old and poor in this country is the loneliness. Harrington notes that we have not only racial ghettos but geriatric ones, in the cheap rooming-house districts of large cities. He gives one peculiarly disturbing statistic: "One-third of the aged in the United States, some 5,000,000 or more human beings, have no phone in their place of residence. They are literally cut off from the rest of America."

Ernest Hemingway's celebrated deflation of Scott Fitzgerald's romantic notion that the rich are "different" somehow—"Yes, they have money"—doesn't apply to the poor. They are different in more important ways than their lack of money, as Harrington demonstrates:

> Emotional upset is one of the main forms of the vicious circle of impoverishment. The structure of the society is hostile to these people. The poor tend to become pessimistic and depressed; they seek immediate gratification instead of saving; they act out.

Once this mood, this unarticulated philosophy becomes a fact, society can change, the recession can end, and yet there is no motive for movement. The depression has become internalized. The middle class looks upon this process and sees "lazy" people who "just don't want to get ahead." People who are much too sensitive to demand of cripples that they run races ask of the poor that they get up and act just like everyone else in the society.

The poor are not like everyone else. . . . They think and feel differently; they look upon a different America than the middle class looks upon.

The poor are also different in a physical sense: they are much less healthy. According to *Poverty and Deprivation*, the proportion of those "disabled or limited in their major activity by chronic ill health" rises sharply as income sinks. In reasonably well-off families, 4.3 percent are so disabled; in reasonably poor families, the proportion doubles, to 8 percent; and in unreasonably poor families, it doubles again, to 16.5 percent. An obvious cause, among others, for the very poor being four times as much disabled by "chronic ill health" as the well-to-do is that they have much less money to spend for medical care—in fact, almost nothing. This weighs with special heaviness on the aged poor. During the fifties, Mr. Harrington notes, "all costs on the Consumer Price Index went up by 12 percent. But medical costs, that terrible staple of the aged, went up by 36 percent, hospitalization rose by 65 percent, and group hospitalization costs (Blue Cross premiums) were up by 83 percent." This last figure is particularly interesting, since Blue Cross and such plans are the AMA's alternative to socialized medicine.

Mental as well as physical illness is much greater among the poor, even though our complacent cliché is that nervous breakdowns are a prerogative of the rich because the poor "can't afford" them. (They can't, but they have them anyway.) This bit of middle-class folklore should be laid to rest by a study made in New Haven: *Social Class and Mental Illness*, by August B. Hollingshead and Frederick C. Redlich (Wiley). They found that the rate of "treated psychiatric illness" is about the same from the rich down through decently paid workers—an average of 573 per 100,000. But in the bottom fifth it shoots up to 1,659 per 100,000. There is an even more striking difference in the *kind* of mental illness. Of those in the four top income groups who had undergone psychiatric treatment, 65 percent had been treated for neurotic problems and 35 percent for psychotic disturbances. In the bottom fifth, the treated illnesses were almost all psychotic (90 percent). This shows there is something to the notion that the poor "can't afford" nervous breakdowns—the milder kind, that is—since the reason the proportion of *treated* neuroses among the poor is only 10 percent is that a neurotic can keep going, after a fashion. But the argument cuts deeper the other way. The poor go to a psychiatrist (or, more commonly, are committed to a mental institution) only when they are completely unable to function because of psychotic symptoms. Therefore, even that nearly threefold increase in mental disorders among the poor is probably an underestimate.

The poor are different, then, both physically and psychologically. During the fifties, a team of psychiatrists from Cornell studied "Midtown," a residential area in New York City that contained 170,000 people, of all social classes. The area was 99 percent white, so the findings may be presumed to understate the problem of poverty. The description of the poor—the "low social economic status individual"—is blunt: "[They are] rigid, suspicious, and have a fatalistic outlook on life. They do not plan ahead. . . . They are prone to depression, have feelings of futility, lack of belongingness, friendliness, and a lack of trust in others." Only a Dr. Pangloss would expect anything else. As Harrington points out, such characteristics are "a realistic adaptation to a socially perverse situation."

On the isolation that is the lot of the American poor, Harrington is good:

> America has a self-image of itself as a nation of joiners and doers. There are social clubs, charities, community drives, and the like. [One might add organizations like the Elks and Masons, Rotary and Kiwanis, cultural groups like our women's clubs, also alumni associations and professional organizations.] And yet this entire structure is a phenomenon of the middle class. Some time age, a study in Franklin, Indiana [this vagueness of reference is all too typical of *The Other America*], reported that the percentage of people in the bottom class who were without affiliations of any kind was eight times as great as the percentage in the high-income class.

Paradoxically, one of the factors that intensifies the social isolation of the poor is that America thinks of itself as a nation without social classes. As a result, there are few social or civic organizations that are separated on the basis of income and class. The "working-class culture" that sociologists have described in a country like England does not exist here. . . . The poor person who might want to join an organization is afraid. Because he or she will have less education, less money, less competence to articulate ideas than anyone else in the group, they stay away.

One reason our society is a comparatively violent one is that the French and Italian and British poor have a communal life and culture that the American poor lack. As one reads *The Other America*, one wonders why there is not even more violence than there is.

The main reason the American poor have become invisible is that since 1936 their numbers have been reduced by two-thirds. Astounding as it may seem, the fact is that President Roosevelt's "one-third of a nation" was a considerable understatement; over two-thirds of us then lived below the poverty line, as is shown by the tables that follow. But today the poor are a minority, and minorities can be ignored if they are so heterogeneous that they cannot be organized. When the poor were a majority, they simply could not be overlooked. Poverty is also hard to see today because the middle class ($6,000 to $14,999) has vastly increased—from 13 percent of all families in 1936 to a near-majority (47 percent) today. That mass poverty can persist despite this rise to affluence is hard to believe, or see, especially if one is among those who have risen.

Two tables in *Poverty and Deprivation* summarize what has been happening in the last thirty years. They cover only multiple-person families; all figures are converted to 1960 dollars; and the income is before taxes.

The first table is the percentage of families with a given income:

	1935–1936	1947	1953	1960
Under $ 4,000	68%	37%	28%	23%
$4,000 to $ 5,999	17	29	28	23
$6,000 to $ 7,499	6	12	17	16
$7,500 to $14,999	7	17	23	31
Over $15,000	2	4	5	7

The second table is the share each group had in the family income of the nation:

	1935–1936	1947	1953	1960
Under $ 4,000	35%	16%	11%	7%
$4,000 to $ 5,999	21	24	21	15
$6,000 to $ 7,499	10	14	17	14
$7,500 to $14,999	16	28	33	40
Over $15,000	18	18	19	24

Several interesting conclusions can be drawn from these tables:

(1) The New Deal didn't do anything about poverty: The under-$4,000 families in 1936 were 68 percent of the total population, which was slightly *more* than the 1929 figure of 65 percent.

(2) The war economy (hot and cold) did do something about poverty: Between 1936 and 1960 the proportion of all families who were poor was reduced from 68 percent to 23 percent.

(3) If the percentage of under-$4,000 families decreased by two-thirds between 1936 and 1960, their share of the national income dropped much faster in those twenty-five years: by four-fifths, or from 35 percent to 7 percent.

(4) The well-to-do ($7,500 to $14,999) have enormously increased, from 7 percent of all families in 1936 to 31 percent today. The rich ($15,000 and over) have also multiplied—from 2 to 7 percent.

(5) The reduction of poverty has slowed down. In the six years 1947–53, the number of poor families declined 9 percent, but in the following seven years only 5 percent. The economic stasis that set in with Eisenhower and that still persists under Kennedy was responsible. In the *New York Times Magazine* of November 11, 1962, Herman P. Miller, of the Bureau of the Census, wrote, "During the forties, the lower-paid occupations made the greatest relative gains in average income. Laborers and service workers . . . had increases of about 180% . . . and professional and managerial workers, the highest paid workers of all, had the lowest relative gains—96%." But in the last decade the trend has been reversed; laborers and service workers have gained 39 percent while professional-managerial workers have gained 68 percent. This is because in the wartime forties the unskilled were in great demand, while now they are being replaced by

machines. Automation is today the same kind of menace to the un-skilled—that is, the poor—that the enclosure movement was to the British agricultural population centuries ago. "The facts show that our 'social revolution' ended nearly twenty years ago," Mr. Miller concludes, "yet important segments of the American public, many of them highly placed Government officials and prominent educators, think and act as though it were a continuing process."

"A reduction of about 19% [in the under-$6,000 families] in more than thirty years, or at a rate of about 0.7% per year, is no ground for complacency," the authors of *Poverty and Deprivation* justly ob-serve. There is even less ground for complacency in the recent figures on *extreme* poverty. The authors estimate the number of families in 1929 with incomes of under $2,000 (in current dollars) at 7,500,000. By 1947 there were less than 4,000,000, not because of any philanthropic effort by their more prosperous fellow citizens but entirely because of those glorious years of war economy. But six years later, in 1953, when the economy had begun to slow down, there were still 3,300,000 of these families with incomes of less than $2,000, and seven years after that, in 1960, "there had been no further reduction." Thus in the last fifteen years the bottom dogs have remained on the bottom, sharing hardly at all in the advances that the income groups above them have made in an ascending scale that is exquisitely adjusted by the automatic workings of capitalism. I.e., it is inversely proportionate to need.

There are, finally, the bottomest bottom dogs; i.e., *families* with incomes of *under $1,000*. I apologize for the italics, but some facts insist on them. According to *Poverty and Deprivation*, the numbers of these families "appear to have risen slightly" of late (1953–60), from 800,000 to about 1,000,000.

The post-1940 decrease in poverty was not due to the policies or actions of those who are not poor, those in positions of power and responsibility. The war economy needed workers, wages went up, and the poor became less poor. When economic stasis set in, the rate of decrease in poverty slowed down proportionately, and it is still slow. Kennedy's efforts to "get the country moving again" have been unsuccessful, possibly because he has, despite the suggestions of many of his economic advisers, not yet advocated the one big step

that might push the economy off dead center: a massive increase in
government spending.

Some of the post-1940 gains of the poor have been their own
doing. "Moonlighting"—or holding two or more jobs at once—was
practiced by about 3 percent of the employed in 1950; today this
percentage has almost doubled. Far more important is what might be
called "wife-flitting": Between 1940 and 1957, the percentage of
wives with jobs ˙outside the home doubled, from 15 percent to 30
percent. The head of the United States Children's Bureau, Mrs.
Katherine B. Oettinger, announced last summer, not at all triumphantly, that there are now two-thirds more working mothers than
there were ten years ago and that these mothers have about fifteen
million children under eighteen—of whom four million are under six.
This kind of economic enterprise ought to impress Senator Goldwater and the ideologues of the *National Review*, whose reaction to
the poor, when they think about such an uninspiring subject, is
"Why don't they *do* something about it?" The poor have done something about it and the family pay check is bigger and the statistics
on poverty look better. But the effects on family life and on those
four million preschool children is something else. Mrs. Oettinger
quoted a roadside sign, "IRONING, DAY CARE AND WORMS FOR FISHING
BAIT," and mentioned a baby-sitter who pacified her charge with
sleeping pills and another who met the problem of a cold apartment
by putting the baby in the oven. "The situation has become a
'national disgrace,' with many unfortunate conditions that do not
come to public attention until a crisis arises," the *Times* summed up
her conclusion. This crisis has finally penetrated to public attention.
The President recently signed a law that might be called Don'tcare. It
provides $5 million for Daycare facilities this fiscal year, which works
out to $1.25 for each of the four million under-six children with
working mothers. Next year, the program will provide all of $2.50
per child. This is a free, democratic society's notion of an adequate
response. Almost a century ago, Bismarck instituted in Germany
state-financed social benefits far beyond anything we have yet ventured. Granted that he did it merely to take the play away from the
Social Democratic Party founded by Marx and Engels. Still, one imagines that Count Bismarck must be amused—in the circle of Hell
reserved for reactionaries—by that $2.50 a child.

It's not that Public Opinion doesn't become Aroused every now and them. But the arousement never leads to much. It was aroused twenty-four years ago when John Steinbeck published *The Grapes of Wrath*, but Harrington reports that things in the Imperial Valley are still much the same: low wages, bad housing, no effective union. Public Opinion is too public—that is, too general; of its very nature, it can have no sustained interest in California agriculture. The only groups with such a continuing interest are the workers and the farmers who hire them. Once Public Opinion ceased to be Aroused, the battle was again between the two antagonists with a real, personal stake in the outcome, and there was no question about which was stronger.* So with the rural poor in general. In the late fifties, the average annual wage for white male American farm workers was slightly over $1,000; women, children, Negroes, and Mexicans got less. One recalls Edward R. Murrow's celebrated television program about these people, "Harvest of Shame." Once more everybody was shocked, but the harvest is still shameful. One also recalls that Mr. Murrow, after President Kennedy had appointed him head of the United States Information Agency, tried to persuade the BBC not to show "Harvest of Shame." His argument was that it would give an undesirable "image" of America to foreign audiences.

There is a monotony about the injustices suffered by the poor that perhaps accounts for the lack of interest the rest of society shows in them. Everything seems to go wrong with them. They never win. It's just boring.

Public housing turns out not to be for them. The 1949 Housing Act authorized 810,000 new units of low-cost housing in the following four years. Twelve years later, in 1961, the AFL-CIO proposed 400,000 units to complete the lagging 1949 program. The Kennedy administration ventured to recommend 100,000 to Congress. Thus, instead of 810,000 low-cost units by 1953, the poor will get, if they are lucky, 500,000 by 1963. And they are more likely to be injured than helped by slum clearance, since the new projects usually have higher rents than the displaced slum-dwellers can afford. (There has

---

* (1973) The workers have found their most effective expression in Chavez's United Farm Workers union. But the question of relative strength has not as yet been resolved in their favor.

been no dearth of government-financed *middle*-income housing since 1949.) These refugees from the bulldozers for the most part simply emigrate to other slums. They also become invisible; Harrington notes that half of them are recorded as "address unknown." Several years ago, Charles Abrams, who was New York State Rent Administrator under Harriman and who is now president of the National Committee Against Discrimination in Housing, summed up what he had learned in two decades in public housing: "Once social reforms have won tonal appeal in the public mind, their slogans and goal-symbols may degenerate into tools of the dominant class for beleaguering the minority and often for defeating the very aims which the original sponsors had intended for their reforms." Mr. Abrams was probably thinking, in part, of the Title I adventures of Robert Moses in mucking up New York housing against the poor. There is a Moses or two in every American city, determined to lead us away from the promised land.

And this is not the end of tribulation. The poor, who can least afford to lose pay because of ill health, lose the most. A National Health Survey, made a few years ago, found that workers earning under $2,000 a year had twice as many "restricted-activity days" as those earning over $4,000.

The poor are even fatter than the rich. (The cartoonists will have to revise their clichés.) "Obesity is seven times more frequent among women of the lowest socio-economic level than it is among those of the highest level," state Drs. Moore, Stunkard, and Srole in a recent issue of the *Journal of the American Medical Association*. (The proportion is almost the same for men.) They also found that overweight associated with poverty is related to mental disease. Fatness used to be a sign of wealth, as it still is in some parts of Africa, but in more advanced societies it is now a stigma of poverty, since it means too many cheap carbohydrates and too little exercise— as may be confirmed by a glance at the models in any fashion magazine.

The poor actually pay more taxes, in proportion to their income, than the rich. A recent study by the Tax Foundation estimates that 28 percent of incomes under $2,000 goes for taxes, as against 24 percent of the incomes of families earning five to seven times as much. Sales and other excise taxes are largely responsible for this curious statistic. It is true that such taxes fall impartially on all, like the blessed rain from heaven, but it is a form of egalitarianism that perhaps only Senator Goldwater can fully appreciate.*

The final irony is that the Welfare State, which Roosevelt erected and which Eisenhower didn't dare to pull down, is not for the poor, either. Agricultural workers are not covered by Social Security, nor are many of the desperately poor among the aged, such as "unrelated individuals" with incomes of less than $1,000, of whom only 37 percent are covered, which is just half the percentage of coverage among the aged in general. Of the Welfare State, Harrington says, "Its creation had been stimulated by mass impoverishment and misery, yet it helped the poor least of all. Laws like unemployment compensation, the Wagner Act, the various farm programs, all these were designed for the middle third in the cities, for the organized workers, and for the . . . big market farmers. . . . [It] benefits those least who need help most." The industrial workers, led by John L. Lewis, mobilized enough political force to put through Section 7(a) of the National Industrial Recovery Act, which, with the Wagner Act, made the CIO possible. The big farmers put enough pressure on Henry Wallace, Roosevelt's first Secretary of Agriculture—who talked a good fight for liberal principles but was a Hamlet when it came to action—to establish the two basic propositions of Welfare State agriculture: subsidies that now cost $3 billion a year and that chiefly benefit the big farmers; and the exclusion of sharecroppers, tenant farmers, and migratory workers from the protection of minimum-wage and Social Security laws. One reaches the unstartling conclusion that rewards in class societies, including Communist ones, are according to power rather than need.

It seems likely that mass poverty will continue in this country for a long time. The more it is reduced, the harder it is to keep on reducing it. The poor, having dwindled from two-thirds of the population in 1936 to one-quarter today, no longer are a significant political force, as is shown by the Senate's rejection of Medicare and by the Democrats' dropping it as an issue in the elections last year. Also, as poverty decreases, those left behind tend more and more to be the

---

* (1973) Or President Nixon.

ones who have for so long accepted poverty as their destiny that they need outside help to climb out of it. This new minority mass poverty, so much more isolated and hopeless than the old majority poverty, shows signs of becoming chronic. "The permanence of low incomes is inferred from a variety of findings," write the authors of the Michigan survey. "In many poor families the head has never earned enough to cover the family's present needs." They give a vignette of what the statistics mean in human terms:

> For most families, however, the problem of chronic poverty is serious. One such family is headed by a thirty-two-year-old who is employed as a dishwasher. Though he works steadily and more than full time, he earned slightly over $2,000 in 1959. His wife earned $300 more, but their combined incomes are not enough to support themselves and their three children. Although the head of the family is only thirty-two, he feels that he has no chance of advancement partly because he finished only seven grades of school. . . . The possibility of such families leaving the ranks of the poor is not high.

Children born into poor families today have less chance of "improving themselves" than the children of the pre-1940 poor. Rags to riches is now more likely to be rags to rags. "Indeed," the Michigan surveyors conclude, "it appears that a number of the heads of poor families have moved into less skilled jobs than their fathers had." Over a third of the children of the poor, according to the survey, don't go beyond the eighth grade and "will probably perpetuate the poverty of their parents." There are a great many of these children. Harrington writes, "The character of poverty has changed, and it has become more deadly for the young. It is no longer associated with immigrant groups with high aspirations; it is now identified with those whose social existence makes it more and more difficult to break out into the larger society." Even when children from poor families show intellectual promise, there is nothing in the values of their friends or families to encourage them to make use of it.

The problem of educating the poor has changed since 1900. Then it was the language and cultural difficulties of immigrants from foreign countries; now it is the subtler but more intractable problems of internal migration from backward regions, mostly in the

South. The old immigrants wanted to Better Themselves and to Get Ahead. The new migrants are less ambitious, and they come into a less ambitious atmosphere. "When they arrive in the city," wrote Christopher Jencks in an excellent two-part survey, "Slums and Schools," in the *New Republic* last fall,

> they join others equally unprepared for urban life in the slums —a milieu which is in many ways utterly dissociated from the rest of America. Often this milieu is self-perpetuating. I have been unable to find any statistics on how many of these migrants' children and grandchildren have become middle-class, but it is probably not too inaccurate to estimate that about 30,000,000 people live in urban slums, and that about half are second-generation residents.

The immigrants of 1890–1910 also arrived in a milieu that was "in many ways utterly dissociated from the rest of America," yet they had a vision—a rather materialistic one, but still a vision—of what life in America could be if they worked hard enough; and they did work, and they did aspire to something more than they had; and they did get out of the slums. The disturbing thing about the poor today is that so many of them seem to lack any such vision. Mr. Jencks remarks:

> While the economy is changing in a way which makes the eventual liquidation of the slums at least conceivable, young people are not seizing the opportunities this change presents. Too many are dropping out of school before graduation (more than half in many slums); too few are going to college. . . . As a result there are serious shortages of teachers, nurses, doctors, technicians, and scientifically trained executives, but 4,500,000 unemployables.

"Poverty is the parent of revolution and crime," Aristotle wrote. This is now a half truth—the last half. Our poor are alienated; they don't consider themselves part of society. But precisely because they don't they are not politically dangerous. It is people with "a stake in the country" who make revolutions. The best—though by no means the only—reason for worrying about The Other America is that its existence should make us feel uncomfortable.

The federal government is the only purposeful force—I assume wars are not purposeful—that can reduce the numbers of the poor and make their lives more bearable.

The effect of government policy on poverty has two quite distinct aspects. One is the indirect effect of the stimulation of the economy by federal spending. Such stimulation—though by wartime demands rather than government policy—has in the past produced a prosperity that did cut down American poverty by almost two-thirds. But I am inclined to agree with Dr. Galbraith that it would not have a comparable effect on present-day poverty:

> It is assumed that with increasing output poverty must disappear [he writes]. Increased output eliminated the general poverty of all who worked. Accordingly it must, sooner or later, eliminate the special poverty that still remains. . . . Yet just as the arithmetic of modern politics makes it tempting to overlook the very poor, so the supposition that increasing output will remedy their case has made it easy to do so too.

He adds that there is now a hard core of the specially disadvantaged —because of age, race, environment, physical or mental defects, etc. —that would not be significantly reduced by general prosperity.

To do something about this hard core, a second line of government policy would be required; namely, direct intervention to help the poor. We have had this since the New Deal, but it has always been grudging and miserly, and we have never accepted the principle that every citizen should be provided, at state expense, with a reasonable minimum standard of living regardless of any other considerations. It should not depend on earnings, as does Social Security, which continues the inequalities and inequities and so tends to keep the poor forever poor. Nor should it exclude millions of our poorest citizens because they lack the political pressure to force their way into the Welfare State. The governmental obligation to provide, out of taxes, such a minimum living standard for all who need it should be taken as much for granted as free public schools have always been in our history.

It may be objected that the economy cannot bear the cost, and certainly costs must be calculated. But the point is not the calculation but the principle. Statistics—and especially statistical forecasts— can be pushed one way or the other. Who can determine in advance to what extent the extra expense of giving our forty million poor enough income to rise above the poverty line would be offset by the lift to the economy from their increased purchasing power? We really don't know. Nor did we know what the budgetary effects would be when we established the principle of free public education. The rationale then was that all citizens should have an equal chance of competing for a better status. The rationale now is different: that every citizen has a right to become or remain part of our society because if this right is denied, as it now is in the case of one-fourth of our citizens, it impoverishes us all. Since 1932, "the government"—local, state, and federal—has recognized a responsibility to provide its citizens with a subsistence living. Apples will never again be sold on the street by jobless accountants, it seems safe to predict, nor will any serious political leader ever again suggest that share-the-work and local charity can solve the problem of unemployment. "Nobody starves" in this country any more, but, like every social statistic, this is a tricky business. Nobody starves, but who can measure the starvation, not to be calculated by daily intake of proteins and calories, that reduces life for many of our poor to a long vestibule to death? Nobody starves, but every fourth citizen rubs along on a standard of living that is below what Michael Harrington defines as "the minimal levels of health, housing, food, and education that our present stage of scientific knowledge specifies as necessary for life as it is now lived in the United States." Nobody starves, but a fourth of us are excluded from the common social existence. Not to be able to afford a movie or a glass of beer is a kind of starvation—if everybody else can.

The problem is obvious: the persistence of mass poverty in a prosperous country. The solution is also obvious: to provide, out of taxes, the kind of subsidies that have always been given to the public schools (not to mention the police and fire departments and the post office)—subsidies that would raise incomes above the poverty level, so that every citizen could feel he is indeed such. *"Civis Romanus sum!"* cried St. Paul when he was threatened with flogging—and he was not flogged. Until our poor can be proud to say *"Civis Americanus sum!,"* until the act of justice that would make this possible has been performed by the three-quarters of Americans who are not poor—until then the shame of The Other America will continue.

—*The New Yorker*, January 19, 1963

Afterword

"Our Invisible Poor"—reprinted here with drastic cuts—was the most effective political article I've written (no great boast—my forte is not practical criticism), analogous to my critique of James Gould Cozzens' *By Love Possessed* which single-handed reversed the almost unanimous favorable critical opinion—I reviewed the reviews as well as the book—so that the novel didn't get either the Pulitzer Prize or the National Book Award; and to my review of the third edition of *Webster's New International Dictionary* (Unabridged), which played some part—though here I had many allies—in its debacle. (See "By Cozzens Possessed" and "The String Untuned" in *Against the American Grain*, Random House, 1962.)

Between us, Mike Harrington and I made a difference. Although I didn't hear from any residents of Camelot at the time, I later learned that the President read it and, after consultation with Moynihan, Heller, and Sorensen, formally declared war on poverty.* I'm sure they were all as shocked, and surprised, as I was to learn that mass poverty still existed despite three decades of new deals, fair deals, and new frontiers, and that this was why they leaped to arms; mostly. But they must also have realized that a War on Poverty was the perfect crusade for the Democratic Party, one that could

* (1972) "The evidence of economic imbalance [the persistence of chronic mass poverty despite general prosperity since 1940] piled up, but few paid attention to the congressional hearings or the scholarly monographs," Sar A. Levitan writes in *The Great Society's Poor Law* (Johns Hopkins Press, 1969). "Even the impassioned argument of Michael Harrington's *The Other America* . . . was at first hardly noted. (The book was published in March, 1962, and sold only a few thousand copies during the balance of the year. After a review by Dwight Macdonald in *The New Yorker* early in 1963, some 7,000 copies of the second printing were sold. The paperback reprint that fall sold several hundred thousand copies.) Macdonald's review . . . reached the White House and was read by Theodore Sorensen, and presumably by the President himself. Harrington's book was also given to the President by Walter Heller, then chairman of the Council of Economic Advisers, although it is not known whether the President read it."

unite its discordant parts as had World War II. The Northern liberals would be for it on principle, and the Southern reactionaries could not oppose it in practice. Whatever their private misgivings about creeping socialism, coddling the nigras, and invasion of states' rights, the Southerners would have to support it—publicly—because theirs is a notably poor region and its politicians are in no position to reject federal funds—publicly. A perfect issue, both idealistic and practical, and no wonder Johnson expanded his predecessor's crusade (until more vital trans-Pacific projects drained off the money—and, more important, attention). Even Nixon, initially prodded by Moynihan, took several years to get up the nerve to declare an armistice, officially.

It's odd, or perhaps not, that despite these Herculean efforts on the highest governmental levels, the poor seem to be as much with us as ever. Like that other high-level campaign against racial injustice that has been going on even longer.

To bring "Our Invisible Poor" up to date or even to touch on the high spots in the later literature—for a few years a new book on poverty seemed to appear monthly—would take another article of the same length. The piece has been reprinted in a score of textbook-anthologies and one or two requests a year still come in—always granted, if they're not tired of it, I'm certainly not. So many inquiries about reprints came in that for the first year I ran a little nonprofit business from my office at The New Yorker—with their help in printing and mailing—disposing of some 20,000 copies @ 10¢ each (reduction on bundle orders).

After-Afterword

"Over the past three to four years, our nation's needy have become hungrier and poorer," said Ronald Pollack, director of the Food Research and Action Center of New York, who headed a 26-member study panel on "nutrition and special groups.". . ."The sad and tragic truth is that, over the past several years, we have moved backwards in our struggle to end hunger, poverty and malnutrtion." Mr. Pollack's testimony [before a Senate committee headed by Senator George McGovern, whose first response to the worldwide hunger problem, which is even worse than our own, was to substitute for the outmoded "food for peace" slogan a more catchy battle cry: "plowshares for peace"] was based on a 185-page report by his group, which illustrated the slide of the needy into deeper poverty.

—The New York Times, June 20, 1974

A Critique
of the
Warren Report

Report of the President's Commission on the Assassination of President John F. Kennedy; U.S. Government Printing Office, 1964; 912 pages, $3.25.

This thick volume with the Great Seal of the President of the United States stamped in gold on its dark blue cover is a tax-subsidized steal at $3.25. The sturdily sewn binding and tough paper stand up to hard use, as in writing this review. The typeface, used in all GPO publications since the nineteenth century, is as legible as it is homely. The GPO goes in for utility, not flash. The solid craftsmanship, however, does not extend to the text.

The Warren Report is an American-style *Iliad*, i.e., an anti-*Iliad*, full of anti-heroes, retelling great and terrible events in limping prose instead of winged poetry. And what prose! The lawyer's drone, the clotted chunks of expert testimony, the turgidities of officialese, the bureaucrat's smooth-worn evasions. For the Homeric simile, Research; for the epic thunder, the crepitating clutter of Fact.

> But Achilleus, gathering the fury upon him, sprang on the Trojans / with a ghastly cry, and the first of them he killed was Iphition. . . . / Great Achilleus struck him with the spear as he came in fury / in the middle of the head, and all the head broke into two pieces. / He fell, thunderously.

At 12:30 P.M., Central Standard Time, as the President's
open limousine proceeded at approximately eleven miles per
hour along Elm Street toward the Triple Underpass, shots
fired from a rifle mortally wounded President Kennedy and
seriously injured Governor Connally. One bullet passed through
the President's neck; a subsequent bullet, which was lethal,
shattered the right side of his skull. Governor Connally sus-
tained bullet wounds in his back, the right side of his chest,
right wrist, and left thigh.

The heroes of our antiepic are not Hector and Lysander "and
such great names as these," not Diomedes, Agamemnon, Sarpedon,
Menelaus, not even Patroclus. They are that quintessence of the
antihero, Lee Harvey Oswald, resentful underdog trying to give
meaning to his failed life by elbowing his way into History; Jack
Ruby, hero-worshiper of cops and presidents, who killed Oswald to
avenge Jackie and the kids; Judge Joe Brown who presided over
Ruby's trial chewing tobacco and occasionally leafing through magazines on the bench; Police Chief Curry who led the fatal motorcade
and whose appetite for publicity made his headquarters a televised
chaos which Ruby easily penetrated; District Attorney Wade who
tried and convicted "the suspect" on TV during Oswald's miraculous
survival for almost two days in the custody of the Dallas cops; J.
Edgar Hoover, whose G-men had efficiently kept Oswald "under sur-
veillance" as a defector to the U.S.S.R. and a pro-Castro agitator, but
who neglected to tell the Secret Service about it, and whose response
to a reproof in the Report was "Monday-morning quarterbacking."

Not that there weren't epic parallels, of a sort. Chief Curry, or
D.A. Wade, will do as Ajax, Shakespeare's "beef-witted" Ajax
("Mars his idiot"). Nor is the Commission's chairman, Chief Justice
Warren, badly cast as Nestor: honorable, respected, but slow-witted,
the Polonius type. Pretty as she is, Marina Oswald isn't up to Helen;
Cressida maybe. The one hero who is definitely missing, among the
authors of the Report as well as among the unheroes they celebrate,
is that man of many counsels, the clever Odysseus.

But the greatest hero of all, oddly, is here. The late President
Kennedy will more than do for Achilles, strong and handsome and
all-conquering (except for the House Rules Committee), a prince
among men. But his Myrmidons, the scores of Secret Service agents

whose job it was to protect him, were in the American style: "Under established procedure, [they] had instructions to watch the route for signs of trouble, scanning not only the crowds but the roofs and windows of buildings"—except, it seems, the sixth floor of the Texas School Book Depository. Somehow the established procedure didn't quite work out and the President got killed. Achilles' Myrmidons did better, but then they were Greeks.

However, the Warren Commission did not undertake its enormous labors in order to write an *Iliad*. "The President directed the Commission to evaluate all the facts and circumstances surrounding the assassination and the subsequent killing of the alleged assassin," states the Foreword, which later comes to the real point: "Because of the numerous rumors and theories, the Commission concluded that the public interest . . . could not be met by merely accepting the reports or the analyses [of the FBI, the Secret Service, and the Dallas police]. Not only were the premises and conclusions of those reports critically reassessed, but all assertions or rumors relating to a possible conspiracy . . . which have come to the attention of the Commission, were investigated." The Commission's task was one of exorcism, to lay to rest once for all those "numerous rumors and theories" that flitted and chittered in the twilight of those two strange days in Dallas.

Europeans generally assumed that Oswald and Ruby could not have achieved their murders all by themselves and for personal—and irrational—motives; nor could they believe that the confusion in the Dallas Police Headquarters and the many contradictory statements that issued from that Bedlam were evidence of bungling rather than of conspiracy. Their own police forces are more professional, more "*sérieux.*" And their assassinations have typically been the work of conspiratorial groups, with clear political aims. But of the seven previous attempts on the lives of our presidents, successful (Lincoln, Garfield, McKinley) and unsuccessful (Jackson, the two Roosevelts, Truman), five have been the work of solitary cranks of dubious mental balance, one (Lincoln) of a political conspiracy, but limited to half a dozen fanatics acting on their own; and only one (Truman) in the European style—it's significant that the party behind it was Puerto Rican and not American.

The American public also had doubts. A Gallup poll shortly after the assassination found that only 29 percent thought Oswald had acted alone, while 52 percent thought "some group or element" was also involved. What group precisely was rarely specified, for then as now there was a complete blank on the most modest kind of evidence connecting (either Oswald or Ruby) to any accomplices. Still the fact was that a bare majority of Americans and a decisive majority of Europeans thought there was something fishy about the case and that the authorities ("they") had either overlooked or were covering up some kind of political conspiracy. So on November 29, 1963, President Johnson appointed the Commission whose report was issued ten months later.

Its most striking aspect is the quantitative. The 912 pages are distilled from some 25,000 interviews and re-interviews by the FBI which were submitted to the Commission in 25,400 pages of reports plus 1,550 interviews by the Secret Service (4,600 pages) plus the testimony of 552 witnesses, 94 of whom appeared before the Commission while the rest were questioned by the Commission's legal staff or submitted sworn affidavits. There were two unsworn statements, those of Mr. and Mrs. Lyndon B. Johnson, Peking papers please copy. Eight weeks after the Report, the Commission published the complete testimony of its 552 witnesses in 15 volumes plus 11 volumes containing photographs of 3,154 Exhibits ranging from President Kennedy's coat and shirt (the rips in the coat made by the frantic doctors and the great patches of bloodstains that blot out the shirt's jaunty stripes were, for me, more moving and horrible than anything in the testimony, even Jackie's narrative) to the Complete Works of Lee Harvey Oswald (every scrap of paper covered with his wretched handwriting and even worse spelling seems to be preserved here for history) and snapshots from his family album ("Me and Marina with Uncle Vasily and Aunt Lubova," also known as Exhibit 2623) and Jack Ruby's (Exhibit 5300-A: "Me and Two of the Girls in front of My Nightclub").

Our heroes, and our villains, have often used this factual, pragmatic approach, so congenial to the national temperament: the early muckrakers like Lincoln Steffens (*The Shame of the Cities*) and Ida Tarbell (*The History of the Standard Oil Company*); Brandeis's

invention of the "sociological brief" with which in 1908 he successfully defended before the Supreme Court the Oregon ten-hour law,
substituting socioeconomic data for legal reasoning on the grounds
that "There is no logic that is properly applicable to these laws except
the logic of facts," a proposition dubious philosophically, since facts
have no logic, but effective practically—Constitutional law was never
the same again. There was Al Smith's rasping battle cry when he was
the reform governor of New York, "Let's look at the record!"; the
late Senator McCarthy's exploitation of Facts ("I hold in my hand a
letter dated . . .") which later proved to be irrelevant Facts—the
letter once was a blank sheet of paper—or even anti-Facts, or lies; the
mountains of Facts, sometimes surpassing even the Warren Commission's hoard, accumulated by the great congressional investigations
from the Pujo Committee's hearings on the "Money Trust" in 1913
down to the late Senator Kefauver's patient, masterly investigation of
monopolistic business practices. Vice-President Nixon summed up
the American attitude when he cried out, incredulously, to a mob of
Peruvian students who were stoning him: "But don't you want to
hear *facts*?" The rocks continued to fly.

So now we have the Warren Commissioners, neither heroes nor
villains, putting their trust in a saturation barrage of factual ammunition. Now Facts are all very well but they have their little weaknesses. Americans often assume that Facts are solid, concrete (and
discrete) objects like marbles, but they are very much not. Rather are
they subtle essences, full of mystery and metaphysics, that change
their color and shape, their meaning, according to the context in
which they are presented.* They must always be treated with skepticism, and the standard of judgment should be not how many Facts
one can mobilize in support of a position but how skillfully one dis-
criminates between them, how objectively one uses them to arrive at
Truth, which is something different from, though related to, the
Facts.

Another aspect of Facts is that there can be too many of them.

---

* (1971) As Norman Mailer explained at the Chicago conspiracy trial when
the prosecutor asked him to "stick to the facts, please": "Facts are nothing
without their nuances, sir."

This the Warren Commissioners don't seem to understand, perhaps because they are representative Americans. A great defect of their report, whether it be considered as literature or as argumentation is an omnivorous inclusiveness. The kitchen stove is omitted but not the Facts, recorded on page 670 at the taxpayers' expense, that the New Orleans house Mother Oswald bought in 1941 (a) cost $1,300; (b) was located at 1010 Bartholomew Street and not at 1011 or 1009; (c) had a backyard; and (d) was in a neighborhood that, "according to John's recollection . . . was not as pleasant as Alvar Street." It is also recorded that in this period "the family kept a dog named 'Sunshine.' "

In Edgar Allan Poe's *The Purloined Letter*, a blackmailer steals a letter and hides it in his house; the Paris police spend weeks systematically going over every room and its contents with probes, microscopes, etc., but fail to find it; Poe's Dupin, first and greatest of fictional detectives, reasons that the blackmailer, a clever man, would have anticipated such a search and would have decided the best way to hide the letter was not to; Dupin finds it in plain sight, thrust with ostentatious carelessness into a cheap card rack "dangling by a dirty blue ribbon" from the study mantelpiece. Americans have a similar technique for concealing by revealing: we publish so much accurate information that only the most acute and diligent reader can find the needle of Truth in the haystack of Facts: the plethora of unedited Facts in the news columns of the *New York Times;* our sociological studies, impenetrably thick with tables, case histories, and masses of dispensable data; and the Warren Report. I don't imply these respectable editors, scholars, and Commissioners intended to conceal anything. Merely that this is the effect of their labors.

For instance, the Report has twelve pages on Oswald's trip to Mexico two months before the assassination and his unsuccessful efforts to get travel visas at the Cuban and Soviet embassies: a crucial point, and the Commission's patient sleuthing establishes to my satisfaction that while Oswald was full of conspiratorial zeal, he failed to infect the Cuban and Russian embassies with it so signally that neither gave him a visa, while the Cubans threw him out. But it could have been done in half the space had they left out the kind of research trivia—Minifacts—one finds on page 305, as: "A hotel guest stated that on one occasion he sat down at a table with Oswald at the restaurant because no empty tables were available [they explain *everything*] but that neither spoke to the other because of the language barrier." The Commission has gone Sherlock Holmes' dog-that-didn't-bark-in-the-night one worse: *their* dog not only didn't bark but also had no significance. Or: "Investigation of the hotel at which Oswald stayed has failed to uncover any evidence that the hotel is unusual in any way that could relate to Oswald's visit." The hotel didn't bark either. Or: "Oswald's notebook which he carried with him to Mexico City contained the telephone number of the Cuban Airlines Office in Mexico City." Aha! But then not aha: "However . . . a confidential check of the Cuban Airlines Office uncovered no evidence that Oswald visited their offices while in the city." There is also quite a lot on one Albert Osborne, "an elderly itinerant preacher," whom, "two Australian girls" said, Oswald had sat next to on the bus to Mexico City but who denied it. However, "Osborne's responses to Federal investigators on matters unrelated to Oswald have proved inconsistent and unreliable," so "the Commission has attached no credence to his denial." However-however, or however squared, "to the other passengers on the bus it appeared that Osborne and Oswald had not previously met," and "extensive investigation" revealed no more Oswald-Osborne meetings, and so, after "investigation of his [Osborne's] background and activities," the Commission found "no basis for suspecting him of any involvement in the assassination." So much, and too much, for the Reverend Osborne. On turning the page, groggily, one is confronted with a full-page map of "Lee Harvey Oswald's Movements in Mexico City" (where nothing happened), with eight Points of Interest beginning with: "Bus terminal of Flecha Roja bus line, Calle Heroes Ferrocarrileros No. 45." Just what one wanted to know.

The Commissioners seem to have a thing about buses. Although I realize that in selecting Exhibits it is better to err on the inclusive side since what may seem trivial may later turn out to be important —since Facts take on meaning only from the context, and the right context may not have occurred to anybody at the time the Exhibits, or Facts, were chosen—still, leafing through those eleven volumes left me with the feeling that no remotely conceivable context could give significance to many of the Exhibits. Nos. 372 through 380, for example, are devoted to a Dreiserian brooding on the intimate details of the bus that Oswald took after the assassination. In No. 373 we get "Diagram of Cecil McWatters' bus," in 375 "Photograph of a side view of Cecil McWatters' bus," in 379 "Photograph of the interior of Cecil McWatters' bus, taken from the rear," which is logically enough followed by 380 ("Photograph of the interior of Cecil McWatters' bus taken from the front"). We also are able to decide for ourselves—nothing up the sleeves, you see—by inspection of No. 372 ("Sample of punchmarks made by Cecil McWatters' punch") whether Cecil McWatters, practically a family friend by now, did or did not punch the transfer that the Dallas police found in Oswald's pocket. Personally, I'm convinced he did.

The structure of the Report may be described cinematically. The first chapter is an "establishing" long shot which summarizes the events and the conclusions the Commission has drawn from them: that Oswald all by himself killed President Kennedy and Officer Tippit, that Ruby all by himself killed Oswald, and that there was no conspiracy. In the seven remaining chapters the camera moves in closer, to middle-distance shots, at first narrative (II: The Assassination; III: The Shots From the Texas School Book Depository; IV: The Assassin; V: Detention and Death of Oswald) and then expository (VI: Investigation of Possible Conspiracy; VII: Lee Harvey Oswald: Background and Possible Motives; VIII: The Protection of the President). The latter half of the volume consists of eighteen appendices which are mostly closeups: medical reports; identification of guns, bullets, cartridges, handwriting, etc.; a Brief History of Presidential Protection, etc. The most interesting of these closeups is Appendix XI.

Appendix XI is thirty-eight pages of photostats of reports by Captain Fritz of the Dallas police, FBI agents Hosty, Bookhout, and Clements, Inspector Kelly of the Secret Service, and Postal Inspector Holmes on the interrogations of Oswald. Why Inspector Holmes was included is not explained—that Oswald rented post-office boxes under a false name seems the only connection—but it was fortunate because his account is the most intelligent, with Inspector Kelly second, Captain Fritz third, and the FBI agents in the awkward squad. Captain Fritz's opacity is more personal than official and so his report gives us a few glimpses of reality. But Messrs. Hosty and

Bookhout are professionally stupid: their thinking has become so bureaucratized that it excludes unofficial reality, i.e., real reality. In their report Oswald doesn't say, he admits. When "he admitted . . . to having resided in the Soviet Union for three years" is shortly followed by "Oswald admitted to having received an award for marksmanship while a member of the U.S. Marine Corps," one begins to wonder about this "Marine Corps" and its so-called marksmanship awards. Maybe some kind of cover?

But the quality of these reports isn't the point. The best of them add little to what we already knew, but Oswald was an uncooperative witness, either clamming up or recklessly lying whenever the questions brought up hard evidence tying him to the assassination, and perhaps here we have all the meat there was in the approximately twelve hours of interrogations. What is appalling, unbelievable, is that these reports, written later in part from memory, in some cases days later, are all we shall ever know. There was no stenographer or tape recorder. The Dallas police are capable of anything, but I cannot explain why the FBI and Secret Service agents present didn't think of making a record. Were they as inefficient as the cops? Did they, too, fail to recognize this was a fairly important murder case and that a transcript of those nearly twelve hours of questioning might be worth some trouble and expense? The Report offers no explanation or criticism, seems unaware of any problem. In my much-too-cursory looking through the complete testimony, which was not published until I was in the final stages of this article, I ran across the following:

> Mr. Ball: Did you have any tape recorder?
> Captain Fritz: No, sir. . . . We need one, if we had one at this time we could have handled these conversations far better.
> Mr. Ball: The Dallas Police Department doesn't have one?
> Captain Fritz: No, sir; I have requested one several times but so far they haven't gotten me one.

Mr. Ball didn't ask the obvious next question, "Why didn't you or somebody think of renting or borrowing one?"* The subject was

---

* (1973) Nor did he ask why nobody thought of having an old-fashioned stenographer present to take short-hand notes.

simply dropped. I conclude that the Commission drew back from a line of inquiry that would have discredited the Dallas cops and, more important, the FBI and the Secret Service. And I'm sorry to say this is not the only time such a conclusion may be drawn from the Warren Report.

Judging the Report as a literary work, I find the style and the form are not calculated to produce the desired effect on the reader, i.e., that he is getting at last the definitive account, complete and objective, of what happened in Dallas. What was wanted was a tightly organized presentation of the "hard" evidence (ballistic and other identification tests, dates and places and documents) plus a tough-minded evaluation of the "soft" evidence, mostly eyewitness testimony, which would not try to conceal or explain away places where it contradicted whatever general theory the Commission had formed. (It was proper, indeed necessary, that it should have such a theory since it couldn't have made sense out of the facts without some hypothesis providing a provisional context to which they could be related; but when a fact collides with a theory, it is the latter that should be altered.) Something like the early Sherlock Holmes. Or that laconic, understated, and deadly work two young English booksellers, John Carter and Graham Pollard, published in 1934 which concealed under its demurely drab title, *An Enquiry into the Nature of Certain Nineteenth Century Pamphlets*, a cargo of high-explosive research that blew up the reputation of Thomas J. Wise, who was until their book appeared the highly respected "dean of English bibliographers," exposing him as the fabricator and marketer, in his youth, of some fifty bogus first editions.

No, this is not what the Warren Report gives us. Its prose is at best workmanlike but too often turgidly legalistic or pompously official. It obscures the strong points of its case, and many are very strong, under a midden-heap of inessential Facts of which I've given samples above. Its tone is that of the advocate, smoothing away or sidestepping objections to his "case," rather than the impartial judge or the researcher welcoming all data with detached curiosity. Its structure is clumsy, confused, and repetitious. Oswald's biography, for example, is scattered in three places. Why this obsessive returning to Oswald, why the disproportionate space devoted to him—almost a fourth of the Report? The Commissioners build in a Romanesque style that seems needlessly massive, but their Oswald buttress is so thick as to suggest to the cynical that the builders may have felt their fabric was weakest at that point.

These defects don't necessarily invalidate the Report's conclusions: a sound theory may be poorly presented, a prejudiced judge may arrive at a correct decision. The publicists who have insisted that Oswald was framed or was part of a conspiracy naturally give sinister explanations of the Report's one-sidedness. The most informed and rational of them is Leo Sauvage, the American correspondent of the Paris daily *Le Figaro*, whose book on the assassination Les Éditions de Minuit is about to publish. He is the only one I know of who doesn't have a large, left-handed political ax to grind. On a very different level are Joachim Joesten's *Oswald: Assassin or Fall Guy?* and Thomas Buchanan's *Who Killed Kennedy?* Also the articles and speeches of the New York lawyer and politician, Mark Lane. Or Bertrand Russell, who, according to I. F. Stone, calls it the American Dreyfus Case, with Lane cast as Zola,* and has smeared the Warren Commissioners with such charges as that Congressman Ford of Michigan was "a leader of his local Goldwater movement" when in fact Mr. Ford nominated Romney at the Republican Convention in the hope of stopping Goldwater. "Demonology," Mr. Stone, hardly a supporter of the Establishment, calls it in the October 5, 1964, issue of his newsletter. These diehards wouldn't have been convinced by the Warren Report if Jehovah had descended in Person and had the Recording Angel engrave it on tablets of stone before their eyes. They often refer to Murray Kempton's article in the October 10, 1964, *New Republic*, the best evaluation I've seen, and especially to his conclusion, with which I agree, that it is essentially a brief for the prosecution. But they seldom quote the full sentence: "In sum, he [Earl Warren] has given us an immense and almost indisputable statement for the prosecution." ("Almost indisputable" seems to me just right.) Nor do they say much about an earlier sentence: "It is hard to believe [after reading the Report] that Oswald did not kill John F. Kennedy, and that he did not act alone."

---

* (1970) Rather like casting Brann the Iconoclast—or Mark Rudd—as Voltaire.

Partisanship does infect the Report, however, and it won't do to pretend otherwise. In two ways. *The Prosecutor's Brief*: accepting or rejecting testimony according to how it fits into what the Commissioners want to prove. And *The Establishment Syndrome*: the reflexive instinct of people in office to trust other officials more than outsiders, and to gloss over their mistakes.

Mr. Kempton has noted the Report's tendency to "tidy up its case with evidence that is not evidence . . . to convince the unpersuaded by the desperate sort of carpentry which trims every piece to make it neat, even though the whole is untidy." He gives two examples: the escalation of Howard Brennan's distant glimpse of a man firing a rifle from a sixth-floor window of the School Book Depository into a "positive identification" of Oswald, although all he could tell the police at the time was that the man was white, slim, and in his early thirties, and although when he first saw Oswald in the police lineup, Brennan would only say he might be the man. Later he became positive, explaining that on that wild first day he had feared it was a Communist conspiracy whose agents might kill him and his family if he had identified Oswald. Could be, could be, but, as Kempton observes, "The case against Oswald badly needs an unimpeachable eyewitness." His other instance is the Report's claim that Oswald's firing three accurate rounds in under eight seconds was not fantastic luck but quite expectable, although his marksmanship record in the Marines was mediocre, and although, in a later test, three crack shots, firing at a moving target at the same angle and distance, didn't do much better, and sometimes worse, than Oswald had.

There are other examples of *The Prosecutor's Brief* and/or *The Establishment Syndrome*. To cite a few:

The murder of Officer Tippit is usually considered the weakest link in the chain of evidence against Oswald. The testimony is even more confused and contradictory than in the assassination of the President although (or perhaps because) there were more eyewitnesses, three to the murder itself and seven to the flight of the killer. The Report claims that nine of them "positively identified" Oswald, an exaggeration since some did so after seeing him on TV and others weeks later from photographs. And there were those extraordinary lineups staged by the Dallas police. A taxi driver, William Whaley, for example, made a "positive identification" of Oswald as having taken his cab right after the assassination. "You could have picked him out without identifying him," he told the Commission, "by just listening to him, because he was bawling out the policeman, telling him it wasn't right to put him in line with these teen-agers [Oswald was twenty-four] and all of that. . . ." The Commission's comments are: (1) Whaley was mistaken about the lineup: he said there were five teen-agers plus Oswald in it but in fact there were only three; (2) "Whaley believes that Oswald's conduct did not aid him in his identification 'because I knew he was the right one as soon as I saw him' "; (3) "The Commission is satisfied that the lineups were conducted fairly."

The Dallas police are let off easy all through the Report—officials of a feather stick together—as its passing over their failure to make a record of Oswald's interrogation; its blandness about their letting their prisoner get killed right in headquarters ("The Abortive Transfer" is the wonderful title it gives *that* episode); its blaming the press and TV almost as much as Chief Curry for the bedlam in the corridors, which Captain Fritz testified had upset Oswald and made it harder to interrogate him, and which was responsible for enabling Jack Ruby simply to stroll in and shoot Oswald. It's not that the reporters didn't behave badly but that the Report pictures Chief Curry as helpless under their pressure. But of course he could have cleared them out any time he liked. Only he didn't like. As he told the Commission: "I didn't order them out of the building, which if I had to do over I would. In the past, like I say, we had always maintained very good relations with our press, and they had always respected us." His men also cherished "good relations with our press," i.e., publicity, especially on television. Watching the screen those two days I came to expect anybody in uniform, from patrolman to chief, to begin to talk the minute a camera was pointed his way, nor was I surprised to notice that at the moment Ruby darted out with his gun, the tall, ten-gallon-hatted deputy whose wrist was chained to Oswald's, the better to guard him, was looking with a bemused smile in the other direction, where the cameras were.

The three eyewitnesses to the Tippit murder who testified before the Commission were Domingo Benavides, a truckdriver, William Scoggins, a taxi driver, and Mrs. Helen Markham, a waitress. They must have been disappointing, though the Report maintains its usual composure. Benavides said he couldn't make a positive identification; Scoggins did pick Oswald out of "a lineup of four persons," which sounds like the teen-ager farce Whaley had described; also, the lineup was a day later and Scoggins "thought" he had by then seen a picture of Oswald in the newspaper. That left Mrs. Markham, and the Report makes the most of her. Mrs. Markham's testimony is vivid: "He fell to the ground and his cap went a little way out on the street." She is also definite; the trouble is she is differently definite at different times. She first told reporters the killer was short and stocky, with bushy hair; next made a "positive identification" of Oswald, who was slender and thin-haired, at one of those lineups; then was called from New York by Mark Lane who momentarily elicited her agreement that the killer was "slightly heavy" (but "not too heavy") and that his hair was "uh, yeh, uh, just a little bit bushy, uh-huh"; then testified before the Commission that the man was the slim, non-bushy-haired Oswald and denied she had ever spoken to, or heard of, Mark Lane; then later, when a Commission lawyer played for her a tape recording of the phone call that Mr. Lane, a New York rather than a Dallas type, had presciently made, admitted it was her voice and explained she had thought she was talking to a local cop and so had been confused when she was asked about a call from a New York lawyer. Not the most solid of witnesses, even in the discreet prose of the Report, and much less so in her unexpurgated testimony. At the opening of one session, she is evidently so agitated that Mr. Ball, the Commission's laywer, tries to soothe her: "Take it easy, this is just—" Mrs. M.: "I am very shook up." Mr. B.: "This is a very little informal conference here." She pulls herself together. "I had came, I come one block, I had come one block from my home," she begins, pinning grammar to the mat on the third fall. But a few more questions reduce her to chaos: "Now you have got me all mixed up on my streets." She is also frightened: "And I was scared, which I was scared of everybody. . . . I don't want to do something wrong." She clings to her identification of Oswald as a lifeline that will save her from everybody except Mr. Lane, who isn't a policeman, let alone a Supreme Court justice like Mr. Warren. Mr. Lane couldn't budge her on that even when she thought he was a cop. Apropos of her picking Oswald out of the lineup, "I took my time," she tells him proudly, adding, "Of course, I was passing out all the time." A rich character for a novelist, one would think, but an alarming witness. Not at all. She saw what she was supposed to see, and the Report makes a stately bow of appreciation: "Addressing itself solely to the probative value of Mrs. Markham's contemporaneous description of the gunman and her positive identification of Oswald at a police lineup, the Commission considers her testimony reliable." "Probative" is one of *its* most useful euphemisms: it means the testimony doesn't stand up by itself but with all that other testimony in the same direction, it'll do. Sometimes two or three probative cripples seem to be holding each other up—in a probative, or Pickwickian, sense. *The Witnesses*, the Bantam paperback edited by the *New York Times*, prints extracts from the testimony of seventy-seven witnesses. But nothing from Mrs. Markham. Journalists are sometimes smarter than Commissioners.

Toward those whose testimony doesn't fit, the Commission is less gallant. In his introduction to *The Witnesses*, Anthony Lewis describes Chairman Warren as "a friendly, grandfatherly figure to . . . Marina, but a relentless questioner of other witnesses." Exactly. They can't get enough of Marina's testimony and treat her with a respect—"a brave little woman," their chairman has described her— that seems to me excessive. She is a far better witness than Oswald's mother, not a high standard, but the Commission's softness toward the wife and hardness toward the mother seem also due to the fact that the former thinks Oswald guilty while the latter doesn't.* Marina seems a little too eager to please, as when she told a story of Oswald's planning an attack on Nixon which the Report shows couldn't be true because Nixon wasn't in Texas anywhere near that time. Vice-President Johnson was, however, and when asked whether it might have been he, Marina replied, à la Markham: "Yes, no. I am

---

* (1972) More precisely: she doesn't most of the time but she does some of the time—depends on her mood and her polemical needs of moment. When she's angry with Marina, she accuses her of framing Lee Harvey, aided by two Secret Service agents and an unidentified "high official" in the government ("I'd rather not give the name."). When she is angry with President Johnson for snubbing her, she protests to reporters: "I am not just anyone and he is just President by grace of my son's action. . . . I will go down in history too." See end of article for a pale sketch of "Mother" Oswald, an improbable type to whom only Dickens could do justice—and in fact has in his portrait of another nurse, Sairey Gamp.

getting a little confused with so many questions. I was absolutely convinced it was Nixon and now after all these questions I wonder if I am right in my mind." The Commission decided her evidence on that point was "of no probative value."

The Report states that the man who on the night of April 10, 1963, took a potshot at the ultraright General Walker in his Dallas home was Oswald. Apart from Marina's story, there is one solid bit of evidence: a note she said Oswald left her before setting out that night giving her instructions about rent, money, disposal of his personal belongings, etc., and ending: "11. If I am alive and taken prisoner, the city jail is located at . . ." The handwriting was identified as his and, from internal evidence, the date of the note was placed around the time of the attack on Walker. She also gave them photographs of Walker's house that were identified as taken by Oswald's camera. With so much evidence, it is curious the Commission doesn't go very much into the circumstances of the attack, and especially curious it couldn't find room among its 552 witnesses for Kirk Newman, a fourteen-year-old boy who told reporters he had seen "several men jump into an automobile after the shooting and speed away." He may have been mistaken, or perhaps there was an innocent explanation (services were in progress in a church next door), but all we know is that his testimony didn't fit.

Such are some of the defects of the Warren Report. They can be explained as indications either of a deliberate attempt by the Commission to cover up, for *raisons d'état*, a broader conspiracy; or of a professional deformation of intelligence. I believe the first explanation unlikely, for reasons to be considered later, and the second likely.

The trouble with the Warren Report is that it was written by lawyers. All seven of the Commissioners graduated from law school and made their early careers as lawyers. It could hardly have been otherwise: our governmental establishment has always been trained in the law. From the early years of the Republic the vast majority of our senators, congressmen and administrators have been lawyers.*

---

* (1973) De Tocqueville explains why. "The people in democratic states does not distrust the members of the legal profession," he writes in Chapter XVI of *Democracy in America*, "because it is well known that they are interested

This is a legal-minded country and while one or two nonlawyers might have been wedged into the Commission had anybody thought about it, a distinguished group of Americans like the Warren Commission was bound to be monopolized by lawyers because of their preponderance in the Establishment.

The Commission was composed of Chief Justice Warren, Senators Russell and Cooper, Congressmen Ford and Boggs, Allen Dulles, late head of the CIA, and John J. McCloy, a Wall Street banker who doubles in top-level governmental missions. All seven of them lawyers by training—granted, expectable. But there were also twenty-seven others who were important enough to get their names attached to the Report, and not granted that all but five of them should also have been lawyers. I suppose the General Counsel, J. Lee Rankin, had to be a lawyer, but did all of his fourteen Assistant Counsel—the plural is the same as the singular, like fish—have to come from that esoteric profession? Also, to a nonlawyer, it seems disproportionate that the seven Commissioners, all lawyers themselves, needed fifteen other lawyers, or Counsel, to advise them on points of law. Was that the main issue?

It's more complicated than this, however, only fair to admit. As the Foreword to the Report explains, those fifteen Counsel didn't just advise the Commissioners about libel and torts and the Constitutional aspects of shooting the President and the rights of a dead defendant, if any. They "undertook the work of the Commission with a wealth of legal and investigative experience and a total dedication to the determination of the truth." They did the job, in short. "The Commission has been assisted also by highly qualified personnel from several Federal agencies," namely the Staff, who are thus relegated to the "also-assisted" level. Not that it would have made much difference had the Staff been on top, since seven of the twelve were also lawyers. And of these seven, three were to become law

in serving the popular cause. . . . Lawyers belong to the people by birth and interest, to the aristocracy by habit and taste, and they are the natural connecting link between the two great classes of society. . . . As the lawyers constitute the only enlightened class which the people do not mistrust, they are naturally called upon to occupy most of the public stations. They fill the legislative assemblies, and they conduct the administration." As then, so now a century and a half later.

clerks to Justice Warren, Judge Medina, and Justice Matthew Tobriner and the year before one had been Justice Harlan's law clerk —that is, ambitious young chaps who were not going to step out of the lines drawn by their chiefs. So of the thirty-four persons—Commissioners, Counsel, and Staff—who were important enough to get their names in the Report, just five were not lawyers, three being from the Internal Revenue Service and two being "Air Force historians."

A layman might think those four law clerks plus some of the fourteen Assistant Counsel could have been replaced by, say, a psychiatrist (plenty of lay analysis practiced in the Report's over two hundred pages on Oswald's twisted life, including a speculation that Marina's rejection of him as a husband the night before the assassination might have been an immediate motive, as it might—but an expert opinion would have been interesting), a detective or two, a couple of political experts (Lippmann?, Reston?,* Kempton?, Rovere?), and some real historians—not from the air force—who knew something about extremist politics and psychology, Left or Right: Richard Hofstadter? C. Vann Woodward? Henry Steele Commager? Daniel Bell? Erle Stanley Gardner might have been a useful Staff Member, less for his detective stories than for his work in "The Court of Last Resort"—just the kind of resourceful defender of the legal underdog the dead Oswald needed, and didn't get.

The lawyers were in charge, however, twenty-nine to five, and they messed it up.† D.C. wits call Earl Warren "the Washington of the Supreme Court" and certainly his rectitude was as important to

---

* (1971) Delete "Reston," substitute "Wicker." (1973) Add "Anthony Lewis."

† (1973) Perhaps because, trained in an esoteric discipline, they lacked the common touch—and the common sense—to successfully conduct an investigation which was more political than legal. Again de Tocqueville is illuminating: "The special information which lawyers derive from their studies ensures them a special station in society, and they constitute a sort of privileged body in the scale of intelligence. Their notion of this superiority constantly recurs to them. . . . They are masters of a science which is necessary but which is not generally understood . . . and the habit of directing the blind passions of parties in litigation to their purpose inspires them with a certain contempt for the judgment of the multitude." Unhappily, it was precisely this judgment that President Johnson set up the Warren Commission to convince.

the Commission as Washington's was to the infant Republic. But, like Washington, his character is as solid as his intellect is not, and the Commission could have done with a Disraeli or a Metternich to supplement Warren's unimpeachable rectitude with impeachable cleverness.

They might have, in that case, handled better the awkward business of the chief, indeed the only, suspect's being dead. "The Commission has functioned," states the Foreword, "neither as a court presiding over an adversary proceeding nor as a prosecutor determined to prove a case, but as a fact-finding agency committed to the ascertainment of truth." But American lawyers are trained in "adversary proceedings," which work well enough in trials, where a rough balance of truth can be arrived at by the dialectic clash of prosecution and defense. But the Commission faced the unprecedented problem of a defendant who couldn't defend himself, making the "adversary" dialectic impossible. They took the fact-finding-agency-committed-to-truth line, but they seem to have doubted, as well they might, their ability to cleave to it and so, three months after they began their labors, they gave in to outside objections and "in fairness to the alleged assassin and his family . . . requested Walter E. Craig, President of the American Bar Association, to participate in the investigation and to advise the Commission whether in his opinion the proceedings conformed to the basic principles of American justice." He accepted this vague mandate and carried it out even more vaguely. Although he and his "associates" (names not given) were made free of all data in the Commission's files, plus "opportunity to cross-examine witnesses, to recall any witnesses prior to his appointment," and to suggest new witnesses, they seem to have exercised these privileges sparingly, if at all. There may be traces of Mr. Craig's activity in the complete testimony, though I found none in the interrogations of Mr. Brennan or Mrs. Markham, witnesses one would expect to be a cross-examiner's delight. Nor has he left any impress on the Report, whose index doesn't list him. So I suspect this is a lawyer's idea of "making the record" and that, after appointing the fantasmal Craig to watch over Oswald's interests, the Commission felt free, morally and in a public-relations sense, to go to town for the prosecution.

The suspicion hardened when I read, "This procedure was

agreeable to counsel for Oswald's widow," and remembered that Oswald's widow was a leading witness for the *prosecution*. Oswald's mother, who insisted he was framed, was the one the procedure should have been "agreeable to." But her lawyer, Mark Lane, had asked to be recognized as defense attorney long before Mr. Craig was drafted, and had been decisively snubbed by Earl Warren. I sympathize with the chairman: if Mr. Craig was King Log, Mr. Lane would have been King Stork. He strikes me less as a truth seeker than as a crude, tireless, and demagogic advocate, and I can imagine the publicity circus, the confusion, the waste of time had he been given status before the Commission as lawyer for a client that only an embattled partisan would have wanted to represent: Mother Oswald, whose mental processes are even more "shook up" than Mrs. Markham's. Any serious investigating body might well draw back from such a counsel representing such a client. But I think a less lawyer-like commission could have hit on something between the extremes of Mr. Craig and Mr. Lane: an energetic but responsible Devil's Advocate who would have asked the important questions that were not asked. Erle Stanley Gardner would have been a big improvement on President Craig of the American Bar Association.*

The American legal mind is often subtle and complex, but its "adversary" training pushes it toward an Either/Or solution which treats Facts not as ever-changing pointers toward an ever-changing hypothesis, but as uniformed troops to be strategically massed so as to overwhelm the enemy by sheer numbers. The irony is that a much shorter report, which concentrated on the "hard" evidence instead of relying on great accumulations of often dubious testimony, would have been more effective because it would have presented a shorter, and stronger, defensive front. But lawyers are always out for total victory. (I attribute the Commission's "adversary" bias against Oswald simply to the fact that the prima-facie case against him was so strong.) But—another irony—it was just this insistence on total victory that caused the Report to defend every position when it would have been tactically shrewder to abandon the more vulnerable ones.

---

* (1973) Or, anachronistically, Senator Sam Ervin of North Carolina whose conduct of the Watergate hearings combines acumen, persistence, fairness, and respect for, and knowledge of, our Constitution.

Why not admit that Mrs. Markham was a poor witness, that the Dallas police lineups were absurd, that a record should have been made of the interrogations of Oswald, etc.? No serious damage would have been done to the Commission's basic case, the diehard skeptics would have had less ammunition, and those "rumors and speculations" the Report was intended to exorcise would have been more effectively deflated.

In a Lou Harris poll taken after the publication of the Report, 87 percent of the respondents believed Oswald shot the President, but 31 percent still thought he had accomplices that have not yet been discovered. Thus, with a third of the American public—and undoubtedly a larger percentage of Europeans—the Warren Report has not succeeded in its chief object. The ghost of conspiracy still walks.

The ghost may never be laid, if only because so many people have accreted so much information and misinformation about those two days in Dallas, and have developed such elaborate systems of casuistry to explain them, that discussions tend to be as inconclusive as those that used to grind on for hours about the symbolism in Bergman movies.

But perhaps I can rescue the Warren Report from its authors. Its shortcomings are serious but not fatal. It proves its big point beyond a reasonable doubt—which doesn't mean beyond all doubt—namely that Oswald killed the President and there were no accomplices. It achieves this partly because it has the virtue of its defect: the abundance of data I've objected to as confusing is sometimes, to the patient reader, illuminating. In criticizing the Report's verbosity, one shouldn't forget its many little triumphs in bringing to bear on specific points the Facts amassed in thirty thousand pages of FBI and Secret Service reports, a lot of man-hour sleuthing. For instance, pages 256–257 show that Oswald paid for his trip to the Soviet Union without help from either the CIA or the Kremlin; page 274 convinces me that his membership in the Belorussian Society of Hunters and Fishermen was not a cover for secret training as a Soviet agent; pages 322–323 trace his movements on September 26–27, 1963, in such detail as to show he couldn't have been in Dallas then and so couldn't have been the man that Mrs. Odio, a Cuban exile, thought she had met as "Leon Oswald" under conspiratorial circumstances.

But the most convincing aspect of the Report is the "hard" evidence:

(1) On March 13, 1963, Klein's Sporting Goods Company in Chicago received a purchase order, with a $21.45 postal check, for one Mannlicher-Carcano Italian military rifle, Model 91/38, equipped with a Japanese sighting scope. The order was from "A. Hidell," P.O. Box 2915, Dallas, Texas, and the rifle was shipped to that address. ("Hidell" or "Hydell" was Oswald's favorite alias, perhaps because, as Benjamin DeMott suggested in the December 26, 1963, *New York Review of Books*, "Within the soft blur of the name fantasy selves whirled like the blades of a fan: Hydell, Hidell: hide, hell, hideous, idle, idol, Fidel, Hyde, Jekyll.") The application form for Dallas P.O. Box 2915 and the purchase order sent to Klein's were both identified, by two "questioned document experts" from the FBI and the Treasury Department, as in Oswald's handwriting.

(2) A Mannlicher-Carcano Italian military rifle was found shortly after the shooting on the sixth floor of the Texas School Book Depository, where Oswald worked and where fellow workers have placed him on the morning of the assassination. Its barrel was stamped with the serial number C2766, which was the number of the rifle sent to "A. Hidell," Box 2915, Dallas, according to Klein's records. The Italian armed-forces intelligence stated that "this particular rifle was the only rifle of its type bearing the number C2766." On the underside of the barrel a palm print was found which was identified as Oswald's by Sebastian Latona, of the "Latent Fingerprint" division of the FBI. No other prints were found on the rifle.

(3) One whole bullet and fragments of other bullets were recovered from the car in which the President was riding and the stretcher on which Governor Connally was carried into the Parkland Hospital. Three spent cartridges were found on the sixth floor of the School Book Depository. Four ballistics experts, three from the FBI and one from the Illinois police, agreed that the bullet, the bullet fragments, and the cartridges had all been fired in the C2766 Mannlicher-Carcano rifle "to the exclusion of all other weapons."

(4) When Oswald was arrested in the movie theater a half

hour after the Tippit shooting, the police took a revolver from him, they testified he tried to shoot Officer McDonald with it, inconsistencies have been pointed out in their testimony, cops are not my favorite kind of witnesses, let it go, not essential. What cannot be disputed is that the gun was a .38 Smith & Wesson special two-inch Commando, serial number V510210. Nor is there any doubt that it was bought from Seaport Traders Incorporated, of Los Angeles, who shipped it on March 20, 1963, to A. J. Hidell, Post Office Box 2915, Dallas, or that the handwriting on the order coupon was Oswald's. The four bullets recovered from Tippit's body were consistent with this gun but could not be "positively" identified with it to the exclusion of all other guns of its type because they were a trifle too small for the barrel and so were mangled passing through it; technical stuff, see page 559. But three eyewitnesses had turned over to the police four spent cartridges: the truckdriver, Benavides, who saw Tippit fall and later picked up two shells he had seen the killer eject from his revolver as he ran away; and two young women living in the neighborhood who heard the shots, ran to the door, saw a man running across their lawn emptying his gun, and later gave the police two shells they had found near their house. Two ballistics experts, Mr. Cunningham of the FBI and Mr. Nicol of the Illinois police, positively identified these four cartridges as having been fired from the 38 Smith & Wesson Commando, serial V510210, that was found on Oswald when he was arrested.

If we accept the evidence summarized above, we must conclude that Oswald almost certainly killed the President and that he certainly killed Tippit. If we reject some or all of it as faked, then we must assume two conspiracies, one for the assassination and a second to cover up the first by framing Oswald.

There are four possibilities:

(1) Oswald was innocent, just a case of mistaken identity—the most unfortunate innocent bystander in history.

(2) He was innocent but was framed by the real criminals.

(3) He was part of a conspiracy; he may or may not have done one or both killings; he may or may not have been betrayed by his confederates and made to appear the sole assassin of the President.

(4) He did both killings alone; there were no accomplices and no conspiracy.

Whether one believes the "hard" evidence or not, (1) is ruled out, since if one believes it is true, he was guilty, and if one believes it is doctored, the only possibilities are (2) or (3). It seems almost impossible to believe (2) in the face of all the evidence, hard or soft, that ties him to the incriminating guns and documents and puts him at the scene of the assassination and has him running away and then shooting down a cop who stops him on the street for questioning.

Parenthetically, I think it interesting that the direct, or eye-witness, testimony on the Tippit murder is the weakest against Oswald, while the "hard" evidence (ballistics, handwriting, etc.) is the strongest. I have never understood the popular prejudice against "'just circumstantial evidence." Why the "just"?

In his classic *Convicting the Innocent* (1932), a study of American and British trials in which this happened, Edwin A. Borchard, then of the Yale Law School, writes: "Perhaps the major source of these tragic errors is an identification of the accused by the victim of a crime of violence. . . . These cases illustrate the fact that the emotional balance of the victim *or eyewitness* [my emphasis—D.M.] is so disturbed by his extraordinary experience that his powers of perception become distorted and his identification is frequently most untrustworthy." In almost half the cases (twenty-nine out of sixty-five) Borchard found that mistaken eyewitnesses were solely responsible for the error, while he lists only eleven cases of defendants wrongly convicted on circumstantial evidence alone. As Thoreau observed, "Sometimes circumstantial evidence is very strong, as when you find a trout in the milk."

And sometimes eyewitness testimony can be very weak, as when the audience at Ford's Theater on April 14, 1865, saw John Wilkes Booth jump down onto the stage from the presidential box and . . . what? Some saw him turn around, wave the bloody dagger with which he had just slashed Major Rathbone, declaim the state motto of Virginia, *"Sic Semper Tyrannis!"* and disappear backstage. And some saw him limp (his ankle was broken, circumstantially) directly into the wings without any dagger-waving heroics.

The advantage of hypothesis (3) (Oswald was part of a conspiracy) is that it explains so many puzzling details: Oswald's lucky shooting (a more expert marksman used his rifle), how the police got a description of him so quickly (they had already framed him), the killing of Tippit (Oswald realized his fellow conspirators were framing him when Tippit stopped him), and the cops letting Ruby in to kill Oswald. Indeed (3) explains practically anything that needs explaining. For instance: Mrs. Odio thought she met Oswald when she couldn't have, a gunsmith found a work tag marked "Oswald" for installing a sighting scope (Oswald's rifle already had a scope when he bought it), a sportsman at a local target range identified Oswald as a man he saw practicing there, getting into a noisy row, and driving off in a car (Oswald couldn't drive), etc. Oswald was not unusual-looking and a double might have been busy planting incriminating clues. A double really makes detective work child's play: maybe Oswald didn't even kill Tippit, maybe that double stole his gun, shot Tippit with it, rushed it to the cops who planted it on Oswald a half hour later after he had obligingly called attention to himself by hurrying down the street, ducking into the movie lobby when he heard police sirens, and running into the theater without buying a ticket (which led the woman in the box office to call the police). Well, no, I guess even a double doesn't explain all that. But now suppose there were *two* doubles . . . and if all three got mixed up somehow . . . and Ruby killed an Oswald facsimile . . . and Oswald is living right now in the Argentine next door to a German with a small moustache. . . .

The drawback of (3) or any other conspiracy theory is that it soon faces a dilemma. Either: (a) Some or all of the many investigators knew about a conspiracy in advance, perhaps were part of it, or discovered it later and then covered it right up again. Or: (b) They knew of no conspiracy, were part of none, and although one existed, their best efforts were unable to find any trace.

To believe (a), it is not enough to pin it on the Dallas police or "certain elements" in the FBI or the CIA or whatnot. We must go all the way to the top, to President Johnson, to J. Edgar Hoover, to Chief Justice Warren, because if the conspiracy did not reach that high, then some investigator who worked for a boss who was not in the conspiracy and was of a higher rank than any of the officials who were would have run across something fishy, some loose end, have tugged at it with innocent zeal and pulled up another odd fish, would have innocently told his innocent boss, and that would be it.

The Dallas cops couldn't possibly have covered up a conspiracy from the FBI, nor the FBI from the Warren Commission. Nor can I conceive of any *raison d'état* that would make a man of Earl Warren's character falsify his report on the assassination of his president, or one that would have caused the then attorney-general of the United States, an able, energetic, and aggressive man with great resources at his command for criminal investigation, agreeing to let the murderers of a beloved brother go unpunished.

Alternative (b), that an honest investigation of the scope of this one would not turn up one accomplice of Oswald or Ruby, this is possible in formal logic but not probable in real life. I can't believe that among the many hundreds of detectives, FBI and Secret Service agents, and workers for the Warren Commission, assuming, as (b) does, they were really trying to find what there was to be found, not one would be bright, or lucky, enough to discover, or stumble across, some clue if there were any there. Nor that any conspiracy could be so perfectly managed as to defy such a massive investigation, and not to yield one stray bean to be spilled by one imperfect human instrument. And if I were planning to murder a president of the United States, Jack Ruby and Lee Oswald would be far down on my list of reliable instruments.

But no beans *have* been spilled.* Those who believe the Warren Report is deliberately hiding some explosive truth can cite chapter and verse, as I have, on its obfuscations, but when they try to de-

---

* (1973) The evolution of the Watergate scandal shows the tendency of beans to spill if there are any in the pot in the first place. In less than a year, what seemed at first an aberration of overzealous (and underscrupled) Republican small-fry has been traced, by press and congressional investigation, to the top levels of the White House—by the time this appears perhaps to the tip-toppest level—new beans are spilling, new cats emerging from that capacious bag every week. A conspiracy, to vary the metaphor, is a fabric, and if there is enough interest in unraveling it—as was the case with both Watergate and the Kennedy assassination—it is hard to imagine that some conspirator won't break (McCord began it) or that some investigators (like that pair on the *Washington Post*) won't find a loose thread and pull on it and find it unravels others, etc. It is now ten years since Dallas, and all the efforts of Mark Lane, Big Jim Garrison, and other more serious and reputable investigators have yet to find a thread that leads away from Oswald and toward some other person, or persons, with faces, names, postal addresses, and other attributes of concrete existence.

scribe the precise nature of this political land mine and to relate it to specific evidence in the report, they abandon chapter and verse for the hymnal. M. Sauvage sings very low: his Gallic logic tells him the Report couldn't be *that* bad unless it is hiding something, but he prudently refuses to speculate on what.

It is true the "Dallas oligarchy" had reason to dislike Kennedy's policies, as did General Walker, H. L. Hunt, the Birchites, the Klan, Governor Wallace of Alabama, et al. And as also did Castro, the Kremlin (the *détente* wasn't all that *détented*), and Red China, although none of the conspiracy-mongers ever mention *them* for reasons that leap to the eye. (I can't quite see how the FBI or CIA come in, motivewise.) But if motives were conspiracies, then journalistic beggars might ride. And speaking of motives, it seems not to have occurred to the conspiratorialists that the Kennedy-Johnson government, which was and is in control of the agencies that are alleged to have covered up the damning truth, would not at all object to discovering that the assassination was the work of Mr. Hunt and other Dallas millionaires, or General Walker, or any of the right-wing persons and groups they are supposed to be masochistically protecting. But it's not worth arguing when political passions reach this point. A Mr. Ousman Ba, then foreign minister of Mali, arose in the United Nations Security Council on December 10, 1964, and "charged . . . that President Kennedy's assassination, the murder of Patrice Lumumba and Dag Hammarskjöld's death were all the work of forces that were behind the recent U.S.-Belgian rescue operation in the Congo. [Mr. Ba] did not elaborate beyond denouncing what he called 'imperialistic forces of reaction, obscurantism and racism.' " The most elaborate nonelaboration of the year.

"Depend upon it, my dear Watson, once you have eliminated all the other possibilities, the remaining one, however improbable, is the correct solution," Sherlock Holmes once observed. So we are left, or stuck, with (4), that Oswald and Ruby did it all by themselves, and, since Holmes was always right, we must accept that hypothesis even though the Warren Report says it's true. But is it really so hard to accept?

The arguments most commonly advanced against Oswald's being the assassin (aside from matters of evidence, with which I've already dealt) are: (1) As a leftist, who may well have taken that shot at General Walker, he had no political motive to shoot Kennedy. (2) Why did he insist he was innocent if he had done it, since political murderers usually proclaim their deed proudly? (3) He couldn't have done it alone: too much skill and planning needed.

(1) The Report shows in detail that underdog resentment and envy together with a desperate ambition to make his mark on History (when he lacked the talents even to hold down a job, or get himself taken seriously by that beleaguered little pro-Castro committee) were his chief motives. He may have had also a secondary political motive—his pathetic struggles to distinguish himself from the common herd often took a "Marxist" form. And from my Trotskyist days, I can testify that for a real ultraleft sectarian a Kennedy would seem a more dangerous enemy of World Revolution than a Walker precisely because Kennedy *pretended* to be on the side of the people while Walker was an *open* reactionary. In Oswald's case there was also Kennedy's hostility to Castro and his rapprochement with Khrushchev, which Oswald would have seen as a conspiracy to "sell out the revolution"—he left Russia partly because it was "too bourgeois."

(2) But why didn't he proclaim his act, as one would expect if it was either a political gesture or an attempt to get into the history books (the awful thing is he has)? I think the clue is the cocky smirk one noticed whenever he appeared on TV those two days, as if to say, I know something but these dumb cops and reporters aren't going to get it out of me. He was split between two gratifications which were hard to combine: that of being one up on everybody, putting it over on them—"Don't you wish you knew?"; and that of impressing the world as the nobody who had become somebody by his extraordinary, and successful, deed. He was similarly split between making good his escape after he had shot the President, in which case he wouldn't have been famous, and letting himself be caught, in which case he would have achieved "fame" but at the possible expense of his life. His behavior after the assassination shows this ambivalence. He did try to escape but in such a way as to insure his getting caught. Had he really wanted to escape —not only consciously, but also unconsciously—Oswald would have headed out of town not back to his room, he would not have taken

only $13.87 that morning (hardly enough to get out of Texas) and left Marina $170 which would have come in handy for a fugitive on the lam, he wouldn't have gunned down Tippit nor behaved so queerly on his flight through the streets to the movie theater and he would not have attracted the ticket-seller's attention by trying to sneak in without paying. So—unless he was even more of a bungler than one would think possible, though with Lee Harvey bungling was admittedly a fine art—he "escaped" in such a way as to insure he would be caught. . . . Similarly, I think that, had Ruby not altered his game plan permanently, Oswald would have confessed—or rather boasted about—his success as a presidential killer after he had exhausted the pleasures of frustrating and mocking the police and the press.

(After I'd worked out all this, I was reassured to see that a Dr. William Offenkrantz, of the University of Chicago, had arrived at the same line: "Criminals who unconsciously arrange for their own capture are not rare. A more bizarre possibility is that by refusing to talk, he was not just waiting for a lawyer, but perhaps enjoying the sadistic pleasure of rendering the police impotent and helpless.")

(3) On the impossibility of Oswald's having done it all by himself: Garfield and McKinley were killed by lone crackpots of the Oswald type, and both Roosevelts came near it. And there is, for our European friends, Fritz Tobias's *The Reichstag Fire* (G. P. Putnam's Sons, 1962; introduction by A. J. P. Taylor), which demonstrates to my, and Professor Taylor's, satisfaction that Van der Lubbe did it all by himself, and that it was not, as everybody at the time assumed was obvious (including me, but excepting the Berlin detectives who worked on the case), the work of either the Nazis (my view, remember *The Brown Book of the Hitler Terror*, one of the more inspired fabrications of Stalin's Goebbels, Willi Münzenberg—complete with a map of the "secret tunnel" from Göring's residence to the Reichstag which the painstaking Mr. Tobias shows was a phony?) or, as the Nazis tried to prove in court unsuccessfully, the Communists. Both sides made great play with political motivations and it was obvious to everybody that no single arsonist could have set so many fires in such a short time, just as Oswald couldn't have made three hits in under eight seconds. Yet alas for What Must Have Been: it appears that What Was was that one fanatic, in-

spired by anarchistic ideas as vague as Oswald's "Marxism" (Van der Lubbe actually believed he was helping the workers' cause against the Nazis), did it all by himself.

Robert Frazier, an FBI firearms-identification expert, after explaining to the Commission the techniques of his trade and how he had used them to identify a cartridge found on the sixth floor of the Texas School Book Depository as fired by Lee Oswald's "fateful rifle" and no other rifle in the world, concluded his testimony:

> Dissimilarities may or may not be present, depending on whether there have been changes to the firing pin through use or wear, whether the metal flows are the same, and whether the pressures are the same or not.
> So I don't think we can say that it is an absence of dissimilarities, but rather the presence of similarities.

This about sums up my view of the Warren Report's basic case. It is not the absence of dissimilarities that is convincing, for there are plenty in the evidence, but rather the presence of similarities too chronic and consistent to be explained by any hypothesis except: (4) Oswald alone killed the President; there were no accomplices and there was no conspiracy.

It is our *Iliad*. Homer's plot line has suffered a most American wrench. The great Achilles is killed by the base Thersites, "who knew within his head many words, but disorderly; /vain, and without decency, to quarrel with the princes. . . . /This was the ugliest man who came beneath Ilion."* Homer's emphasis on Thersites' deformed body ("bandy-legged . . . lame of one foot . . . shoulders stooped," etc.) I take as a metaphor, in an ante-psychiatric age when personality was assumed to express itself in physical appearance, for a moral ugliness one senses in Oswald. After reading the Report's documentation on Oswald's life and character, I understood the heroes' revulsion from Thersites ("Beyond all others, Achilleus hated him.") although I don't share their contempt for his speech abusing Agamemnon, which seems to the modern reader sensible and justi-

---

* These (and earlier) lines are from Richmond Lattimore's translation of the *Iliad*.

fied social criticism—the only passage of its kind in the whole poem, in fact. But three thousand years ago even the intellectual Odysseus had never heard of social justice. After a demagogic rebuttal, not up to his usual standard, Odysseus beats Thersites with his scepter "and a bloody welt stood up between his shoulders under/the golden scepter's stroke, and he sat down again, frightened,/in pain, and looking helplessly about wiped off the tear-drops." Homer had no higher opinion of Thersites than the Commissioners do of Oswald, but he is more just; Thersites is a man, whatever else he is, and so Homer assumes his humiliation is moving to other men, and renders it so. I found nothing like that in the Warren Report, but of course Homer was a poet, while the Commissioners were lawyers.

Homer drops Thersites after his brief moment in Book II. Thersites was then just an oddity, a man before his time, good for a small scene of sixty or seventy lines. By the sixteenth century Thersites has moved toward the center of the stage, under different names, as the malcontent, the cynical underdog who takes out his resentment against his "betters" in words, snarling and snapping at their heels but not daring the bite of action. He has a long part in Shakespeare's *Troilus and Cressida*, though none of the principals, except the ox-stupid Ajax, take his raillery as anything more than rodomontade. "Thou core of envy!" Achilles sums him up contemptuously. But they should have eavesdropped on his soliloquy "before Achilles' tent" in Act II, Scene 3. (It's in prose, Shakespeare wouldn't have thought such a clown worthy of verse.)

> How now, Thersites? What—lost in the labyrinth of thy fury? Shall the elephant Ajax carry it thus? He beats me and I rail at him—O worthy satisfaction! Would it were otherwise: that I could beat him whilst he railed at me. 'Sfoot! I'll learn to conjure and raise devils, but I'll see some issue of my spiteful execrations. Then there's Achilles—a rare engineer! If Troy be not taken till these two undermine it, the walls will stand till they fall of themselves. . . . I have said my prayers and devil envy says Amen.

In the post-Homeric legends, Achilles kills Thersites whom he instinctively "hated beyond all others." But on that day in Dallas, Thersites conjured up the devil of his envy, found an issue from his spite and a way out of the labyrinth of his fury and at long last dared the bite of action and showed he was the equal of Achilles, indeed his superior, by killing him with a Mannlicher-Carcano rifle, $21.45, postpaid, from Klein's Sporting Goods Company, of Chicago.

The place of the gods as the movers and contrivers of the tragic action in the *Iliad* is taken, in our American version, by the modern sense of History.

The President was undone by three trivial decisions: to ride in a "motorcade" through Dallas; to leave off the plastic bubbletop; and to remove the two Secret Service men who usually stood on running-boards on each side of the back seat. All three decisions were made in order to give the President "maximum exposure" to the public, "his" public. The motorcade, which the Dallas *Morning News* announced "will move slowly so that crowds can 'get a good view' of President Kennedy and his wife," was opposed by some of his aides precisely on that ground. They remembered that Adlai Stevenson had been roughed up a few weeks earlier in Dallas, and they thought the city's reputation for violence and political extremism hadn't changed much since the twenties, when it was known as "the Southwest hate capital of Dixie."* The bubbletop was not bullet-proof but it might have deflected a shot. The two Secret Service men shielded the President somewhat but this also meant they concealed him somewhat from "his" people.

An interesting study could be made of "Presidential Exposure." That it is dangerous is clear, yet recent presidents, and none more than Johnson, who seems to have a manic compulsion to make physical contact with as many citizens as possible, have considered it a necessary part of their job. Perhaps it is. A nation of almost two hundred million cannot be governed democratically; the decisions, and the power, must be concentrated in a few men at the top, with everybody else looking on as impotent spectators after the event. When President Kennedy lost the Bay of Pigs, or when he won the showdown on the Cuban missile bases, "the American people" could

---

* (1971) Curio collectors in the Dallas area have bought, by mail, over a hundred Mannlicher-Carcano rifles like the one Oswald used, and several of the wealthier have offered large sums for the original, which luckily is federal property. "They keep telling you, 'It could have happened anywhere,'" Art Buchwald reported after a visit down there. "Maybe. But it did happen in Dallas."

lament or applaud from the grandstands, *ex post facto*. "Presidential
Exposure" is one way of symbolically bridging the chasm between
the powerful insiders and the powerless outsiders: a ritual compensation for an imbalance that makes both sides uneasy. The kind
of autocratic power exercised by Louis XIV is past, at least
in the West. "*L'état, c'est nous*," the American president says, and
he needs reassurance from "his" people that he is their democratic
equal as much as they need from him the reverse assurance. Hence
the slow-moving motorcades. But of course they aren't equals, no
matter how many times our current president grabs three or four out-
stretched hands at once in a frantic effort to make contact. "My"
public, "my" people can turn in a wink into Alexander Hamilton's
"The people, Sir—the people is a great *beast!*"

The presidential party landed "in bright sunshine" at the Dallas
airport—it is called Love Field—and after cheering crowds all along
the way, Mrs. Connally, who was riding in the Kennedys' car with
her husband, the governor of Texas—the state motto is "Friendship"
—turned to the President as the motorcade was (slowly) approaching the Texas School Book Depository—what a very American site
for an assassination!—and said, possibly in some relief: "Mr. President, you can't say Dallas doesn't love you," to which he replied,
"That is very obvious." A minute later, "shots from a rifle mortally
wounded President Kennedy and seriously injured Governor Connally." The President had said his last words, but the Governor was
able to gasp, before he lost consciousness, "My God, they are going
to kill us all!" We and My had suddenly become They, the Great
Beast.

"It is considered certain," a *Time* correspondent wrote the same
day, ". . . that the informality of office under recent Presidents,
especially President Kennedy, will be sharply curtailed. President
Johnson is expected to be less publicly accessible, less in the public
view."*

---

* (*1970*) On the contrary, during his first two years in office, Johnson insisted on "pressing the flesh" with street crowds to a manic degree. This lust
for touching and being touched by "his" people had to be repressed after
popular opposition to his Vietnam caper began to escalate. By the end, he
didn't dare even to show his face at his own birthday party staged, *in absentia*,
at the 1968 Democratic Convention—cake by Mayor Daley, icing by Hubert
Humphrey.

"He looked upon the eyes of future people as some kind of tribunal, and he wanted to be on the winning side so that ten thousand years from now people would look in the history books and say, 'Well, this man was ahead of his time.' The eyes of the future became the eyes of God. He was concerned with his image in history." So Kerry Thornley remembered Oswald in the marines. For it wasn't only the President who was conscious of an historic role. Oswald seems to have had History on the brain. He grandly titled the semiliterate notebook he kept in Russia: "Historic Diary." Marxism for him was a skeleton key to History, theoretically—he doesn't seem to have read Marx. On October 3, 1956, he wrote the Socialist Party of America asking if there was "a branch in my area" he could join, adding: "I am a Marxist, and have been studying Socialist principles for well over fifteen months." On October 18, he became seventeen and on October 24 he enlisted in the marines. A record of some kind, three weeks from the revolution to boot camp, from Marxism to the marines. But the transition, for one with Oswald's free-floating dreams of glory, was just a step from one kind of powerhouse into another. It's not impossible that he opened negotiations with the Socialists so as to have somewhere to go if the marines turned him down.

The pathos of Oswald's life was that he had unlimited aspirations and extremely limited talents. He failed in everything he tried: defecting to the Soviet Union, holding down a fifty-dollar-a-week job, making a go of it with Marina. And the more he failed, the grander became his aspirations. "I'll be prime minister in twenty years!" he told Marina just before he took the bus to Mexico City to get his Russian and Cuban visas, which he didn't get. Nothing seemed to go right, nobody took him seriously, not even the Fair Play for Cuba Committee, not even the Socialist Workers Party. The one success in his whole life seems to have been the assassination of President Kennedy. But that was a relatively simple job. No people. And a footnote in History. Like Herostratus, who set fire to the great temple of Artemis in Ephesus, in order to immortalize himself. That same night in 356 B.C. a Macedonian prince named Alexander was born who was to get much more space in the history books than Herostratus, as President Kennedy will than Oswald. But these were small men, and the reach of their ambition didn't go beyond a footnote recognizing that, while others might create, they could destroy.*

"Don't worry," Lee Oswald told Marina when she visited him in the Dallas jail. "Everything will be all right." He was, for once, right. (About *her* future, anyway.) Within a fortnight she had signed a contract with one James Martin, who was to be her "personal manager," empowered to "advise and counsel with me in any and all matters pertaining to publicity, public relations, and advertising . . . news releases . . . public appearances . . . for television . . . sale of any movie rights, magazine rights, book rights . . . caricatures . . . contracts for my services, talents, memoirs, history story. . . ." Not bad for only two weeks after what Marina calls "the fateful rifle of Lee Oswald" had done its work. The contract (Exhibit 276 in Volume XVI of the Commission's complete testimony) gives the impression that Marina thinks she has suddenly become Doris Day. She even has ghostwriters. Elizabeth Hardwick quotes a former one: "I quit because Marina has come to believe she is as important as the President of the United States." *The Americanization of Marina* would make an interesting movie, though I'd hate to have to dicker with her for the rights.

Lee Oswald's fateful rifle didn't do badly by his mother either. Like Marina, she automatically became part of History. Being older, less pretty, and considerably more scatterbrained than her daughter-in-law, Marguerite (or "Mother Oswald" as the media at once dubbed

---

* History-consciousness can also operate in reverse. Nine of the twenty-eight Secret Service operatives who guarded the President that day in Dallas had violated regulations by going to late parties, with drinks, the night before. The Report, with its usual blandness about official blunders, concedes this was unfortunate, but concludes probably they couldn't have reacted any quicker anyway (though Senator Yarborough of Texas, who was in the motorcade, testified differently). In any case their chief, Mr. Rowley, did not fire or discipline them, on Historical grounds. "I do not think in the light of history," he hold the Commission, "that they should be stigmatized with something like that." Americans have a right to avoid, as well as to make, historical footnotes.

her, rather like "Mother Macbeth") hasn't been so visible, though she's done her best. According to *Time* (February 14, 1964) she was indignant when President Johnson brushed her off with a form letter telling her to consult the Commission when she demanded that a defense lawyer be appointed to defend her late son's interests at the hearings. She had a point—for once—but what seems to have graveled her was that Johnson didn't reply personally. "I am not just anyone and he is just President by grace of my son's action," she declared firmly, adding: "I understand that I will go down in history, too." She also felt hurt when she didn't get a note of condolence on her son's death from—Jackie Kennedy. "Everybody has sympathy for Mrs. Kennedy," she complained. "Doesn't anybody feel sorry for me? . . . I did my best for my boys." She is also reported to have exclaimed: "They can't push us around any more. We're in the history books now!"*

---

*(1972) For the lowdown—*le mot juste*—on Mother Oswald see Jean Stafford's "The Strange World of Marguerite Oswald" (*McCall's*, October, 1965 —later published as *A Mother in History*) in which she records her interviews with Mother O in her Dallas lair. Her account is factual and low-keyed, and it suggests with brilliant precision, right out of Mother O's mouth, how Lee Harvey got that way. The mass public, expectably, missed the point—both ways. "The mail that came into *McCall's* was 99% denunciatory," Miss Stafford wrote me. "On the one hand, I had taken advantage of this poor widow woman bereft of her son; on the other, I was outrageous to take as gospel the ravings of this mad bitch whose son had killed our beloved President. I was the subject of the lead editorial in the Mormon paper of Salt Lake City—the title was 'SHAME'—and a representative from Connecticut was remarkably vituperative."

See also, for supporting evidence, Volume I, pages 169–200, of the Warren Commission Hearings, beginning with Mother O's flat statement to the horrified Commissioners: "I think our trouble in this is our own Government. And I suspect these two [Secret Service] agents of conspiracy with my daughter-in-law in this plot [to assassinate President Kennedy]." In the next thirty pages she gives her evidence (with many and lengthy side-trips—the commissioners were very permissive) whose hard core (relatively) is that the two Secret Service agents were more polite to Marina than to her, that one of them was allegedly flirting with Marina and vice versa, that Marina talks "broken English" and isn't a good American and wasn't a good wife to Lee and she can't stand Marina and was a good mother to Lee and is a good American and Lee was framed by Marina and the two agents plus an unidentified "high official" ("I have my own very strong suspicions as to the official who he might be but I would rather not give a name." The Com-

And so they are in the history books, all three of them. The Greeks had only Herostratus to put up with but we have also Mrs. Herostratus and Mother Herostratus.

Even Jack Ruby seems to have had a sense of History. At the notorious midnight "press conference" in the jail when the reporters and cameramen swarmed all over Oswald and even Chief Curry was appalled and cut it short—at this saturnalia, Jack Ruby, who was there along with anybody else in Dallas who felt like dropping in ("No identification was required," the Warren Report notes), appointed himself as a kind of liaison officer between District Attorney Wade and the reporters, since he knew him and many of them. "I was carried away by history," he said later. His brush with History seems to have changed him. Up to then he had been weepingly upset by the President's murder. But a local announcer named Duncan was surprised to find that "Ruby did not appear to be grieving but, instead, seemed pleased about the personal contact he had had with the investigation earlier in the evening." Perhaps that was when Jack Ruby discovered History and got the notion that he, too, could take the center of the stage, just like Oswald . . . and speaking of Oswald . . . why not? The President's blood called out for vengeance, not to mention Jackie and those marvelous kids, and everybody would praise the man who killed the monster. . . . Jack the Monster Killer. It may be that Ruby's state of "fugue" at his

---

missioners didn't press her, I think—for once—wisely.) though of course Lee may also have been part of the conspiracy ("I realize he is a human being and could possibly be involved, yes, sir.") and she has no evidence against the two Secret Service agents except their bad manners ("I will answer that emphatically, no. What I have stated is the way they treated me, sir.") and Marina became uppity and brushed her off once Marina began to rake in some media dough and her "impression is that Marina came here and didn't speak English at all." *Mr. Rankin*: "How does that show she conspired to assassinate the President?" *Mrs. Oswald*: "Because Marina is not happy. . . . Marina became discontented with Lee. Lee couldn't give her the things she wanted, what he told her about America. And Marina has now become discontented with me." Q.E.D.

The prospect of Mother Oswald *and* Mark Lane doing a duet before them understandably struck terror into the Commissioners. The only lawyer I myself would have allowed to represent her would have been Calvin Coolidge.

trial was caused by his realization that everybody didn't applaud. Quite the contrary.*

Appendix:
Dr. Johnson on
Excessive Skepticism

Many Americans have always believed that Oswald was probably part of a conspiracy which, whether by chance, bungling, or design, has not been unearthed by the authorities. The hard core of this mass skepticism has been the young and/or alienated. For many and good reasons—though not as good as they think they are—they have developed an instinctive mistrust—almost a reflex below the conscious level—of the American Establishment that seizes on every contradiction, obscurity, and mistake in a most complex, murky, and bungled affair as a feedback justifying their initial prejudice. So in the first year after the assassination, they scrutinized the normal, expectable

---

* (1973) Ruby's dazed expression at his trial reminded me of Van der Lubbe's at the Reichstag Fire trial, and this may not be a coincidence. Ruby thought he was punishing Oswald and avenging the Kennedys but he soon discovered that in fact he had let Oswald off the hook—Historically speaking—and made it impossible for the President to be avenged since a trial could have set to rest some of the doubts and suspicions that swarmed in the popular mind after he'd destroyed the one key that might have unlocked the puzzle. So, too, Van der Lubbe actually thought he was striking a blow *against* the Nazis by burning down the Reichstag building which he saw as a symbol of the State. To his anarchist scatterbrain, the State was the State, whether Weimar or Nazi, and the destruction of its chief icon would spark proletarian revolt. (Cf. our own ultraleft simpletons who plotted to blow up the Statue of Liberty a few years ago from equally pure motives.) When he discovered that his heroic act (for such it was in conception and execution—to burn down the Reichstag all by his dedicated lonesome!) had in fact given the Nazis just the big show trial they needed to solidify their power by framing up their chief opponents, then he collapsed like Ruby. One remembers him slumped in his seat, head lolling low, mumbling incoherent answers, stupefied, sodden with despair, pole-axed by History.

inconsistencies of daily TV and newspaper journalism with a scholarly rigor more appropriate to Ph.D. theses. So they flocked to Mark Lane's revival meetings on some of our most sophisticated (or so one would have thought) university campuses, their enthusiasm undimmed by his manipulation of the evidence, which was even more blatant than the Commission's. Long before the Warren Report came out, they were sure "there must have been a conspiracy." To their suspicions of the Ruling Class was added a habituation to Marxist historical determinism that made it impossible for them to take seriously the hypothesis that an isolated oddball had killed the President of the United States for his own personal, cranky, and utterly ahistorical reasons.* I suspect this conviction, or rather prejudice, would have persisted had the Warren Report been far more convincing than it was.

There's another factor in this skepticism. As the Oxford don, John Sparrow, Master of All Souls College, argues in his skeptical, rigorous little analysis of the "conspiracy-mongers," *After the Assassination: a Positive Appraisal of the Warren Report* (Chilmark/ Vintage, 1967), it is extremely difficult, logically, to prove a negative.

Dining at the Mitre with Boswell one evening in 1763, Dr. Johnson playfully worked out a line of argument that is perhaps relevant two centuries later.

> "It is always easy to be on the negative side [he began]. If a man were now to deny that there is salt upon the table, you could not reduce him to absurdity. Come, let us try this a little further. I deny that Canada is taken and I can support my argu-

---

* That few of them had probably read much, if any, of Marx is irrelevant. As Joyce and Eliot shaped our literary tastes by diffusion in the postwar cultural atmosphere, so to speak, whether we read them or not, so with Marx and the liberals in the same period: they breathed in his system through their pores. It was in the 1930–1960 air: History is an understandable working-out of the conflict, dialectically progressive, between large, dignified, and abstract forces, and is definitely not a chancy game in which small, trivial individuals can absurdly and accidentally affect the outcome. So "of course" there "must have been" something, or somebody, serious behind Oswald. Else History makes no sense (which, by the way, it doesn't). So the Mark Lanes were listened to respectfully as shamans whose magic assimilated smoothly into the Marxist tribal beliefs a discordant, threatening event.

ment by pretty good arguments. The French are a much more numerous people than we, and it is not likely that they would allow us to take it."

"*But the Ministry have assured us, in all the formality of* The Gazette *that it is taken.*"*

"Very true. But the ministry have put us to an enormous expense by the war in America and it is to their interest to persuade us that we have got something for our money."

"*But the fact is confirmed by thousands of men who were at the taking of it.*"

"Aye, but these men still have some interest in deceiving us. They don't want you to think the French have beat them.

"Now suppose you should go over and find that Canada is really taken. That would satisfy only yourself, for when you come home, we will not believe you. We will say you have been bribed."

"Yet, sir," Johnson concluded, "notwithstanding all these plausible objections, we have no doubt that Canada is really ours." And according to the history books, Wolfe had beaten Montcalm long before that dinner at the Mitre, and Canada had, in fact, been "taken" by the British despite all historical probabilities.

But come, let us try it a little further:

"I deny that Oswald could have killed Kennedy all by himself. His politics were leftist and it is not likely he would have shot a liberal President. Since Dallas is, as you, sir, must agree, a notorious nexus of reaction, it is reasonable to suppose the assassination was the work of a right-wing cabal. If Oswald was involved, it must have been as an unwitting catspaw—Bedlam was ever pressing on his poor brain—for mighty principals with very different interests."

"*But the Johnson Administration have assured us, in all the formality of the* Warren Report, *that Oswald did it and did it unaided. Also that Ruby acted alone in murdering Oswald.*"

---

* I have italicized the counterarguments. I take them to be not Boswell's objections (he wouldn't have so bluntly contradicted the Doctor) but rather Johnson's hypothetical man of reason, the limitations of whose rationality he is demonstrating.

"Very true. But it is to their interest to persuade us that these were acts of isolated fanatics if not indeed Bedlamites, and not of any conspiracy, lest the political sickness of the realm be exposed and the Presidential consensus be broken. Let sleeping dogs lie is ever a wise maxim in governing deca-dent-bourgeois states."

"But the fact is confirmed in twenty-seven volumes covering the interrogation of over five hundred witnesses as well as a mountain of data amassed by hundreds of police, FBI, Secret Service, and Commission investigators."

"Aye, but these men have still more interest in deceiving us: they don't want us to think the case has beaten them.

"Now suppose you have gone through those twenty-seven volumes and had found no clues leading toward a conspiracy and you should tell us the Warren Commission is right. We will not say you have been bribed. We will say you have been co-opted by The Establishment."

A Day
at the
White House

"President and Mrs. Johnson are
planning the most extensive arts festival ever held in the White
House," reported the *New York Times* on May 27, 1965. It would
last thirteen hours, there would be exhibitions of current American
painting, sculpture, and photography; programs of American plays,
movies, ballet, and music; and readings by two novelists, Saul Bellow
and John Hersey, two poets, Robert Lowell and Phyllis McGinley,
and one popular biographer, Catherine Drinker Bowen. The
Johnsonian consensus: Bellow and Lowell balanced against Hersey
and McGinley, with Miss Bowen added to the democratic side of
the scale to make it more consensual. As the drunk said about the
books in Jay Gatsby's library: "Absolutely real—have pages and
everything. . . . See! It's a bona-fide piece of printed matter. . . .
This fella's a regular Belasco! What thoroughness! What realism!
Knew when to stop, too—didn't cut the pages. But what do you
want? What do you expect?" Our president, too, is a regular Belasco
for realistic stage settings and, like Gatsby, he knows when, and
where, to stop: just beyond Miss Bowen. He doesn't cut the pages.
But what do you want, what do you expect? A consensus is a
consensus.

A week later, the consensus was broken by Robert Lowell, who
wrote a letter to the President that appeared on the front page of the
June third *Times*:

. . . Although I am very enthusiastic about most of your domestic legislation and intentions, I nevertheless can only follow our present foreign policy with the greatest dismay and distrust. . . . We are in danger of imperceptibly becoming an explosive and suddenly chauvinistic nation, and we may even be drifting on our way to the last nuclear ruin.

I know it is hard for the responsible man to act; it is also painful for the private and irresolute man to dare criticism. At this anguished, delicate and perhaps determining moment, I feel I am serving you and our country best by not taking part in the White House Festival of the Arts.

In the same issue of the *Times*, statements appeared by Bellow and Hersey explaining why they had decided not to join Lowell. Neither expressed disagreement with his "dismay and distrust" (though Bellow seemed to accept Vietnam, criticizing only the Dominican occupation; I'm told he had first written a much stronger letter but then, like his Herzog, didn't send it; there was to be plenty of Herzogian behavior at the Festival). Bellow reasoned that it was not "a political occasion which demands agreement with Mr. Johnson on all the policies of his administration. . . . Moreover, Mr. Johnson is not simply this country's principal policy-maker. He is an institution. When he invited me to Washington, I accepted in order to show my respect for his intentions and to honor his high office." This makes no sense to me. President Harding had good intentions and he was also "an institution" to whose "high office" honor was, on this reasoning, due. But I don't think Bellow, had he been anachronistically invited to the White House then, would have accepted, any more than Emerson and Thoreau would have agreed to read from their works if President Polk had staged an arts festival during the Mexican war.

Mr. Hersey said he was "deeply troubled by the drift toward reliance on military solutions in our foreign policy" but that he felt he could "make a stronger point by standing in the White House, I would hope in the presence of the President, and reading from a work of mine entitled *Hiroshima*."*

---

* (1973) How James Russell Lowell would have reacted to such an invitation is an interesting question. On the one hand, he was a solid, conventional Boston Brahmin. On the other, he had his moments: he broke ranks to support that impossible, and hostile, outsider, Poe, whom even Emerson couldn't

The day Lowell's letter appeared in the *Times* I was asked to sign a telegram to the President supporting Lowell's position, which I gladly did because I agreed with its content and admired its unrhetorical style. The statement appeared in the next morning's *Times* (June 4) and the same morning I received a telegram: "THE PRESIDENT AND MRS. JOHNSON INVITE YOU TO THE WHITE HOUSE FESTIVAL OF THE ARTS TO BEGIN AT 10 AM ON JUNE 14TH AND CONTINUE THROUGH THE EVENING . . ." After some thought, and consultation, I decided that while the most consistent course would be to refuse—also the easiest—it might be more fruitful to accept, so that at least one critical observer would be there to report on what happened. So I wired my acceptance to the Festival's impresario, Dr. Eric Goldman—Professor of History at Princeton and President Johnson's chief cultural adviser—stating that, as he probably knew by then, I supported Lowell's stand and should feel free to comment publicly on the Festival. On these terms I sacrificed, not for the first time, consistency and good taste in the interest of a larger objective.

It turned out to be worth it. For one thing, I secured a copy of a document of primary importance, whose significance none of the newspaper reports, including Howard Taubman's copious account in the *Times*, seem to have grasped: the guest list.* I've seen no mention, for instance, that there were *two* guest lists, one for the first sitting, from 10:00 A.M. on, and the other for the second, from 7:00 P.M. on. Each contained roughly 175 persons, but the first group was invited for the major part of the Festival while the second came in only for a cocktail party on the lawn followed by the President's

---

swallow (as he could Whitman) calling him "the jingle man." Also, Lowell detested the Mexican war as proslavery and imperialist. My guess is he would either have refused, like his collateral relative of our day, or else taken the Hersey line: accepted with the hope he could read to the President from *The Biglow Papers.*

* How many others beside Lowell declined, and for what reasons, I don't know. Two refusals because of our present foreign policy have been made public: those of the photographer Paul Strand, and the sculptor Alexander Calder. And two have not: those of Jack Levine, the painter, and Robert Brustein, the drama critic—both have authorized me to state the fact. As for the rest of the absentees, who include practically the entire literary establishment, from Edmund Wilson to Thornton Wilder, all that can be said is that they were not there.

speech of welcome, a buffet supper, and two hours of ballet and jazz. The most enjoyable part of the day in fact, but still they were placed below the salt. The only rationale of this discrimination I can detect is that all the artists without exception—all the painters, sculptors, and photographers—were relegated to the second sitting. A mistake, if one purpose of the Festival was, as a White House "source" suggested, to bring together the patron and the artist. But further examination of the guest list shows the aims to have been different. "Does anyone know exactly why this particular group of people is here or why this Festival is being held in the first place?" Mildred Dunnock asked. (*She* was there to give two soliloquies from *Death of a Salesman*—but, still, why?) Asked the same question later, Jack Valenti, a presidential assistant, answered: "This is a wonderful thing to show the White House's great interest in the arts. It doesn't matter why, just that it was." Theirs not to reason why . . . So one purpose was to give the Johnson administration a cultural image, a consensus of artists and writers reciprocating "the White House's great interest in the arts" by turning out for the Festival.

But the main purpose was to impress not the actual producers of art or thought with the "White House's great interest" but rather our cultural fuglemen ("a trained soldier stationed in front of a military company as a guide for the others in their exercises"), that is, directors and patrons of art museums, presidents of symphony orchestras (i.e., the money holders or raisers—no directors or composers of any note were present, not Stravinsky or Copland or Thomson or Carter or Stokowski or Barber or Harris or Bernstein or Menotti), organizers of local "arts councils," and various pundits from TV, newspapers, and big-circulation magazines. Whether this purpose was achieved or not I don't know, but that it was paramount an examination of the guest list shows.

Excluding the *ex officio* invitees who were asked because they were reading or acting or dancing or playing music or because their pictures or sculptures or movies or plays were on view—eighty would be a generous estimate, most of them in the below-the-salt 7:00 P.M. sitting—there were present at either 10:00 A.M. or 7:00 P.M. the following who might be considered to have some direct connection with arts and letters: Alfred H. Barr, James Johnson Sweeney, Ralph

Ellison, Reed Whittemore (this year's poet in residence at the Library of Congress), Thomas Hess (editor of *Art News*), José Limon, Russell Lynes, Paul Horgan,* Pauline Kael (movie critic), Harold Taylor, Henry Geldzahler (Metropolitan Museum of Art), Frank Getlein (art critic), and myself. Adding, to be generous, ten or so newspaper critics (if there can be such a creature) and the art editor of *Time*, this comes to twenty-five participants who were some kind of artist or writer (and who were invited as part of the audience). Add five senators and congressmen (who seem to have been selected for political rather than cultural reasons—Javits, Lindsay, Morse, Robert Kennedy, Paul Douglas, and Fulbright are not on the list while Congressmen Brademas, Farnsley, and Thompson are, also Senators Cooper and Yarborough) and another five names I've at least heard of: Earl Warren, Sol Hurok, Abe Fortas, Irv Kupcinet (a Chicago columnist and TV impresario—"Kup's Show"—whose iridescent jacket livened things up) and the Hon. William Walton, chairman of the Washington Commission of Fine Arts and one of the few Kennedy intimates who were present.† Adding these ten to the artists and intellectuals mentioned above, we get 113 names or about one-third of the participants, active or passive, in the Festival.

---

* (1970): "I was not present," Mr. Horgan wrote the *New York Review* after my piece came out. "But I was honored to be invited, I regretted my inability to attend, I applauded the interest on the part of the President and Mrs. Johnson which resulted in a salute to our arts, and I see no occasion in either the idea of the Festival or its staging by Professor Goldman for the sustained jeers of Mr. Macdonald." Whether my jeers should have been sustained or intermittent as to "idea" and/or "staging" (*le mot juste*) of what Mr. Horgan aptly calls "a salute to our arts" may be judged by reading on. Meanwhile, it's depressing that this blurb for a White House arts festival Mr. Horgan hadn't time to attend was written on the letterhead of the Center for Advanced Studies at Wesleyan University of which he was then director.

† Arthur Schlesinger, Jr., for instance, was not invited, although he had ridiculed Lowell's letter and, earlier that spring, had dismissed Lewis Mumford's presidential address at the American Academy of Arts and Letters (which had departed from academic objectivity to criticize Johnson's Vietnam escalation) as "an anxious blast of a somewhat inchoate sort." Mr. Schlesinger, a historian by trade, added that the reaction of the American Academicians to their president's speech reminded him of the "wild, unleashed emotionalism" of Hitler's Nuremberg rallies. What more could Lyndon Johnson have asked? But he is a hard man with an elephantine memory. No invitation.

What of the other two-thirds? A good number, perhaps thirty, are not identified nor do their names wake any resonance in my ear. No doubt Fred Lazarus and Mrs. Irma Lazarus, both of Cincinnati, Mrs. R. Max Brooks of Austin, Texas, and Dr. Abdul Hamid, the Rector of the University of Kabul, all had some reason for being there.

There is no doubt, however, as to the identity of the great majority of participants. They were patrons, bureaucrats, or entrepreneurs of culture: Dempster Christenson, Pres., Sioux Falls-Augustana Sym. Orch., S. Dak.; R. Phillips Hanes, Jr., Pres., Arts Council of America, Winston-Salem, N. C.; John D. Rockefeller III, Chr. Bd. Trustees, Lincoln Center, NYC; Mrs. Hugh Bullock, Pres., the Academy of American Poets, NYC; Col. Eben Henson, Pres., Kentucky Council of the Performing Arts, Danville, Ky.; J. Paul Hewitt, Chr., Louisiana Commission on Culture and the Performing Arts—*tutti quanti.*

I entered the White House on the dot of ten and was greeted cordially by an attractive young matron who gave me a smile, a luxurious program with the President's seal embossed on its laid-paper cover, and a large card with my name (misspelled "McDonald") inscribed in bold calligraphy over a pale blue vignette of the White House. She pressed the gummy back side to my chest—rather like being decorated—and it stuck there all through that long day's journey into night. I was then briefed on my next move ("Straight up the stairs, sir, then sharp *right*") by one of the pleasant young officers who chivvied us about all day like respectful sheepdogs. Their crisp, incredibly clean white uniforms were accented by brass buttons, silver shoulder bars, and one of those military corsages of gold cords and tassels looped over the left shoulder.

The first familiar face I saw, on emerging from the labyrinthine corridors, was Saul Bellow's. He didn't look happy. We greeted each other in a Stanley-Livingstone mood, two exiles meeting amid all those strange natives. Nor was the mood dissipated for me, when we instantly began to argue, violently, about The Lowell Problem. Arguments are part of the New York ambience I'm used to and, for a few moments, I felt at home at the White House Festival of Arts. Our argument—can't really call it a "dialogue," not even a "discussion"—was cut short by one of the military sheepdogs who began to arrange us in line to be presented to the first lady. ("You must be pleased to see so many able-bodied young men not fighting in Vietnam," a cynical museum director observed to me.) We filed past Mrs. Johnson, murmuring our names to an officer-footman who repeated them to her, whereupon she smiled and shook hands with every appearance of delight. Since the President didn't appear until eight o'clock that evening when he gave a brief speech of welcome, after which he disappeared without any handshakes or, from where I sat, smiles, I cannot report on him as a host. But his wife was a charming hostess, agreeable and indefatigible.

"10:25–10:30 A.M. East Room. Mrs. Johnson opens the Festival with brief remarks" stated the program and so it came to pass. Logistically, the Festival was a great success. "A festival is a time for feasting and there is a rich feast indeed before us," she began, optimistically. "The arts will be presented in many forms, all of which are warmly welcome in this house. For as Aristotle told us long ago, in part the arts imitate nature but in part they also 'complete what nature cannot elaborate.' " She omitted the second sentence—I quote from the text given to the press—perhaps feeling, as a sensible woman, that her ghost-writer had overestimated the capacity of her audience for a willing suspension of disbelief. But she did include the next three sentences, which perfectly sum up the consensual approach to culture: "There is something here for the taste of everyone. Each of us will like or dislike particular things. All contribute to the enormous vigor and diversity of the creative life in America." Well, maybe, but only an omnivorous Walt Whitman could have swallowed what was served up to us at that Festival. She concluded, as per script: "You have earned the gratitude of every American for the beauty, the meaning and the zest you are contributing to our lives." That "you" was disturbing, surrounded as I was by treasurers of symphony orchestras, chairmen of state cultural commissions, and John D. Rockefeller III. I was reminded, *proportions gardées*, of Henry Wallace's postwar tour of Siberia in which he innocently saluted his audiences, composed of officials in charge of forced-labor camps, as free-spirited pioneers taming the wild frontier in the best American tradition. "Men born in wide free spaces will not brook injustice and will not even temporarily live in slavery," Mr. Wallace declaimed to the stupefied prison wardens of Irkutsk.

Mark Van Doren, the *compère* of the literary session, now rose, looking very solemn, and began by noting with regret "the absence of Lowell": ". . . I have been troubled as to whether I should speak of it at all; I do so now, after several previous attempts, merely as honoring the scruple of a fine poet who, in his own terms, was 'conscience-bound' to stay away." Originally, Mr. Van Doren had planned to say a great deal more—his "merely" above is accurate—and a typescript had been given out to the press. Some of it may be of interest:

> . . . Surely it is no secret that many share his concern—I do, for one—and perhaps it is true that all of us, without exception, are somewhat uneasy. But the main point I wish to make is that Mr. Lowell, by acting and speaking as he did, honored an ancient tradition in the arts. . . . He spoke out of his deepest conviction. . . . Nothing prevents a poet from being a citizen, too; and if Mr. Lowell thought that his duty as a citizen was to be absent from this place, it is not for us who are present to doubt that he was as serious as he was sensitive, or that it was difficult for him to stay away. History will show whether his dismay and distrust were justified; meanwhile, however, he himself has made history, and it seems fitting to record that simple fact.

Why did Van Doren omit, when he came to give the talk, all the politics and most of the praise for Lowell? Howard Taubman quotes Van Doren as saying he "had decided to shorten his comments after a talk with Bellow and Hersey," while Drew Pearson writes that "Eric Goldman diplomatically persuaded Van Doren to eliminate most of the criticism." Not a good show either way.

After Catherine Drinker Bowen had read, with spirit, an amusing extract from her biography of the late Justice Holmes, Saul Bellow, looking even more solemn than Mr. Van Doren, read, with less spirit, an extract from *Herzog* which was more amusing than Miss Bowen's passage and, in every way, much the best writing we heard that morning.

Next came Phyllis McGinley, a pleasant-looking matron in a flowered hat who was introduced by Mr. Van Doren with the admonition that light verse can be fine poetry, too, and in Miss McGinley's case, was: "She is nothing less than a poet." The warn-

ing was wasted on me, since I am fond of light verse. The trouble
was that Miss McGinley's seemed on the heavy side. After "Apolo-
gia," a soggy pastiche of Housman and Millay, she swung into her
big number, lasting eight or nine minutes, "In Praise of Diversity,"
an updated "Essay on Man":

> *Counting no blessing but the flaw*
> *That difference is the moral law.*

(Could I have got that down right?) I don't think Pope would have
rhymed "sexes" with "Texas" or "beginning" with "original sinning"
or "knee" with "courtesy." Pop Pope, you might say. That this work
was originally composed for recitation at a Columbia commence-
ment is something to think about. Ever the obliging poetaster, Miss
McGinley inserted, for the occasion, six new lines which took a firm,
positive stand in favor of both and indeed all sides:

> *Applaud both dream and commonsense,*
> *Born equal; then with all our power,*
> *Let us, for once, praise Presidents*
> *Providing Dream its festival hour.*
> *And while the pot of culture's bubblesome,*
> *Praise poets, even when they're troublesome.*

John Hersey next rose to read passages from *Hiroshima*, not in
the presence of the President, but with Mrs. Johnson in the first row.
He prefaced them, speaking slowly and emphatically.

> I read these passages on behalf of the great number of citizens
> who have become alarmed in recent weeks by the sight of fire
> begetting fire.
>   Let these words be a reminder. The step from one degree
> of violence to the next is imperceptibly taken and cannot easily
> be taken back. The end point of these little steps is horror
> and oblivion.
>   We cannot for a moment forget the truly terminal dangers,
> in these times, of miscalculation, of arrogance, of accident,
> of reliance not on moral strength but on mere military power.
> Wars have a way of getting out of hand.

Mr. Hersey is a reserved, gentlemanly fellow—also the newly appointed master of a Yale college—and it must have pained him to

make such ungracious comments about her husband's policies in the presence of his hostess. But he evidently shared Lowell's "dismay and distrust" to such an extent that he insisted on making a statement that was impolite—and necessary.

From 11:20 to 12:10 the program advised "viewing of the works of art." There was a lot of viewing of the works of art: again from 5:00 to 7:00 and, at the very end: "10:30 P.M.: Mrs. Johnson closes the Festival and guests will view the art." Fortunately, the art proved to be the best thing at the Festival (except for Duke Ellington's music at the end): a broad representation of every kind of contemporary American painting and sculpture that was selected with sophisticated taste, all the more remarkable because it was assembled in three weeks from thirty museums. The photographic exhibition, however, was disappointing: poor examples of such masters as Stieglitz, Evans, and Abbott and too many chestnuts like Capa's "Death of a Loyalist Militiaman."

Luncheon was, as the card said, "hosted" by the National Art Gallery, to which we were transported in special buses, landing at the "rarely used Presidential entrance," also called "the VIP entrance." After lunch, George F. Kennan, former ambassador to the Soviet Union and Yugoslavia, now of the Institute of Advanced Studies at Princeton, and also President of the National Institute of Arts and Letters, addressed us on the subject of "The Arts and American Society." Fair enough. Mr. Kennan is an admirable man, an original and independent political thinker who writes well and has —or so I'd thought before he began to talk—a cultural background more common in the past among Establishment figures than today. Like Adlai Stevenson. And like Stevenson, he was disappointing. What I could hear of his speech—the echoes in the stone-walled Garden Court were deafening—was not promising: "Beauty is openended . . . The artist is an odd ball . . . the helping hand of the Maecenas . . . he [the artist] must do what he can to shield the public from artistic frivolity and charlatanism." (But frivolity I think an essential trait of the artist. "A little charlatanism is permitted to genius," said Baudelaire of Poe.)

Reading the text confirmed my suspicion that Mr. Kennan is a distinguished philistine. The central theme is that the artist must be tolerant of the public, and vice versa, because each needs the other. An American Civil Liberties Union approach: "These rules of mutual forbearance are the prerequisites, then, as I see them, for a successful relationship between American society and the arts." I don't think many practicing artists would feel elated by this compromise. Luckily, none were present.

There was also the curious matter, especially for such a stiffnecked character as Mr. Kennan, of a page and a half of additional remarks that was given out to the press just before lunch, but which he failed to deliver. They were addressed to what by that time had become The Lowell-Hersey-Van Doren Problem:

> I do not wish to aggravate feelings that are already tense [he began, or rather had intended to begin]. . . . The worker in the vineyard of the arts has, God knows, no obligation to agree with the government in matters of political policy, or to conceal his disagreement . . . [BUT] government is made up, in overwhelming majority, of honorable and well-meaning people charged with preserving the intactness of our national life, without which it is hard to picture any national culture at all. . . . [BUT] People in government . . . will have to bear in mind . . . first of all, that in the moral spirit of this country, of which the arts are one of the great interpreters and custodians, we have a very special and precious thing—the very soul of the nation. . . . Secondly, that artists and writers feel themselves today—more, I think, than ever before—a responsible part of the public conscience of the nation, and are recognized in this capacity by many others, particularly among the youth, and finally, this being so, and for their own sake as well, that there is reason to view with concern the anguish many of them feel over these problems, and to respect their need and their longing to be permitted to identify with the methods and the tone of American diplomacy no less than with its objectives.

Why Mr. Kennan decided at the last minute not to pronounce in public words he had already given to the press I do not know. The Washington *Evening Star* (which quotes most of the above) suggests that Kennan himself was of two minds even after he had nonsaid his additional remarks: "He told at least one reporter he had no objection to their being quoted anyhow, even though undelivered, and told another reporter he didn't want them quoted at all. Then he went off to catch a plane for Yugoslavia, where he is to make a speech today, leaving behind with White House cultural adviser Eric Goldman a brief 'clarifying' statement that didn't seem to clarify anything."

Back to the White House for an hour of music, which I don't pretend to judge, but I'm told the Louisville Symphony Orchestra played well and Roberta Peters was in good voice when she sang Gershwin's "Summertime." Then to the East Room again (3:45– 4:15 P.M.) where Helen Hayes introduced gracefully (all too) ten-minute excerpts from two "classics" (*The Glass Menagerie* and *Death of a Salesman*) and two recent plays by young writers: Frank Gilroy's *The Subject Was Roses* and Millard Lampell's *Hard Travelin'*. The last was the only one that came off: written with style and pace, and well played by Moses Gunn and Tom Ligon. Miss Hayes was fluttery and exalted. The First Lady of the American Stage. She wondered why plays had become so "grimly realistic" since "the joy and fun of my salad days." But she soon cheered up: the new playwrights "sometimes draw the picture a little *too* dark" but "Oh what power they put into their words!" There was also some Kennanesque talk about the role of art in "helping people to understand themselves."

Back to the dining room to view a half hour of "The Motion Picture," very brief film clips from movies by Hitchcock, Wyler, Kazan, Stevens, and Zinneman which, except for the famous taxicab scene between Marlon Brando and Rod Steiger from *On the Waterfront*, were mediocre or worse. They consulted six film critics—but not me, possibly because they suspected I would have recommended giving the whole thirty minutes to Kubrick's *Dr. Strangelove*. The chief interest was provided by Charlton Heston, the "narrator," a fine figure of a man bursting with health and ideas. "The salt shaker is essential to cinema, especially to the American movie," he began. I'm not sure just what he meant; not *cum grano salis* as I'd hoped, but probably the literal object since he went on "Bogart with a toothpick, Chaplin with a cane, these are hard to beat. . . . Film has been described as the most uniquely American of all the arts." From this seed Mr. Heston nurtured a healthy growth of chauvinism until finally all the great directors abroad were getting their stuff, really, by copying Hollywood. His introductions to the film clips were also memorable: "We know what Hitchcock can do with Janet Leigh and a bathtub. . . . His style is subjective because his ideas don't exist as persuasion but as experience." (That's what my notes say.)* "To define Stevens's style is to trace the melodic line of Mozart."†

After a two-hour recess, we assembled at seven for the home stretch: a cocktail party in the garden with Mrs. Johnson circulating amiably and unweariedly, the President's speech from the stage that had been erected to be used later, after an alfresco supper on the lawn, for a ballet performance "hosted" by Gene Kelly and then an hour of Duke Ellington's band.

The President's speech had its Hestonesque moments. But the passage which scared me was:

> Every President has known that our people look to this city, and this House, not only to follow but to lead, not only to listen but to teach, not only to obey their will but to help design their purpose. The Presidency is . . . a wellspring of moral leadership. We are using this great power to help move toward justice for all our people, not simply because American freedom depends on it. And we are trying to stimulate creation, not because of our personal tastes or desires but because American greatness will rest on it. This is the true meaning of this occasion.

I don't like that "leadership," moral or not, nor do I want my purpose to be designed by anybody else, not even McGeorge Bundy. And I'd be much easier in mind if the President's attempt to "stimulate creation" grew from his own "personal tastes or desires," however unsympathetic I might find them, and not from his hope to use our arts and letters as underpinning for "American greatness," for which I don't give a damn.

The President didn't look any happier than Saul Bellow did. Perhaps both realized they'd gotten into a false position. "Some of them insult me by staying away and some of them insult me by coming," the President grumbled to a reporter. (A good crack, I

---

* (1973) They also say it was not a bathtub but a shower.
† (1973) My notes have several "?"s.

thought. He meant Lowell and me—I circulated a little statement among the guests backing up Lowell's stand against Mr. Johnson's war; see below.) There was a bad moment when he departed from the text to growl briefly but ominously at his guests. Also at Dr. Eric Goldman (who looked most unfestive throughout his festival—the only really happy-looking people, in fact, were Duke Ellington and his bandsmen). The text reads: "You have been asked to come not because you are the greatest artists of the land, although some of you may be [but] because you have distinguished yourselves in the world of American art." In delivering the speech, the President gave a twist to this tepid encomium: "You have been asked to come not because you are the greatest artists of the land, although in the judgment of those who made up this guest list, you may have been." Tom Donnelly, who writes a sophisticated column in the Washington *Daily News*, interpreted this: "The President was thus indicating his displeasure with certain of his guests and certain of his list-makers." Other indications were his failure to receive his guests formally or talk to them informally (or at all) and his quick exit from the party as soon as he'd got through his speech. Poor Dr. Goldman, caught like Polonius ("wretched, rash, intruding fool!") between the fell and incensed points of mighty antagonists! He had to invite a few artists and intellectuals to leaven the dough, no pun intended, of all those patrons and *kultur-apparatchiks*, but it turned out badly and his boss is a man who doesn't easily accept defeat.

The President's "forward" policies in Vietnam and the Dominican Republic have not only, in a few months, alarmed and disgusted the intelligentsia (the academic community, writers and artists, and the better-educated part of the professional classes) so much as to split them off from him, but they have also produced another split, between the intelligentsia and the rest of the country, which is getting as marked as it was during the McCarthy era. Johnson's popularity, according to the pollsters, is greater today than it ever was. But not among the kind of people who were invited to the White House Festival of the Arts—or, more accurately, among perhaps a third of them, the artists, writers, and intellectuals that Dr. Goldman simply had to include. For example, I circulated a two-sentence "Statement to the Press" while I was there: "We wish to make it clear that, in accepting the President's kind invitation, we do not mean to repudiate the courageous stand taken by Robert Lowell nor to endorse the Administration's foreign policy. We quite share Mr. Lowell's dismay at our country's recent action in Vietnam and the Dominican Republic." Tom Hess and I showed this to those of our fellow guests we knew—some forty or fifty. We got nine signatures—among them Willem DeKooning, Herbert Ferber, Isamu Noguchi, and Reed Whittemore—but it was significant that nobody refused to sign because he favored the President's foreign policy. "I'm an artist, I don't know anything about politics," they said; or "Okay—but this isn't the time or place"; or, most frequent, "We're here as guests, it's rude, in bad taste." Charlton Heston, with whom I had an eyeball-to-eyeball confrontation in the rose garden—he's really *tall*—told me, in the nicest possible way, that it was "arrogant" for mere intellectuals to question our President's decisions since he "must" know far more than we do. Mary McGrory, in the New York *Post*, reported that Ralph Ellison "turned Macdonald down cold," complaining to her: "It's adolescent, he's boring from within at the White House." Ralph's objections, however, although delivered *fortissimo*, were tactical rather than political: he felt that circulating such a "stupid" document might frivolously imperil the *rapprochement* between the White House and Culture, or us, that was symbolized by the Festival.

But the symbol was obsolete before any of us checked in at the East Gate on June fourteenth, as the extraordinary effect of Robert Lowell's letter showed. Rarely has one person's statement of his moral unease about his government's behavior had such public resonance. I think it was because the letter was so personal, so unexpected, and yet so expressive of a widespread mood of "dismay and distrust." Herzen writes, in his memoirs, of the effect on the Russian intelligentsia, stifled under Nicholas I, who had his own methods of getting a national consensus, of the publication of Chaadayev's *Philosophical Letters to a Lady*, another individualistic and unexpected protest: "It was a shot that rang out in the dark night. . . . It forced us all to awake."

—*New York Review of Books*, July 15, 1965

The Chicago
Conspiracy Trial
as *Kulturkampf*

 U_{nited} *States of America, Plaintiff,*
vs. *David T. Dellinger et al., Defendants, No. 69 Crim. 180* began
in the Federal District Courthouse in Chicago on September 26,
1969, before the Hon. Julius J. Hoffman (and a jury) and ended
five months later after some 200 witnesses had been heard—more or
less, depending on the Judge's iron whim; Mayor Daley didn't get
much beyond giving his name, not to his displeasure—and 22,000
pages of transcript had been accumulated. *The Tales of Hoffman,*
a title that understates the fantastic atmosphere of the trial, is a
mosaic of the more significant moments.*

It is hardly news by now, at least here in the effete East, that if
the defendants were out to show up American bourgeois justice, as
they were, Judge Hoffman aided and abetted them beyond their most
alienated dreams of revolutionary glory. Even editors of the *New
York Times* have perceived this, even Max Lerner. Let me pass over,
for the moment, the Judge's courtroom manner, arrogant without
dignity, wisecracking without wit, a combination of Torquemada
and a Borscht-circuit *tummler.* I'm also willing to stipulate that his

---

* *The Tales of Hoffman,* edited from the official transcript by Mark L.
Levine, George C. McNamee, and Daniel Greenberg (Bantam Books, 1970).

sustaining all the prosecution's objections and overruling all the defense's—to be fair, the ratio was maybe only ninety-eight to two— that these rulings were called as he saw them, honestly and without bias or prejudice. But there is something peculiar, assuming the Judge was not in cahoots with the defendants to undermine our legal system, already reeling from the assaults of our attorney general, about the consistency with which he perpetrated injudicial outrages from beginning to end of the trial. He rushed through jury selection in half a day, solo, refusing to question the panel on most of the points the defense asked him to, including previous exposure to the case from press and television. He tried to arrest for contempt four lawyers who didn't show up on the first day because they had been engaged by the defense only for pretrial work, a position he backed down from under pressure from the legal establishment. He refused to postpone the trial until Bobby Seale's lawyer, Charles Garry, recovered from an operation, refusing to let Seale defend himself and thus goading him into constant interruptions—always sensible and rarely obscene, by the way, if you read the complete transcript and not just the press reports—which the Judge solved catastrophically by having Seale gagged and bound, finally severing him from the case with a four-year contempt sentence to give him a head start on his separate trial later. He excluded basic defense documents and witnesses such as Ramsey Clark, who as attorney general at the time had had the responsibility of insuring a peaceful Convention and who had tried to negotiate with Mayor Daley to that end. Judge Hoffman wound it all up in an orgy of sabotage of due process, sentencing all of the defendants and both their lawyers to prison for contempt of court before the verdict. When the jury, after being hung up for four days (unexpectedly, and a tribute to them but not to Judge Hoffman) acquitted two defendants on both charges (conspiring to incite a riot, and actually doing so) and the other five on the conspiracy charge, the odd—and to a hopeful believer (like me) in the jury system, the intolerable—outcome was they were all sentenced anyway for contempt, from six months to two years.

Their lawyers got the works: four years, thirteen days for William Kunstler; one year, eight months, five days for Leonard Weinglass. These neat calculations show an unexpected rationality, in a way. Hitherto the accepted maximum sentence for refractory lawyers had been six months; by slicing up Kunstler's crime into twenty-four separate offenses, the Judge was able to give him a lenient two months on each and still come out with four years. A pity to see a brain like that wasted on the right side of the law. Finally, despite the jury's long hesitation and eventual compromise, the Judge gave the five defendants still within his reach the maximum five years, adding a Hoffmaniac turn of the screw with $5,000 fines apiece plus "the costs of prosecution," no doubt a tidy sum once the Judge's slide rule gets into action, say $58,612.57 apiece, give or take a few cents.

In short, Judge Hoffman made the kind of legal history Tom Hayden, David Dellinger, Rennie Davis, Abbie Hoffman, and Jerry Rubin wanted him to make. It looks fishy—a federal judge playing into the hands of the revolutionaries he appeared to be persecuting. And who, or what, is behind him? That's the interesting question. How can we account for the present situation unless we believe that men high in the government are concerting to deliver us to disaster? This must be the product of a great conspiracy, a conspiracy so immense as to dwarf any previous such venture in the history of man. What can be made of this unbroken series of decisions and acts contributing to the strategy of defeat? They cannot be attributed to incompetence. If Hoffman were merely stupid, the laws of probability would dictate that part of his decisions would serve his country's interest.

The last five sentences above are, of course, not mine—one hopes the reader sensed the style had become rather gamey. Except for substituting "Hoffman" for "Marshall," they are quoted from the sixty-thousand-word speech the late Senator McCarthy delivered in the Senate on June 14, 1951, exposing the then Secretary of State, George Marshall, as a traitor working for the Kremlin. I didn't believe then that General Marshall, granted his incompetence, was an agent of Stalin, nor do I now believe that Judge Hoffman, granted his, is an agent of the New Left. But a clever prosecutor—not Mr. Foran or Mr. Schultz—could make as good a case for this paranoiac hypothesis as they did for their own in the trial.

Chicago has become our new Dallas: first the "police riot" against demonstrators (and others, anybody within club reach) at the 1968

Democratic Convention, and a year later, a judicial riot when the leading demonstrators went on trial for having tactlessly provoked the police riot: they insisted on exercising their rights as defined in the First Amendment to the Constitution; which guarantees "freedom of speech [and] the right of the people peaceably to assemble, and to petition the government for a redress of grievances." It is true that the Chicago Eight weren't respectful to their judge and prosecutors any more than they had been to Mayor Daley's cops. But in both cases the repressive reaction was disproportionate to the provocation, and their disrespect fed and grew on the professional incompetence of the forces of law and order—policemen are supposed to control themselves, judges are supposed to "have ice water in their veins." Whatever was in Judge Hoffman's veins, it wasn't ice water. He was spoiling for confrontation from the first day, and as the months wore on, it becomes obvious from the evidence in the present book that he was enjoying it. And not just sadistically, though that too, but also in a sly, masochistic way—he was asking for it, begging for it, and often he seems to deliberately provoke the disrespect he instantly complains about. One understands why Kunstler at the end says he feels "nothing but compassion" for Hoffman, also why the other Hoffman, Abbie, was given a relatively light contempt sentence although he, of all the defendants, was the most personally, and effectively, insulting to his namesake. A complex neurotic, Julie. (I apologize for the familiarity, Judge; it's not my style, but I feel I really know you after reading this book—you're so freely self-expressive on the bench. *Hoffman's Complaint.*)

The defense lawyers have been criticized for not sitting down when told to and for not controlling their clients (though, as Weinglass says to the Judge at one point, "Do you really think we could?") and for talking back and other nonprofessional practices, such as making an issue about when and where their clients may go to the bathroom and, on a higher level, asking for relaxation of procedure on various irrelevant, and political, occasions. As to the low-comedy scenes about going to the bathroom—they aren't much to my taste but the Court takes part with gusto. Likewise with Kunstler's request for unlegal favors such as a recess on October 15 to allow the defendants to participate in Moratorium Day activities, permission to have his clients present in court a cake to Bobby Seale on his thirty-third birthday, a "moment of silence for Dr. King" on January 15, et cetera. The Judge rejects them all, I think properly, but with unjudicial side remarks that are here pleasant enough—"I won't even let anybody bring *me* a birthday cake. . . . This is a courthouse and we conduct trials here. I am sorry."—but that become nasty and provocative when the same uncorseted style is applied to serious matters.*

His constant ridicule of the two defense lawyers would alone be grounds for a mistrial, I should think. In one session we get first:

Mr. Weinglass: That is permissible procedure?
The Court: I said it was. You don't have to ask me after I said it.
Mr. Weinglass: I am sorry. I object to it.
The Court: Sometime I am going to take an oath before I talk to you, you ask me so many questions.

Then:

Mr. Kunstler: Your Honor, there is an old maxim in law that if the police are brutal to one group, there is an inference they may be brutal to other groups, and that is a—
The Court: That is a maxim of the law I never heard of, and I sustain the objection.
Mr. Kunstler: You heard the maxim that "False in one thing, false in all." That is what I am saying: "Falsus in uno, falsus in omnibus." That is the maxim.
The Court: You ought to put on your striped trousers and be a professor.
Mr. Kunstler: Your Honor, I am afraid I don't have striped trousers.
The Court: I didn't ask you for a lecture. . . . I don't know all of those fancy phrases that you used.

This simple-guy put-down of the Eastern city slicker was one of the Judge's favorite ploys, as:

The Court: You speak of the Constitution as though it were a document printed yesterday. [A very good way to speak of it.

---

* One of the Judge's few witty remarks—as against his usual *tummler* cross talk—came after he had granted a five-minute recess so that the defendants could consult Dr. Spock, who had dropped in to see the show. "We would like to introduce him to your Honor," suggested Kunstler, ever alert with the innocent needle. "My children are grown, Mr. Kunstler," replied his Honor.

—D.M.] We know about the Constitution way out here in the Middlewest, too, Mr. Kunstler.

Mr. Kunstler: Oh, your Honor, this is a little unfair, isn't it?

The Court: We really do. You would be amazed at our knowledge of constitutional law.

Mr. Kunstler: Isn't that a little unfair, your Honor? We are not here from different parts of the country—

The Court: I am getting a little weary of these thrusts by counsel and I don't want any more of them. [The Judge should move to New York and find what thrusts can be. —D.M.] I had occasion to admonish you before.

Mr. Kunstler: I know, but you said I could argue as long as I wanted.

The Court: As long as you are respectful, sir.

Mr. Kunstler: I am respectful.

The Court: No, you haven't been.

Mr. Kunstler: You implied, I thought, Chicago people didn't understand the Constitution, only Easterners understand it. That isn't true.

The Court: Bring in the jury.

The dominant impression I got from *The Tales of Hoffman* was how sensible and courteous the defense lawyers were (their clients were also sensible but not polite) and how unsensible and rude the Judge. I skip over his Honor's personal remarks (as when he asked Kunstler if he used Chanel No. 5) and his frequent questioning of the defense lawyers' competence, in front of the jury, item number 78 on the mistrial docket ("a defense, if you can call it that" and, when they asked for explanations of his bizarre rulings, advising them to consult a competent lawyer). I will conclude, your Honor, with item number 79, The Weinglass Mystery, or The Case of the Amnesiac Judge. For some antic, Torquemada-*tummler* reason, Hoffman throughout the trial affected to forget the junior counsel's name, calling him Weinstein, Feinstein, Fineglass, Weinberg, Weinramer, forever being corrected and forever apologizing.* Toward the end, the

---

* This doubtless accompanied by one of those rubberlipped smirks I'm told he indulged in—unlike the defendants' laughter that bothered him so much, they don't appear in the record. Nor do his intonations, which are reported to have been so expressive in merely reading the indictment at the beginning of the trial that a lady juror felt she couldn't give a fair verdict and got herself excused.

resourceful defense table produced a large placard inscribed "WEIN-GLASS" which they hoisted up on occasion to refresh the Judge's memory. But he still got it wrong. At the very end, after he had modulated to "Weinrob," his victim wearily observed: "I was hope-ful when I came here that after twenty weeks, the Court would know my name. . . ." To which, the Court: "Well, I am going to tell you about that. . . . I have got a very close friend named Weinruss and I know nobody by the name of Weinrob—[something wrong here with the transcript, or the Judge—D.M.] and somehow or other the name of Weinruss stuck in my mind and it is your first appearance here. You have seen lawyers pass before this bar all during your four to five months here whom I know intimately and I scarcely ever forget a lawyer's name even when he hasn't been in for twenty years." This garrulity makes no sense as an explanation, since "Weinruss" was not even the most common of the pseudonyms by which he ad-dressed Mr.—it *is* "Weinglass," isn't it? And, as an apology, it is also defective, the last sentence adding the clinching insult. Not the most consecutive mind, his Honor's. But still, why? What method in his madness? I think the clue is his remark, overheard by a reporter in an elevator: "Now we are going to hear this wild man Weinglass." (For once, he got the name right.) It reminds me of another injudi-cious remark made in a public place, the bar of a country club as I recall, by another unjudicial judge, the Hon. Webster Thayer of the Massachusetts bench, apropos a trial he was about to conduct with all due legal decorum, including that great black maxirobe: "I'm going to get those anarchist bastards!" The Hon. Thayer did get Sacco and Vanzetti but I don't think the Hon. Hoffman will do well in the appellate courts. If he does, I'll have to agree that Tom Hayden for once is right about something.*

What Judge Hoffman and his two more sober but equally obtuse allies at the Government table, Mr. Foran and Mr. Schultz, didn't realize—a fatal error that played into the receptive hands of the defense and made a shambles of the trial—was that dissidents have lately developed a new kind of courtroom behavior which makes

---

* (1973) He didn't: all but two of his salami contempt convictions were dismissed, with comments, and the convictions on the conspiracy charge have been set aside. So the only thing I'm forced to concede Tom Hayden was right about is marrying Jane Fonda.

unheard-of demands on the judge. In old-style political trials, from the pre-Revolutionary trial in which Peter Zenger was successfully defended against His Majesty's prosecutors on a charge of publishing seditious matter to the recent trial of Dr. Spock et al., in Boston, both sides, in dress and behavior, accepted the conventions of the ruling establishment. The lawyers sat down when the judge told them to and didn't ask for permission to bring birthday cakes into court; the defendants wore business suits and neckties (or stocks and tie-wigs) and not purple pants, Indian headbands, or—as Abbie and Jerry did at one point—judicial robes; nor did they laugh or make abusive or witty remarks; nor did the spectators shout "Right on!" or "Oink!" or, indeed, anything at all. Repression reigned. The defense behaved as if they shared the values and life-style of the Court, even when they didn't, as in the big IWW trial in 1918 under the Espionage Act. There were over a hundred defendants, the entire leadership (plus a few innocent bystanders) of the Wobblies, the only American anarchists who ever got through to the people. Their trial lasted five months—there were seventeen thousand separate offenses, a salami-slicing record beside which Judge Hoffman's is amateurish—the jury took sixty-five minutes to find one hundred of the defendants guilty, and Judge Kenesaw Mountain Landis, later the "Czar" of baseball after the "Black Sox" scandal, also made Judge Hoffman look like a piker, handing out sentences ranging up to twenty years, plus a cool $2.3 million in fines, plus costs. That was the end of the Wobblies. But although the defendants were anarchists to a man, as bold and ingenious in anti-Establishment disruption outside the courtroom as their lineal descendants, Tom Hayden's SDS and Abbie Hoffman's Yippies, they behaved themselves inside it. Judge Landis, as mean a patriot as Judge Hoffman and fully as tough a jurist, didn't feel obliged to hand out any contempt sentences. The defendants respected those sacred precincts not from any civic illusions—they were as cynically antibourgeois as the next Yippie—but because, like most radicals before the present generation, their public style was separate from their personal style. Today's radicals have merged the two and have created a functioning community which, unlike the nineteenth-century Fourierist and Owenite experiments, is not set apart geographically but lives in and takes part in everyday life, swimming against the current but in the common river. As Chairman Mao well puts it, "The people are to the revolutionary as the water is to the fish." In the case of our New Left, read "mass media" for "people."

The Spock trial, which took place only a year and a half ago, how time flies, was perhaps the last in the old mode we shall see. Dr. Spock, after sitting in on the Chicago jurodrama, had second thoughts: "We sat like good little boys called into the principal's office. I'm afraid we didn't prove very much." He meant that, as Jessica Mitford's excellent book showed, the moral and political issues the defendants hoped to promote by their defiant acts and by the trial were never brought out. Judge Ford was as repressive as Judge Hoffman (though more dignified). And so, given an old-style defense by old-style lawyers (for such they were, even Leonard Boudin, the most sophisticated in left-wing defense cases) who shut up when they were overruled, the Boston judge was in control and could repress the meaning of the trial in a way the Chicago judge, confronted by new-style defendants and lawyers, could not. Toward the end, one of the prosecutors complained that Kunstler and Weinglass were part of the same radical ambience as their clients. (It was one of his few perceptive remarks.) The closeness revolted him, as a professional gladiator might be outraged if his opponent hacked away at him in the name of some abstract doctrine like Christianity.

In the new-style radical courtroom tactics, either the lawyers share the alienation and often the hair-style of their clients, or there are no lawyers. Also, as in the Living Theatre and other avant-garde dramatic presentations, the audience gets into the act; the spectators raise their voices, or, worse, their laughter, at crucial moments despite all those beefy marshals. And the defendants, hitherto passive except when they had their meager moment on the witness stand— "Please answer the question, yes or no"—feel free to make critical comments on the drama when the spirit moves them. The Chicago trial is the richest specimen of the new free-form trial to date* owing to the ingenious tactics of the defense (and the Judge's collabora-

---

* (1973) Alas, such an interesting historical insight—and now so faded! Where are the "new free-form trials" of yesteryear? Vanished with the SDS, campus rebellion, and America-greening in a mere four years. The Chicago conspiracy trial has had no successors but quite the contrary, as a glance at later radical courtroom behavior and tactics shows: Harrisburg, Camden, Angela Davis, Daniel Ellsberg: all have been old-style legal proceedings, restrained and dignified before and behind the bench—all have also been triumphs for the defense.

tion), but there are two other examples that compare, and contrast, interestingly with it: the current trial of Black Panthers in New York before a city magistrate, Judge Murtagh, on charges of conspiracy to blow up various business and police premises; and the trial a year ago of the "Milwaukee Fourteen" before Judge Larson, of the Wisconsin state judiciary, on charges of having incinerated ten thousand draft cards with homemade napalm.

The Black Panther trial hasn't begun yet, technically—in its first three weeks only two of sixteen pretrial motions have been disposed of—and it promises to last even longer than the Chicago one did. But already a quite different pattern has emerged. The defendants are as indignant as the Chicago Eight were at what is being done to them in the name of legality, and with even more reason. They have been imprisoned for almost a year under $100,000 bail apiece, which means no bail. The Chicago Eight were free on bail. The Panthers aren't charged with any actual bombings, only with a conspiracy to intend to bomb, while the bail for four white radicals recently indicted in New York on charges of complicity in some real bombings was set at a reasonable $20,000 each. A year's imprisonment, and possibly two if the trial drags on at its present pace, seems excessive for innocent people, as the Panthers are until they are proven guilty in court. So there has been flak from the defendants— what have they to lose, they're in jail already—and outbursts from the spectators. Judge Murtagh's response has been tough but cool. He has ignored static from the defendants when he could—"Let's get on with it"—and when he couldn't, engaged in chilly dialogue like a hostess with a drunk on her hands. He has established some control over the spectators by making it clear he would jail them for contempt if they persisted in shouting "Right on!" to the defendants' morning greeting, "Power to the People!" and has sentenced two on the spot, after summary courts-martial, to thirty days. At this writing, he seems to have established a precarious control over the courtroom. It may blow up any day, but it is at least a possible approach to the problem from the old-style viewpoint: play it by ear, modulating between fatherly admonitions and drumhead executions, and above all, don't get involved the way Julie did.*

---

* (1973) Judge Murtagh's courtroom didn't erupt but his jury didn't convict, either.

Judge Larson's approach was different from either Murtagh's or Hoffman's: he did get involved, but in a sympathetic way, like a psychiatrist. His problem was easier than theirs, it is true: the fourteen defendants were mostly Catholic priests, scholars, and laymen; the crime they were accused of was destroying records that might send American youths to die in what many Americans think an unjust war; they admitted their guilt, indeed insisted on it as an act of conscience; and they defended themselves—no lawyers, old or new style, around to recall the judge to his professional role. This last was perhaps the decisive factor in making the Milwaukee trial a benign and sensible expression of our court system as against the Boston blank, the New York minuet, and the Chicago circus. Judge Larson allowed the defendants considerable leeway in expressing the ideals and ideas that had led them to their illegal action, whether from sympathy with them as moralists or as babes in the legal woods, or both. And when he sentenced them—leniently—he was regretful and, when it came to Father Mullaney, a Benedictine monk with a Ph.D. in clinical psychology who had been especially eloquent and moving in his courtroom discourse, he cried.*

The legal basis for the Chicago trial was as rickety as its conduct under the Master of the Revels, also called the Lord of Misrule in the old days, the Honorable Julius J. Hoffman—namely, the 1968 "Anti-Riot Act," fathered by Strom Thurmond. The antiriot act (commonly known as "the Rap Brown Act") was a congressional reflex to the ghetto riots following the murder of Martin Luther King and to such forgotten black bogeymen as H. Rap Brown and Stokely Carmichael. It is worthy of its sire. It makes it a federal offense (five years, $10,000) to cross state lines with the *intention* of inciting, promoting, encouraging or participating in a riot, which is defined as any assemblage of three or more persons in which one or more

---

* For a detailed account of this remarkable trial, see Francine Gray's article in the *New York Review of Books* for Sept. 25, 1969—as imaginative reportage as I've read in a long time. The *Review* has also printed, in its Dec. 4, 1969, and Feb. 12, 1970, issues, the complete transcripts of the parts of the Chicago trial record concerning Bobby Seale and Allen Ginsberg, with excellent introductions by Jason Epstein, which give a sense of context and continuity that is of necessity lacking in the present volume. It is reassuring that the mosaic excerpts here give about the same general picture as the *Review's* complete-text episodes do.

persons injure another person (or more) or *damage property*, or *threaten to do so*. (My emphasis.) It seems obvious that such a "law" would convict anybody—and, in the case of the Chicago Five, did so—who travels any distance with the aim of exercising his First Amendment rights to talk and assemble for redress of grievances, since if the demonstration is a success, somebody is bound to get knocked around by the cops and a window or two may be broken in the heat of the moment. So who's to say what his *intentions* were? That's for a psychiatrist not a judge or jury. It seems likely the higher courts will throw out this Thurmondity as unconstitutional, but Judge Hoffman botched up the Chicago trial so thoroughly that they will be able to avoid the issue, with some relief, one imagines, by limiting themselves to correcting his errors.

From the legal viewpoint, the trial was—disappointing. But it was of unique significance in a way the defendants understood from the start and the prosecution and judge never caught on to: as a head-on collision, a public confrontation between the extremes of American politics and life-styles: the radicalized, alienated youth versus the bourgeois Establishment. A *kulturkampf* which the young won hands down, on points. (Not that they were *really* young, the Chicago Five—Dellinger was a senile fifty-three, and the others were close to the age barrier of thirty; even revolutionaries grow old, if not up.) This is not a vaudeville theater, the Judge complained, asking the marshals to make the defendants stop giggling. And another time he asked the marshals to exclude from the courtroom anyone who applauded. The court, he said, isn't a theater. But Jerry Rubin was right when he said, explaining he had been unavoidably detained and hadn't meant to walk out on the trial: "I like being here. It is interesting. . . . It is good theater, your Honor."

A long procession of singers, writers, and intellectuals took the witness stand during the five months, and the contrast between their minds and feelings and those of the Court was dramatic. The testimony of Allen Ginsberg (who was allowed three O-o-m-m-ms and no more) and Norman Mailer (who replied to Prosecutor Schultz's request to stick to the facts—"Facts are nothing without their nuance, sir") was especially educational. It was all wasted on the Judge, however. When Mr. Schultz complained Mailer was not being "responsive" to his questions—i.e., was trying to tell the complicated truth—the Judge said: "You are too high-priced a writer to give us all that gratis, Mr. Mailer. Just answer the question." And to Tom Hayden's "So, your Honor, before your eyes you see the most vital ingredient of your system collapsing because the system does not hold together," the Judge replied: "Oh, don't be so pessimistic. Our system isn't collapsing. Fellows as smart as you could do awfully well under this system. I am not trying to convert you, mind you."

The tone of the whole affair was set by Abbie Hoffman; it was his show, a chance to act out in largest publicity his ideas about radical politics as theater, about "putting on" the squares and goosing the media. His testimony is the crux of the trial, the most extensive and intensive expression of the new-radical style. Abbie combines wit, imagination, and shrewdness in a way not so common, and he has mastered his peculiar style so thoroughly that he can play around in and with it like a frisky dolphin. They can't even get him to give his name and address. When the Judge asks him for the former, he replies "Just Abbie. I don't have a last name, Judge. I lost it." (He told the press he was going to legally change his name after getting a load of his Honor.) Later: "My name is Abbie. I am an orphan of America." "Where do you reside?" "I live in Woodstock Nation." "Will you tell the Court and jury where it is?" "Yes. It is a nation of alienated young people. We carry it around with us as a state of mind in the same way the Sioux Indians carried the Sioux nation around with them. It is a nation dedicated to cooperation versus competition. . . ." "Just where is it, that is all." "It is in my mind and in the minds of my brothers and sisters." Even his age provokes a poetic cadenza:

Q. Can you tell the Court and jury your present age?
A. My age is 33. I am a child of the 60's.
Q. When were you born?
A. Psychologically, 1960.

. . .

Q. Can you tell the Court and jury what is your present occupation?
A. I am a cultural revolutionary. Well, I am really a defendant—
Q. What do you mean?
A. —full time.

It is a wonder the trial ever got finished at all. And that the Judge, Government lawyers, and federal marshals were physically able to stay in the same room with such defendants. Some of them may have been educated by the experience. I have been, and I've enjoyed it.

—Introduction to *The Tales of Hoffman*, 1970

2

THE ARTS

On
Selling Out

I've sold but not, with one large exception, out. That is, I've had to make my living by my typewriter but I've written as well as I could and on subjects of my own choice. The large exception was 1929–1936 when I was a staff writer on *Fortune*, a hack in Luce's stables; the subjects were assigned and the style was a "house" style, not my own. Excuses swarm: I was young; the articles weren't signed; hard times, and I needed the dough to support my aging mother, and myself. Also I learned the tricks of the trade—professional education: how to research the facts and how to present them (everything on the same topic should go into the same place, an editor once explained, worth the whole six years). By 1936, I'd learned all I could from Luce journalism and had become profoundly bored with its dynamic simplifications. I was tempted, morally, to keep on selling out—I was by then getting $10,000 a year, an interesting salary in those primitive days—but it had become neurologically impossible: I kept falling asleep in the very act of prostitution.

This suggests that "selling out" is possibly a false concept. Does anybody, *can* anybody sell out, really, in the sense of deliberately writing, or acting, below one's best in order to make money (or achieve power)? There used to be much clucking in the thirties over allegedly brilliant talents who had "sold out to Hollywood," but the horrible examples, when examined closely, always turned out to be

modestly endowed; one suspected they would have produced the
same junk, with "avant-garde" rather than "commercial" secondary
cultural characteristics, had they remained in Greenwich Village.
Faulkner and Fitzgerald sold out to Hollywood in the minor sense
that they wrote scripts indistinguishable, judging by the resulting
movies, from those of the hacks. But not in the major sense. They
used Hollywood more than they were used by it: Faulkner saved his
fairy gold to finance an annual retreat to Oxford, Mississippi, for
writing novels, and Fitzgerald employed his experience, and fees, to
write *The Last Tycoon*, which promised to be one of his most interesting works.

It's not so easy to sell out if you have anything to sell. Cf. Henry
James' "The Next Time," a story about a distinguished nonselling
novelist who tries to escape penury by writing a potboiler—and produces one more unpopular masterpiece. Or cf. the late Delmore
Schwartz's attempts to raise some cash by writing one of those short
short stories (1,000 words, $1,000) a national magazine used to fea-
ture; he tried twice, no go either time, he just couldn't get down to
the level convincingly. (It takes a whole heart to sell out.) Or cf. the
late Edgar Allan Poe, a calculating, unprincipled money-writer,
always hard up, always with an eye to the main chance, always laboring to come up with something that would "go" and make him rich or
at least solvent. That he always failed is another matter, having to do
with his own neuroses; his *will* to sell out was intact to the end. He
turned his hand to all the popular genres of the day: the Gothic tale
of horror, after Hoffmann and *Blackwood's*, the sentimental ladies'-
book poem ("Helen, thy beauty is to me . . ."), the romantic thren-
ody on the death of a female Loved One ("Once upon a midnight
dreary . . ."). And, in desperation, he invented some new genres that
became popular: the detective story and science fiction. But he was
helpless in the grip of his genius: despite the worst intentions, Poe
transmuted these clichés into his own idiom so that they became
literature and not commodities. Poor fellow, the classic failure of
classic American letters, his life a cautionary tale—Poe couldn't even
sell out.

It would seem that the first condition for selling out is that one
has nothing to sell out in the first place. Older readers may recognize
this as what used to be called in more rational, or logical, times "an

Irish bull," the traditional definition being that if ten cows are lying down in a field, the one that is standing up is an Irish bull. For ambitious youth my advice is: sell out if you can, since if you can you don't have anything of value and you might as well cash in on it.

Norman Cousins'
Flat *World*

I have been complaining for a long time without much effect except on those already in agreement (a common deficiency of American *kultur*-critics from Poe on) that the trouble with our culture is that it's neither proletarian nor aristocratic but petty bourgeois.* Middle-class, middlebrow—the all-too-democratic expression of the first great modern nation to begin its history unencumbered by either a peasantry or a nobility. As de Tocqueville noted, with prescient foreboding, all Americans belong, psychologically, to one class, the middle. Or as Alexander Herzen (not Herzl), the nineteenth-century founder of Russian socialism (not Zionism), observed in his memoirs: "The Americans present the spectacle of one class—the middle class—with nothing below it and nothing above it; petty bourgeois manners and morals are all that remain."

The objection to middlebrow, or petty-bourgeois, culture is that it vitiates serious art and thought by reducing it to a democratic-philistine pabulum, dull and tasteless because it is manufactured

---

* I've complained about this for twenty-eight years if you count from my first full-dress formulation, "A Theory of Popular Culture," in the February, 1944, number of my late magazine *Politics*; forty-five, if you begin with "The Teaching of English at Yale" (*Yale Lit.*, 1927), a long grouse about the crowd-pleasing pop-romantic antics certain eminent English profs went in for to hold the interest of a lecture hall full of future stockbrokers.

for a hypothetical "common man" who is assumed (I think wrongly) to be even dumber than the entrepreneurs who condescendingly "give the public what it wants." Compromise is the essence of midcult, and compromise is fatal to excellence in such matters.

In my own by now rather extensive time, the textbook example of middlebrow cultural journalism has been the *Saturday Review*, a successful (circulation-wise) amalgam of *de jure* high seriousness and *de facto* low accommodation. (Recently, by entrepreneurial fission, it has become four magazines, a solemn thought indeed.) The *Saturday Review* began shakily in the twenties under the genteel-academic aegis of Henry Seidel Canby, and it was firmly taken in hand some thirty years ago by a nonacademic, but also genteel, midcult entrepreneur named Norman Cousins, who hyped the circulation from 15,000 to over 600,000. I didn't think much of it under Professor Canby (whose course in "creative writing" I didn't think much of either, in 1927 at Yale; sorry, must be a congenital allergy) and Mr. Cousins' jazzed-up S.R. didn't seem any better or any worse; just mediocre in a different way.* The *Saturday Review* used to proudly add *of Literature* until Mr. Cousins had accreted so many unliterary but popular departments—travel, pop science, records, movies, consumerism, etc.—that even he was embarrassed and dropped the last two words.

The end of the old *Saturday Review* came in the spring of 1971 when it was sold to John Veronis and Nicolas Charney, two younger midcult entrepreneurs, and Norman Cousins went with it. The agreement was that he and his old staff were to continue to edit the magazine, which they did for six months. Then, in the November 27 issue, Cousins announced their exit in a long and cloudy "Final Report to

---

* The more successful (by a factor of about twenty) *Reader's Digest* is not middlebrow but lowbrow, or maybe by now upper-lowbrow; let's say pale blue-collar. It lacks the cultural pretensions, the little finger crooked over the teacup of Canby's and Cousins' *Saturday Review*. It's just a simple mid-American *kaffeeklatsch*, easy and relaxed ("My Most Unforgettable Character," Herman Wouk on The Zionist in Me, Admiral Byrd on My Antarctica), except when incendiary stimuli like Communism or Abortion on Demand turn it into a mid-Amerikan barbecue. But it's no longer just American: the success of its international editions in French, Italian, Spanish, and other civilized tongues is ominous. A little touch of vulgarity makes the whole world subscribe.

the Readers," never making clear just what caused him to change his mind.

"*We have seldom known a more compatible partnership.* . . . *John and Nick* . . . *went out of their way to express appreciation of 'S.R.'s' staff members. It isn't difficult to develop strong bonds of affection for such men. Our personal and working relationships have been satisfying rather than merely satisfactory. Despite this, I feel I cannot continue as editor. Nick and John have strong ideas about the future of the Saturday Review. This is as it should be.*" The Nixon touch; but the only thing he made perfectly clear was that "Nick" and "John" were going to divide S.R. into four monthlies, one appearing each week in rotation: the *Saturday Review of Science*, the *Saturday Review of Education*, the *Saturday Review of the Arts*, and the *Saturday Review of the Society*. "*John and Nick have emphasized that the four monthly magazines are a natural outgrowth of* . . . *present* ['*S.R.*'] *supplements. A number of the basic features of the existing 'S.R.' will be retained* . . . *to provide continuity.*" So far, so good, or so bad, depending on one's view of the old S.R.

But then "the strong bonds of affection" begin to show strain. Nothing unpleasant or explicit, you understand, that's not the S.R. style. Only a Jeevesian admonitory murmur: "*It is not my purpose here to enter a detailed discussion of that plan. It is sufficient to say* ["m'Lord," Wodehouse would have added] *I find myself in philosophical and professional disagreement. I object strongly to the commercial use of the 'Saturday Review' subscription list for purposes that have nothing to do with the magazine.* [No details; Jeeves was good on details.] *I also object to the exploitation of the name of the 'Saturday Review' for sundry marketing ventures.* . . . [Again no specifics; did John and Nick franchise sweatshirts?] *As I write this I have the feeling that I am slipping into an error I was determined to avoid. I have no wish to argue a case or justify a stand.* [Why in the world not? We'll never understand each other. My life has been devoted to those two activities.] *My purpose is to state the fact of an honest difference of opinion and to announce my resignation.*" How an "honest difference of opinion" can be "stated" by refusing to specify what it was I don't understand.

In the next *Saturday Review* another long editorial, signed "John J. Veronis," excretes some even less penetrable clouds of printer's ink: *"Norman Cousins is an extraordinary man.* [The last adjective that I'd have thought of; his career seems to me an exploitation of the opposite quality.] *He is part editor, part world citizen . . . lecturer, author, humanitarian, president of World Federalists.* [So they're still around!] *. . . We have developed respect, admiration, and an abiding affection for this unique person. . . . Norman Cousins and his staff have edited what many consider to be America's foremost thought weekly . . . in the forefront of man's continuing struggle to build a just and secure peace, to strengthen the United Nations, to defend civil liberties and organize a more compassionate society . . . improve the environment* [etc., etc.]."

But it seems that—Veronis edges into the point—John and Nick had taken over with some "objectives" in mind, not being in business for their health. *"These objectives entail development of circulation, promotion, advertising, finance . . . and ancillary activities* [ah!] *as well as the editorial product itself* [ah, squared!]. *. . . Norman Cousins . . . understandably was most interested in them. As might be expected, he understood and embraced a good part of what we were doing. On the other hand, he also seemed a bit uncomfortable with a few new developments."* As the headmaster, another evasive type, would put it: "Norman has had a little difficulty adjusting but he has made many friends and we hope he will come back to see us soon." Again, no vulgar specifics. Just a few crocodile sympathies.

What the new masters of S.R. will do with its barnacled hulk, beyond adding fresher barnacles, I can't predict; I haven't seen any of those quadruple amoebic spin-offs, there being a limit to my appetite for midcult. But it's a bad omen that President Veronis of "Saturday Review Industries," in puffing his colleague, the new Czar Of All The S.R.'s, Nicolas H. Charney (*"an uncommonly gifted thirty-year-old . . . son of . . . Jule Charney, the noted meteorologist now at M.I.T."*), mentions among their achievements as "equal partners" the "launching" of Communications Research Machines, Inc., which in turn launched *Psychology Today* and *Intellectual Digest.*

I've missed the former but its ads are as aggressively vulgar as those of Time-Life Books. I did catch one issue of the latter, though, because it had digested an article of mine. Next time I'll forgo their

$100, since it's not an ambience I feel comfortable in: cramped format tarted up with mini-pictures and the editors' *hard-sell* come-ons above each truncated article. *Hurry! Hurry! Hurry!* The spiel for mine was: "A SOCIAL CRITIC EXPLORES THE 38-YEAR HISTORY OF DOROTHY DAY'S CATHOLIC WORKER AND THE PARADOX OF ITS TRADITIONAL THEOLOGY AND RADICAL POLITICS." Fair enough, in fact quite ingenious—and accurate. But why not let *me* make the points—and the reader discover them, or not, all by himself? Why do midcult editors do all our work? Same reason the old Hollywood "mood music" told the suckers just what they were feeling at any given moment.

Three months after the minuets I've described were danced in the *Saturday Review*, there appeared in the *New York Times* of March 19, 1972, a full-page ad (repeated a week later), signed by Norman Cousins and headed: "AN OPEN LETTER TO THE READERS OF THE NEW YORK TIMES." The text says: ". . . *My colleagues and I have decided to launch a new magazine. . . . It will be called World* [and] *will be concerned with ideas and the arts. Our arena, however, will be the world.*" (Why "however"? Are art and ideas assumed to be geographically limited? To continents? nations? congressional districts?) Three months after the ads (plus a lot of "personalized" direct mail and prerecorded phone calls: "This is Norman Cousins, I hope you forgive the intrusion") he was doing business at the old stand.

A *Times* interview on June 22, inaccurately headed "IT'S A NEW WORLD FOR NORMAN COUSINS," revealed that *World* was about to appear with an initial press-run of 175,000 copies, of which 100,000 went to subscribers, most of them veteran S.R. addicts. Cousins calls the latter his "family" and defines them with unexpected specificity: "*When I think of a 'Saturday Review' reader, I think of a professor of biochemistry at, oh, S.M.U. His wife is a community leader. She helps to put on art festivals. . . . Or, I think of a company vice president who lives in New Canaan. His wife plays the organ. . . . They have musicales and serious discussions in their home. . . . It's a whole family. . . . After my resignation a 12-year-old girl called me. She said, 'Mommy wanted to write you, but each time she tried she broke down and cried.' We've been through things together. . . . I began to realize a long time ago that we were developing not so*

much readers as a constituency, a family." Parody is disarmed before
such candor. And what parodist would dare give *World's* publisher
the name S. Spencer Grin?

Volume I, Number 1 of *World* is dated July 4, which is probably a
coincidence but does touch all bases, the patriotic along with the
global. The proud rubric "A REVIEW OF IDEAS, THE ARTS AND THE
HUMAN CONDITION" was dropped before Number 2, perhaps because
it was too confining; certainly not because Mr. Cousins felt it was a
bit gaseous—his gaseosity threshold is very high. I remember the only
time I ever saw and, worse, heard him—at the Waldorf (or maybe
the Roosevelt) for some Worthy Cause. My wife and I were free-
loading off some friends, and the food and drinks were okay, and
first Franklin D. Roosevelt, Jr., so big and handsome, said nothing
for thirty-five minutes in the most dignified way and sat down at last
(whew!); and then Norman Cousins, smaller and less handsome,
arose and for forty minutes matched FDR's vapidity (though in a
more sincere style, of course), a feat I'd have thought impossible.
What *were* they talking about? My wife can't remember either. She
says I shouldn't attack Cousins "personally," though his speech was
lethal precisely because it was so smoothly impersonal. Well then,
let's get down to printed matter and the subject.

  *"This first issue of 'World Magazine' is dedicated to the future
of print, and to our colleagues on other magazines, newspapers, and
books,"* Mr. Cousins begins his lead editorial, making me feel like a
heel right away. *"We are confident that print will not only endure
but will continue to be a primary force in the life of the mind. Nothing yet invented meets the intellectual needs of the human brain so
fully as print."* Now if "brain" is defined in the narrow nineteenth-
century way, "intellectual" is tautologous; if in broader post-Freudian
terms, a lot of other "needs" are not covered by "intellectual." At all
events, this ringing but uneasy defiance ("we are confident" means
"we are not confident" in such official rhetoric, just as "undoubtedly" means "perhaps" and "obviously" "maybe") seems to be
aimed at Marshall McLuhan—though typically he isn't mentioned.
Cousinsland is like Eden before Adam got around to naming the
animals: naming names, as Adam unhappily realized after he'd eaten
that knowledgeable apple, only lowers the tone and raises doubts.

It's also typical in Cousinsland that the horse being beaten, anonymously, is safely dead; McLuhan's anti-Gutenberg flash expired from the pan several years ago.

" 'World' seeks to become a magazine on the human situation," the editor plunges on, like a hippopotamus trying to extricate himself from a slough of molasses, to borrow Mencken's description of an earlier orgiast of the imprecise word, Warren G. Harding. "In philosophy, editorial content, and direction, it seeks to become a journal of creative world thought and activity." This print conveys no meaning to me, "intellectual" or otherwise. Maybe the S.R. family—Mr. Cousins' cousins, you might call them—respond to certain code words like "human" or "creative" as the George Wallace family does to "law" and "order"; they get the emotive point and feel virtuous and that's enough for them. The editor goes on to explain—can't complain of a paucity of print here—but the trouble is, the more he explicates the more his meaning vanishes into the mists.

There is, for instance, a crucial paragraph on "a new and larger kind of wisdom . . . needed to keep humankind from becoming inimical to its own survival." This new (and larger) wisdom is of four kinds: Wisdom One "can deal with basic causes of breakdowns between the national aggregations." I take these as code words for the Biafran and Bangladesh horrors, the Ugandan racist expulsions, and the Arab guerrilla massacres at Tel Aviv airport and the Olympic Games plus Israel's eye-for-eye retaliation for these outrages on Lebanese villagers unfortunate enough to live near Arab commando camps. (Jehovah didn't make fine distinctions either.) Whatever Mr. Cousins had in mind in July, no specific implementations of Wisdom One have surfaced to date, either theoretically in his journal or practically in that United Nations he is hooked on. Unreasonable to expect it: Marx, Lenin, Metternich, and Huey Long combined couldn't patch up these "breakdowns." But why pretend there exists such a "wisdom"? Wisdoms Two and Three are, respectively, ecological ("Halt the poisoning of the natural environment . . . establish a balance between resources and needs") and what was, until even liberal columnists saw that the problem was more complex, called in the thirties "technocracy" ("Apply technology to the upgrading of the whole of human society"). Okay both, but hardly new.

"And, finally," the editor winds up at Four, rising into the thin air of the heights of noble platitude where he breathes most easily,

*"wisdom that can help men regain their essential trust in one an-
other and restore their sensitivities to life. It is folly to expect that
genuine creativity—whether in the individual or society—can exist
in the absence of highly developed sensitivities."* As suggested above,
I can see "creativity" only as a much-abused modern code (or cant)
word, like "relevant," and Mr. Cousins doesn't help: "genuine creativity" implies that there exists a false creativity, but I'd think that
that wouldn't be "creative" but . . . well, false; I suspect he threw in
"genuine" because it's the kind of enheartening, enriching, positive
adjective his "family" responds to. The general sense—if one may use
such a noun with the prose of this peroration—seems to me unex-
ceptionable. I positively admire "whether in the individual or society"; a less conscientious stylist might have left it up in the air.
    " 'World' Magazine, therefore, is devoted to ideas and the arts."
I don't understand "therefore"; no mention of "ideas" or "the arts"
up to now, nor what is meant by these grand terms, which he
doesn't define later either. Always apologize, never explain is the
Cousins armorial motto. *"One may make a distinction between the
two, but one cannot separate the two. Both are part of the same
creative process."* He's got the bit between his teeth. *"Survival is
impossible without ideas, but the arts give sense and excitement to
survival."* Oh *that's* what he means! *"The ultimate adventure on
earth is the adventure of ideas."* Whoa! *" 'World' would like to be
part of that adventure."*

Norman Cousins reminds me of an earlier heartwarming liberalistic
spellbinder in his rhetoric and in his mental confusion; I refer to
Henry Wallace. Away back in 1947 I wrote "A Note on Wallese"
("a debased provincial dialect" produced by "the warm winds of the
liberal Gulf Stream coming in contact with the Soviet glacier"),
pointing out that "adventure" was an important word in Wallese
because "it suggests something Different (and God knows we're sick
of what we've got now), Positive, Exciting; something, in short, to
which the old critical categories, which have proved so lethal in the
hands of Irresponsible and Destructive critics, cannot be applied."
To go back even further, to 1929, I dimly recall a prospectus by my
then boss, Henry Luce, proclaiming: "Business is the great American adventure. *Fortune* would like to be part of that adventure."
    "The times favor new ideas. Old dogmas and ideologies are los-

ing their power to inspire or terrify," Mr. Cousins' lead editorial
continues. (I know how Hercules felt when he grappled with
Proteus, or was it the Old Man of the Sea—some monster of im-
precision, and persistence.) As a veteran observer of what Mr.
Cousins would call "the world scene," I cannot, alas, agree. But as a
writer, I find old dogmas and ideologies preferable to his formulations: they're definite, at least. You know where you are. "*Com-
partmentalized Man is giving way to World Man. The banner
commanding the greatest attention has human unity stamped upon
it.*" No comment; I'm getting tired. "*The century of Marx and
Engels has ended. Marxian doctrine is breaking up, both outside and
inside the Soviet Union. . . .*" A truth, at last, but long since a
truism. The calendars are out of date in Cousinsland (the better
name might be "Cousinsville"). My two-part essay "The Root Is
Man," published in *Politics* in 1946, was far from the first study of
the obsolescence of Marxism as a revolutionary ideology.

"*The end of the isolation of China, one of the great events of
the 20th century, removes a great wall of separation and exposes
the largest single human grouping to the new winds of change
sweeping the globe. . . .*" The great event is the admission of the
real China to the UN as a result of the Nixon Peking Ploy, already
rather faded; I predict that the Nimzo-Indian Defense will outlast
it (a smaller game, of course). Cousins often confuses the UN with
the real world, perhaps because it is as empty yet portentous as his
prose style, perhaps because it's as safe a cause as motherhood except
to a few difficult oddballs: "The U.N. is not a parliament of peace-
loving peoples," I wrote in 1946; "it is not an arena of history-in-
the-making. . . . It is, quite simply, a bore." The first two reactions,
by the way, of the unwalled Chinese delegation to the new winds of
global change have been (1) to insist, successfully, that the UN
eliminate Taiwan not only from membership but also from all its
statistics henceforth, which will make the same curious distortion—
Taiwan is more populous than many UN member nations—that
Stalin's similarly magical-paranoiac erasing of Trotsky from the text-
books (except as a secret agent of British Intelligence) had on Soviet
historiography; and (2) to use its veto in the Security Council to
deny admission to Bangladesh.

"*Old ideas of separatism and group identity don't move men as much as new perceptions of human solidarity."* See the *New York Times*, July 11 last: "PAKISTANI TOLL 47 IN LANGUAGE RIOTS. . . . At least 47 persons have been killed since Friday night in clashes over the choice of Sindhi as Sind province's official language. . . . The demonstrators want equal status for Urdu." By "men" Mr. C. must mean his S.R. "family," who, to a man—and woman—are, I'm sure, not moved by "old ideas of group identity," at least not to the point of murder. But they are not mankind any more than the UN is the world. Maybe he doesn't see the *Times*.

"We are excited by the prospect of publishing a magazine with a world purpose," Mr. C. gamely concludes his fight-talk. There's a cadenza about how the editors *"do not regard this* [first] *issue as a definitive expression,"* but since Number 7 looks and reads about the same as Number 1, I take this as only a graceful arabesque. That Mr. Cousins and his family might ever arrive at anything "definitive" is improbable.

I do hope that Cousins is correct in his confidence that "print will endure," but a careful reading of the first two issues of *World* and his founding editorial have caused me to wonder, for the first time, whether Marshall McLuhan may not have had a point.

The first issue's feature article is blurbed: "THE NO. 1 HEROIN SUPPLY LINE—Eyewitness report on the world's largest source of narcotics— Who does the dealing and how." A comedown from the editor's lofty exordium, for the article displays no "ideas" and damned little "art": a pedestrian muckraking job by one Santi Tara, "the pseudonym of an English-speaking expert on Southeast Asian affairs." The expert gives us only stale revelations of the complicity of Kuomintang, Laotian, and Siamese warlord racketeers in the transit of the stuff from Asian poppy fields to American consumers. Since this is old information to readers of the *Times* and the newsmagazines, it isn't clear why the expert needed a false name. What is clear is that editor Cousins had been pre-scooped by editor Manning of *The Atlantic*,* who had already printed extensive portions of the real exposé, both serious and sensational: *The Politics of Heroin in Southeast Asia* by the unpseudonymous Alfred W. McCoy. Mr. Mc-

---

* (1973) It was Shnayerson of *Harper's*. See Appendix.

Coy, a young ex-CIA employee, spilled a lot of awkward beans about American high-level connivance, for the better prosecution of the Vietnam "war," with a wide variety of Southeast Asian warlords, including some in Thieu's cabinet, who were (1) "on our side"; (2) making a buck out of the heroin traffic; and (3) had connected (1) and (2) so as to blackmail our anticommunist crusaders.

Whether from diplomatic tact or simple ignorance, "Santi Tara" omits the whole American involvement and our Saigon *compradores'* part in the racket as well. But one shouldn't underestimate either simple ignorance or diplomatic tact in Norman Cousins, as an editor or writer. Except in rhetorical posture, he's always been decently respectful of the powers that be, or as we say now, the Establishment: when SANE's executive committee extruded Dr. Benjamin Spock as a too-fiery particle, Cousins was an active fire-fighter. And he is extensively, I sometimes think a mite deliberately, uninformed on awkward questions, Establishment-wise. In any case, he has been able to infect the contributors to *World* with this mini-meaching style of thought, as he did on *Saturday Review*; with exceptions, of course; he's only human like the rest of us, as he would be the first to admit. To describe it as a melding of Uriah Heep's humility and Mr. Pecksniff's pomposity is the kind of simplistic insult our alienated young radicals would have hurled at him had they ever gone to the library, and I reject it as what they would call "overexaggerated." Slightly.

But it's ammunition wasted to criticize *World* as if it were a journalistic effort like *The Atlantic* or *The New Yorker* or *Newsweek* or *The New York Review of Books* or *The Columbia Forum.* It's both more and less, and criticizing it by the usual standards is both easy and beside the point, like shooting fish in a barrel.* Since that's the only kind of criticism I know, however, I must continue that way, with a feeling which must often afflict anthropologists: that making judgments on tribal mores is useless to the tribe. But then, I'm not writing for the tribe but for the readers of this magazine—so *en avant!*

---

* A striking phrase, but has anyone ever done it?

Cousins is, in *World*, as he was for thirty years in *Saturday Review*, after something above, or beneath, criticism—the creation and maintenance of a middlebrow, midcult "family": a moral-cultural ambience so self-contained and cohesive that it is as impervious to "outside troublemakers" as a real family is. He is after what Lyndon Johnson called "a consensus." In this endeavor, Cousins has been even more successful than the late Father Divine, whose own "family" never came near the 600,000 readers of the old Cousinsville *Saturday Review*, nor even the 150,000-plus faithful who so far have rallied to his *World*. I am amazed that the latter figure isn't higher, considering it's the same old formula. But they'll come, they'll come, like flies to this honeypot of banality and deep-stuff Uncle Norman has been serving up in his first seven numbers. I do hope I'm wrong.

But I doubt it. In choosing his two big-gun regular contributors, for example, Cousins was wonderfully perceptive of his family's kinky appetites. The anchorman in the "Peace and Politics" department is no other than U Thant, who accomplished so much for world peace in his years as head of the United Nations; and in the "Planetary Planning" department one can depend on a biweekly vaticination by Buckminster Fuller in person, assuming he exists that way. The two most eminent global bores I can think of. (Henry Wallace, Wendell Willkie, and Hendrik Willem Van Loon are with us no more.) Thant is the official, Bucky the avant-garde bore.

"There are certain advantages that go with the Observation Post on the 38th floor of the United Nations," the former began his first column. *"One of them is the opportunity to observe trends in the world without the limitations on one's vision that are inevitable to the observer from one particular nation or region. This perspective was what enabled me to call attention several years ago to the rapidity with which major world problems were converging to create a crisis of nothing less than planetary dimensions."* Even without benefit of that thirty-eighth floor, I've never felt any "limitations" on my "vision," and certainly not from my inhabiting "one particular nation or region." Thus I can dislike our flag—a design-botch, off-center and too "busy" compared to the British, French, and Japanese; and our national anthem, hysterical and unsingable compared to the Marseillaise and the one Haydn ran up for Austria. Since U Thant has always struck me as a time-serving

officeholder—a "pork-chopper," in trade-union slang—timid and bureaucratic and a great comedown from Dag Hammarskjöld, and since a few random sentences of his prose confirmed my suspicions, I didn't finish his "Reflections of a Mediator."

I did read through Bucky Fuller's first "Geoview." (Not the least of Uncle Norman's talents for amazing the kids in the "family" is devising interesting names for *World*'s departments, others being "Human Resources" and "World of Research.") Bucky weighs in with the modest title "The World Game and How to Make It Work." The column was only a page long, and I have a weakness for avant-garde rhetoric. I wasn't disappointed: a heady cocktail of nostalgic ideologies—futurism, technocracy, cybernetics—with a dash of Bucky's Angostura sweets: ". . . *We are going to undertake an extraordinary computerized program to be known as 'How to Make the World Work.'* " Fair enough; fills a long-felt need; and the specifics are even more exciting: "*Major world individuals* [Norman? Solzhenitsyn? U Thant? Senator Fulbright? Susan Sontag? me?] *and teams* [Rand Corporation? Ford Foundation? Pittsburgh Pirates?] *will be asked to play the game. The game cannot help but become major world news. As it will be played from a high balcony* [no locale given; maybe Thant's thirty-eighth floor?] *overlooking a football-field-sized Dymaxion World Map with electrically illumined data transformations* [sounds like the Houston Astrodome scoreboard] *the game will be visibly developed and could then be live-televised the world over by a multi-Telstar relay system.*"

In *World*'s second issue, Thant deserts "Peace and Politics" to join Bucky in "Planetary Planning," his article being called "The U.N. and the Planetary Concept" (what else?), while Bucky's "Geoview" takes off into the wide blue yonder with a three-page explosion of that freeform sub-Whitmanesque doggerel he has lately invented. You know it's poetry because the right-hand margin isn't squared off. Bucky concludes, if that is the word I want: "*Einstein said, 'What a faith in the orderliness of Universe/ Must have inspired Kepler/ To spend the nights of his life alone with the stars',/ Which inadvertently revealed Einstein's own faith/ And that of the billions before him/ In the integrity of Universe/ Which has ever inspired humans/ To commit themselves in all-out love,/ Hopeful thereby of increasing human understanding/ Of the a priori mys-*

tery/ Of the ever comprehensively embracing/ Yet micro-cosmically permeating/ Omni-exquisitely concerned/ Eternal Integrity." Well, I suppose he had something or other in mind. (On second thought, it sounds more like Don Marquis's Archie the Cockroach—after he'd learned to work the capital shift on the boss's typewriter, of course.)

They are both still plugging away in Number 7, U Thant on "A New Deal for Europe?" (I wouldn't read a piece by that title if it were by George Bernard Shaw) and Bucky, ever hopeful, with "Geosocial Revolution" (I might read a piece so entitled if Benchley or Thurber had signed it). In fact I did peek at the last sentence of that one—the weakness for avant-garde bull already noted—and was fascinated: *"There is, therefore, a deep subconscious passion in man which now stimulates his intuitions to strike for realization of the historically held 'impossible' and now looming reality of physical success for all humanity."* I wondered if he meant by "physical success" what I do—namely feeling good when I wake up—and when he expected this "reality" to progress from the looming to the actual. (In my case, next September is the deadline.) Or by "physical success" did he mean immortality. So I began at the beginning and immediately ran into a roadblock: *"Though dwarfing all other of history's revolutions in relative magnitude of transformation of human affairs in the universe, the vital characteristics and overall involvements of the twentieth-century revolution have gone on entirely unapprehended for one half of a century."* Impressive but marking time, you might say; nor did the rest of the paragraph advance towards that looming "physical success"; on the contrary, a distinctly circular, retrograde movement seemed to be setting in. So I decided to reread *My Life and Hard Times*. I'm a busy man.

In 7 as in 1, the other regular columnists persist and are still competitive with the two stars, Fuller and Thant, the lead-dust twins. Hollis Alpert still does movies; he's better than his predecessor on the old S.R., Arthur Knight, but who isn't? Goodman Ace ("veteran humorist—remember radio's 'Easy Aces'?" he is blurbed; I do indeed) still gives out with labored stand-up jocosity in "Top of the World." John Ciardi, an S.R. oldtimer, still reminisces with tepid garrulity in "As I Was Saying," the ancient mariner of midcult. And Cleveland Amory still runs his scrapbook of clippings. Amory's opening shot was an odd misfire, by the way: he heads a reprint from the London *Economist* "Parody of the Fortnight"; either he has a very extensive idea of a fortnight or Willard Espy, whom he thanks for it, neglected to tell him it originally appeared in 1959 (and may be read in my own 1960 anthology of parodies). Amory's column is headed "Curmudgeon at Large" but he is a very amateur curmudgeon (speaking as an expert one).

The publisher of *World* is still S. Spencer Grin.

—*The Columbia Forum*, Fall, 1972

Appendix:
The Critic at Bay

Author's Note: The following exchanges appeared in the Winter, 1973, issue of The Columbia Forum.

Re: Dwight Macdonald's article on Norman Cousins' new *World* magazine: doesn't *The Forum* have more constructive use for its pages? If *World* is too "midcult" for Mr. Macdonald's sophistication, he is under no obligation to read it, and I doubt that *Forum* readers are enlightened by his fulminations.

A. H. Griffing
Granville, N.Y.

Dwight Macdonald writes:

Mr. Griffing's note strikes at the *raison d'être* of my career. I've always specialized in negative criticism—literary, political, cinematic, cultural—because I've found so few contemporary products about which I could be "constructive" without hating myself in the morning. Mr. Cousins' unfortunate magazine and cultural influence are the latest of a series of impostures and vulgarizations I've thought needed to have the mickey taken out of them *pro bono publico.* Earlier examples of this effort include the third edition of Webster's Unabridged Dictionary, Henry Wallace's Progressive Party campaign, the Revised Standard Version of the Bible, the Adler-Hutchins fifty-volume set of Great Books complete with two-volume Syntopicon, and too many movies to record.

So when Erik Wensberg sent me the first two issues of *World* and suggested that, in view of the discrepancy between their quality and Mr. Cousins' prestige as an editor, I might like to have a look and make a few remarks, I gritted my teeth and plowed through them; they were, in fact, even worse than I'd expected from Cousins' old *Saturday Review* days; thus, I felt it was my duty (*and* pleasure) to rise, or sink, to the occasion. Rosinante to the road again! A few "fulminations" may have inadvertently crept in, and if so, I do apologize, my only excuse being a desire to relieve the reader's and my own ennui in exploring so flat a world. Whether *Forum* readers in general were "enlightened," I don't know; but I do know that those I heard from directly were unexpectedly numerous and applausive. It seems that letting the hot air out of Norman Cousins' inflated reputation as a thinker and moralist filled, as he might put it, a long-felt need.

I enjoyed, if that's the word, the midcultification or evisceration of Mr. Cousins in *The Columbia Forum*, though it might be nice if Dwight Macdonald picked on someone his own size.

Nonetheless, it falls to me, I fear, to note an error that somewhat pains us. Alfred W. McCoy is anything but what Mr. Macdonald called him—a former CIA man. He's a Yale graduate student. Furthermore, the magazine that first (last July) published a portion of McCoy's heroin exposé was *Harper's*, not *The Atlantic*. I spent months developing and excerpting that piece, and while Robert Manning is a great fellow, immodesty compels me to inform you that in this (rare) case, Macdonald cited the wrong Robert.

Robert Shnayerson
Editor-in-Chief
Harper's Magazine, New York, N.Y.

Dwight Macdonald writes:
Sorry about crediting *The Atlantic* instead of *Harper's* for the real McCoy; apologies all the more abject because my own clips indicate *Harper's*. But I don't quite know what Mr. Shnayerson

means by "it might be nice if Dwight Macdonald picked on someone his own size." He seems to be both deriding Cousins and feeling sorry for him—a tricky stance. "Size" is also a tricky term here.
Agreed that qualitatively Cousins is David to my Goliath—or so I
read Mr. Shnayerson's point, a modest encomium—but in quantitative terms it's the other way around, as it was with the midcult
products I recalled above for Mr. Griffing. Myself, I assume it's a
useful function to criticize such influential Goliaths. If critics like
me only fought in their own intellectual weight class—I'm in those
matches too, often enough—who would and could take on the mass-
market heavyweights?

Dwight McDonald's article on Norman Cousins and *World* in *The
Columbia Forum* . . . contains criticisms with which I disagree, but
which undeniably you have a right to publish. I do question the
basic decency, however, of allowing Mr. McDonald to ridicule Mr.
Cousins' and Mr. Grin's names.

  Perhaps I am sensitive because my own name has been ridiculed
so much. But it is improper to make a public joke of a person's
name, his ethnic origin, his color, his creed, his politics, or his
clothes if he is poor. I recall the attacks made on Franklin Roosevelt,
including the crude, insensitive, and anti-Semitic statements about
"that Jew, Rosenfeld." Mr. McDonald's remarks about Mr. Cousins'
and Mr. Grin's names disturbingly reminded me of that sort of thing.

David F. Brinegar
Executive Editor
The Arizona Daily Star, Tucson, Arizona

Dwight Macdonald writes:
  Two or three other readers have objected to my making fun of
Mr. Grin's name, but only Mr. Brinegar has also charged me with
lèse-majesté about Mr. Cousins' name. On rereading my essay I
find no kidding of Mr. Cousins' name, unless a mild, nonpejorative
pun on "cousin" is so considered by my hypersensitive correspondent. I did have fun, twice, with "S. Spencer Grin" as a name, and
God knows I'd have refrained—Mr. Grin's magazine affords many
other, and better, laughs—had I foreseen that it would upset Mr.
Brinegar so much. How depressing that in my golden, or sunset,

years, I should be amalgamated with those Liberty League racists I fought in my youth. "Insensitive" seems an inadequate adjective for them, especially from an editor. (If only FDR *had* been Jewish! He might have returned from Yalta with his pants.)

I joked about "Grin" not for an ethnic put-down, since I have no idea of its provenance—Finnish? Czech? Scandinavian? German? Turkish? Serb?—but because it is, after all, a noun meaning "a wide smile" and so struck me as the perfect *nom de guerre* for a midcult entrepreneur. ("How cheerfully he seems to grin, / How neatly spreads his claws, / And welcomes little fishes in / With gently smiling jaws!"—Lewis Carroll.)* I admit I consider "Grin" a funny name in some contexts, including my article. If I'd inherited it, I'd have changed it to something like, say, "Grinegar." And if I was unwilling to let down the ancestral house, I'd have called myself "S. S. Grin," or "Samuel S. Grin" but never, never "S. Spencer Grin," which strikes just the note of fusty pomposity that invites a hot-foot.

Finally, I don't understand why Mr. Brinegar's name has "been ridiculed so much." Because it echoes "vinegar"? Even I would pass that one up.

Finally finally, if Mr. Brinegar is so persnickety about names, why does he misspell mine three times in a brief note? "MacDonald" is the normal mistake; "McDonald" takes real talent.

The silence from the editors of *World* has been, as they might say, deafening. Erik Wensberg invited every one of those I mentioned to defend, attack, correct, object, protest, explain—anything—generously offering them all the space they needed to set the record straight; a real First Amendment editor. No go and no comment. I wasn't surprised. The objects, or victims, of my "fulminations" have rarely

---

* (1973) Cf. also Poe's essay, "Diddling / Considered as one of the Exact Sciences." The ninth, and climactic, trait of the diddler is: "*Grin*:—Your *true* diddler winds up all with a grin. But this nobody sees but himself. He grins when his daily work is done . . . at night in his own closet, and altogether for his own private entertainment. He goes home. He locks his door. He divests himself of his clothes. He puts out his candle. He gets into bed. All this done, and your diddler *grins*. This is no hypothesis. . . . I reason *a priori*, and a diddle would be no diddle without a grin."

riposted (in print, anyway) and never in the case of the quantitative Goliaths. Their reasons, I'm immodest enough to think, have been prudential: too many specific criticisms that questioned the assumptions on which their commercially flourishing and culturally jejune enterprises were founded. Keep away from *that* tar-baby, Brer Fox!

So I didn't expect any comeback, publicly, from anybody on *World*. There were some private back-stairs cudgelings, though, suitable for upstarts of low degree. One contributing editor wrote Wensberg a note of seventy-five words, not for publication, which said that the writer had long since decided to "ignore" me and my "twelve-word glossary," and which reproached Wensberg for opening his pages to someone who could make another man's name into a "private joke." As a choice of issues, I'd say that shows a certain desperation. I don't know what the reference to my "twelve-word glossary" means. My hunch is that the secretive letter-writer extrapolated from "masscult," "midcult," and "parajournalism," and would be hard put to specify the other nine. Then too, someone's secretary at *World* wrote that her boss thanked Wensberg for calling my article to "our" attention (regal, that "our") but considered me a foeman unworthy of his steel because of my "unjustifiable tirade" against "such great minds as Buckminster Fuller and Norman Cousins."

Afterword

On February 9, 1973, too late to be noticed in the above rundown—perfect timing—the Master of the Revels and Lord of Misrule himself, Norman Cousins, wrote Mr. Wensberg the following Masterful note: "Sorry to be so late in thanking you for your courtesy in letting me see the article by Dwight McDonald. Yes, what he said hurt. But I hope we learned something from it." Well, class, the first lesson is how to spell my name. . . . Naturally, after my conscientious debunking of Mr. Cousins and his magazine, I should have expected his career would zoom sharply upward, and so in fact it soon did:

"SATURDAY REVIEW IS BANKRUPT; NORMAN COUSINS TO RUN IT AGAIN" was a front-page headline in the *Times* of April 25, 1973, with a followup on July 6: "COUSINS'S WORLD WILL BE EXPANDED / The Saturday Review/World Plans to Publish Soon." Those two young *kultur*-hustlers, Veronis and Charney, overextended themselves financially ("about three million in debts, largely for printing, according to well-placed sources"); their quadruple splitting of the *S.R.* atom blew up in their faces.* Uncle Norman is picking up the pieces, taking over 800,000 subscribers to *S.R.* Sciences, Arts, Education, and Society and adding them to the 178,000 *World* subscribers; whether he can digest such a 300 percent overnight expansion in circulation is by no means clear—the whole deal has murky aspects—and his July 6 press release was still extremely vague: "The new *Saturday Review/World* will have a highly contemporary flavor. I expect the design will be stronger, brighter and more accessible. . . . Our aim is to publish for a very compact, high-value readership of 550,000." Last fall, when I was more confident as a Cassandra, I'd have thought the new name not inspired and would have questioned each of the above adjectives. But now—who knows? Not me. When the midcult audience is the problem, I feel (not for the first time, but more poignantly than hitherto) that my vision is a reversed-mirror image of the reality—the practical or sales reality, that is. Cf. my deflation of Swanberg's biography of Henry Luce, later in this section, which was of course followed in a few months by the book's winning a Pulitzer award. Every knock a boost.

---

* For a detailed, fascinating inside view of the hows and whys of the debacle, see William H. Horan's "The Morning After The Saturday Review," in *Esquire* for November, 1973.

Massachusetts
vs. *Mailer*

It began as just another D & D case—Drunk & Disorderly. It won't be found in the lawbooks—there wasn't even a court stenographer—but it's already part of the folklore of Provincetown, also known as Eighth Street by the Sea. Every summer, this Cape Cod seashore town becomes what the sociologists would call a focus of conflicting cultures. The *kulturkampf* is waged between the natives—mostly either Protestant New Englanders or Portuguese-descended Catholic fishermen, two breeds not notable for the breadth of their morality—and the summer people, whose morals are latitudinarian: a rich mixture of artists, writers, beats, hipsters, homosexuals, and other estival hedonists. The police force is definitely on the side of the native culture.

The case of the *Commonwealth of Massachusetts* vs. *Norman Mailer* began on Commercial Street at about one-ten on the morning of June 9, 1960. The bars close at one in Provincetown, and Mailer and his pretty brunette wife, Adele, who was acting at the Province-town Playhouse that summer, were walking home after some pub-crawling. They were making for the Hawthorne House, a big place on a hill and one of the town's landmarks, which was built by the turn-of-the century painter Charles Hawthorne; they had rented it for the season for themselves and their two small children. A police car came nosing along the deserted street in that unsettling way police cars have, like Melville's pale shark slipping ominously through tropical waters.

"Taxi! Taxi!" Mailer called out, mocking the tribal enemy.

"Be quiet, you damn fool!" said Mrs. Mailer, in a wifely fashion.

"TAXI!" he insisted, in satisfactory defiance of both police and wife.

The car glided sharkily on, went around the block and came back—this is the moment in the nightmare at which you wake up if you're lucky—and pulled around a corner in front of the Mailers just as they were about to cross the street. Two cops got out.

"Did you yell 'Taxi'?"

"Yes."

"Does this car look to you like a taxi?"

"Well, you know—that thing on top."

"All right, move on!"

"I'll move on when you get out of my way."

At this point, the cops grabbed Mailer and pushed him into the car. With considerable presence of mind, he called out as he disappeared, "Adele! You're my witness. I'm not resisting arrest." The car drove off, leaving Adele on the street, as alone as Ariadne. Provincetown cops have been known to drop the wife at her home in such late arrests, but the present acting police chief, Francis H. (Cheyney) Marshall, has put a stop to such gallantry.

During the ride to the jail—both sides agree—no one said anything. When they arrived, the cops got out. They were Patrolman George St. Amand and Special Patrolman—that is, on the summer force only—William Sylvia, known throughout town as Cobra. Still without a word, Cobra reached in and pulled Mailer out of the car. What happened next was described by the victim in a letter written several weeks later to the New York *Post*. The letter is a good specimen of Basic Mailerese.

> The rumble was a touch copacetic. It began when we got out of the police car outside the station house, and they would not let me walk in, but endeavored to assist me in. The scrimmage started because I did not want their hands on me. Yet all the way through, I was afraid of a flip, afraid I would begin to hit a uniform. I had the sustained image of a summer or a year in cellular, and so I did no more; let us say I was reduced by this caution to no more than ducking, spinning, slipping, blocking, and sidestepping. At one point one of the policemen tripped

and fell, but I was on my feet all the way, a point to take no vast pride in because the cops were smaller than me, and did not know how to fight. And maybe I was yellow not to hit them back. A difficult point. When I was hit with something heavier than his fist . . . it was from behind and I kept standing but I think it took a bit away from my pride to resist because the form my thoughts next took were liberal rather than radical: Give up a little or they'll beat your head in. So I relinquished the defense of an arm, and let one of the cops manage to apply the grip he had been trying to apply for the last minute—he was proud when he got it—and then he bent me over the trunk of a parked car, and liquid started falling in dark half-dollar drops on the polish of the automobile, and I said, "Okay, you happy now? I'm bleeding," and that seemed to cool them a little, and in we went, into the jailhouse which was safe.

The clubbing resulted in a thirteen-stitch cut on the back of Mailer's head. After permitting him to make a telephone call to his wife, the cops put him in a bare cell, without bed or toilet. He improvised an antiphonal barrage of anti-police insults with a young boy in the next cell, another D & D case. Officer St. Amand came around and explained to Mailer that he had cut his head on a car bumper.

"Are you a Catholic?" asked Mailer.

"Yes."

"You'll go to Hell for lying!"

Chief Marshall soon showed up. He and Mailer got into an exchange of insults, like Homeric heroes before battle.

"I could beat up those two toy cops of yours, and you know it, kid."

"Listen, boy, I could take you with one hand."

"Maybe you could and maybe you couldn't, but you picked the wrong pigeon this time. You cops are used to dealing with people who can't defend themselves. Well, I'm a writer and I know how to use words, and, boy, I'm going to use them."

At three-thirty, Mrs. Mailer arrived, bringing fifty dollars bail, but Mailer had to wait till the bondsman appeared, two hours later, for release. Although her husband had warned her on the phone that he had been clubbed, when Mrs. Mailer saw his bandaged head she was furious. "Look what you've done to my husband. You'll wish you'd never begun this!" It is not known precisely when the cops realized that they had beaten up not an anonymous beatnik but a writer of reputation, and that both the writer and the writer's wife were not going to be good sports about it.

I went up to Provincetown to cover the trial.* Upon my arrival—on July 22d, the day before the trial—Mailer told me that he had decided to undertake his own defense, because he felt that an out-of-town lawyer would be resented and a local lawyer, while he might win the case, would be inclined not to attack the police. That night, the Mailers and I spent several hours drinking with the local beatniks in the Old Colony Bar, at the east end of town. (The homosexuals' turf is the other end.) Mailer was a kind of big brother to them, both a leader and a confidant; he clearly enjoyed not only talking to them but also listening to them. I heard a lot about the police: that the former chief, now ill with heart trouble, was relatively mild but that Cheyney Marshall, who had been acting chief for the past three months, had been cracking down on the summer latitudinarians; that the slightest public exuberance after the bars close might land one in jail suddenly; that Franz Kline, the painter, was arrested, without warning, for playing records in his home late at night; that homosexual bars and night clubs were being closed down by legalistic hokeypokey about licenses; that the police tried to get restaurant and night-club proprietors to fire homosexual employees; that one officious young cop diverted himself by stopping people who looked odd to his untraveled eyes and demanding that they "identify" themselves—this from a young Negro artist, who thought it was his paint-stained trousers, and from a white artist, who thought it was his beard.

The next morning, I joined the Mailers for breakfast. Over

---

* (1973) I covered the trial as a correspondent for *Esquire*, but they didn't think much of the article—"trivia" sticks in memory—so I showed it to Shawn at *The New Yorker* and he accepted it. The piece is unusual in being taken by *The New Yorker* after it was rejected by *Esquire*—the current normally runs the other way.

coffee, Mailer revealed to his wife that he was going to put her on the stand, explaining that he had said nothing about it earlier, lest she get tensed up. She showed signs of alarm.

"All you have to do is tell the truth and look the judge in the eye and don't get angry," he said.

"Yes, I know, but—"

"Don't worry, baby. I'll take care of you. It'll be all right."

Mailer decided that he and his wife should both dress in sober black for the occasion. The three of us were about to set off for the trial, in the Mailers' car—he had decided, for tactical reasons, to use the ancient family sedan instead of an English sports roadster, something low and dashing called a Triumph TR-3, he had recently acquired—when he noticed that she was not wearing stockings. He sent her back for stockings.

The courtroom, done in the usual police-court light oak, with the usual flags, was packed. Chief Marshall and his two cops sat along one wall, in civilian clothes, and so did various local dignitaries, including S. Osborn Ball, landlord, realtor, lawyer, and the town's leading offbeat eminence.

"Hey, Norman!" Mr. Ball called across the room. "I'll visit you in state's prison!"

"Okay, Ozzie, don't forget," Mailer called back, grinning.

The judge entered, and everybody stood up. He was the Honorable Gershom Hall, a circuit judge from Harwichport, up the Cape. He was long and lean and composed, with an impassive New England expression and a voice that was low but audible, and slightly chilling.

Two short cases first—a bored young man in dungarees who pleaded guilty to dangerous operation of a motor scooter, and a red-eyed, unshaven workingman who pleaded guilty to Drunk & Disorderly, and clowned around a bit, scoring once. The Judge asked him, "Why do you drink?" and he replied, "I like it."

Then the main event. Mailer began by asking to have not only his wife sworn as a witness but also me. I scrambled up and raised my hand, my notes tumbling about my feet; he hadn't alerted *me* at breakfast. Can one report a trial in which one is a witness? I wondered uneasily. Always willing to try anything once, Mailer had thought I could testify that he had had more drinks the night before than on the night of the arrest, and yet had shown no signs of being drunk. True. But the Judge pointed out that since I hadn't been there on June ninth, my testimony was irrelevant. I sat down, and began taking notes again.

Chief Marshall, who was doubling as prosecuting attorney, took the stand as a witness—a well-set-up man with a big brown face, hot of eye and jutting of jaw. When he got to the jail, he testified, he had found the defendant drunk and abusive. "I detected a strong odor of liquor on his breath," he said. The defendant had called up Mr. Ball and asked him to come down and get him out; when Mr. Ball had demurred, because of the lateness of the hour, the defendant had shouted angrily into the phone, "You're a lawyer, aren't you? Why don't you get down here?" When Dr. Daniel Hiebert, summoned from his bed, had wanted to shave the defendant's head, the latter had indignantly refused to let him, saying he was going to a dance the next night; he had made many loud and uncomplimentary remarks to the doctor (though he had finally let him bandage his head). "Why don't you sober up?" Dr. Hiebert had said as he left.

Mailer rose to cross-examine Chief Marshall. He walked up with a slight swagger—something between the new gun in town and Perry Mason—and his first questions were delivered in a sinister Texas drawl; throughout the hearing, he shifted gears between this accent and his normal one (Brooklyn-Harvard), according to the dramatic voltage he felt was required.

"Why did you come to the jail at two in the morning?" Mailer began.

This drew a blank. The chief had been called out to look into a possible case of drowning—he had the record sheet to back him up —and had dropped in at the jail as a matter of routine.

Mailer opened up a second front. "Before I dismiss you"—the chief's large jaw tightened—"I want to ask one thing: Do you insist I was going to a *dance* the next night? Actually, I was going to the Robinson-Pender fight in Boston. I haven't been to a dance in years."

"You said a dance."

"Have you ever been wrong?"

"Yes, I suppose so."

"Mr. Marshall, you are not an electronic machine. You might be in error."

The chief admitted that he was not an electronic machine.

The nonbelligerent cop, Patrolman St. Amand, next took the stand—pale, puffy, eyeglassed, somewhat bald, more like a book-keeper than a policeman. He seemed uneasy, and stared at his shoes as he was testifying. He went through the story, stating that when the police cruiser arrived at the station, the defendant had jumped out swinging at Officer Sylvia; that there was "a little mealie" (melee); that all three of them fell down; and that when the defendant got up, "I noticed his head was lacerated and bleeding; I don't know how it happened." He had apparently given up the car bumper theory.

"Did you find it offensive that I called the police car a taxi?" asked Mailer, cross-examining. "Is driving a taxi a contemptible occupation?"

"No."

"Then why did you circle back around the block?"

"We didn't. We completed our regular tour as far as the Ace of Spades and then came back."

There followed some virtuoso questioning in which Mailer got the witness to place him on the street the first time the car passed and then the second. Mailer pointed out that these two spots were less than two hundred feet apart, and then drew his conclusion: The police car could not have gone to the Ace of Spades, a night spot a half mile away, in the interval. (Point unimportant, except to show that the police did resent being called taxi drivers, and that their testimony was not to be relied upon.)

"Did you put me into a bare cell?" asked Mailer.

"Yes."*

---

* (1973) I showed the MS to Mailer before publication and he suggested a number of corrections, most of which I accepted. At this point in the original MS there followed this passage:

"Is it your practice to put a man with a head wound into such a cell?"

"There was no other cell free."

Mailer got him to admit there was perhaps another cell free.

Patrolman St. Amand found his shoes more and more fascinating.

I recalled there had been quite a lot of cross-examination here but this was all I could dredge from my notes, so I wrote in the margin: "Norman—

"This cell had no bed to lie on. No toilet, not even a pail. I had a bad cut, which was still bleeding. Is it possible you were being vindictive?"

"No. I just put you in the first handy cell."

"Mr. St. Amand, how long have you worked for the police force?"

"Five years."

"How many cells are there in that wing?"

"Four."

"In five years you haven't been able to learn the separate characteristics of those four cells?"

"Well, there was no other one open."

"Are you certain? At the time I was brought in, there were only two other men in the cells."

"The fourth cell is the women's cell."

"I was transferred to that hours later. It had no bed, but it had raised planks on which you could lie down. It also had a pail. Is that the women's cell?"

"I guess it isn't."

"So you had a choice of putting me in a cell where I could lie down, or one where I couldn't, and you put me in the bare cell."

Patrolman St. Amand found his shoes more and more fascinating.

Please reconstruct this—terribly sorry." I needn't have worried—nothing he enjoys more than such paleontology. From my six-line bone he reconstructed the thirty-line skeleton that follows in the printed text. I used it because it was both dramatic and plausible. It sounded the way I remembered his cross-examining technique, and it had the same tone as other examples I did have full notes on. Whether it all went just this way is, of course, doubtful (a lot of paleontology needed to flesh out my own notes, too) but not, I think, important—the essence of the truth was here—*se non è vero, è ben trovato*. I was struck, in reading *The Armies of the Night*, with how "right" his account of scenes I was involved in seemed, including dialogue I knew he hadn't taken notes on. I asked him if he had total recall. "No, but I do have a good memory for the mood of a scene and for the key words and actions that express it, and I kind of feel my way back to reconstructing it through them." . . . All this is significant because a few months after the Provincetown trial Mailer covered the 1960 Democratic Convention for *Esquire*. The resulting piece, "Superman at the Supermarket," was the first of a series of reportage articles and books that he did for the next decade, and in which, I'm not alone in thinking, he finally discovered his literary métier.

Mailer: When we arrived at the station, did Cobra reach in and—

Chief Marshall: I object.

Judge: Mr. Mailer, the officer's name is Sylvia, not Cobra.

Mailer: Your Honor, I have heard this man called nothing but Cobra since I've been in town. I will try to call him Sylvia, but if I slip I wish to assure Your Honor it will not be an intentional trick. (*To witness*) Did Officer Sylvia pull me out of the car?

St. Amand: He did assist you from the cruiser, yes. (*Laughter in court*)

Judge: If there are any more demonstrations, I will clear the court. (*To witness*) You stated the defendant came out of the car swinging. Did you see him throw any punches?

St. Amand: He was fighting and aggressive and—

Judge: *Did you see him throw a punch?*

St. Amand: I did not actually see him swing at Officer Sylvia.

Special Officer William Sylvia took the stand—small, stocky, sharp-featured, hard-eyed. As he was rehearsing the tale again—with that wooden-faced impassivity cops assume in court—the Judge interrupted. "You back there, you with the cigarette, come up here!"

A callow young beatnik, with whom I had drunk the evening before, made his way forward. One could fairly hear the Judge ticking, like a grenade. It was an awful moment.

"Were you *smoking?*"

"Yes. I'm sorry."

"Don't you know I could send you to jail for contempt? This is not a circus." To the officer of the court: "Officer, get this man out at once. Get him out of the building."

Officer Sylvia resumed. When he had finished, the Judge asked him, "Did he refuse to get out of the car?"

"No."

"Do you know how he got the cut on his head?"

"No."

Mailer had planned to cross-examine Officer Sylvia along psychiatric lines (he had written the questions out in advance on cards): "Are you aware that your nickname in this town is Cobra?" "Do you know what Cobra means? Webster defines it as 'any of several very venomous Asiatic and African snakes.'" He had also written down such questions for Police Chief Marshall as "Are you aware that people in the town believe they have a bullying and brutal police force?" and "Do you know that the nickname for the police here is the Gestapo?" Judge Hall, however, had made it clear almost immediately that such questions, interesting as they were, did not fall within his concept of cross-examination, and Mailer had forgone them. But he found it difficult to abstain from interpretation. As the trial progressed, the Judge gave the defendant-*cum*-attorney-for-the-defense an elementary course in courtroom procedure. "You have no right to comment on proceedings at this point," he kept repeating as Mailer kept inserting conclusions into his questions. "Mr. Mailer is not a lawyer," the Judge usually added. "We'll give him a little leeway."

It was the legal versus the novelistic mind, and the latter always gave way politely—and temporarily. For, as a writer, Mailer had done a rough draft before he entered the courtroom, and, also as a writer, he couldn't bear to have this draft wholly wasted; he worked it in wherever he saw an opening, like a beaver instinctively using what comes to hand.

> Mailer: You grabbed my arms from behind—isn't that right, Cobra?
> Chief Marshall: Objection!
> Mailer: I'm very sorry, Your Honor. I forgot. I should have said "Mr. Sylvia."
> Sylvia: Yes.
> Mailer: Have you been in this sort of trouble before, Mr. Sylvia? I mean have there been violent episodes in your past?
> Judge: We're not interested in the past. Only in what happened on June ninth.
> Mailer: Yes, Your Honor . . . Now, have you no fear of getting out of control?
> Sylvia: No.
> Mailer: Do you ever have bad dreams about violence?
> Chief Marshall: *I object!*
> Judge: That is not a proper question, Mr. Mailer.
> Mailer: I'm sorry, Your Honor.

The prosecution rested, and the defense called Mrs. Mailer. She took the stand, looking very pretty and nervous and unprofessional—a pleasant contrast to the three wooden-faced cops.

"What did we have for supper on the night of June ninth?" Mailer asked her, sensing her nervousness.

"Steak," she replied triumphantly.

"And where did we go after supper?"

"To the Ace of Spades."

Mailer looked a little dashed. "But didn't we go somewhere else first? To a drive-in movie, for instance?"

"Oh, yes, that's right."

"And after that to the Atlantic House, where we had one drink each?"

"Yes, we did."

At this point, the Judge said something about leading the witness. Mailer said earnestly that he had no such intention, adding, "Your Honor, I think it is clear that the testimony of this witness has not been rehearsed."

Mrs. Mailer then fixed the number of further drinks that evening at one for her, three for him, all at the Ace of Spades, and identified them as gin-and-tonic.

"Could you be in error?" Mailer asked ruminatively. "Was it not possibly gin-and-tonic for you and gin-on-the-rocks for me?"

Mrs. Mailer agreed that it might indeed have been so.

After this display of candor, her testimony went along smoothly enough, except that the Judge had to ask her to address herself to him rather than to the spectators. The important point came at the end, when she testified that her husband had called out to her as the cops hustled him into the squad car, "You're my witness. I'm not resisting arrest."

Mailer now took the stand as his own witness and told, in more conversational terms, the story of the "rumble" already given above in his letter. He admitted he had been "a little coy" with the cops, but explained that his aggressiveness was due to the lack of tobacco rather than the presence of alcohol. "I was a little high but I don't get drunk on four drinks," he said. "That night, I was irritable, because I had stopped smoking two days earlier. I was worried about myself when they began hitting me. I have a bad temper. They may have thought I was a dangerous beatnik; maybe they look at television too much." He admitted he had insulted Dr. Hiebert. "I'm very sorry about that—I was angry and he seemed to me at that moment just a representative of the police and I hated the police. I was cocky, sassy, arrogant—call it what you will. When they took me into the station, I was in a state of great anger and I remained angry for hours. Shaving my head I thought was the last indignity."

Chief Marshall's cross-examination centered on the call to Mr. Ball, which he cited as an example of drunken belligerence, and on Mailer's rudeness to the doctor (ditto).

Mailer then called S. Osborn Ball to the stand, and asked him if he concluded from their phone talk that he (Mailer) was drunk.

After a rather dramatic pause, Mr. Ball replied, "You showed no signs of drunkenness."

"Was I offensive when I asked you if you were a lawyer?"

"No. You had dealt with me only as a tenant. And some have had doubts about the matter anyway."

"Mr. Ball, you have upstaged me forever," said Mailer.

"Don't put me into your next novel, that's all I ask," said Mr. Ball, getting in the last word. Mr. Ball just happened to be in court, on another case; neither side had thought of subpoenaing him. For all his advance preparation, Mailer forgot to include in his testimony that it took thirteen stitches to sew up the cut on his head. At the post-mortem after the trial, over a pitcher of beer at the Old Colony, someone asked why he hadn't mentioned this. "Didn't I?" he said. "Damn!" It was that kind of trial—sort of free-form. The police forgot to subpoena Dr. Hiebert—an omission that the Judge commented on unfavorably, as he also did on the failure of the police witnesses either to report or deny Mailer's parting words to his wife about not resisting arrest. Nothing-up-his-sleeve Mailer *had* asked Dr. Hiebert's wife, informally, the evening before, to ask him to appear, but he didn't.

Mailer summed up his case: "A middle ground may apply here. A man has had a few drinks and is sassy, but I question whether this is a cause for arrest. . . . I don't want to be flowery. I've been coming here ten times in the last fifteen years. I like Provincetown, and there's no reason it can't have a police force that is as good as the rest of the town."

Chief Marshall's summary was long on rhetoric: "This man is an intelligent man. He did not ask for a drunk test. Is this the action of a normal person? Is this the action of a sober man? He presents himself here clean as the new-fallen snow. But we have seen he behaved in a rude and disorderly manner."

> Judge: Was it rude and disorderly to call your men hack-drivers?
> Chief Marshall: Police officers are called many things.
> Judge: Rightly so.

Chief Marshall then finished his speech.

After a short recess, Judge Hall pronounced his decision: "I'm going to say pretty frankly what I think about the whole business. I think the defendant had enough to drink to act like a fool. On the other hand"—turning to the cops—"you police officers were too thin-skinned. You have to deal with many summer visitors here, and you can't manhandle a man because he says something you don't like. If any more cases like this come before me, there will be some action taken. I say that in this case the police went too far. . . . I find you"—turning to Mailer—"guilty of drunkenness, and I advise you in future to show more respect to the police. The verdict will be filed"—i.e., no fine or sentence; nothing on the record, unless it happens again. "I find you not guilty of disorderly conduct."

Finis. Subdued jubilation in the audience. Reporters from the local and Boston papers leave to write their stories. Attorney Ball congratulates Mailer on his handling of the case. Much handshaking and backslapping, centering on Mailer, who finally slips off to retrieve his fifty dollars bail from the clerk of the court. General *détente,* and *exeunt omnes* with a sense of having been in on a bit of legal and literary history in the making.

—*The New Yorker*, October 8, 1960

Afterword

The following is the original conclusion of "Massachusetts vs. Mailer." It was omitted in The New Yorker *because the editors felt (a) it was otiose ("We're not all that interested in the Provincetown police department") and (b) Chief Marshall had been given enough lumps already. I'd never agree to (b) at any time—"Roll on, thou deep and dark blue watergate!" is my motto. As for (a), the interview seems to me to throw new (and sinister) lights on the kulturkampf of which the Mailer case was a symbol, also to suggest that the defendant (in making an issue of his arrest) and the judge (in finding against the police) were even more justified than the courtroom proceedings indicated. So my own editorial judgment is to restore the coda.*

The next day I went around to the police station and asked to interview Chief Marshall. Somewhat to my surprise, he agreed. (I cannot imagine a British or French police chief doing so; one small dividend from our democratic tradition and our informal manners—also from our perhaps exaggerated respect for the press.) I asked him whether there would be any policy changes because of Judge Hall's criticisms. "No. The judge saw the evidence one way. I saw it different. It's a matter of opinion." "Will Officer Sylvia be disciplined?" "No. I think he was telling the truth. That big-mouth Mailer!" Then, shifting gears: "Sylvia's never been in trouble before. I think every man is entitled to one mistake." Blank wall. "There's an impression around town the police have been tougher on beats and homosexuals since you took over from Chief Rogers." "There's been no change in policy. [Pause.] We don't want that type here. But what can I do? It's not illegal. I can't line them up and shoot them, can I?" There was a wistful note in his voice, but I had to agree he couldn't. I suggested it was inconsistent to want "them" to go away and yet to depend on them economically. "We don't depend on them. One normal decent family with a few kids [I thought of the Mailers' ménage] will spend more than a hundred of that kind.

We have a saying here: A beatnik comes in the spring with a clean pair of dungarees and a five-dollar bill and when he leaves in September he hasn't changed either."

I left with the impression that Chief Marshall is honest and efficient and more than adequate to cope with crime in Provincetown. I believed him when he told me that he had been an intercollegiate boxing champion, that he had kept himself in condition ever since—he seemed to be in the pink—and that he had come out on top in brawls without using a gun. I was also convinced that he was not afraid of Mailer: "That guy! He said he could beat up my officers. He couldn't beat up my sister! Any time he wants to take me on, I'll be glad to oblige."*

But the issue is perhaps not one of relative prowess, or even of efficiency. "You can't manhandle a man because he says something you don't like. . . . In this case the police went too far," said Judge Hall. Chief Marshall and his police like very little about Norman Mailer and his friends. When to this is added Drunk & Disorderly, then the Bill of Rights looks tenuous indeed. As Chief Marshall put it to me: "I'm definitely in favor of humane treatment of prisoners. But you take some of these goddam drunks you gotta protect yourself." Cobra—that is, Special Officer William Sylvia—protected himself.

The Mailer case is interesting for several reasons. Although the judge was an austere New England type, never in living memory have the Provincetown cops been so thoroughly worsted by a summer latitudinarian. It is also a curious episode of literary history because Mailer conducted his own case, and conducted it with an aggressive resourcefulness rarely seen off television—which was, in fact, his law school. The Duke of Wellington, with the contempt of a man of

---

* (1973) Norman suggested adding here: "When I told this to Mailer, his response was: 'I've never met Mr. Marshall's sister, so maybe she could do me in, and I'm not at all sure I could take Cheyney, but any time he wants to spend an evening drinking with me. . . . Maybe I could be lawyer for both sides in court next day.' " He added: "If this wrecks the rhythm of the end of your piece, or is too complicated, let it go, but I do think his remarks uncontested will give inordinate pleasure to all the people who think I'm insufferable."

action, dismissed intellectuals as "the scribbling set," on which the late economist Joseph Schumpeter commented: "Intellectuals are in fact people who wield the power of the spoken or written word, and one of the touches that distinguish them . . . is the absence of direct responsibility for practical affairs." Because of this "lack of that first-hand knowledge which only actual experience can give," Dr. Schumpeter concluded that the Iron Duke was right and that the scribbling set tends to be ineffective in action. Since I have been of the opinion, ever since I saw big-business leaders at close quarters years ago as a *Fortune* writer, that any intellectual worthy of the name could run a railroad or a bank better than the pros because he would be smarter and because making money and such "practical" activities are child's play compared to constructing a good paragraph, for this reason I was delighted when Norman Mailer proved me right and both the Duke and Dr. Schumpeter wrong.

Armies of
the Night,
or Bad Man
Makes Good

In a day somewhat late in November, in the year of the first and he hoped the last March on the Pentagon, the phone on Dwight Macdonald's disorderly desk rang and instantly a piranha school of apprehensions began to swarmingly nibble away at the carcass of his disorderly mind as he scrabbled about to find the receiver among the drifts of unanswered letters and unsolicited manuscripts he was supposed to have long since passed on to some of the all-too-many editors he had become acquainted with in the course of a long and not entirely dishonorable career and also many invitations to press screenings of movies he wouldn't have gone to see even had he not given up his film column two years ago, their persistent appearance on his desk reminding him unpleasantly of the growth of hair on a corpse; plus windrows of second-class matter he had not yet quite decided to throw away, for reasons which reflected, he reflected, little if any credit on his character. The piranha thoughts had now become little round balls darting through the pinball machine that passed for his brain: anal-retentive personality (flash! ping!), petty-bourgeois sense of property (flash! ping! *ping!*), and finally (flash! ping! TILT!) that all-American cancer. So Macdonald mused, hmmm, hmmm, hmmm, as he tried to face the shrilling challenge with the grace, the blunt, battered but tenacious realism about one's existential being, also one's left hook, he had admired in certain aging club fighters, not necessarily always the most skillful.

As he put the retrieved and still-shrilling receiver to his rather large ear, Macdonald pondered some of the too-many mysteries of his too-long career. A somewhat younger writer was shortly to write in *Armies of the Night*: "Dwight was by now one of the oldest anti-Communists in America," and Dwight was to feel again that old club-fighter ache. Or perhaps "curiosities" would be more descriptive than "mysteries"; for Macdonald was a modest, unpretentious chap *au fond* and out of the spotlight. How had he gotten into the odd habit, for instance, of answering his phone although, looking down the rapidly diminishing perspective of his years, he had long ago concluded that practically all his incoming calls were from people who wanted something from him, rather than from people who wanted to give him something. A suave-voiced foundation official had seldom called to offer him a $10,000 Prize for Distinguished Service to American Criticism, tax free, while there was never any dearth of calls inviting him to panel discussions at the New School or the YMHA on The Future of the Novel, or New Directions in Cinema; or to be interviewed on The American Crisis by some foreign journalist or on some educational radio or TV station; or to review big books for small periodicals; all at modest if any fees. Had forty years of professional journalism habituated him to the umbilical cord of Mr. Bell's, or was it Mr. Edison's, malign invention? Had his instinct for self-preservation been destroyed? Or were his nerves not sufficiently sensitive to keep them well covered with flesh? (And what did *that* mean, exactly, he flash-ping pondered as the little round balls scampered through his mind in much less time than it has taken to put it all down here, the tracks having been worn deep by similar reveries each time the thing rang.) Or was it, a truly cancerous thought, that at sixty-one he still had never acquired a secretary, unlike, say, a certain somewhat younger writer he refused to think about, in print, since he was fond of him and therefore was resolved not to be in any way petty or envious about him, in print.

By now, these problems were beginning to bore even Macdonald. With That Sinking Feeling once celebrated in the Lydia E.

Pinkham ads and now all too familiar to his ravaged eld, worn thin
as an early Victoria penny of the "bun" design, so called from the
coiffure of the imperial bitch in her plump Teutonic bloom before
dear, beloved Albert, her one and only true stud, had succumbed to
her *Backfisch* avidities, Dwight Macdonald now realized that his
thoughts as transcribed above for more paragraphs, and more lengthy
ones, than he cared to think about had been about as fascinating as
the "bun" penny and, dear reader, you can shove up the prig prince
too if you feel so inclined. A whiff of the ceremental odor of dissolu-
tion suddenly invaded Macdonald's nostrils. Was it the end, he
wondered?

Before he could decide, the voice of an old friend, rough in
timbre, tough in accent but soothingly affectionate in some curious
way for all its anfractuosities, rushed into his ear with its usual
restrained urgency: "Hi, Dwight? . . . Listen, I'm doing a long piece
on that Pentagon weekend. . . . For *Harper's*. . . . Yeah, my idea. . . .
No, it's really long—they agreed to twenty thousand words and I've
done sixty thousand and it looks like another thirty thousand anyway. . . . I know, but they say okay. . . . I'd like to talk to you and
Cal about it, what you remember that I don't, what happened after I
got arrested. . . . Can we make a date soon?" Macdonald wasn't
wholly delighted with this call from Norman Mailer, for it was he.
He wasn't sure Mailer had a better character than he did, in fact he
was pretty sure he didn't. But then he remembered that Mailer was
as clever as he was, a more important consideration; also that they
had managed to remain friends for some twenty-five years in spite of
a radical incompatibility of temperaments. It was partly because of a
large tolerance on both sides, on his of Mailer's personal and literary
vagaries, and on Mailer's of Macdonald's chronic objections to same
—which must have been all the more irritating because they were so
monotonously right. But chiefly, Macdonald thought, because this
tolerance, after all a negative or at best a neutral matter, was lubri-
cated by a common addiction to the great American folk art of kidding, which they both indulged in copiously and *ad libitum* whenever they met, aggression calling unto aggression but, you understand,
always just kidding and no bones broken. All this went through
Macdonald's mind in his usual split second flat and he said okay and
the date was made, the talk was talked and absolutely nothing at all

from this forgathering of Mailer with his two comrades of the Pentagon weekend, "noble Lowell" and "stout Macdonald"—the latter,
conceded grudgingly the latter, a masterpiece of adjectival ambiguity
—appeared in print, so far as Macdonald's practiced eye could tell.
Mailer must have had something else in mind, the suspicious Macdonald later suspected, after he had read the piece, but he didn't
really care what, for—to abandon the parodic voice—I thought it a
journalistic masterpiece and a literary triumph.

"NORMAN MAILER'S BEST WORK," blares the cover of the March *Harper's*, whose editorial content is given over wholly, excluding departments, to the ninety-five pages of "The Steps of the Pentagon." For
once, a blurb is accurate—I think it really may be Mailer's best work
—the only exceptions that occur to me are the first half of *Barbary
Shore* and the two short stories, "The Time of Her Time" and "The
Man Who Studied Yoga." The cover blurb continues: "A documentary report about the famous Washington weekend during which
thousands of Americans marched across the Potomac in the name of
peace, and some—the author among them—ended in jail. Along the
way, many of our most basic problems are illuminated, while a cast
of brilliant and wonderfully entertaining characters play out their
roles in the action." This is also true but not the whole truth: the
documentary report also covers another subject better than Mailer
has ever covered it before: himself. Not more fully—cf. *Advertise-
ments for Myself, passim*, also *An American Dream* almost *in toto*
—but better: subtlety, awareness of his own motivations, objectivity,
and, most notable innovation in Mailer's previous self-exposure,
objectivity's ultimate seal and signal, humor about himself. The subject proves to be of considerable value both in itself and as a way of
getting into other topics. Once he was forced to abandon—under
pressures we shall look into later—the Messianic-*cum*-Superman nonsense he has too often in the past indulged himself with, and tries to
seriously think about—and explain—himself, Mailer proves to have a
more complex and interesting mind than he has hitherto revealed.
This revelation, his ruminating awareness of himself and the insights
into others he gets from this fixed vantage point, makes "The Steps
of the Pentagon" also superior, I think, to Mailer's justly celebrated
reportage pieces about political conventions, prizefights, and other

events in which he was less personally involved. "Curious," Lowell said to me after reading it, "when you're with X [another novelist], you think he's so sensitive and alert and then you find later he wasn't taking in anything, while Norman seems not to pay much attention but now it seems he didn't miss a trick—and what a memory!" What a memory indeed—he took no notes that I observed and yet he reproduces, with few errors or omissions I detected, the scenes and dialogues of the weekend; doubtless he reconstructed them by ear, but his reconstructions ring true, and sometimes they border on the prodigious, as that play-by-play account, at the end, of the duel between the WASP commissioner, Scaife, and the scrappy, indefatigably ingenious Jewish civil-liberties lawyer, Hirschkopf—a real hero —over Mailer's release on bail. I wasn't there but, as an amateur of legal processes, it sounds right; the technical jockeying back and forth is reproduced with the expertise and verve of a Dickens; or a sportswriter.

Mailer was annoyed when Lowell said, "Norman, you are the best journalist in America"; he explains just why. But what neither of them could have realized, since the present work hadn't been written, was that Mailer was about to carry journalism into literature in the way that Agee had done in *Let Us Now Praise Famous Men*: by planting himself squarely in the foreground and relating the whole composition to his own sensibility. Just the opposite method Truman Capote used in his "nonfiction novel," *In Cold Blood*, which falls into fragments every paragraph because of the author's mistake in keeping himself antiseptically out of it—a gimmick that "worked" well enough commercially, of course.

"The Steps of the Pentagon" is an astonishing literary performance: the style is both free and dignified throughout, the tone is maintained with few of the lapses into journalese one might expect from such a subject. It reminds me of Henry James. Mailer has devised a consistent rhetoric which he sustains with Jamesian control. It is even the same kind of rhetoric, a flexible mixture of the formal and the colloquial—takes a steady hand to bring it off— which can rise to elaborate metaphors and sink to the easiest slang, sometimes in the same paragraph, without going off key in either direction, the vulgar or the "literary." See the last two paragraphs on page 62, for instance—also note the Jamesian *density* of style, all the water squeezed out, every word expressive, necessary, pulling its weight. Or the marvelous science-fiction metaphor of the sarcophagus on the first page, elaborated with the patient exuberance of James, also with his baroque comic touch. Excessive as it may sound, I venture that "The Steps of the Pentagon" is often as funny as *The Spoils of Poynton.*

A literary gem. Specifically a pearl, secreted layer by layer to enclose, smooth over, and neutralize a most painful gritty particle that had intruded itself into the author's soft psyche between the hard shells of his ego: Mailer's scandalous, drunken, endless (it seemed), and mindless (it was) eruption of scatological exhibitionism at a "literary reading" on Thursday night—Paul Goodman, Lowell, myself, and Mailer—for which several hundred people had paid $3 up to attend, for the benefit of the coming Pentagon march that Saturday. A less self-aware (and less egotistical) writer might have let it pass ("I was tight") and a less clever writer would have attempted to tone down or omit some of the more gruesome details, but Mailer meets it head on, beginning with the full text of *Time's* waspish, no pun intended, account of his behavior, to which he appends: "Now we may leave *Time* in order to find out what happened." Actually, the *Time* story was, for once, reasonably accurate —it would have been difficult for even a *Time* editor to improve on the raw material for snide comment so copiously provided by Mailer. What the author had in mind when he promised to reveal "what [really] happened" is not clear to me, since the fifteen pages he devotes to the episode include everything in the *Time* story plus a great deal more detail about what he did or said that night which I had mercifully forgotten. This is his subtler method of coating the gritty particle: he confesses he is a Jekyll-Hyde character (sometimes he turns into "an absolute egomaniac, a Beast—no recognition existed of the existence of anything beyond the range of his reach. And when he appeared, it was often with great speed") and thus disarms readers by revealing, nay insisting, that he is much worse than they are, or could ever hope, or dread, to be. And then proving it at length. The more obvious ploy is his five and a half pages on "The Liberal Party" which preceded the catastrophe. It revolted him by its academic-liberal anemia—"a party lacked flavor for him unless some one very rich or social was present"—to such an extent that he

refused the food—which was not at all anemic, a rich boeuf Bour-
guignon. So he establishes a physiological alibi for what happened
later. Myself, I found the company pleasant—Mailer takes care of
that: "Macdonald was the operative definition of the gregarious and
could talk with equal facility and equal lack of personal observation
to an Eskimo, a collector from the New York Department of Sani-
tation, or a U.N. diplomat—therefore was chatting happily with the
world fifteen minutes after his entrance." Shrewdly observed—one
finds Mailer holding up an only slightly distorted mirror to one's
nature throughout the piece. But in fact I did personally observe an
attractive, and original, Argentinian girl and managed to eat the
burgundy beef enjoyably in her company. If only Norman had been
more personally observant—what a different turn the history of that
evening might have taken! But then we shouldn't have had *The
Armies of the Night.*

—Esquire, May, 1968

Incomplete Nonsense:
The McLuhan Massage

Understanding Media: The Extensions of Man is one of those ambitious, far-ranging idea-books that is almost certain to be a *succès d'estime* and may well edge its way onto the bestseller lists.* It has all the essentials: a big, new theory about an important aspect of modern life—in this case what is called Mass Media, or Communications—that is massively buttressed by data and adorned with a special terminology. An early example was James Burnham's *The Managerial Revolution*, which wasted a great deal of print, talk, and time two decades ago. Later, and more respectable, examples are *The Lonely Crowd* ("other-directed"), Norman O. Brown's *Life Against Death* ("polymorphous perverse"), Paul Goodman's *Growing Up Absurd*, and C. Wright Mills' *The Power Elite*.

Marshall McLuhan's book outdoes its predecessors in the scope and novelty of its theory, the variety of its data (he has looted all culture, from cave paintings to *Mad* magazine, for fragments to shore up against the ruin of his System), and the panache of its terminology. My only fear is he may have overestimated the absorp-

---

* (1973) It shoved its way to the top a few months after this appeared. (The subtitle is not a misprint, by the way: *The Message Is the Massage* was the title of a later McLuhancy.) Media Marshall went up like a rocket—and has fizzed down, and out, like one.

217

tive capacities of our intelligentsia and have given them a richer feast of Big, New ideas than even their ostrich stomachs can digest. I have a sneaking sympathy for "the consternation of one of the editors of this book" who, we are told on page 4, "noted in dismay that 'seventy-five percent of your material is new.'" Not that this fazes our author. "Such a risk seems quite worth taking at the present time when the stakes are very high and the need to understand the effects of the extensions of man becomes more urgent by the hour." If the worse comes to the worst, as the hours tick by, no one can say that Marshall McLuhan, director of the Center for Culture and Technology at the University of Toronto and a former chairman (1953–1955) of the Ford Foundation Seminar on Culture and Communication, didn't do his best to wise us up.

Compared to Mr. McLuhan, Spengler is cautious and Toynbee positively pedantic. His thesis is that mankind has gone through three cultural stages: a Golden Age of illiterate tribalism that was oral, homogeneous, collective, nonrational, and undifferentiated; a Silver Age (the terms are Ovid's, not his) that set in after the invention of the alphabet during which the spoken word began to be superseded by the written word, a decay into literacy that was facilitated by the fact that alphabetic writing is easier to learn and use than Egyptian hieroglyphs or Chinese ideograms, whose desuetude he deplores; and the present Iron Age that was inaugurated by movable-type printing—an even more unfortunate invention—that is visual, fragmented, individualistic, rational, and specialized. McLuhan's *The Gutenberg Galaxy* (University of Toronto Press, 1962) is really Volume 1 of the present work, describing the sociocultural changes, mostly bad, brought about by the post-Gutenberg multiplication of printed matter, with its attendant stimulation of literacy. A gloomy work.

Understanding Media is more cheerful. It is about a fourth Age into which for over a century we have been moving more and more rapidly, with nobody realizing it except Mr. McLuhan: the Electronic Age of telegraph, telephone, photograph, phonograph, radio, movie, television, and automation. This is a return to the Golden Age but on a higher level, as in the Hegelian synthesis of thesis and antithesis. (Or a spiral staircase.) These new media are, in his view, making written language obsolete, or, in his (written) language, the Electronic Age "now brings oral and tribal ear-culture to the literate West [whose] electric technology now begins to translate the visual or eye man back into the tribal and oral pattern with its seamless web of kinship and interdependence."

This preference for speech over writing, for the primitive over the civilized—to be fair, McLuhan's Noble Savage is a more advanced model than Rousseau's, one equipped with computers and other electronic devices that make writing, indeed even speech, unnecessary for communication—this is grounded on a reversal of the traditional hierarchy of the senses. Sight, Hearing, Touch was Plato's ranking, and I imagine even in the Electronic Age few would choose blindness over deafness or touch over either of the other two. But McLuhan's 75 percent of new material includes a rearrangement to Touch, Hearing, Sight, which fits his tropism toward the primitive. He seems to have overlooked the even more primitive Taste and Smell, which is a pity, since a historical-cultural view based on them would have yielded at least 90 percent new material.

If I have inadvertently suggested that *Understanding Media* is pure nonsense, let me correct that impression. It is impure nonsense—i.e., nonsense adulterated by sense. Mr. McLuhan is an ingenious, imaginative, and (above all) fertile thinker. He has accumulated a great deal of fresh and interesting information (and a great deal of dull or dubious information). There is even much to be said for his basic thesis, if one doesn't push it too far (he does). I sympathize with McLuhan's poetic wisecrack about "the typographical trance of the West"—he is good at such phrases, maybe he should have written his book in verse, some brief and elliptical form like the Japanese *haiku*. It is when he develops his ideas, or rather when he fails to, that I become antipathetic.

One defect of *Understanding Media* is that the parts are greater than the whole. A single page is impressive, two are "stimulating," five raise serious doubts, ten confirm them, and long before the hardy reader has staggered to page 359 the accumulation of contradictions, *non sequiturs*, facts that are distorted and facts that are not facts, exaggerations, and chronic rhetorical vagueness has numbed him to the insights (as the chapter on Clocks, especially the pages on Donne and Marvell which almost make one forget the preceding page, which tries to conscript three Shakespeare quotations that simply won't be bullied) and the many bits of new and fascinating information: the non-English-speaking African who tunes in to the BBC news broadcast every evening, listening to it as pure music, with an overtone of magic; the literate African villager who, when he reads aloud the letters his illiterate friends bring him, feels he should stop up his ears so as not to violate their privacy.

If he had written, instead of a long book, a long article for some scholarly journal setting forth his ideas clearly—and once—Mr. McLuhan might have produced an important little work, as Frederick Jackson Turner did in 1893 with his famous essay on the frontier in American history. At the worst, it would have been Provocative, Stimulating, maybe even Seminal. And Readable. But of course he wrote the book because he couldn't write the article. Like those tribesmen of the Golden Age, his mind-set doesn't make for either precision or brevity.

"Mr. McLuhan has an insoluble problem of method," Frank Kermode observed in his admirable review of *The Gutenberg Galaxy* in the February, 1963, *Encounter*. "Typography has made us incapable of knowing and discoursing otherwise than by 'a metamorphosis of situations into a fixed point of view'; that is, we reduce everything to the linear and the successive, as computers reduce everything to a series of either/ors. And since he himself is unable to proceed by any other method, he cannot avoid falsifying the facts his book sets out to establish." He goes on to paraphrase a letter he received from McLuhan: "He says the ideal form of his book would be an ideogram. Or perhaps it could be a film; but otherwise he can find no way 'of creating an inconclusive image that is lineal and sequential.' " Alas. A writer who believes that truth can be expressed only by a mosaic, a montage, a Gestalt in which the parts are apprehended simultaneously rather than successively, is forced by the logic of the typographical medium into "a fixed point of view" and into much too definite conclusions. And if he rejects that logic, as McLuhan tries to, the alternative is even worse: a book that lacks the virtues of its medium, being vague, repetitious, formless, and, after a while, boring.

One way of judging a polymath work like this (or an omniscient magazine like *Time*) is to see what it says about a subject you know.

On movies, *Understanding Media* is not very understanding, or accurate. McLuhan is a fast man with a fact. Not that he is careless or untruthful, simply that he's a system-builder and so interested in data only as building stones; if a corner has to be lopped off, a roughness smoothed to fit, he won't hesitate to do it. This is one of the reasons his book is dull reading—it's just those quirky corners, those roughnesses that make actuality interesting.

▪ Page 18: "The content of a movie is a novel or a play or an opera." This suits a McLuhan thesis: "the medium is the message," the content of a medium is always another medium, so the only *real* content is the technology peculiar to each medium, and its effects. Many movies, especially Hollywood ones, are made from novels and plays. But many are not, and those usually the best. "Even the film industry regards all of its greatest achievements as derived from novels, nor is this unreasonable." (By "not unreasonable" McLuhan means It Fits.) "All" is the kind of needlessly large claim McLuhan often makes: common sense would suggest there might be a few films not derived from novels that are well regarded by the industry. In fact, there are many. I imagine that even Hollywood—which has given Oscars to Bergman and Fellini, after all—would include among the cinema's "greatest achievements" *Potemkin, Caligari, Ten Days That Shook the World, Citizen Kane, Intolerance, 8½, Children of Paradise, L'Avventura, Grande Illusion, Wild Strawberries,* and the comedies of Keaton, Chaplin, Vigo, Clair, and the Marx Brothers.

▪ Page 287: Pudovkin and Eisenstein did not "denounce" the sound film. Quite the contrary: their famous 1928 Manifesto begins, "The dream of a sound film has come true" and concludes that, if sound is treated nonrealistically as a montage element, "it will introduce new means of enormous power . . . for the circulation . . . of a filmic idea." Again McLuhan knew this, for he refers to the Manifesto, but he suppressed this knowledge for Systematic reasons.

▪ Page 293: "This kind of casual, cool realism has given the new British films easy ascendancy." On the contrary, British films of the last decade—as the chief British film journal, *Sight & Sound,* constantly laments—now stand low on the international scale. McLuhan makes this misjudgment because one of his theories is that "cool" media suit the Electronic Age better than "hot" ones—I'll explain shortly—so since British films are indeed on the casual-cool side, either they must be ascendant or the theory must be wrong.

An occupational disease of system-building that is perhaps even worse than the distortion of reality is a compulsion to push the logic of the system to extremes. The climactic, and much the longest, chapter in *Understanding Media* is the one on television. A happy ending: TV is reforming culture by bringing us the real stuff, tribal, communal, and analphabetic—none of that divisive book larnin'—and restoring the brotherhood of man. It is the finest flower of mankind's finest Age, the present or Electronic one.

In *The Gutenberg Galaxy*, McLuhan with his usual originality denounces the "open" society of individual freedom we have kept alive, with varying success, since the Greeks invented it. He prefers a "closed" society on the primitive model ("the product of speech, drum and ear technologies") and he looks forward, as the Electronic Age progresses, to "the sealing of the entire human family into a single global tribe." TV is the demiurge that is creating this transformation. Already it has changed things in many ways, most of them beneficial—I predict a brisk sale for the book on Madison Avenue. Among them are: the end of bloc voting in politics; the rise of the quality paperback (had thought Jason Epstein was the demiurge there, but maybe he got the idea from Jack Paar); the recent improvement in our criticism ("Depth probing of words and language is a normal feature of oral and manuscript cultures, rather than of print. Europeans have always felt that the English and Americans lacked depth in their culture. Since radio, and especially since TV, English and American literary critics have exceeded the performances of any European in depth and subtlety." Well, an *original* judgment anyway.); "the abrupt decline of baseball" and the removal of the Dodgers to Los Angeles; "the beatnik reaching out for Zen"; the picture window; the vogue for the small car; the vogue for skiing ("So avid is the TV viewer for rich tactile effects that he could be counted on to revert to skis. The wheel, so far as he is concerned, lacks the requisite abrasiveness." Skis seem to me *less* abrasive than wheels, but let it pass, let it pass.); the twist; and the "demand for crash-programming in education."

TV has been able to accomplish all this because it is not only Electronic but also very Cool. Hot media (radio, cinema, photography) are characterized by "high definition" or "the state of being well filled with data." Thus comic strips are Cool because "very little visual information is provided." He rates speech Cool ("because so little is given and so much has to be filled in by the listener"). McLuhan's own style, incidentally, is one of the Hottest since Carlyle: cf. the chapter headings: "The Gadget Lover: Narcissus as Narcosis"; "The Photograph: the Brothel-without-Walls"; "The Telephone: Sounding Brass or Tinkling Symbol?"; "Movies: the Reel World" (now reelly).

TV is the Coolest of medias because the engineers haven't yet been able to give us a clear picture. Or, in McLuhanese: "The TV image is of low intensity or definition and therefore, unlike film, it does not afford detailed information about objects." (You can say that again, Mac.) So the viewer is forced to participate, to eke out imaginatively the poverty of what he sees, like the readers of those Cool comic books—all very stimulating and educational. In the McLuhanorama, Picasso is inferior to Milton Caniff because he goes in for "high definition." Another virtue of TV is that it "is, above all, an extension of the sense of touch, which involves maximal interplay of all the senses." Touch would seem to me to involve *less* interplay than, say, sight, and I have always thought of TV as oral and visual. But touch is No. 1 in the McLuhan hierarchy of the senses and TV is No. 1 in the McLuhan hierarchy of media and so . . .

Watching TV is also gregarious—"the TV mosaic image demands social completion and dialogue"—with the spectators chatting while *Gunsmoke* flickers by, and this is also Good. (It doesn't seem to have occurred to McLuhan that TV may Demand Social Completion simply because there isn't much of interest on the screen.) How different are the passive, isolated, mute movie-goers, who must put up with clear, complete, and sometimes even beautiful images that give them nothing to fill in (Cinema is Hot) and no chance for creative or social activity. They might as well be looking at a Mantegna or a Cézanne or some other high-definition, nonparticipatory image. "Since TV nobody is happy with a mere book knowledge of French or English poetry," McLuhan writes or rather proclaims. "The unanimous cry now is 'Let's *talk* French' and 'Let the bard be heard.' " Unanimous cries I doubt ever got unanimously cried. But I do like that "mere."

I found two statements I could agree with: TV is "an endless adventure amidst blurred images and mysterious contours"; and "TV makes for myopia." For the rest, the chapter reveals with special clarity two severe personal limitations on his usefulness as a thinker about media: his total lack of interest in cultural standards (he praises Jack Paar because his low-keyed, personal manner is well suited to a Cool medium like TV—as it is—but has nothing to say about the quality of the material Paar puts across so Coolly); and his habit—it seems almost a compulsion as if he wanted to be found out, like a kleptomaniac—of pushing his ideas to extremes of absurdity.

The most extreme extreme I noticed was the millennial vision that concludes the chapter on "The Spoken Word: Flower of Evil?":

> Our new electric technology that extends our senses and nerves in a global embrace has large implications for the future of language. Electric technology does not need words any more than the digital computer needs numbers. Electricity points the way to an extension of the process of consciousness itself, on a world scale, and without any verbalization whatever. Such a state of collective awareness may have been the preverbal condition of men. . . . The computer promises by technology a Pentecostal condition of universal understanding and unity. The next logical step would seem to be . . . to bypass languages in favor of a general cosmic consciousness which might be very like the collective unconscious dreamt of by Bergson [Only McLuhan would see the conscious as "very like" the unconscious; in his case, the resemblance may be close.—D.M.] The condition of weightlessness that biologists say promises a physical immortality may be paralleled by the condition of a speechlessness that could confer a perpetuity of collective harmony and peace.

I think Madame Blavatsky would have envied the writer capable of the above paragraph.

—*Book Week*, June 7, 1964

Afterword

McLuhan began as a debunker of Madison Ave. and masscult in his first book, *The Mechanical Bride* (1951), and ended as a rebunker of both in his third, the one considered above. The transitional work, and his best book, was *The Gutenberg Galaxy* (1962). . . . Those still curious about Marshall's Meteor should consult two recent collections of critical (and uncritical) essays on the phenomenon: Gerald Stearn's *McLuhan: Hot & Cool* (Dial, 1967) and Raymond Rosenthal's *McLuhan: Pro & Con* (Funk & Wagnalls, 1967). Both are interesting in different ways. Rosenthal's is more solid to my exoteric taste. Stearn's goes in heavily for esoterica from the Master and his disciples, including a thirty-six-page coda in which the editor interviews his subject under the McLuhanesque title "Even Hercules Had to Clean the Augean Stables but Once!" (The above essay is reprinted in both collections.)

Readers of "Incomplete Nonsense" may be interested in McLuhan's reaction to it, which is in his grandest manner. "A number of critics suggest that your books are repetitious and, in Dwight Macdonald's words, 'ultimately boring,'" prods Mr. Stearns and gets, as usual, a two-page response which I found more interesting than the book. (As noted above, I think McLuhan is better at the hundred-yard dash than at the marathon.)

> Macdonald's is the kind of confusion that comes to the literary mind when confronted with a drilling operation [McLuhan begins]. Repetition is really drilling. When I'm using a probe, I drill. [So does my dentist, but he's less painful.] You repeat naturally when you're drilling. But the levels are changing all the time. Macdonald thinks *that's* repetition. There is a complete unawareness of what's going on in the book. His remark that the book might have been an article reveals another fallacy of the literary mind—that the purpose of facts is for classification. The idea of using facts as probes—as means of getting into new territories—is utterly alien to them. They use facts as classified data, as categories, as packages. [Rinse, please.]

Literally *Understanding Media* is a kit of tools for analysis
and perception. It is to *begin* an operation of discovery. It is
not the complete work of discovery. It is intended for practical
use.*

Most of my work in the media is that of a safecracker. In
the beginning I don't know what's inside. I just set myself
down in front of the problem and begin to work. I grope, I
probe, I listen, I test—until the tumblers fall and I'm in. That's
the way I work with all these media. [Page omitted.]

Macdonald (and other literary critics) have never thought
for one minute about the book as a medium or structure and
how it related itself to other media as a structure, politically,
verbally and so on. It's not peculiar to Macdonald. [Thanks.]

It's true of the entire academic world, of the whole journalistic world. [Seems to include everybody but M.M.] . . .
Classification, for the literary man, is the be-all and end-all of
observations. That's why Macdonald attempts to classify me.
. . . Most nineteenth-century minds are helpless in discussing
contemporary forms. . . . Macdonald has no verbal strategies
for even coping with the movies, let alone more subtle or
more recent forms like radio or television.

Admitting I have "a literary mind" (though McLuhan wields
a mean pen himself) I'd remark on the above: (a) I like that "even"
re. the movies, a medium I've been writing extensively about since
1929 (see *Dwight Macdonald on Movies*, Prentice-Hall, 1969, $9.95;
Medallion paperback, $1.50) without realizing I lacked verbal strate-
gies. . . . (b) My mind may be "nineteenth-century" (sometimes
I suspect it's eighteenth-century), but I'm as veteran a discusser of
contemporary forms as the Great Panjandrum himself, my preoccupa-
tion with mass media dating back to "A Theory of Popular Culture"
which I wrote for the first issue of my magazine, *Politics* (February,

---

* Brilliant, original, stimulating *Understanding Media* may be (at times and
in small doses), but a practical handbook it is not. Madison Ave. and the TV
industry pored raptly over the book and sat at the master's feet in plush
seminars, but the quality of TV gets lower every year. Or is that what the
book was intended to justify—to reassure the media boys that only "nineteenth-
century literary minds" worried about that archaic linear concept, "quality"?
The medium is the massage. If so, *Understanding Media* has been horribly
practical, judging by the decade of TV that followed its publication.

1944). In those days Marshall and I were lonely pioneers in that then still largely unexplored wilderness—we used to exchange notes on our peculiar "field" sometimes. My verbal strategies seemed to satisfy him in those days, but of course we were then on the same side (critical, worried) re. the mass media: cf. the piece he wrote for my "Popular Culture" department in *Politics* (September, 1946), or his 1951 *Mechanical Bride*. . . . (c) I like the safecracker metaphor—he's good at metaphors, being more a poet than a thinker—but I recall that when a professional yeggsman like Jimmy Valentine cracked a safe by listening to the tumblers, he had a very good idea of what was inside: something valuable. McLuhan is more the oil-wildcatter type, one hit in ten if he's lucky; most of the safes he cracks prove to contain canceled checks and confederate money.

Finally, my chief criticism of *Understanding Media* was precisely that its "spirit" was *not* "clinical" (which I take to mean detached and objective) but rather that of a rousing revival meeting.

Parajournalism,
or Tom Wolfe
and His Magic
Writing Machine

A new kind of journalism is being born, or spawned. It might be called "parajournalism," from the Greek *para*, "beside" or "against": something similar in form but different in function. As in parody, from the *parodia*, or counter-ode, the satyr play of Athenian drama that was performed after the tragedy by the same actors in grotesque costumes. Or paranoia ("against-beside thought") in which rational forms are used to express delusions. Parajournalism seems to be journalism—"the collection and dissemination of current news"—but the appearance is deceptive. It is a bastard form, having it both ways, exploiting the factual authority of journalism and the atmospheric license of fiction. Entertainment rather than information is the aim of its producers, and the hope of its consumers.*

Parajournalism has an ancestry, from Daniel Defoe, whose

---

* (1973) This paragraph much too dismissive. True about Tom Wolfe *e tutti quanti*, but in more talented hands, parajournalism is a legitimate art form. How could I have forgotten James Agee's *Let Us Now Praise Famous Men* (1942)? And Norman Mailer's early essays in the genre—his fact-fiction reportage on the 1960 Democratic and the 1964 Republican conventions— which later culminated in *The Armies of the Night*?

Journal of the Plague Year was a hoax so convincingly circumstantial that it was long taken for a historical record, to the gossip columnists, sob sisters, fashion writers, and Hollywood reporters of this century. What is new is the pretension of our current parajournalists to be writing not hoaxes or publicity chitchat but the real thing; and the willingness of the public to accept this pretense. We convert everything into entertainment. *The New Yorker* recently quoted from a toy catalogue:

> WATER PISTOL & "BLEEDING" TARGETS! Bang! Bang! I got 'cha! Now the kids can know for sure who's [sic] turn it is to play "dead"! New self-adhesive "stick-on" water wounds TURN RED WHEN WATER HITS THEM! Don't worry, Mom! Won't stain clothing! "Automatic" pistol is a copy of a famous gun. SHOOTS 30 FT. Water Pistol & Wounds . . . 59c. 40 Extra Wounds . . . 29c.

And there was the ninety-minute TV, pop-music, and dance spectacular put on at Sargent Shriver's official request, by a disc jockey who calls himself Murray the K, in the hope of "getting through" to high school dropouts about what Mr. Shriver's Office of Economic Opportunity could do for them. Some Republican senators objected on grounds of taste and dignity—the message was delivered by Murray the K jigging up and down in a funny hat as the big beat frugged on—but the program did stimulate a great many teen-age inquiries. It "worked" in the same sense that parajournalism does.

The genre originated in *Esquire* but it now appears most flamboyantly in the New York *Herald Tribune*, which used to be a staidly respectable newspaper but has been driven by chronic deficits —and by a competitive squeeze between the respectable, and profitable, *Times*, and the less substantial but also profitable *News*—into some very unstaid antics. Dick Schaap is one of the *Trib*'s parajournalists. "David Dubinsky began yelling, which means he was happy," he begins an account of a recent political meeting. Another is Jimmy Breslin, the tough-guy-with-heart-of-schmalz bard of the little man and the big celeb:

> Richard Burton, who had just driven in from Quogue . . . went straight for the ice-cubes when he came into his sixth-floor suite at the Regency Hotel. "Oh, I'd love a drink,"

he said. "Vodka." . . . "Humphrey Bogart," he laughed.
"Bogey . . ." Burton has his tie pulled down and his eyes
flashed as he told the stories. He tells a story maybe better
than anybody I've ever heard. The stories are usually about
somebody else. The big ones seem to have very little trouble
thinking about something other than themselves. His wife
kept hopping up and down getting drinks for everybody. She
has long hair and striking eyes.

Right out of Fitzgerald, except he would have made a better job of
describing Mr. Burton's wife.

But the king of the cats is, of course, Tom Wolfe, an *Esquire*
alumnus who writes mostly for the *Trib*'s Sunday magazine, *New
York*, which is edited by a former *Esquire* editor, Clay Felker, with
whom his writer-editor relationship is practically symbiotic. Wolfe is
thirty-four, has a Ph.D. from Yale in "American Studies," was a
reporter first on the Springfield *Republican*, then on the *Washington
Post*, and, after several years of writing tepid, old-fashioned parajournalism for *Esquire*, raised, or lowered, the genre to a new level. This
happened when, after covering a Hot Rod and Custom Car show at
the New York Coliseum and writing a conventional, poking-mild-
fun article about it (what he calls a "totem story"), he got *Esquire*
to send him out to California where the Brancusis of hot-rod custom, or kustom, car design are concentrated. He returned full of
inchoate excitements that he found himself unable to express freely
in the usual condescending "totem" story because he was inhibited
by "the big amoeba god of Anglo-European sophistication that gets
you in the East." At the ultra-last deadline, Byron Dobell, Felker's
successor at *Esquire*, asked him just to type out his notes and send
them over for somebody else to write up. What happened was a
stylistic breakthrough: "I just started recording it all [at 8:00 P.M.]
and inside of a couple of hours, typing along like a madman, I could
tell that something was beginning to happen." By 6:15 next morning
he had a forty-nine-page memo, typed straight along no revisions at
five pages an hour, which he delivered to Dobell, who struck out the
initial "Dear Byron" and ran it as was. A historic breakthrough.

The Kandy-Kolored Tangerine-Flake Streamline Baby is a collection
of twenty-four articles written by Wolfe in the fifteen months after

his stylistic retooling. It is amusing if one reads it the way it was written, hastily and loosely, skipping paragraphs, or pages, when the jazzed-up style and the mock-sociological pronouncements become oppressive. Since elaboration rather than development is Wolfe's forte, anything you miss will be repeated later, with bells on. He writes about topics like Las Vegas, Cassius Clay, Baby Jane Holzer, demolition car derbies, a pop-record entrepreneur named Phil Spector, and a stock-car racing driver named Junior Johnson. A good read, as the English say. The fifth and last section, "Love and Hate, New York Style," is more than that. He is a good observer, with an eye for the city's style, and he would do very well as a writer of light pieces for, say, *The New Yorker.* "Putting Daddy On" and "The Woman Who Has Everything" are parajournalism at its best, making no pretense at factuality but sketching with humor and poignancy urban dilemmas one recognizes as real. "The Voices of Village Square" and "The Big League Complex" are shrewd and funny social comments—not the bogus-inflated kind he makes in his more ambitious pieces. Even better was "Therapy and Corned Beef While You Wait," which was in the advance galleys but doesn't appear in the book. Doubtless for space reasons, but why is it always the best parts they can't find room for?

A nice little book, one might say, might go to five thousand with luck. One would be wrong. The *Kandy-Kolored* (etc.) is in its fourth printing, a month after publication, has sold over ten thousand and is still going strong. The reviews helped. Except for Wallace Mark-field in the *Tribune's* Sunday *Book Week,* and Conrad Knicker-bocker's penetrating analysis in *Life,* they have been "selling" reviews. That Terry Southern should find it "a groove and a gas" and Seymour Krim "super-contemporary" is expectable, but less so other reactions: ". . . might well be required reading in courses like American studies" (*Time*); "He knows all the stuff that Arthur Schlesinger, Jr., knows, keeps picking up brand-new, ultra-contemporary stuff that nobody else knows, and arrives at zonky conclusions couched in scholarly terms. . . . Verdict: excellent book by a genius who will do anything to attract attention." (Kurt Vonnegut, Jr., *New York Times Book Review*). *Newsweek* summed it up: "This is a book that will be a sharp pleasure to reread years from now when it will bring back, like a falcon in the sky of memory, a whole world that is cur-

rently jetting and jazzing its way somewhere or other." I don't think
Wolfe will be read with pleasure, or at all, years from now, for the
same reason the reviewers, and the reading public, are so taken with
his book: because he has treated novel subjects—fairly novel, others
have discovered our teen-age culture, including myself, seven years
ago, in a *New Yorker* series—in a novel style. But I predict the subjects will prove of ephemeral interest and that the style will not wear
well because its eccentricities, while novel, are monotonous; those
italics, dots, exclamation points, odd words like "infarcted" and
expressions like *Santa Barranza!* already look a little tired in his
recent *Trib* pieces. As Mr. Knickerbocker writes, "There is no one as
dead as last year's mannerist."*

The distinctive qualities of parajournalism appear in the lead to "The
Nanny Mafia":

> All right, Charlotte, you gorgeous White Anglo-Saxon Prot-
> estant socialite, all you are doing is giving a birthday party for
> your little boy. . . . So why are you sitting there by the
> telephone and your old malachite-top coffee-table gnashing on
> one thumbnail? Why are you staring out the Thermo-Plate
> glass toward the other towers on East 72nd Street with such
> vacant torture in your eyes?
> "Damn it, I knew I'd forget something," says Charlotte. "I
> forgot the champagne."

---

* (1973) Eight years later, I think my prediction was accurate. Perhaps because his style has become boring to himself, Mr. Wolfe has written, or at
least published, less and less of late years. He did edit a big anthology of what
he calls "the new journalism" recently, with a nervously assertive preface
staking out big claims to ultramodernity, but this I take to be whistling in
the dark. Those who can, write; those who can't, anthologize. . . . I must
admit, however, that a few years ago he did produce one indubitable parajournalistic triumph: *Radical Chic and Mau-Mauing the Flak Catchers,*
a long report on the famous "cause party" Leonard Bernstein gave for the
Black Panthers. It was as nasty, ungenerous, unfair, slanted, reactionary, racist,
fascist—take your pick—in viewpoint as it was successful aesthetically and
polemically. I mean that his observation was acute, his style under perfect
control, and his low-comedy kidding very funny in that exaggerated/grotesque
style we all admire when Dickens uses it on the Veneerings or Mr. Pecksniff.
Also that he had, I'm afraid, a real, solid sociocultural point, for once: there
was in fact a vast amount of bad faith, hypocrisy, and role-playing on both
sides; a false position all around; and Wolfe wolfed it up to the last bleeding
morsel.

The "knowing" details—Charlotte's malachite coffee table and her Thermo-Plate windows (and, later, her "Leslie II Prince Valiant coiffure") are fictional devices that remind me of similar touches in the young Kipling's *Plain Tales from the Hills.* But Wolfe, who has publicly promised to write eight novels by 1968* and the sooner he gets at it and gives up journalism the better, is no Kipling but a mere reporter who is, ostensibly, giving us information—in this case that there is a mafia of superior, British-born nurses who tyrannize over socially insecure Park Avenue employers like Charlotte to such an extent that they don't dare give a children's party without providing champagne for the nurses. This may or may not be true— he rarely gives data that can be checked up on—but if it isn't, I don't think we would be quite as interested. Unlike Kipling's tales, it doesn't stand up as fiction. Marianne Moore defines poetry as putting real toads into imaginary gardens. Wolfe has reversed the process: his decor is real but his toads are synthetic. Junior Johnson and Murray the K and Phil Spector and the kustom-kar designers are real persons—or so I assume—but somehow in his treatment come to seem as freely invented as Charlotte.

Stylistically, the above passage has the essential quality of *kitsch*, or a pseudocultural product manufactured for the market: the built-in reaction. The hastiest, most obtuse reader is left in no doubt as to how he is supposed to react to Charlotte with her malachite table and—later—"her alabaster legs and lamb-chop shanks . . . in hard, slippery, glistening skins of nylon and silk." As T. W. Adorno has noted of popular songs: "The composition hears for the listener." The specific *kitsch* device here is intimacy. Intimacy with the subject not in the old-fashioned sense of research, but an intimacy of style: the parajournalist cozies up, merges into the subject so completely that the viewpoint is wholly from the inside, like family gossip. "All right, Charlotte, you . . ." There is no space between writer and topic, no "distancing" to allow the most rudimentary objective judgment. Inside and outside are one. It might be called topological journalism after those experiments with folding and cutting a piece of paper until it has only one side. There is

* (1973) Five years after the deadline Wolfe's Three-Year Plan is 100 percent unfulfilled.

also an intimacy with the reader, who is grabbed by the lapels—the buttonhole school of writing. I've never met Jimmy Breslin but he often addresses me as "you"—in print.

It is hard to say just what Wolfe thinks of Charlotte, or of the real people he writes about. He melts into them so topologically that he seems to be celebrating them, and yet there is a peculiar and rather unpleasant ambivalence, as in his piece on Mrs. Leonard ("Baby Jane") Holzer, a rich young matron with lots of blond hair whom he says he made "The Girl of the Year" (that is, last year; there's another one now). I'm willing to grant this claim, but his piece seems to alternate between building up Baby Jane and tearing her down, damning with loud praise, assenting with not-so-civil leer. As for his readers, flattered though they may be to be taken so intimately into his confidence, made free of the creative kitchen so to speak, they are in the same ambiguous position. "Bangs manes bouffants bee-hives Beatle caps butter faces brush-on lashes decal eyes puffy sweaters French thrust bras" one article begins, continuing for six more unpunctuated lines of similar arcana and if you don't dig them you're dead, baby.

But there is one value Tom Wolfe asserts clearly, constantly, obsessively: old he bad, new he good. Although he is pushing thirty-five, or perhaps because of it, he carries the American teen-ager's contempt for adults to burlesque extremes. His forty-seven-page ode to Junior Johnson, "The Last American Hero," ends: "up with the automobile into their America, and the hell with the arteriosclerotic old boys trying to hold onto the whole pot with their arms of cotton seersucker. Junior!" He contrasts his teen-age tycoon, Phil Spector, with "the arteriosclerotic, larded adults, infarcted vultures . . . one meets in the music business." Even Baby Jane—Baby! Junior!—loses her cool when she thinks of all those . . . adults: "Now she looks worried, as if the world could be such a simple and exhilarating place if there weren't so many old and arteriosclerotic people around to muck it up."

Those ten-thousand-plus purchasers of Wolfe's book are probably almost all adults, arteriosclerotic or not, since there are so many of them still around mucking it up and also in a financial position to lay $5.50 on the line. So it's not a literal business of age—Junior and Baby Jane aren't exactly teen-agers. Maybe more like how you *feel*

sort of—"in" (new) or "out" (old)? I think the vogue of Tom Wolfe
may be explained by two *kultur*-neuroses common among adult, educated Americans today: a masochistic deference to the Young, who
are also, by definition, new and so in; and a guilt feeling about
class—maybe they don't deserve their status, maybe they aren't so
cultivated—that makes them feel insecure when an articulate young—
well, youngish—type like Wolfe assures them the "proles," the *young*
proles that is, have created a cultural style which they either had
been uncultivated enough to think vulgar or, worse, hadn't even
noticed. Especially when his spiel is on the highest level—Wolfe is
no Cholly Knickerbocker, he's even more impressive than Vance
Packard—full of hard words like "ischium" and "panopticon" and
heady concepts like "charisma" ("the [automobile] manufacturers
may well be on their way to routinizing the charisma, as Max Weber
used to say") and offhand references to "high-status sports cars of
the Apollonian sort" as against, you understand, "the Dionysian
custom kind." Or: "The people who end up in Hollywood are mostly
Dionysian sorts and they feel alien and resentful when they are confronted with the Anglo-European ethos. They're a little slow to note
the differences between topside and sneakers, but they appreciate
Cuban sunglasses." A passage like that can shake the confidence
of the most arrogant Ivy League WASP. Or this:

> The educated classes in this country [Wolfe writes in his Intro-
> duction] the people who grow up to control visual and printed
> communication media are all plugged into what is, when one
> gets down to it, an ancient, aristocratic aesthetic. Stock car
> racing, custom cars—and for that matter the jerk, the monkey,
> rock music—still seem beneath serious consideration, still the
> preserve of ratty people with ratty hair and dermatitis and cor-
> roded thoracic boxes and so forth. Yet all these rancid people
> [one assumes "ratty," "rancid," etc., are rhetorical irony but one
> can't be sure; with Wolfe for the defense you don't need a
> D.A.] are creating new styles all the time and changing the
> whole life of the country in ways nobody even seems to record,
> much less analyze.

The publisher's handout puts it more frankly: "Tom Wolfe describes his beat as 'the status life of our time.' As he sees it, U.S.
taste is being shaped by what were once its subcultures, largely

teenage. . . . He zeroes in on the new, exotic forms of status-seeking of a young, dynamic social class, 'vulgar' and 'common' to the Establishment, that has emerged since the war and that expresses the ordinary American's sense of form and beauty." No wonder the book is selling. In addition to appealing to our adult masochisms, it also promises a new sociology of taste. The postwar "culture boom" has greatly increased the number of Americans who are educated, in the formal sense they have gone through college, without increasing proportionately the number who know or care much about culture. There is, therefore, a large and growing public that feels it really should Take An Interest and is looking for guidance as to what is, currently, The Real Thing. The old *kitsch* was directed to the masses but the reader of Edna Ferber or even Will Durant would be put off, if only by its title, by *The Kandy-Kolored Tangerine-Flake Streamline Baby*, which is *kitsch* addressed to what might be called a class-mass audience, smaller and, educationally, on a higher level but otherwise not so different from the old one.

I don't think they will get their money's worth, for their *arbiter elegantiarum* is as uncertain as they are, his only firm value being old-bad, new-good. Not enough. It forces him to abstract "style" so aseptically from all other contexts that it becomes ambiguous even as a guide to taste. Writing of those kandy-kolored automotive aberrations, he drops names desperately—Miró, Picasso, Cellini, the Easter Island statues, "If Brancusi is any good, then this thing belongs on a pedestal"—but his actual description of them and of their creators runs the other way. "Jane Holzer—and the Baby Jane syndrome —there's nothing freakish about it," he protests. "Baby Jane is the hyper-version of a whole new style of life in America. I think she is a very profound symbol. But hers is not the super-hyper-version. The super-hyper-version is Las Vegas." Rodomontade, whistling in the dark. He doesn't explain why Baby Jane is not freakish or why she is a profound symbol of the new American style or why Las Vegas is a super-hyper-profounder one, and his articles on her, and on Las Vegas ("the Versailles of America") lead me to opposite conclusions, which he often seems to share as a reporter if not as an ideologue. His most extreme effort is his praise of Bernarr Macfadden's New York *Daily Graphic*: "Everybody was outraged and called it 'gutter journalism' and 'The Daily Pornographic.' But by god the whole thing had style. . . . Even in the realm of the bogus, the *Graphic* went after bogosity with a kind of Left Bank sense of rebellious discovery. Those cosmographs, boy! Those confession yarns!" But the "cosmographs" were merely faked news photos, the confessions dreary fabrications, and that dear old *Graphic* in fact *was* gutter journalism in which no kind of rebellion, Left or Right Bank, was involved. Wolfe's term for its subtle quality is "the *aesthetique du schlock*"—*schlock* being Yiddish for *ersatz* or phony—and it applies to his other discoveries in "the new American style." Oh, we're tenting tonight on the old camping ground!

There are two kinds of appropriate subjects for parajournalism. The kind Tom Wolfe exploits in the present book is the world of the "celebs": prizefighters, gamblers, movie and stage "personalities," racing drivers, pop singers and their disc jockeys like Murray the K ("The Fifth Beatle"), impresarios like Phil Spector ("The First Tycoon of Teen"), entrepreneurs like Robert Harrison (whose *Confidential* magazine, the classic *old* one [1952–1958] you understand, Wolfe salutes as "the most scandalous scandal magazine in the history of the world," adding: *"Confidential* was beautiful. This may be a hard idea to put across . . . but the fact is the man is an aesthete, the original *aesthete du schlock,"* who as a teen-age employee of the *Graphic* received the stigmata direct from Bernarr Macfadden) and pop-art-*cum*-society figures like Andy Warhol, Huntington Hartford (an antipop popper), and Mrs. Leonard Holzer.* The other kind of suitable game for the parajournalist—though not Tom Wolfe's pigeon—is the Little Man (or Woman) who gets into trouble with the law; or who is interestingly poor or old or ill or, best, all three; or who has some other Little problem like delinquent children or a close relative who has been murdered for which they can count on Jimmy Breslin's heavy-breathing sympathy and prose.

---

* Wolfe unaccountably missed Christina Paolozzi, a young Italian noblewoman who achieved celebdom by no more complicated strategy than stripping to the waist and allowing *Harper's Bazaar* to photograph her, from the front. But Gay Talese, an *Esquire* alumnus who now parajournalizes mostly in the *Times*—in a more dignified way, of course—includes her in his recent collection, *The Overreachers*, along with Joshua Logan, Floyd Patterson, Peter O'Toole, Frank Costello, and such.

Both celebs and uncelebs offer the same advantage: inaccuracy will have no serious consequences. The little people are unknown to the reader and, if they think they have been misrepresented, are in no position to do anything about it, nor, even if such a daring idea occurred to them, to object to the invasion of their privacy. The celebs are eager to have their privacy invaded, welcoming the attentions of the press for reasons of profession or of vanity. While the reader knows a great deal, too much, about them, this is not real knowledge because they are, in their public aspect, not real. They are not persons but *personae* ("artificial characters in a play or novel" —or in parajournalistic reportage) which have been manufactured for public consumption—with their enthusiastic cooperation. Notions of truth or accuracy are irrelevant in such a context of collusive fabrication on both sides; all that matters to anybody—subject, writer, reader—is that it be a good story. To complain of Wolfe's Pindaric ode to Junior Johnson that his hero couldn't be all that heroic is like objecting to Tarzan as unbelievable.

But of late Tom Wolfe has attempted more solid, resistant subjects. As his colleague, Mr. Breslin, might put it, he's been fighting above his weight. There was that front-page review of Norman Mailer's *An American Dream* in the Sunday Tribune's *Book Week* (which Richard Kluger edits in a more substantial and, to me, interesting way than Clay Felker's set-'em-up-in-the-other-alley technique with *New York*). As the French say, the most beautiful parajournalist cannot give any more than he has, and the only way Wolfe could explicate his low estimation of the novel was to jeer at the author's private life and personality—or rather his *persona*, this being the aspect of people Wolfe is at home with—followed by some satirical excursions on tangential matters like the ludicrous discrepancy between Mailer and Dostoevsky and the even more laughable crepancy between Mailer and James M. Cain. *C'est amusant mais ce n'est pas la critique.* Not that I disagree with his low estimate of *An American Dream.* Mr. Kluger asked me to review it and I declined for lack of time. If I had accepted, I should also have slated it but I don't think I would have thought of going into Mailer's personality and private life if only because there is so much in the printed text to criticize. But Tom Wolfe doesn't seem to be much of a reader.

A week or two later, he took on a subject of much greater mass and resistance: *The New Yorker*, with which he grappled in the April 11 and 18, 1965, issues of Felker's *New York*. The perfect target for two young(ish) men on the make with a new magazine competing for the same kind of readers and advertisers. Part One was headed "Tiny Mummies! The True Story of The Ruler of 43rd Street's Land of the Walking Dead!" It sketched in bold strokes, letting the facts fall where they may, an action painting of a bureaucratic, arteriosclerotic, infarcted organism that was dead but didn't know enough to lie down and of William Shawn, its editor, "the museum curator, the mummifier, the preserver-in-amber, the smiling embalmer" who took over after Harold Ross died in 1952.* The second part debunks the magazine itself: "For forty years it has maintained a strikingly low level of literary achievement"—compared, that is, to *Esquire* and the *Saturday Evening Post*. There is no space here to consider the truth of these propositions or the methods by which Wolfe attempts to demonstrate them beyond noting that, as a staff writer with an office at *The New Yorker* for the last thirteen years, I find his facts to be often not such, especially when some atmospheric touch depends on them; his snide caricature of Shawn to be a *persona* (convenient for his purpose) rather than the real person I know; and his evaluation of the magazine to be hung on a statistical gimmick it would be courteous to call flimsy. His "research" wouldn't get by the editor of a high school yearbook; and his ignorance of *The New Yorker*'s present and past—he thinks Ross was trying to imitate *Punch*—is remarkable even for a Doctor of American Studies.

Somehow Tom Wolfe has managed to miss a target broad enough to have profited by sensible criticism. He has also revealed the ugly side of parajournalism when it tries to be serious. What with his own reading block and Shawn's refusal to be interviewed— his privilege, I should think, perhaps and in fact constitutional right, cf. Justice Brandeis on "the right to privacy"—Wolfe was reduced to

---

* "Infarcted" sums up Wolfe's stance: "*Pathol.* a circumscribed portion of tissue which has been suddenly deprived of its blood supply by embolism or thrombosis and which, as a result, is undergoing death (necrosis), to be replaced by scar tissue." Necrosis! Scar tissue! Santa Barranza! Eeeeeeeeeee!

speculations on the nature of the magazine and its editor. These are
sometimes plausible, sometimes not, but they always fit into a pattern
that has been determined in advance of the evidence, like Victorian
melodrama or the political tracts we used to get from Germany and
Russia in the thirties.* It is not surprising that Wolfe got away with
it, making an instant reputation as a rebel and bad man which
didn't do any harm to his book later. The first resource of a parajournalist is that his audience knows even less than he does—and it
was a bold, slashing attack on a sacred cow, an Institution, the Establishment. That fellow Wolfe, he really gave it to *The New Yorker*!
David and Goliath. It's hard for the class-mass audience to see that,
today, Goliath is sometimes the good guy. He's so much less entertaining than David.

—*New York Review of Books*, August 26, 1965

---

* These are generalizations and parajournalism, which thrives on generalization, cannot be understood unless it is examined in specific detail. For such
an examination of Tom Wolfe's *New Yorker* Caper see my analysis of his
technique, from boldly asserted unfacts to rhetorically insinuated untruths, in
a forthcoming issue of this paper.

(1973) See the February 3, 1966, issue for perhaps the most complete,
certainly the most detailed debunking job I've ever done. Even my case-
hardened spirit began to falter (but managed to stagger on) as I discovered
the extent of Wolfe's imposture. Practically every inference was either in-
genuous or disingenuous, and almost the only actual fact was the magazine's
address. "Tom Wolfe doesn't tell lies," I concluded, because "he seems to be
honestly unaware of the distinction between fact and fabrication."

Egyptian Antiquities:
A Touristic Notebook

Foreword: In the fall of 1956, I traveled to Egypt for the first time. My mission: to report on "the Nasser Revolution" (it was shortly after the colonel's take-over of the Suez Canal) for Encounter, *of which I was then a temporary editor. Four days after I deplaned in Cairo, the Israelis sent their armed forces into the Sinai, to be followed shortly by the Anglo-French military occupation of Port Said. (Hungary was the other possibility we considered for this, my first and to date last safari as a foreign correspondent. We thought there was an interesting situation there, too. We were right on both.) My study of the Nasser revolution never got off the ground for obvious reasons, but I was immobilized for three rather edgy (for nonnatives) weeks in Egypt and, ever a tourist at heart, passed the time (when I wasn't pursuing interviewees, with indifferent success) seeing the sights.* *

Visiting the remains of Pharaonic Egypt is a trip to the moon: impressive, but no connection; only the Mayan ruins seem as alien. While I was in Cairo, waiting for the Eden-Mollet filibustering adventure to become history (of a sort), I

---

* (1973) Need I add I was appalled by the Israeli-Anglo-French armed intervention, which struck me as an anachronistic—and revolting—throwback to Kiplingesque colonialism? Yes? Then see my article, "Ten Days in Cairo," in the January, 1957, *Encounter.*

went out to the Pyramids and the Sphinx, spent a morning in the
Cairo Museum and two days at the vast Luxor-Karnak-Thebes complex of tombs and temples. I also roamed around Cairo, searching
out some of the famous old mosques that are buried, like forgotten
jewels, in the dusty, swarming city. The most impressive ones were
Tulun (ninth century) a great square of arcades with massive arches
supported on multiple rows of handsomely carved piers, the whole
effect severe and noble; and Sultan Hassan (fourteenth century),
four gigantic pointed arches enclosing a courtyard, with a large tomb
chamber. The decoration here is already more elaborate but is limited
to wide bands around the walls, which are plain; a few corners drip
that hideous stalactite decor, like a melting honeycomb, which later
will infest Arabic architecture. I also visited, across the street, the Al
Rifai mosque, a nineteenth-century pastiche that echoes Hassan but is
drowned in that vulgar overornamentation, that senseless prolifera-
tion of geometrical designs which blights Arabic buildings of the
last few centuries. The.Tulun mosque was centuries in advance of
anything in Europe, but in the last five hundred years the situation
has been drastically reversed. Tulun to Al Rifai is a capsule history
of the deterioration of Islamic culture.

Sightseeing conditions were ideal: there was nobody else about.
No riders for the rows of undulating camels and nervous Arabian
horses in the sheds near the Pyramids; no tourists, except me, to
disturb the millennial hush of Karnak; a scant dozen guests in the
huge pink Winter Palace Hotel at Luxor, whose corridors are as
wide as some London streets, eating in silence in the blacked-out
cavern of a dining room by flickering candles; no one else unpack-
ing his box lunch at the Thomas Cook Rest House across the river;
no other buyers for the real-genuine-antique carved fragments offered
me with dramatic furtiveness—real real-genuine-antiques belong to
the State—for three pounds, two, one, sixty piasters, forty, okay
twenty (four shillings); nobody else to be ferried across the Nile by
the grizzled Sudanese boatman in his tattered, catastrophic craft at
a *prix fixe* of fifteen piasters the round trip, the boat waiting all
day for my return, making his total earnings for the day (including
my ten-piaster tip) five shillings. It is a weighty responsibility to be
The Last Tourist. Also expensive: one is the only visible means of
support, the only cash customer, the only source of tips, the sole

target of all the highly skilled extractors of small sums that lurk, like piranha fish in a Brazilian stream, in the crevices of every Egyptian ruin; while each bite is minute, they come so fast and many as to reduce one's wallet to a skeleton in a surprisingly short time.

The Pyramids and the Sphinx. The oldest and greatest trademarks ever devised are twenty minutes by bus from downtown Cairo. They are technically in the desert, or at least on the edge of it, but it's not at all like the postcards. One of Farouk's "rest houses"—its courtyard has been turned into a public picnic ground—squats like a great brown toad literally in the shadow of the Great Pyramid. (It has been left as he left it, with its granite desk, translucent hollow alabaster columns with red lights inside them—sunset in the abattoir —and other expensive vulgarities open for public inspection at ten piasters a ticket.) Although the Sphinx and the Great Pyramid are surrounded by genuine authentic Egyptian sand, the whole area has been ravaged by the archaeologists, whose excavations give an effect more like a new sewer project than the eternal mystery of the desert. The Great Pyramid survives all this, rearing up majestically in shelving tiers over one's head, ocean-vast. (But it is the detached awe one feels before Niagara or the Grand Canyon, not the thrill of sympathy communicated by the works of man.) The Sphinx doesn't survive its squalid ambience. A village has grown up in front of it; the archaeologists have diligently uncovered its clumsy, botched-together brick body which detracts from the effect of the head; a Coca-Cola stand has ventured within a hundred yards of its right paw. Like so many monuments of ancient Egypt, including the Pyramids, the Sphinx is picturesque rather than beautiful, imposing because of its scale and hence best seen from afar. The back of its head, for instance, is a smooth round bowl, childish and graceless, more like a haystack than a head; the face is undeniably large but crude and trivial—the Mamelukes improved it by using it as a target for artillery practice: all its celebrated mystery comes from those scarred eyes, that shattered nose. . . . My visit was made pleasant by an elderly guide, agile and erect in his dark blue robes, who captured me with his opening line, under the Great Pyramid: "Shall we go to the top, sar? I took Professor Mark Twain, long time back,

1905 I think, he put me in his book, Mohammed Ali." He also claimed to have been chief hunting guide for Kitchener, Cromer, and Lawrence. I believed him. Or wanted to. I was determined to get *some* sense of the past from the place.

Luxor-Karnak-Thebes. An overnight trip from Cairo, £16 first-class round-trip, extremely comfortable sleeper. . . . Luxor temple, on the Nile bank, built between 1500 and 1350 B.C. by Amenhotep III and Ramses II, is practically an annex of the Winter Palace Hotel; a twenty-minute carriage ride away is Karnak, a half-mile-square jumble of temples begun by the Pharaohs of the Twelfth Dynasty (*circa* 3000 B.C.) and added to every now and then by their successors, all the way down to the Ptolemies; since the time of Breasted, Karnak has been the colonial sphere of interest of the University of Chicago, whose archaeologists, operating from a compound on the outskirts of the town, are still digging up parts of the great jigsaw puzzle and patching them together; as with their university's sociological tradition, the results are impressive quantitatively rather than qualitatively. And finally, across the river, is the even vaster necropolis of Thebes, hundreds of temples and tombs scattered for miles along the edge of the desert. . . . The general effect is a series of bombed and roofless museums. Like Cairo, it looks best from a distance, the strange sloping bulks of the pylons rearing up through palm trees, the coarseness of detail merging into awkward grandeur. . . . The ruins are an ugly yellow-brown, the original granite, limestone, sandstone, or marble being coated with several thousand years of dust. Photographs don't show this. . . . They also minimize the dilapidation by selecting the better-preserved details and vistas. The columns are battered, chipped, with often great holes gouged out; the statues are usually headless or with smashed features. One is appalled by the fury of destruction evident everywhere, like a shriek still resounding down the centuries. The colossal statue of Ramses II, weighing a thousand tons, the nose bigger than a man, lies in scores of fragments in the grass, shattered as if by dynamite. In a niche far at the back of an underground tomb, dark and lost, someone has patiently hacked away at the seated statues of a noble and his wife until only the scarred outlines remain on the wall, like shadows. Some of this devastation was done at the order of later Pharaohs, jealous of their predecessors, some by idol-hating early Christians, some by Persians, Romans, Arabs. . . . A few things give pleasure: the great Lotus columns at Karnak, as majestic and mysterious as in those romantic early Victorian engravings (which give a better idea, by the way, of Egypt than do most photographs); the handsome inner court of the Ramses III temple at Medinet Habu; the colored ceilings at Karnak and the gay painted walls of Der El-Bahri; the two seated colossi of Memnon, whose hooded, obliterated heads brood over the green fields;* one or two of the tombs of the kings where harmonious color and design have got the better of ritual needs; a few sculptures, such as a delicate-featured wife of a Pharaoh at Luxor (she is one-sixth his size, scale being always related to status and not to either art or reality). . . . But the general impression is at best fantastic, at worst grotesque. As the senseless repetition—why is a mile of sphinxes more beautiful than a single one? Why repeat the same colossal statue of Ramses III in front of *every one* of a dozen pillars? The effect is not rhythmical—as with repeated simple patterns like the egg and dart—because each item is complicated, full of distracting details. It is just overpowering, like a great deal of money. And the mass production! Those ram-headed sphinxes at Karnak, crudely carved by journeymen following a standard design, and an atrocious one—each kneeling sphinx has a small human figure (if one can call any of these stiff, one-dimensional statues human) wedged between its knees, awkwardly placed and out of scale. . . . These people were not artists, their minds were at once too literal and too abstract. . . . *Too abstract*: their art—there are exceptions, of course, especially in the earliest dynasties—lacks sensuous feeling for form and color; its primary aim is intellectual: to convey an abstract meaning; buildings are treated not as masses or even as surfaces to be decorated but rather as books, as blackboards;

---

* One of them is the celebrated "Singing Memnon" of the ancients, Juvenal's *"Dimidio magicae resonant ubi Memnone chordae,"* which was said to give forth musical strains at sunrise; ordinary tourists heard only one note, or none at all, but it greeted celebrities, like the emperor Hadrian, with two and even three performances. Modern investigators think the sound was either a priestly trick (there is a suspicious cavity in the lap, big enough to hide a man) or was produced by the expansive action of the hot sun on the night-chilled stone blocks. Nobody any longer thinks it was magic, and so the statue sings no more.

every wall, every pylon, even most columns, are written on, covered
with hieroglyphs, that strange mixture of art and alphabet, or with
bas-reliefs that are not decorative—that is, not adapted to the area
they cover—but communicative, monotonously the same in their
standardized elements, and designed merely to put on record the
Pharaoh's triumphs—to "get it down in writing." . . . *Too literal*: in
another sense, they were unable to get far enough away from life
to create art; the carved and painted victories, slaves, food, wives,
sports, divine relations of the Pharaoh were thought of not as symbols but as actually accompanying him into the next world to repro-
duce literally all the elements of his grandeur in this one; there is
something compulsive about this frenetic, ceaseless talking from every
surface about himself, with hardly ever a blank space (a silence). . . .
The Egyptians were the first graffiti artists. Instead of "Tony loves
Mae" they scrawled on their walls "Isis loves Ramses." . . . Re.
graffiti: they range from the chiseled comments of Roman travelers
to the latest Cook's tourist; twelve feet up on a column at Medinet
Habu is cut, in the elegant lettering of the period: "Sir B. and Lady
Chichester, Jan 4 1844"; America is also in the running—a few
courtyards away a lintel is neatly inscribed "H. H. Humphrey, Jan.
7, 1840, Boston, USA." . . . The brutality of the message often
matches that of the art—those endless rows of kneeling captives,
arms tied behind them, the trunk ending at the neck, painted along
the walls of the tomb of Ramses VI. Also disturbing are the people
merging into animals and vice versa, as the columns in Queen
Hatshepsut's rock temple at Der El-Bahri in which her head, form-
ing the capital, has the eyes and ears of a cow (to indicate her
descent from Hathor, the cow-headed goddess). This temple, incidentally, looks stunning in photographs taken from a distance, being
dramatically terraced into the cliffside, but on closer inspection the
stonework proves to be heavily restored and to resemble nothing so
much as a row of shower stalls. . . . Human use or enjoyment,
even the human vanity implied in trying to impress the spectator—
these were not the object of all this building, carving, painting. In
fact, the spectator is literally excluded. The temples were shut off
from view behind high brick walls, and only the priests were allowed
to enter. The tombs of the kings, rabbit holes hundreds of feet long
cut into the crumbling desert hills, broadening out at intervals into

spacious underground chambers, were richly decorated, crammed with treasures, and then sealed up forever and the entrances carefully hidden. But greedy sightseeing humanity soon began to ferret out the concealed entrances, to loot and gape; a dozen or so were well known to Greek and Roman tourists. In the twenties, only a few hundred yards from tombs famous since antiquity, Howard Carter and Lord Carnarvon opened up the still-intact tomb of Tutankhamun; and today there are electric lights and guide-rails. . . . The drive to the tombs winds up through desolation of desolation, hills of crumbling rock glowing palely against the intense blue sky, no plants, birds, insects (except one butterfly), the flinty shards drained of color by the brilliant brutal sun, oppressively hot even in November. In these ash-heaps, the ancient Egyptians, believers not in the divine right of kings but in the literal divinity of kings, buried their god-rulers; worshipers of the life-giving sun, they chose this place where light is death; materialists and ascetics at the same time, they lapped their kings in gold, surrounded them with treasures real and symbolic, and then raked the cindery rubble over them as if they were pariah dogs. . . . Yet life keeps breaking through. They forgot about tourists—and guides. There was the nice old one at Luxor who deftly parried my "I don't want a guide" with a reproachful, "I no guide. I be guardian here." But, although he confidently showed me Alexander the Great's bathroom and was equally positive about who had wrecked the temple ("The Roman when he come here he break all the statues"), his knowledge was mostly the usual, "Here God Ra welcome King Amenhotep, say he his good son." . . . Apropos guides, it occurs to me that they may be the first Egyptians for thousands of years to get into the driver's seat: "Come along now, sar, I show you——" One comes along.

The Cairo Museum. Mysterious sign at the ticket window: "The Clerk is Not Obliged to Give Change." Unmysterious sign inside: "Many Diseases Are Spread by Spitting/*therefore*/PLEASE DO NOT SPIT." . . . The guards not the usual elderly pensioners but restless young policemen, in white uniforms with blue berets, all with pistols, many with rifles also. . . . A great barn of a place, cluttered and musty and badly lit; only the Tutankhamun treasures are displayed with any showmanship. Most exhibits are not marked, and

some that are remain enigmatic: "Limestone head of a woman, of
very fine work. Although it is often published as one of the finest
examples of New Kingdom work, some consider, and with a certain
amount of reason, that it is a forgery." The museum is a vast attic:
the Egyptian climate preserves everything, so that one gets masses of
trivial, ugly objects that elsewhere are allowed to vanish decently
after a few centuries; as in an attic, one is at once fascinated by the
preservation of so many long-dead trivia and depressed by their lack
of interest. Like Swift's Struldbugs, Egypt is cursed with immortality.
Ex.: the rows and rows, twenty to a row, of practically identical
stone or clay foot-high mummy-effigies from Tutankhamun's tomb.
Ex.: those hideous mummy cases, built like Michigan State tackles
and decorated with dreary gaudiness. And one gets very tired of
statues of mummies with crossed arms. The idea of a statue of a
dead person is *echt*-Egyptian; it is easier to freeze in stone a corpse
than a live body and so much of this sculpture is frozen stiff (with
terror?). . . . They seem to have had no sense of boredom; the
same thing is repeated for thousands of years, the same rigid, for-
ward-facing, stiff-armed statues; one is labeled: "It is remarkable for
the fact that the right foot is advanced instead of the left"; some
Picasso of the Twelfth Dynasty (but his daring was exhausted in
putting the wrong foot forward). . . . The animals are often more
human than the people. That seated black dog with long pointed
ears standing up and long club of a tail hanging down. Or the
cats—yet, since ritual and not art was always the artists' aim, they
ruin some of the best by awkwardly placing a sun-symbol between
the ears. . . . Most of this art combines the defects of the religious
and the materialistic approach; it is religious in its ritual abstraction
(the art is subordinated to communication; most of these statues
are really useful objects rather than works of art) but it is materialistic in its emphasis on gigantism and on rich materials (so much of
it is really quite *vulgar*). . . . Some of the Tutankhamun treasures are
beautiful, but most would be commonplace were they not executed
in solid gold. And isn't there something a little repulsive in the
insane profusion of pins, brooches, bracelets, necklaces, amulets,
breastplates, etc., etc., possessed by Tutankhamun and his wife? One
gets the feeling they had them not for use and not even because
they were greedy collectors but simply because their status, their

royal duty required them to have all this stuff, for ceremonial not human reasons. There is something of this in any society, of course, but, like most things, it was overdone in Egypt. One feels sorry for the Pharaoh, the poor little rich boy, as for everyone in this death-obsessed society, where everything means something else, something abstract and not connected with human needs and pleasures, and where nothing, not even art, exists for its own sake. (I could never see why "art for art's sake" is sneered at as frivolous. For what better sake, then?) This, I think, is why Egyptian art is so alien to us. It's not a matter of historical discontinuity, since Egypt was part of the Greco-Roman world, China was not, and yet Chinese art seems familiar, while Egyptian doesn't. There is something unbalanced about this art, repeating its ritual obsessions for thousands of years unaffected by life—or art—like a neurotic so absorbed in his private magic (don't step on the pavement-lines) that he never looks up.

—*Encounter*, February, 1957

Mary Poppins
Is Not
a Junkie

To the *Editor*, New York Times:
I agree with your objections, aesthetic and otherwise, to the proposed Mary Poppins statue in Central Park—though I rather like the Alice group, "dangerously metallic plaything" though it may be—and I share your puzzlement as to why our enlightened and sophisticated parks commissioner should have okayed it. But why has no one raised the most obvious objection to commemorating this woman: that she was a domineering ignoramus who couldn't, or at least wouldn't, answer the simplest questions of her charges. Nor did she give them, as other semiliterate governesses often did, love and imaginative sympathy. For these qualities, Miss Poppins substituted the densest, dreariest conventionality backed up by authoritarianism: "It's right because I say it's right and button up your galoshes and come along *at once!*" Or words to that effect. When their perfectly reasonable questions become too pressing, she evades them by some silly trick like flying up into the air with her umbrella. (We know what *that* means!) They all fall for it, according to the book, and she establishes a charismatic dominance over her brood. But I wonder if the older ones didn't realize she was merely changing the subject, like any other stuffy grownup?

Miss Julie Andrews, than whom no living actress is more wholesomely democratic or democratically wholesomer, gave a rather different impression in the movie, but that's just Hollywood changing the subject. I sympathize with the author's reply when asked what she thought of the movie: "O-o-o-oh! . . . Let me be silent." She at least has the courage of her original texts, no matter how much cinematic marshmallow fudge has been poured over them. But what mean-spirited, snobbish texts they are—and that upper-class snobbery mated with lower-class snobbery makes it all the more depressing. "Mary Poppins is a junkie!" is a popular form of teen-age graffiti wit. If only she had dared that much!

Years ago I used to read books to my children and I remember how bogus and somehow unpleasant that Mary Poppins stuff came out—none of us really *liked* Mary P. very much, for all the magic she used to conceal her lack of either knowledge or feeling—and how quickly we gave her up for the adventures of that free-and-easy savant, Dr. Doolittle, a real intellectual type who loved to explain everything and did so most satisfactorily and charmingly. If we must have another brazen child-trap in Central Park, let it be a statue of the civilized doctor rather than the troglodytic governess.

—Dwight Macdonald, October 15, 1966*

---

* (1973) One of my numerous unpublished letters to the *Times*.

No Art
and No
Box Office

As has perhaps been observed
somewhere, Hollywood is a strange place. I visited it last fall [1958]
for the first time, to talk to Dore Schary about his new film version
of Nathanael West's *Miss Lonelyhearts*. I was prepared for the vast
horizontal scale—it cost me almost $5 to get from the railroad station
to my hotel—for the interminable white boulevards, the theaters like
mosques and the hamburger stands like castles, and the almost complete lack of pedestrians. I was prepared for my room at the Beverly
Wilshire, which had a black and white marble floor, Chinese bamboo
beds with gold silk canopies, a private patio, incredibly powerful air-
conditioning and television, and a closet the size of the hotel bed-
rooms I usually stay in. I was even prepared for Forest Lawn Memorial Park, courtesy of Waugh's *The Loved One*.

But it was at Forest Lawn that the new note first sounded. Culture.
Off-key, but definitely audible. I had not realized that every one of
Michelangelo's major sculptures is to be found there, full-scale and
executed in the most expensive Carrara marble by real Italian sculptors. Nor that the world's largest painting is there, a panorama of the
Crucifixion by "the celebrated Polish artist, Jan Styka." It is so big
that a large auditorium is devoted solely to its display, every hour on
the hour, with a recorded spiel of awesome dignity; the painting,

apart from its size, gives the general effect of a *Saturday Evening Post* illustration. Nor was I aware that there is a full-scale reproduction, in stained glass, of da Vinci's *Last Supper* enshrined in an aggressively Gothic structure which the management hopefully calls "America's Westminster Abbey" and which so far contains just three cadavers, including that of Carrie Jacobs Bond, composer of *I Love You Truly*. The spiel here, also in the loftiest good taste, implies that for all practical purposes this is the original *Last Supper*, since it was executed "from da Vinci's original sketches in the great museums of Europe" and is superauthentic and brand-new, as against that faded, much-restored thing in Milan. The Michelangelo statues are also now really the real originals, since they are much newer and whiter than those worn-out objects in Italy.

This high cultural tone persisted through my week's stay in Hollywood. I lunched at the Brown Derby with an English screen writer who regretted I was leaving too soon to meet Aldous Huxley, Christopher Isherwood, Gerald Heard, and others of the local crowd. I spent an interesting three hours with Stanley Kubrick, most talented of the younger directors, discussing Whitehead, Kafka, *Potemkin*, Zen Buddhism, the decline of Western culture, and whether life is worth living anywhere except at the extremes—religious faith or the life of the senses; it was a typical New York conversation. I visited the set of *Some Like It Hot* and saw Marilyn Monroe in black lace pajamas jump out of an upper berth eleven times, deliver one line, and then run dancingly off the set, with a charming mixture of deerlike grace and parody of deerlike grace, to perch on the lap of the man sitting next to me, who happened to be her husband, a playwright named Arthur Miller. I had an hour at Twentieth Century-Fox with George Stevens and another with Jerry Wald. Mr. Stevens, who was then working on *The Diary of Anne Frank*, is big, rugged-faced, slow-spoken; he looks like one's idea of a rancher; in common with everyone else I talked to, he was optimistic about the "new Hollywood" of independent producers that has broken the monopoly of the great studios and for the same reason: actors and directors, that is, artists, are now in the ascendancy at the expense of the old-style executive moguls like the late Louis B. Mayer. "It was hopefully thought, in the old days, that people didn't make films, that they were turned out somehow by an organization. But only an individual can make a picture. It can't be done collectively." He also felt—another general impression out there—that the grip of the Hays Office has relaxed and that it is now possible to treat more daring themes in a bolder way: "There will be a wonderful period for the movies in the next ten years." Jerry Wald, a plump, baldish, cigar-chewing producer who talks rapidly and freely on any topic, was also full of cultural optimism. His walls were lined with Rouault prints and other O.K. modern art products, and he had just finished a major production of Faulkner's *The Sound and the Fury*. "Mass audiences are hep now," he said. "There are twenty-five million college graduates. There's no such thing as highbrow and lowbrow any more. They get the best TV and radio shows. They can appreciate quality. I'm gonna do Lawrence's *Sons and Lovers* next and I just bought *Winesburg*." I suggested that *Ulysses* would make a splendid movie. "I got an option on it!" he replied instantly, adding: "It's basically just a father searching for a son. Universal theme!"

It is true that discordant notes may still be noted in the general harmony. "We never make a picture for the art houses," Mr. Wald stated firmly. "The most the art-house circuit can do is $600,000 and most pictures cost a lot more than that. You always try to make a *big* picture. Nobody deliberately starts out to make a stinker. Art houses are just a salvage operation for us." I suggested that some artists might prefer a perceptive audience to a big one. This didn't go down: "An artist tries to reach as many people as possible, don't he? He's not talking to himself." The twenty-five million college graduates marched in again. "Now you take Schary's *The Red Badge of Courage*—that was a flop and so it went into the art houses. I'd say it had superior intent, but inferior content." "Hey, that's *good!*" exclaimed Mr. Wald's press agent. There were other discords: a producer referring to "the Baumhaus school of art"; MGM spending fifteen millions on a remake of *Ben Hur*; a director describing a melodrama set in Israel: "We kick off with the Dead Sea scrolls." But the point is that they are discords. Ten years ago they would have been the tune.

With all this Culture proliferating in Hollywood, it is not surprising that Dore Schary, who has long had the modest distinction of being the leading intellectual among the top studio executives, should signalize his return to Hollywood, two years after his resignation as production chief of MGM, with an independent production of Nathanael West's *Miss Lonelyhearts*. But the new Hollywood, for all its fine cultural plumage, is not so different underneath the feathers from the old bird. Palm trees don't make Los Angeles an exotic city and options on *Ulysses* don't make Hollywood a sophisticated one. Just as the "psychological" Western is *au fond* the same sturdy old Model T that once carried William S. Hart into action, so this new production of *Lonelyhearts*, for all its "seriousness," is just another soap opera. It is painful to say this because I really wished Schary well on his return from Elba, so to speak.

It is also painful because I greatly admire West's novel, which seems to me a miraculously pure expression of our special American sort of agony, the horror of aloneness, and of our kind of corruption, that of mass culture. It is a prose poem, except that instead of being fuzzy and long-winded like most prose poems, which prosaicize poetry, it is rather a poeticizing of prose: sharp, stripped, laconic, every word counting—a masterpiece of omission, like *The Great Gatsby*. A chilling wind from the grave blows into one's heart from this anti-epic, which is uncompromisingly negative, with bitter wit mocking religion, love, ambition, the American Way of Life, humanity itself. Its protagonist is hopelessly split between love and hate and finally destroyed by his inability to resolve the conflict. He cannot love the people who write in to him for help in situations where there is no help—the noseless girl, the fifteen-year-old boy whose deaf-and-dumb kid sister has been raped—yet he feels he should love them. Sometimes he hates them: "He was twisting the arm of all the sick and miserable, broken and betrayed, inarticulate and impotent. He was twisting the arm of Desperate, Broken-hearted, Sick-of-it-all, Disillusioned-with-tubercular-husband." Nor can he love his girl, Betty, who is pretty, loyal, kind—and conventional: "Her world was not the world and could never include the readers of his column. Her sureness was based on the power to limit experience arbitrarily. Moreover, his confusion was significant, while her order was not." Counterpointed against Betty's stolid decency is the frenetic nihilism of his editor, Shrike, which he cannot accept either; and counterpointed against his affair with Betty is his frustrating and sordid pursuit of Mrs. Shrike, a romantic teaser, and his disastrous seduction of and by one of his correspondents, Mrs. Doyle, who betrays him to her crippled husband when he tries to bring the couple together again. The book ends with Doyle shooting Miss Lonelyhearts.

If the epigraph of West's novel might be Dostoevsky's "Hell is the inability to love," that of the film might be William Dean Howells' observation to Edith Wharton: "What the American public always wants is a tragedy with a happy ending."

This Mr. Schary has bountifully supplied. Doyle does turn up at the newspaper office to shoot Miss Lonelyhearts, but he is so overcome by Our Hero's sincerity and compassion that he cannot pull the trigger and staggers out, a sadder and wiser man. Even the cynical Shrike, who up to this point has been handing out a poor man's equivalent of the novelistic Shrike's destructive rhetoric, suddenly has a change of heart and begs Our Hero to stay on the paper. When O.H., though "deeply moved," insists on leaving (*with* his girl, of course, whom he is about to marry, of course, and who, of course, happily explains as she exits, "I believe in him"), Shrike gazes after O.H. with ill-concealed affection.

"I feel that pure tragedy, classic tragedy means that the hero can't overcome his obstacles because of his character, or maybe it's his destiny," Schary explained, apropos of this ending. "There is something inescapable about his doom. But I felt that dramatically Miss Lonelyhearts' life did not *have* to have a sad ending." Or, as the film's director, Vincent Donehue, explained to me: "Dore said he didn't believe the Christ figure had to be crucified." The idea of an uncrucified Christ is very American.

Yet Dore Schary is right. His film, unlike the book, does not in fact require a tragic ending, for the simple reason that about all the film has in common with the book is the names of its characters. Miss Lonelyhearts is now an undivided person, an idealistic young man who doesn't drink or smoke, who feels only a deep compassion for his correspondents, and who has no trouble at all loving his girl; indeed, Montgomery Clift and Dolores Hart are as wholesome a pair of young lovers as have come within camera range in months. Shrike (Robert Ryan) is still Shrike, though his tortured wild wit has been smoothed out to the conventional wisecracking of the tough newspaperman. (Hecht and MacArthur have a lot to answer for.) The conflict between love and hate has been brought up out of the murky depths of Miss Lonelyhearts' soul and neatly externalized by concentrating the good in him and the evil in Shrike.

Lonelyhearts is essentially a Western: the good guy arrives in town—or the newspaper office—tangles with the bad guy, and ultimately defeats him. (The tragic element in the Western is, however, omitted—nobody gets hurt.) The other characters have been similarly reduced. Mrs. Doyle, a grotesque in the book ("He made a quick catalogue: legs like Indian clubs, breasts like balloons. . . . Despite her short plaid skirt, red sweater, rabbit-skin jacket, and knitted tam-o'-shanter, she looked like a police captain") is now just another sexy slattern, to be "understood" as well as condemned. Mrs. Shrike ("She returned his kisses because she hated Shrike. But even there Shrike had beaten him. No matter how hard he begged her to give Shrike horns, she refused to sleep with him") has been cleaned up into a sad-eyed, gallant, noble wife (Myrna Loy) whose only interest in Miss Lonelyhearts is a (sad-eyed) maternal one.

"Fay Doyle is a tramp, so I had to change Mrs. Shrike," Schary explains. "We couldn't have two tramps in the same picture." And so for ten years his Mrs. Shrike has been expiating her single infidelity ("I was alone—I was drunk—you had betrayed me a dozen times"), patiently bearing Shrike's abuse, hoping against hope to win her man back. "Few of us get a second chance. Go to him, Justy," she counsels Betty, who has been so renamed for some deep Hollywoodean reason. "You never get a free pass to love, do you?" replies Justy-Betty, only to be topped by: "Some women like you, Justy, have to run after their second chance. Some, like me, have to sit and wait for theirs." Her ten-year vigil is rewarded in the happy ending: the last shot is of Shrike in the office, about to join his wife in Delehanty's bar where she is, as usual, waiting for him (patiently, nobly). He sees some flowers in a vase on a stenographer's desk, picks them up, and with a remote look in his eyes gently wraps their stems in copy paper and exits. The Shrike's marriage has been saved. Slow fade-out. The End.

In short, Dore Schary, who was the script writer as well as the producer, has performed the considerable feat of converting *Miss Lonelyhearts* into *Stover at Yale*. The usual excuse, sometimes a valid

one, that Hollywood makes for changes in some well-known book is
that they are cinematically necessary—it is a matter, after all, of trans-
lating from one medium into another. But this won't work here. The
film is about as cinematic as the proceedings of the American Iron
and Steel Institute.

A producer is said to have observed, years ago, explaining why he
could no longer go along with Paul Muni's series of re-creations of
such culture-heroes as Pasteur and Zola: "Art and box office, okay.
Art and no box office, okay. No art and box office, okay. But no art
and no box office . . ."

I wonder if Sir Laurence Olivier himself could have put over a
line like Ryan's: "Father Shrike, the encyclopædia on 'heels.' Subtitle: every man." Or Clift's: "Even now—full of guilt and shame—
the only clean thing I ever owned was my love for you." And Duse
herself might have been thrown by Miss Hart's line: "Has anybody
ever tried to figure out how many tears you cry in a lifetime?" The
characterizations in general are deeply rooted in the cornfield. Every
word assimilates them to that vast body of clichés that has been slowly
built up—as a coral reef is built by the accretion of tiny, identical
organisms—in our mass culture; a parody of a tradition. Shrike is
especially painful. His first words addressed to the barman ("Charlie,
a double of the usual stomach-lining destroyer") gets us right into
The Front Page groove, and he follows it up with other conventional
postures. *Cynical:* "Love and kindness—man is good? Take a bath,
Little Boy Blue, and wash off the eau de cologne." *Disillusioned:*
"Ah, yes, those years of peace, full of man's kindness to men, with
fascism and Nazism the fashionable purgative. We've come so far,
haven't we? It's now such a happy world." *Tough:* "You're as important to this department as my tonsils, which I lost some forty
years ago." *Witty:* "Mr. White is not available. He's gone to perdition.
Perdition, Nebraska." Adam, or Miss Lonelyhearts, is the other side
of the cob. "Adam is young," reads the script, "with a mind full of
hopes and dreams. But there is muscle to back up the hopes and the
dreams. Adam searches for truth, which at this point he cannot
define. But if he ever stumbles upon it, he will certainly be able to
identify it." Perhaps, but one wishes his mind were furnished more
substantially. He certainly has an odd idea of the newspaper game.
"It's dreary work," he tells Justy. "But in time a byline. And the
chance to write words that count." (Words that are counted would

be more accurate.) He and Justy go through the prescribed exercises of a Nice Young Couple, American-style. "You taste good, like orange," he tells her as they drink a carbonated beverage together. Later he grapples with the problem again: "I love you because you're possessive—a man wants to be wanted. [Rarely has the American male accepted his chains more gracefully.] And I love you for a long list of other things—because you're warm and soft in the right places—and your eyes are like cornflowers. . . . Am I too poetical?" Nathanael West's hero has rather a different style: "Betty the Buddha. You have the smug smile; all you need is the potbelly. . . . What a kind bitch you are."

It is all very strange. Justy is a replica of Betty—the only character, in fact, who is carried over unchanged from the book into the film —that is, a very nice, wholesome, pretty and conventional girl. But Justy is accepted at face value by Schary's hero, who loves and cherishes her, while Betty is sneered at, humiliated, and relentlessly analyzed by West's hero, perhaps because his mind is not furnished exclusively with hopes and dreams. Even more eerie is the way West's hero proposes to Betty: "He begged the party dress to marry him, saying all the things it expected to hear, all the things that went with strawberry sodas and farms in Connecticut. He was just what the party dress wanted him to be: simple and very sweet, whimsical and poetic, a trifle collegiate yet very masculine." This is precisely how Schary's hero presents himself to Justy, except that he means it, while West's hero doesn't, knows he doesn't, and is in fact in the last stages of schizophrenia. In the next, the final chapter, he becomes Christ, and is shot as he rushes to embrace Doyle "with his arms spread for the miracle." Schary's hero walks out into a new life with Justy on his arm: "We're going to start somewhere else, fresh." Why crucify Christ, after all?

"I see *Lonelyhearts* as a modern morality play," Schary says, "a good man who stands for something posed against Shrike's nihilism. It's an unconventional picture. I knew I wouldn't have any chases or much outdoor stuff, none of the sure-fire things. I didn't use color because it's a serious film, not just entertainment, and there's no mood music because it's a film of talk and ideas and I felt that music would intrude. I thought it would go if the talk were good enough." It isn't good enough, nor are the ideas.

"The reason movies are often so bad out here," Stanley Kubrick observed, "isn't because the people who make them are cynical money hacks. Most of them are doing the very best they can; they really want to make good films. The trouble is with their heads, not their hearts."

Schary was one of the few major Hollywood executives with a liberal record. The first script he sold in Hollywood, which he wrote in 1933 with Jerry Wald, of all people, was an indictment of the Hoover bread lines, entitled *The Public Must Eat*. Several years later he won an Oscar with his script for *Boys Town*, an inspirational salute to Father Flanagan's work, which was followed by two tributes to Thomas A. Edison, *Young Tom Edison* and *Edison, the Man*. His career as producer was marked by an extraordinary number of "message" films: *The Boy with Green Hair, Bad Day at Black Rock, The Hoaxters, Crossfire, Journey for Margaret, Joe Smith, American, The Next Voice You Hear, Blackboard Jungle*; most of them were more worthy than interesting. Jerry Wald calls Schary "a Don Quixote, constantly fighting the windmills of opposition." The irony is unconscious but accurate, for Schary's "message" pictures have a way of missing the real problem and tediously examining a false issue, as in *Lonelyhearts*. Dore Schary battles the forces of Mammon on behalf of the little man, decency, democracy, art, love, etc., but Mammon, whose name in this context is sentimentality, has put his seal on him, so that as an artist he is part of the enemy he fights as an idealist. For all his intelligence and good intentions, he has been so thoroughly saturated by mass culture—or, to use a four-letter word, corn—that he instinctively sees the world that way.

In reading Lillian Ross's *Picture*, one cannot but sympathize with Schary in his epic battle over the *Red Badge of Courage* with Louis B. Mayer, the symbol of all that was vulgar and mindless in the old Hollywood; one cannot but rejoice at his victory, soon followed by Mayer's enforced exit from MGM (which was itself, alas, shortly followed by Schary's ditto). Yet when the smoke cleared away, Schary had insisted on cutting out most of the scenes that the director, John Huston, had particularly liked and that the preview audiences had particularly disliked. So, too, *Lonelyhearts* originally ended with Shrike, as Adam leaves the office, turning to the audience: "He hasn't got a chance, you know that. In the market places of the republic, he'll be minced into hamburger. But, if he comes your way, give him a hand. He's a nice guy." (This was omitted before release.) In Henry James's story, *The Next Time*, it will be recalled, Ray Limbert tries to write a facile, sentimental bestseller but art keeps breaking through and he dies in poverty. Dore Schary's problem is in every way the opposite.

After he left MGM two years ago, Schary wrote an inspirational drama about Franklin D. Roosevelt's triumph over poliomyelitis, called *Sunrise at Campobello*, which he produced on Broadway (in collaboration with the Theatre Guild) and which became a major hit. He has just produced another play with the Theatre Guild: Leonard Spiegelgass's *Majority of One*, which concerns a Jewish widow (Gertrude Berg of "Molly Goldberg" fame on the radio) who goes to Tokyo and meets and is wooed by a rich Japanese industrialist (Sir Cedric Hardwick), and while one respects all efforts to reduce racial prejudice sometimes one has the feeling that things are getting out of hand.

Lonelyhearts opened in New York in February (and in London in June), got unfavorable reviews (quite a feat, by the way), and disappeared from its first-run Times Square house speedily and abruptly. Schary has no plans at present for any future movies. His professional base seems to have shifted to the theater. He is selling Schary Manor, his rustic-Tudor mansion in Hollywood, and he and Mrs. Schary are moving permanently to New York. "We felt strange in Hollywood when we went back last year," he says, "really out of things. I'd been in the top-level big-studio crowd, but now I found I was an outsider. We didn't like it at all." Despite its New York fiasco, the film may just conceivably do better in the provinces*— the mass public is a wayward creature—but it seems more likely that Schary's return from Elba will follow the historical script.

—*Encounter*, July, 1959

---

* (1973) It didn't.

Time,
Vol. 1, No. 1

Celebrated last month by potent newsmag *Time*, its fifteenth birthday. To each and every subscriber, a modest gift: a facsimile reprint of Vol. 1, No. 1. As *Time*nthusiasts avidly scanned it cover to cover, they were in high feather to note how scantly had changed since 1923 their favorite newsource. Ticklish indeed has been *Time*'s job as top-chop house organ for the American business community: to give the news an upper-class slant without appearing to violate the creed of "objectivity," or "Let's stick to the *facts*," which that class holds so dear. No one is more adept at this delicate maneuver than kinetic, bush-browed, twice-wed Henry Robinson Luce, founder and boss of *Time, Life, Fortune*. And no more striking evidence of his talent is there than Vol. 1, No. 1 of *Time, The Weekly Newsmagazine*.

Schooled for his high task at Hotchkiss and Yale, armed with fat checks from people with names like Harkness and Lamont and Iselin, young Harry Luce made his journalistic debut at a dramatically inappropriate time. Just as *Fortune*, founded to ballyhoo Success and the Romance of Business, appeared a few weeks after the 1929 market crash, so *Time*, born with a strong belief in the Divine Rightness of government by Business, materialized just as the Teapot Dome and other businesslike scandals of the Harding administration were beginning to ooze into the public press. This first issue of *Time* contains no hint of the widespreading corruption which five months later was to bring President Harding to his grave. Keynote of the "National Affairs" section is: Congress is about to adjourn—Thank God! The first article on page 1 begins: "Seeking only the nation's

welfare, Mr. Harding has suffered defeat at the hands of Congress."
It concludes: "Today Mr. Harding is prepared to draw a deep breath,
for Congressional politics will soon drop over the horizon. After a
short holiday in Florida he will gather about him the business men
of his cabinet and continue to manage the affairs of the nation,
untrammelled until a new Congress rises—from the West."

Thus smart young Harry Luce and his smart young editors got
off to an unsmart but impeccably businesslike start. In the rest of
their first issue, they give further evidence of their capacity to speak
for The *Time* Community. Specifically, they:

■ Give "three good reasons" why President Harding will not
call a special session of Congress during the nine-month recess: "1.
The President and Mr. Hughes can develop a foreign policy more
easily without Congress than with. 2. The new Congress will gen-
erate new opposition to the President in both home and foreign
affairs. 3. Business is happier when the Capitol is deserted. Legislation and rumors of legislation cause prices to fluctuate." (Best
reason of all, No. 4, not mentioned: lest Congress find out what was
going on among the "business men" of the Cabinet.)

■ Pay a sentimental tribute to "Uncle Joe" Cannon (whose portrait adorns the cover), onetime dictator of the House of Representatives: "He represents the Old Guard in the very flower of its maturity, in the palmy days of McKinley and Mark Hanna, when 'a little
group of wilful men' did more than make the gestures of government; they actually ruled Congress, shrewdly, impregnably, and
without too much rhetoric. . . . The American people . . . will long
for the homely democracy of Mr. Cannon, so often expressed by
those homely democratic symbols—Uncle Joe's black cigar and
thumping quid."

■ Pronounce a lengthy elegy over the notorious Theophile
Delcassé, most chauvinist and imperialistic of prewar French politicians: "A statesman whose diplomacy saved his country from ultimate destruction. . . . Without Delcassé France might now be a
German province and Foch a refugee."*

■ Settle the hash of two literary pranksters (James Joyce and
T. S. Eliot) in an article headlined: "Has the Reader Any Rights

---

* (1973) Sure enough, lacking Delcassé, France did become a German
province in 1940.

Before the Bar of Literature?" Excerpts: "There is a new kind of literature abroad in the land, whose only obvious fault is that no one can understand it. Last year there appeared a gigantic volume entitled *Ulysses* by James Joyce. To the uninitiated, it appeared that Mr. Joyce had taken some half million assorted words—many such as are not ordinarily heard in reputable circles—shaken them up in a colossal hat, laid them end to end. . . . *The Dial* has awarded its $2,000 prize for the best poem of 1922 to an opus entitled *The Waste Land*, by T. S. Eliot. . . . It is rumored that *The Waste Land* was written as a hoax."

▪ Demonstrate their objectivity toward literature by praising two serious authors. (No pranksters they.) A novel by one Gertrude Atherton called *Black Oxen* receives twice as much space as Messrs. Joyce and Eliot combined. "Valuable as an examination of social strata and their relationship," pronounce the editors, vaguely but respectfully. And a work by Arthur Train (of "Mr. Tutt" fame) called *His Children's Children* extorts their admiration: "Whatever the accuracy of its depressing picture of modern society, the novel is interesting and often extremely penetrating."

▪ Devote a full page to the implications for The *Time* Community of an advance of ½ percent in the Federal Reserve rediscount rate.

▪ Set down as an item in a column headed "View with Alarm": "A four to one vote to abolish the Wisconsin National Guard. . . ."

▪ Set down as an item in a parallel column headed "Point with Pride": "Castor oil, a cure for popular indifference to the polls." (A reference to the Mussolini technique, described in detail earlier in the issue.)

Thus in their very first issue the editors of *Time* struck and held the classic editorial note. Thus have they held it in the thousands of interoffice memoranda (disguised as magazines called *Time, Life, Fortune*) which for fifteen years they have been distributing among the high-priced, high-powered* executives who make up The *Time* Community. And thus will they continue to hold it, full and true, as long as The Community itself holds together.

—*Partisan Review*, April, 1938

---

* Also: shrewd, able, potent.

More Luce
than *Veritas*

Foreword: The following was part of a symposium on Time's *journalistic record as to accuracy that appeared in the January–February, 1964, issue of a Ralph Ginzburg enterprise called* Fact. *It's only fair to add that* Fact's *claim to that proud noun shortly proved—not to my surprise; Ginzburg is an enterprising chap who will bear watching in every sense—as tenuous as* Time's. *Cf. its cover story a few months later giving the results of its poll of psychiatrists soliciting opinions as to the mental condition of Senator Goldwater, the then Republican candidate for president. Most of the polled sensibly didn't reply but a deplorably large number (several hundred, as I recall) did pronounce horseback judgments, mostly unfavorable, on the psychological stability and competence of a subject they had never examined more closely than in a newsreel theater. The senator later sued* Fact *for libel and collected, as he should have, heavy damages.*

Dear Editors:

Thanks for showing me the issue of *Time* (April 4, 1949) with an account of the Waldorf Conference for World Peace. I've looked up my own account in *Politics* (Winter, 1949) and I find that it differs in important respects from *Time*'s account.

Time gives the impression that the American impresarios, like Howard Fast and Frederick Schuman, were ardently and monolithically behind the extreme anti-U.S.A. line of the Russian delegates (and of the American rank-and-file audience). My account, however, gives much evidence that the Conference leaders took a surprisingly moderate line. This was politically of the first importance—and quite unexpected—but of course *Time*'s story would have blurred its simplistic political line had this fact of life been admitted.

The most striking evidence of the demoralized state of the Party's more eminent fellow-travelers by 1949—the Waldorf Conference proved to be the last time that the American Communists were able to mount an impressive occasion decked out with big names— was the success with which a little group of veteran Communist-fighters-from-the-Left publicly challenged the Conference's good faith. It was an *ad hoc* group, and we called ourselves "Americans for Democratic Freedom." *Time* doesn't mention our activities, nor does it report (beyond a single reference to my own intervention) on the crucial session in which half a dozen of us (including Robert Lowell, Mary McCarthy, Jean Malaquais, Dr. George Counts, and myself) took the floor to ask awkward questions of the Soviet delegates present, notably the writer Fadayev and the composer Shostakovich. Nor does *Time* mention Norman Mailer's speech at this session in which he broke publicly with the comrades, to their immense confusion, since up to the moment he began to talk he was clearly the special darling of the pro-Stalinist rank and file. It merely lists him as one of the "familiar leftist names" who sponsored the Conference, a fact which had become a half-fact by the time he had finished speaking.*

A serious account of the Conference would have mentioned these developments, which foreshadowed the eclipse of the Communists as a factor in American political and intellectual life.† But

---

* (1973) For a detailed account of the Waldorf Conference see my four-page report, "Soviet v. American Intellectuals," in the Winter, 1949, *Politics*.

† (1973) Another indication of deliquescence in the Commie top cadres was the surprising invitation Mr. Fast (who himself left the Party a few years later, no winter soldier he—Citizen Paine must be haunting him) extended to us socialfascist wreckers, as the session broke up, to drop around at a little pay-party the comrades were throwing. We did so, curious and wondering—such gatherings had not hitherto welcomed the likes of us. It was a pleasant occasion but, for me, disappointing: the comrades looked and behaved and talked (if one followed the melody rather than the lyrics) just like my old Trotskyist comrades of 1937–1942. Apparently the only thing that had divided us all those years was a river of blood.

Time was playing cops-and-robbers and such reporting of the Bad Guys edging over toward the Good Guys would have destroyed the journalistic structure of its article.

The funny thing about *Time* is that Luce and Hadden built it on the rock of Facts, nothing but Facts, in the best American empirical style, although in lower-case fact, the fact is that there are Facts and Facts and that one man's Fact is another man's Delete. I'm told that Briton Hadden, who founded *Time* with Luce, was rather a cynic (see Noel Busch's amusing biography) but I arrived there shortly after his death. However, I did work with and for Henry Luce and I can state he was not at all a cynic but on the contrary a true believer in the gospel of All the Facts. I was never able to persuade him of the elementary truth that some choice of facts is always made, if only for space reasons, and that it is much better if one is aware of the prejudices according to which one selects the facts than if one assumes one has a godlike impartiality. This uncynical delusion of Henry Luce is why one has the same experience year after year with his newsmagazine: the degree of credence with which one reads any given news report is always in inverse ratio to the degree of knowledge one has of the situation that is being reported on.

—*Fact*, January–February, 1964

Luce and His Empire:
A Radical Critique
of a Liberalistic
Biography of a
Reactionary Tycoon

L*uce and His Empire* is one of those dinosaur biographies, more bulk than brains, we fact-obsessed Americans go in for. W. A. Swanberg has already given us all too massive tomes on Hearst, Pulitzer, Dreiser (a congenial subject, stylistically) and others. (O that this too too solid data would melt, thaw, and resolve itself into a form!) His life of the late Henry Robinson Luce is not definitive—definition isn't his thing—but it is undeniably big. His energy and scope as a researcher are either awesome or awful, depending on one's appetite for Facts, Unlimited. His seems to be insatiable, like some people's inability to resist just one more peanut.

What emerges from Mr. Swanberg's labors is a mass of raw material that will be invaluable to some future biographer who writes the illuminating book Mr. S. hasn't. Overwhelmed by his research, he shovels in cartloads of information that is trivial or repetitious or both, perhaps because he's dug them up and can't bear to waste them, perhaps because he assumes we want to know everything. As a thrifty writer myself, I sympathize with the first motive, but as an

easily bored reader, I find not even Luce that interesting. There's a lot
I don't want to know about him—which Mr. S. copiously provides.

As a critic, I'd say this indiscriminate plethora of detail destroys
the structure—or would have had there been one in the first place. It
isn't a narrative in time: the author skips back and forth chronologi-
cally like a clumsy antelope. Nor is the structure thematic either,
since the same themes keep cropping up haphazardly in widely separated sections: a modern *Tristam Shandy,* except that Sterne did it
on purpose.*

Mr. Swanberg does have some control over his material, but it is
an ideological not a formal one and the results are distressing. Speaking as a liberal who was radicalized by six years (1929–1936) as a
writer on *Fortune* and hasn't looked back since though maybe a
little sideways (I'd now call myself a conservative anarchist), I see
Mr. Swanberg's ideology as the conventional "liberalism" of 1935–
1960. (The quotes are to distinguish it from the real liberalism
of Burke, Tocqueville, Mill and other giants of a long-extinct species
—they stuck to principles and would have applied them to Stalin and
even to FDR.) Mr. S. carefully adjusts the lights, the camera angles,
and especially the closeups so that his Luce becomes a consistent,
and rather boring, heavy villain. The one I knew was more complex:
pulled one way by his respect for Facts, his personal decency, his
missionary idealism and his genuine intellectual curiosity and the
other way by his obsessive prejudices in favor of God, America,
capitalism and power, the last being the most damaging. He just
couldn't help adoring success whether others' or, worse, his own.
He was also a strange mixture of intelligence and ignorance, a noble
savage, perhaps because he was educated at the prewar Yale. (So was
I, a decade later, but Henry took the place seriously.)

So Henry—as he was to me then (his more equal equals called
him "Harry") in those simple patriarchal days before *Life, Sports*

---

* Had Mr. S. drudged on *Fortune* in his youth, as I did, he might also have
learned the great basic principle of organization: put everything on the same
subject in the same place. I remember, when an editor casually explained
this trick of the trade to me, that my first reaction was "obviously," my second
"but why didn't it ever occur to me?," and my third that it was one of those
profound banalities "everybody knows"—after they've been told. It was the
climax of my journalistic education on *Fortune.*

*Illustrated, Time*books and other grandeurs—struck me as an uncomfortably divided person but on the whole an attractive one. I really liked him—on the whole. Mr. Swanberg fully records the division—he records everything, fully—but the studio lights are always rigged to bring out the shadows.

He strikes the keynote, loudly, in Chapter I, which is a fifteen-page account of a state visit the Luces once made to Chiang Kai-shek. The details are as fascinating as those about any official visitation, and this one, as the author would be the first to admit, had no historical significance whatever. The opening shows why he made this nonevent the prologue to his nonbook: "When Henry Robinson Luce looked down on the muddy Yangtze on October 6, 1945, he had reason to feel exultation in the consummation of one of the great dreams of his life. China had won. Almost a half billion people, a fifth of all humanity, were saved for Christianity and democracy. . . . But his political jubilation was clouded by distress at a momentous decision of his wife Clare, the beautiful and astonishing Congresswoman from Connecticut."

Clare's decision was to become a Roman Catholic, we learn in a lengthy third paragraph that strikes my ear as out of key with the portentous beginning, like segueing from Gibbon to Winchell with no bridge. (Lord Macauley would have avoided such a pratfall, but he was a writer.) Also, to be tedious, could the first two paragraphs possibly be true? Was Luce's "jubilation," if it in fact existed, as he looked down at "the muddy Yangtze" in fact "clouded by distress" by thoughts of his wife's impending Catholicization? Who knows? Who can know? The author is hostile to Lucean journalism politically but not culturally. He uses the same tricks to create a spurious effect of reality—that knowing "muddy"!—he objects to when they are part of Henry's con game. And granted that Luce's lifelong obsession with the Generalissimo was absurd and deplorable, I don't think a less tendentious biographer would begin his book with a fifteen-page unchronological takeout on the subject. Nor would he devote sixty-five pages to the subject—it keeps popping up like King Charles's head.

Swanberg is a Pinkerton ("We Never Sleep") in exposing Luce's political sins (including one that as an illiberalistic libertarian radical I thought, up to Stalin's death, a venial one: his anticommunism) but he nods off when confronted by his cultural short-comings. Luce was impressed by Ortega y Gasset's "thesis on the mass mind" when he discovered it in the thirties. "These crowds, he says, will destroy civilization." Amen—I was impressed too by *The Revolt of the Masses*, though somewhat differently from Luce —or Swanberg. "Luce was determined to save civilization even if a little authoritarianism was necessary," ironically comments the latter. But his irony misses the big point, as always in cultural matters: that Luce was comically self-deceived about his relation to Gasset's "thesis on the mass mind" because he himself was as mass-minded an editor as the civilization-destroying crowds his journalism pleased—else he wouldn't have known how to please them. Like all masscult entrepreneurs, he succeeded by giving the masses what he, as well as they, wanted. The evidence is he enjoyed his magazines as much as the masses he sold them to. His standards were firmly based on their approval. Unexpectedly asked by a radio interviewer to answer accusations by T. S. Matthews in his memoirs that *Time* consistently slanted the news (Matthews should know—he was a top editor for fifteen years), Luce blurted out: "They aren't true! They aren't true! The answer is we have I don't know how many *Time* readers . . . ten millions anyway. . . . The proof is the fact that they continue to read it and renew it at a phenomenal rate."

The real horror of the Lucepress has always been more cultural than political: its crowd-catching, circulation-building formulae make truth almost impossible.* Luce was politically elitist but culturally

---

* I thought this was true even in the thirties, *Time's* sleaziest period politically, when the profascist (Franco, Hitler, and Mussolini were his *beau ideal* states-men) Laird Shields Goldsborough was kept on as foreign affairs editor right up to Munich. That caper finally convinced Henry that "Goldy" had become counterproductive, or inoperative, in terms of American national interests, so he reluctantly kicked him upstairs—a full two years after some of us *Fortune* liberals had tried to wise up Henry about Goldy and other rightist deviations of *Time*. Archibald MacLeish wrote an eloquent memo, to which I appended a thick dossier of examples.

One of them at least (this is from memory) was about style being as important as content in explaining the defects of the Lucepapers. I noted that the radiator of Léon Blum's presidential limousine ("Jew Blum" as Goldy

all too democratic. I'm the reverse—culturally elitist and politically democratic—while Swanberg is democratic both ways. So he shares the Lucean notion of culture—the more the merrier—and is his brother under that skin except that he says "the people, yes" and Luce said "circulation, yes." (I say "the masses, no.") Thus Swanberg has a page on the abortive attempt *circa* 1945 of one Willi Schlamm, then Luce's court astrologer (he impressed Henry with his pseudoculture and his unpseudo anticommunism) to add to the Luce stable an intellectualistic "little magazine." It never got beyond a prospectus; Luce turned, I imagine with relief, to creating *Sports Illustrated*. Our author suggests of course a political reason: that the potential highbrow contributors were turned off because they were his kind of liberal, that is anti-anticommunist. But they weren't: by then that vegetable was long out of season in such circles, I assure him as an insider. The real difficulty, not suggested by a single Swanbergian phrase—he always dozes off before such problems, as noted—was the corny style and philistine values of Schlamm's prospectus.*

I wonder if Swanberg's appetite for printed matter extended to my "Memo to Mr. Luce," not that it would, or has, made any difference. We're different breeds of cats—he's more the canine type—

---

often jovially called him) became an intruding "snout" when it got entangled with ("poked into" was Goldy's phrase) some right-wing *cagoulard* demonstrators who then attacked it and him. Such emotive anthropomorphization of auto parts, I argued, betrayed a virulent political bias and, worse, was lousy journalism.

That snout could poke into a leftist demonstration, too, and may well have in the superheated reportage characteristic of the late, unlamented *P.M.*, a reversed mirror-image of *Time* in news-slanting, which my managing editor on *Fortune*, Ralph McAllister Ingersoll, later published. with a Stalinoid staff, after he'd left Henry's employ and turned his coat 180 degrees.

* See my "Memo to Mr. Luce" in the October, 1945, *Politics*—reprinted in *Politics Past* (Viking/Compass, 1970)—in which I predicted that nothing would come of Schlamm's project and told why: "Time Inc.'s executive committee has made a historical miscalculation. Another generation or two of the kind of progress we are now making and it may be possible to attract the intelligentsia to a magazine whose editorial standards are derived partly from Brander Matthews and partly from Bernarr MacFadden. But the time is not ripe and so I suggest our executive committee [I still had some Time Inc. shares I'd acquired as an employee] wind up the enterprise, take the losses and confine Mr. Schlamm's flow of ideas once more to that audience they best suit: you, sir."

and he never quite gets me in focus—even though he nervously pats me on the head, twice, as "brilliant." He gets my Yale class wrong—it was '28, not '27—and at the end misstates the reason I left *Fortune*: "The brilliant young leftist Dwight Macdonald had just [spring of 1936] quit in anger over it [*Time*'s political line]." As noted above, I was angry about *Time*'s line, but I wasn't on *Time* and would never have thought of resigning on such a general and remote provocation. I was on *Fortune*, from which I did resign on a specific issue (I was also bored with Luce journalism by then, I must admit) namely, the junking of my final article on the U.S. Steel Corporation. It was a very critical, and very well documented, series and Luce had grimly printed the earlier parts despite pressure from friends (and original *Time* backers) in J. P. Morgan and Company, the Steel Corporation's bankers. But I drew large (though logical) conclusions in the last article. I headed it with a quote from Lenin to the effect that monopoly was the last stage of capitalism which "inevitably" leads to socialism and threw in for good measure a lighthearted profile of the board chairman, Myron C. Taylor, which suggested he had achieved his high position not because he had any business acumen or knowledge of the steel industry (he hadn't, in fact) but simply because he looked like a movie director's idea of the chairman of a big corporation (he did, in fact). I was looking for trouble and got it: the long-suffering Luce threw it all out and replaced it with a mealy-mouthed, back-tracking conclusion to the series by Managing Editor Ingersoll, who also ran up a more flattering portrait of Chairman Taylor.

The story is summed up fairly on pp. 253–255 of Robert Elson's *Time Inc.* (Atheneum, 1968), the first volume (1923–1941) of a company-financed history which is better written than *Luce and His Empire* and more objective. Swanberg read it—he refers to it in his Acknowledgments as "excellent"—but he still has me leaving *Fortune* because of *Time*'s politics. Really odd. Could it be that his reading is more extensive than retentive, also a mite tendentious like his book, so that, in all honest forgetfulness he absent-mindedly pinned on me a plausible motive that fitted his general point (that Luce was then profascist) rather than the actual motive that fitted the specific facts? Yes, it could be.

The author's bias further appears in his devoting half his book to the last third of Luce's life, which is much less interesting either biographically or historically than the first two-thirds, but which better fits his simplistic view of Luce as a reactionary stuffed shirt and worse. With the prurient detail, though not alas the wit, of a Saint-Simon he chronicles the global state journeys, the ever-more-pompously retrograde pronunciamentos, the petty intrigues in the Sun King's court. Dull, depressing stuff but not, I hazard, depressing to Mr. S. because it fits his gloomy thesis better than the first two-thirds of Luce's life. Maybe an ancillary reason for this disproportion, combining (research) business with (liberalistic) pleasure, is that there is a lot of wordage available, for obvious reasons, on the world-famous Luce of the fifties and sixties.

As Luce grew older:—he never matured, he was a Yale man of the Troglodyte period—his inner conflicts were not resolved, but rather smothered, by success. In 1950 he was a top-chop VIP: consulted by presidents, even Democratic ones, cosseted by the media, a Press Lord who not only made news but was news. He steadily became narrower in his sympathies and more doggedly retrograde in his politics. True, he backed off from Goldwater in 1964, but he wasn't, after all, senile.

The fact is Luce had made his one original contribution to (or subtraction from) journalism long before the fifties. Before *Fortune* —whose novelty lay solely in its romantic treatment of a subject hitherto considered hopelessly prosaic and not in its editorial "formula" or, God knows, its "house style" which was amateur-clever in my day and since then has risen, or sunk, to professional-sober—we knew a lot about writing but little about business (and proud of it), while they know a lot about business but . . . Also long before *Life*, which might have made a breakthrough had Luce been picture-minded, but he wasn't and it didn't—it was better than *Look* is all one (me) can say.

No, Luce's one original invention was *Time*, and even that wasn't his, mostly, but Briton Hadden's, his friend, partner, and rival from Hotchkiss through Yale to their cofounding of *Time* in 1923. Hadden was the onlie true begetter and licker-into-shape of that monstrous bear cub. It was just beginning to show its claws, and make money, when he died suddenly in 1929, of a streptococcus infection, at the age of thirty-one. The idea of a newsmagazine—

"terse, clear, complete"—to digest and organize each week the news for busy Americans who wanted to "save time" seems to have been worked out between them over some years, but in the first six years of *Time*, and the last six years of his life, Hadden dominated the editorial side—he invented *Time* style—while Luce concentrated on the business side.

They swapped around sometimes—Luce had been as much of an editor and writer in school and college as Hadden—but it was Hadden who must be credited, or blamed, for *Time's* editorial formula. The contrast between their personalities was dramatic. In every way but one they were polar opposites. Luce/Hadden: moral/amoral, pious/worldly, respectable/raffish, bourgeois/bohemian, introvert/extrovert, sober/convivial, reliable/unpredictable, slow/quick, dog/cat, tame/wild, efficient/brilliant, decent/charming, puritanical/hedonistic, naive/cynical, Victorian/eighteenth century.* The one important quality they had in common was an enormous respect for American-style success and a twenty-four-hour determination to achieve it.

If Hadden had survived, Time Inc. would look quite different today. For one thing, he was strongly opposed to *Fortune* because he thought business a dull subject and businessmen Babbitts. But he couldn't possibly have survived. His premature death was an accident but a historical one, i.e., necessary given the time and place. He was too individualistic, impatient, and irreverent to have collaborated with Luce in the drudgery of modern-style empire-building. Once he had created *Time*, his work was done, the fun was over—unlike Luce, he was easily bored—and it was time to die.

—*New York Times Book Review*, October 1, 1972

---

* (1973) A perhaps apochryphal story sums up the difference between them. "Look out, Henry, you'll drop the college!" Hadden drawled to his earnest *confrère* as Luce was purposefully striding across the Yale campus.

3

POLITICKING

Hemingway's Unpolitical
Political Novel

The publishers advertise *For Whom the Bell Tolls* as "the novel that has something for everybody." It is the biggest publishing success since *Gone With the Wind*: almost half a million copies have been sold and it is selling at the rate of fifty thousand a week; Paramount has bought the movie rights at the highest price yet paid by Hollywood for a novel, and Gary Cooper, at Hemingway's insistence, is to play the hero. The book has been praised by the critics, from Mr. Mumford Jones of the *Saturday Review of Literature* (who describes Pilar as a "Falstaffian" character and thinks it is "at least possible that *For Whom the Bell Tolls* may become the *Uncle Tom's Cabin* of the Spanish Civil War") to Mr. Edmund Wilson of the *New Republic*. It is seldom that a novelist gathers both riches and reputation from the same book.

In the face of all this enthusiasm, I have to note that my own experience was disappointing. The opening chapters promised a good deal: they were moving, exciting, they set the stage for major tragedy. But the stage was never filled, the promise wasn't kept. The longer I read, the more I had a sense that the author was floundering around, uncertain of his values and intentions, unable to come up to the pretensions of his theme. One trouble is it isn't a novel at all but rather a series of short stories, some of them excellent—Pilar's narratives of the killing of the fascists and of her life with the consumptive bullfighter; the description of Gaylords Hotel; Andres' journey through the Loyalist lines; and the final blowing up of the bridge—imbedded in a mixture of sentimental love scenes, too much talk, rambling narrative sequences, and rather dull interior monologues by Jordan. So, too, with the characters; they are excellent when they are sketched in just enough for the purposes of a short story, as with El Sordo, the dignified Fernando, and the old man Anselmo. But when Hemingway tries to do more, he fails, as with the character of Pilar, which starts off well enough but becomes gaseous when it is expanded.

The worst failure is the central character, Robert Jordan. Like previous Hemingway heroes, Jordan is not an objectively rendered character but simply a mouthpiece for the author. The earlier heroes had at least a certain dramatic consistency, but Jordan is a monster, uniting—or trying to—the nihilism of the usual Hemingway hero with simple-minded idealism—a sort of Hemingwayesque scout-master leading his little troop of peasants. For the Hemingway who speaks through Jordan is a Hemingway with a hangover, a repentant Hemingway who has been in contact with a revolution and has accepted it enough to be ashamed of his old faith and yet who cannot feel or understand deeply the new values. The result is that Jordan as a character is destroyed by internal friction.

Jordan's confusion is shared by his creator, and this confusion is the root of the failure of the novel. Although Hemingway himself denies it frequently in the course of the book, and although most of the critics take his denial at face value, *For Whom the Bell Tolls* is a political novel in that it deals with a political event, the Spanish civil war, and that its author takes a definite (though largely unconscious) political attitude towards this event. And it is a failure because Hemingway lacks the equipment to handle such a theme. Instinctively, he tries to cut the subject down to something he can handle by restricting his view of the war to the activities of a small band of peasant guerrillas behind Franco's lines (and hence safely insulated from Loyalist politics) and by making his protagonist—in Karkov's words—"a young American of slight political development but . . . a fine partisan record."

Such limitations negate the pretensions of the book, however.

Hemingway's peasants have been so depoliticalized that it seems little more than chance that they are Loyalists rather than Rebels, and so the long novel is reduced to the scale of an adventure story. As for Jordan, on page 17 he admonishes himself: "Turn off the thinking now, old timer, old comrade. You're a bridge-blower now. Not a thinker." But what can be more fruitless than to follow through some five hundred pages the thoughts of a hero who has renounced thought?   .

I think the novel is a failure for precisely the reason that many critics seem to like it most: because of its rejection of political consciousness. "The *kind* of people people are rather than their social-economic relations is what Hemingway is particularly aware of," writes Edmund Wilson in the *New Republic*, and it is clear from the rest of his review that he conceives of "social-economic relations" as somehow conflicting with "the kind of people people are." This false antithesis, between politics and "art," or even between politics and "life," attractive enough always to the empirically slanted American consciousness, is doubly seductive today when political creeds have been so discredited by the events of recent years. Mr. Wilson ends his review: "That he should thus go back to his art, after a period of artistic demoralization, and give it a large scope, that in an era of general perplexity and panic, he should dramatize the events of the immediate past in terms, not of partisan journalism, but of the common human instincts that make men both fraternal and combative —is reassuring evidence of the soundness of our intellectual life."

Of course, posing the alternative in these terms, one must agree that *For Whom the Bell Tolls* is vastly preferable to the "partisan journalism" of *The Fifth Column*. But there is another alternative, namely the treatment of revolutionary struggle as Malraux and Silone have treated it in their novels, on the level of political consciousness. Mr. Wilson describes Hemingway's political understanding as "not so highly developed as it is with a writer like Malraux," adding "but it is here combined with other things that these political novelists often lack." Just what are these "other things"? I find at least as profound an understanding of "the kind of people people are" in Silone and Malraux as in the Hemingway of *For Whom the Bell Tolls*. Far from there being an antithesis between these two kinds of understanding, the human and the political, in these European novelists the one illuminates the other and is integrated with it. Politics is simply one category of human behavior—to the novelist who is writing about a revolution, the most important one.

To Mr. Wilson, however, "politics" seems to mean the threadbare, vulgarized formulae, the treacheries and lies of Stalinism. Thus he actually describes the Hemingway of *The Fifth Column* as infused with "the semi-religious exaltation of communism," whereas in fact Hemingway in that period expressed the most tepid sort of Popular Frontism. And Mr. Wilson can write of the new novel: "Thus we get down out of the empyrean of Marxist political analysis, where the leaders are pulling the strings for the masses and see the ordinary people as they come." It has never occurred to me that the defects of *The Fifth Column* could be attributed to a too close study of the Marxist classics. And as for the leaders pulling the strings for the masses—Mr. Wilson should read again the passages in *For Whom the Bell Tolls* dealing with the necessity for "discipline," and with the "crazies," the Anarchists.

This misconception of the nature of politics leads Mr. Wilson—and others—to conclude that since Hemingway in *For Whom the Bell Tolls* explicitly rejects the political catchwords of Stalinism, he has therefore liberated himself from "politics" in general and from Stalinism in particular. Hemingway himself, whose conception of politics is essentially that of Mr. Wilson, seems to suffer from the same delusion. But those who see no further into a political program than its catchwords are likely to imagine, when they lose faith in the catchwords, that to reject them is also to free themselves from the program. It may be, however, that they merely become *unconscious* of their political values.

Thus it is precisely that lack of political consciousness which Mr. Wilson finds so admirable that prevents Hemingway from really breaking with Stalinism. Jordan "turns off the thinking" only to act the more freely in accordance with the very political formulae he has come to distrust so deeply as not to want to think about.

"Here in Spain the Communists offered the best discipline and the soundest and sanest for the prosecution of the war. He accepted their discipline because, in the conduct of the war, they were the only party whose program and discipline he could respect. What were his politics, then? He had none now, he told himself. But do not tell any one else, he thought. . . ." Hemingway tries to write a nonpolitical political novel and Jordan tries to participate in a revolutionary war and yet reject politics. But these are merely *other forms* of political thought and action.

"He would not think himself into any defeatism. The first thing was to win the war. If we did not win the war, everything was lost." Here we see a false antithesis, between thinking and successful action (thought leads to defeatism) similar to that already noted between politics and human reality. This corresponds in turn to the false antithesis made by the Stalinists in Spain between the task of winning the war (a "practical" matter which must be settled first) and that of creating a new society (a "theoretical" matter, to be left to the distant future, a sort of dessert to be enjoyed after the war). But there was no real antithesis between the two tasks: the war could have been won only by carrying through the social revolution.

I will be told that Hemingway directly attacks the Stalinists in his portrait of Marty and in his rendering of the cynical atmosphere of Gaylords Hotel. It is true that these represent a shift away from Stalinism—but of a superficial nature, like his rejection of the Party catchwords. Hemingway is at pains to indicate that Jordan's first reaction to Gaylords was naive, that war is an ugly business, and that cynicism may be permitted those who are really facing the realities and "doing the job." And Marty is presented as literally half-crazy, his lunacy consisting in a passion for shooting Trotskyists and Anarchists—thus attributing the settled and rational (from its viewpoint) policy of the C.P. in Spain as the vagary of an eccentric individual!

It is notable that in his attempts to define to himself why he finds it increasingly harder to believe in the Loyalist cause, Jordan often blames the Spanish national character (which he feels is treacherous, provincial, cruel, etc.) and sometimes even certain disturbing moral characteristics of individual Stalinists. But he never gives a thought to the really disillusioning development: the slow strangling, by the Stalino-bourgeois coalition, of the revolutionary upsurge of the Spanish masses. The most politically revealing thing in the book is Hemingway's vindictive picture of the Anarchists—"the crackpots and romantic revolutionists," "the wild men," or most often, simply "the crazies." One character thinks of them as "dangerous children; dirty, foul, undisciplined, kind, loving, silly and ignorant but armed." (This character is not Karkov or Jordan but the simple peasant lad, Andres, who might have disliked the Anarchists but would certainly not have disliked them in these drillmaster's terms—a curious example of how Hemingway sometimes violates realism to voice his own prejudices.) What worries Hemingway about the Anarchists is that they were undisciplined and armed, which is a good short description of the masses in process of making a revolution. His counterprescription is expressed in Jordan's evaluation of the Stalinist generals. "They were Communists and they were disciplinarians. The discipline that they would enforce would make good troops. Lister was murderous in discipline. . . . But he knew how to forge a division into a fighting unit."

I find it significant that the Communist Party seems to be undecided as to just what line to take towards *For Whom the Bell Tolls*. While the book has been roundly denounced in classic CP style in the *Daily Worker*, it is being sold in the Party bookshops. And Alvah C. Bessie in the *New Masses* writes more in sorrow than in anger, taking the line that Hemingway, while still sincerely enlisted in the fight against "our common enemy" (reaction), has been misled so that "at the moment he is found in bad company." The Party has evidently not given up hope of welcoming back the straying sheep into the fold at some future (and happier) date. I should say this is a shrewd political judgment.*

—*Partisan Review*, January–February, 1941

---

* (1973) It wasn't. We were both wrong.

Worldly Politics, or "Nobody ever Did Anything very Foolish except from some Strong Principle"

One of the most curious personalities of that great age of eccentrics, the early nineteenth century in England, was William Lamb, later Lord Melbourne, Prime Minister from 1834 to 1841. His Lordship is the subject of *Melbourne*, a biography by Lord David Cecil. Melbourne is now remembered not for any feats of statecraft—which, indeed, he avoided on principle—but for his original style of behavior and for his relations with two women: his wife, Lady Caroline Lamb, and the young Queen Victoria. Lady Caroline's tragicomic affair with Byron, in which she out-romanticized the great romantic until he fled in mingled alarm and boredom, seems to have permanently saddened her young husband, who continued to adore her in his unromantic way. But his position as the loved and trusted adviser of Victoria during the early years of her reign brought him only happiness—while it lasted. It was a strange conjunction—the prim serious young Queen, already gravid with middle-class virtue, and the elderly, cynical Whig, whose eighteenth-century rationalism showed up oddly in the dawn of the prim serious age to which his Queen was to give her name. And when the husband he had approved for her, the impeccably earnest Prince Albert, superseded him, there was nothing left for the aging Melbourne but to die, slowly and ungracefully.

On the surface, a sad life, and yet how free and pleasurable compared to that of most public figures of our own times, barring such aristocratic holdovers as Roosevelt and Churchill. "Be yourself" is for modern politicians even more difficult an injunction than the Socratic "Know yourself." Melbourne was intransigently himself. It was partly a matter of class and time. The British aristocracy of his day was supremely sure of itself, so sure that its members often behaved in public as most of us hardly dare behave in private.* By this standard, the present Soviet ruling class—stolid types like Malik and Molotov—are supremely unsure of themselves, which is no more than Melbourne would expect of their parvenu origins.†

The result was a remarkable number of "originals"—Execution Selwyn, who never missed a public hanging; and Monk Lewis, the Gothic novelist, who slept in a coffin; Beau Brummell, who spent two hours a day tying his cravat; Lord Brougham, at one time Melbourne's Lord Chancellor, who fortified his eloquence with port to such an extent that when he knelt in supplication, at the conclusion of his memorable (though unsuccessful) plea to the House of Lords not to throw out the first Reform Bill, he was unable to rise again until assisted by more sober colleagues. There was also Lord John Russell, the grandfather of Bertrand Russell and a man who carried

---

* (1970) Since this was written fifteen years ago, our young have also largely erased the distinction between public and private behavior. They, too, think of themselves as an elite—an antielite elite—and are therefore "supremely sure of themselves." So they express freely their negative reactions to law courts, congressional hearings, academic commencements, and other solemn public ceremonies conducted by their elders. . . . (1973) This is now inoperative.

† (1973) The Russians have loosened up—cf. Khrushchev's shoe-pounding, "We'll-bury-you!" antics at the UN and his uncorseted peasant joviality in sunnier moods; also cf. Brezhnev's genial clowning throughout his recent sales trip to the White House, as his joking about spilling a drink over himself— Molotov would have been embarrassed to death. . . . Nixon's demeanor was in vivid contrast to Moscow's supersalesman. He's surely our most socially insecure president; even before Watergate, he seemed literally scared stiff on public occasions. The all-American parvenu.

candor to a rare pitch. "On one occasion," Cecil writes, "he described to a friend how at a party he had left the Duchess of
Inverness to talk to the Duchess of Sutherland because she was
sitting further from the fire and he felt too hot. 'I hope you told the
Duchess of Inverness why you left her,' said the friend. 'No,' said
John Russell after a pause. 'But I did tell the Duchess of Sutherland
why I joined her.' "

Even in such an age, Melbourne was considered odd. "He is
certainly a queer fellow to be Prime Minister," Charles Greville
noted in his diary on July 15, 1834, when he heard the news of the
appointment, "and he and Brougham are two wild chaps to have the
destinies of this country in their hands." Melbourne's reputation as
an "original" derived from his rejection of social pretense; "a great
disdainer of humbug," Greville calls him. He was not afraid to be
thought stupid. "I hardly make out what Puseyism is," he remarked
apropos of the Oxford Movement, the existentialism of its day.
"Either I am dull or its apostles are very obscure. I have got one of
their chief Newman's publications with an appendix of four hundred
and forty-four pages. I have read fifty-seven and cannot say I understand a sentence, or any idea whatever." He was not even afraid to be
thought afraid:

> Soon after he went to Eton [Cecil writes] he had to fight a
> boy bigger than himself. "He pummelled me amazingly," he
> related, "and I saw I should never beat him; I stood and re-
> flected a little and *thought* to myself and then gave it up.
> I thought it one of the most prudent acts, but it was reckoned
> very dastardly. . . ."
> From this time forward, he made it his sensible rule never
> to fight with anyone likely to beat him. "After the first
> round, if I found I could not lick the fellow, I said, 'Come,
> this won't do, I will go away; it is no use standing here to be
> knocked to pieces.' "

Such behavior in a trueborn Englishman, not to mention a
public-school boy, was shocking to the contemporaries of Execution
Selwyn. Nor was his attitude toward honors any more reassuring.
"What I like about the Order of the Garter," Melbourne observed,
"is that there is no damned merit about it." At that, his liking was
not exactly passionate. When William IV pressed the Garter on him,

Melbourne refused it: "A Garter may attract to us somebody of consequence whom nothing else can reach. But what is the use of my taking it? I cannot bribe myself." This utilitarian view is again apparent in his comment on the crowds of would-be baronets who besieged him after he became Prime Minister: "I did not know that anyone cared any longer for these sort of things. Now I have a hold on the fellows!" An earl came to him demanding to be made a marquess. "My dear sir," replied Melbourne, "how can you be such a damn fool!"

Melbourne's "style" as a politician was never to behave like one. "On the most dignified public occasions," writes Cecil, "when everybody else was guarded or stilted, William Lamb talked exactly as if he were at home." Ever a late riser ("For recruiting the spirits," he told the young Victoria, "there is nothing like lying a good while in bed"), he often received official visitors and delegations in his dressing gown. When Sir Francis Head, who had just put down a rebellion in Canada, came to complain that the Government had not sufficiently recognized his achievement, he found the Prime Minister shaving. "I saved the Colony!" exclaimed Head. "And so you did," Melbourne answered, going on with his shaving. Presently he put down his razor and turned around. "But you see, you're such a damned odd fellow!" It seems never to have occurred to Melbourne that he was a damned odd fellow himself.

The American politician whose style most closely parallels Melbourne's was the late James J. Walker, New York's "night mayor." The milieus that produced Jimmy Walker—Tammany and Broadway—resembled Melbourne's in being small, provincial worlds by no means in awe of the larger world but rather contemptuous of it, and therefore affording a firm moral base for idiosyncratic behavior. Walker's wisecrack about his ponderously respectable antagonist, Samuel Seabury, was in the Melbourne manner: "Judge Seabury is a snappy dresser, too, but in a sublime way." And so was the opening sentence of Walker's reply, on behalf of the City of New York, to an attack on the five-cent subway fare by another dignified New Yorker, De Lancey Nicoll: "Gentlemen, that was the longest ride I ever had on a Nicoll." One may imagine a senior colleague of bright young William Lamb, M.P. for Leominster, addressing him as Al Smith, in 1925, addressed bright young Jimmy Walker, then

Democratic majority leader in Albany: "If you'd only cut out your tomfoolery on Broadway and watch your step, God only knows how far you'd go in public life." And the reply would be not unlike Walker's: "Yes, it's a great temptation to be like Mayor Hylan. A solid, substantial man. . . ."

Most politicians either do or pretend to do things; the rest "stand for" certain principles. In Melbourne's day, there were Canning, Palmerston, and Peel in the first category; the Duke of Wellington, that rock of Tory obstructionism, was in the second. Melbourne's openly stated rule was to do as little as possible. Nor, for all his temperamental conservatism, was he any Iron Duke: "Nobody ever did anything very foolish," he said, "except from some strong principle." As home secretary in Lord Grey's ministry, which in 1832 passed the first Reform Bill and thus began the modern era of British politics, Melbourne repressed the lower classes with lethargic efficiency while resisting the efforts of panicky noblemen to call out the military. As for Reform, he had little interest in it and less hope, supporting it only because he thought the bill would cause less trouble if it was passed than if it was not. (The avoidance of "trouble" was his chief, and often—it seemed—his only, criterion for political decisions.) During the long uproar over the passage of the Reform Bill, compared to which the stormiest days of the New Deal were halcyon, Melbourne's most memorable statement was "The whole duty of government is to prevent crime and to preserve contracts." A few years later, when William IV asked him to form a cabinet, Melbourne consulted his secretary, a raffish individual named Tom Young. "I think it's a damned bore," said Melbourne. "I am in many minds as to what to do." "Why, damn it all," replied Young, who seems to have modeled himself on his master, "such a position was never held by any Greek or Roman: and if it only last three months, it will be worth while to have been Prime Minister of England." This sporting view appealed to Melbourne: "By God, that's true! I'll go!"

The anecdote explains why Continentals have never been able to take the English seriously as a political people, and also why they are to be taken seriously. Only a race as much at home in politics as a fish is in water could be so offhand about it. Once he was installed in the position never held by any Greek or Roman, Melbourne avoided action with such success that the most durable fruit of his seven years as prime minister is the naming of an Australian city after him.

"The philosophers have only *interpreted* the world," the young Karl Marx wrote a few years before the elderly Melbourne died. "The point, however, is to *change* it." Melbourne thought just the opposite. With a happier, or at least a different, personal life, as Cecil notes, he might have become a minor Montaigne, a milder La Rochefoucauld. He had the essential knack for homemade philosophy—a lively curiosity about every aspect of life, and no conventional prejudices. Victoria set down in her diary many examples. Watching her pet dog lap up a saucer of tea, Melbourne mused, "I wonder if lapping is a pleasant sensation. It is a thing we have never felt." He rejected the prevailing romantic idea about larks and nightingales: "I can never admire the singing of birds. There is no melody in it. It is so shrill. That is all humbug: it is mere poetry." "There's nothing," he insisted, perhaps with a tactful thought about his royal pupil's appearance, "men get so tired of as a continued look of great beauty—very fine eyes, for instance; nothing tires men so much as two very fine eyes."

As for changing the world, Melbourne thought only mischief could result. "Try to do no good and then you won't get into any scrapes," he admonished the reformers who were constantly bothering him. "I say," he remarked to Archbishop Whately, referring to Wilberforce's agitation to outlaw the slave trade, "what do you think I would have done about this slavery business if I had my own way? I would have done nothing at all. . . . There always have been slaves in most civilized countries, the Greeks, the Romans. However, they *would* have their own way and we have abolished slavery. But it is all great folly." He also opposed the secret ballot, popular education, and the introduction of penny postage.

There was a perverse bravado about all this—"he was a better man than he affected to be," a Victorian biographer noted—and he did, after all, let the reformers have their own way when he felt it would be less bothersome to accept a strongly supported reform than to resist it. For he was conservative even in his conservatism. "I cannot think why a man cannot talk of penny postage without going into a passion!" he observed of Lord Lichfield, the postmaster general, who was sure that cheap postage would so stimulate correspondence that the post offices would collapse under the weight of letters. This moderateness of judgment also appears in his remark that if you really wanted to read at Eton, there was nothing to stop you. He was perhaps extreme when he complained, "I do not know why there is all this fuss about education. None of the Paget family can read or write and they do very well." But a century of popular education has not yet disproved his foreboding that "You may fill a person's head with nonsense which may be impossible ever to get out again." And if "shocking fellows!" is hardly adequate as a scientific analysis of those devious visionaries of the strong state, Mazarin and Richelieu, it hits the mark emotionally. One wonders what term Melbourne would have used for their twentieth-century descendants.

Melbourne raises some questions about the impressionistic school of modern biography. The classic style, exemplified by Plutarch and Dr. Johnson's *Lives of the Poets,* clearly distinguishes the data from the author's inferences and comment. But in *Melbourne* one is never quite sure what is fact and what is commentary. Thus Cecil writes, of Melbourne's effect on interviewers, "But then, looking up at him by chance, they would perceive, darting out beneath the half-closed lids, a keen glance that seemed to penetrate to their very hearts." Did a contemporary so describe Melbourne? If so, why not say who it was? If not, how does Cecil know about those half-closed lids and that heart-plumbing glance? Is not this the heightening of reality, the dramatic touching up, that Sargent did so cleverly in his portraits? One feels that Cecil is really a novelist *manqué,* that his personages laugh, weep, storm, dart glances, and otherwise comport themselves with the freedom properly granted only to fictional characters. The suspicion is increased by his trick of talking about the material instead of presenting it, like a guide who covers the "points of interest" with a patter that intervenes between the spectator and the object—that, indeed, often substitutes itself for the object. There is an extraordinary amount of intimate source material about Melbourne and his set. Byron, Lady Caroline Lamb, Queen Victoria, Melbourne's mother, and Melbourne himself kept diaries or wrote copious letters; there are also memoirs like those of Charles Greville and the family records cited in the Countess of Airlie's fascinating *In Whig Society*.

But while some of this richness gets into the book, much doesn't. The Byron–Lady Caroline affair, for instance, is more vivid in the letters of the principals than in Cecil's urbane rendering; more actual, also, in the studies of André Maurois and Peter Quennell, simply because they quote more and paraphrase less. Our author's gentlemanly vagueness is sometimes tantalizing. What was the "fatal disease" in whose "clutches" Melbourne's mother expired? Just what were the "unconventional methods" used by Head to suppress the rebellion in Canada? Cecil states that his hero "sometimes took the opportunity to gratify his more agreeable passions"; surely it would not have been vulgar, in a full-length biography, to be more specific. We are told that William Huskisson, a Whig leader, had "an unfortunate habit of falling down on the most embarrassing occasions," and not a word more. Later we learn that he "had recently let himself be run over by a railway train going twelve miles an hour"—nothing more, not even whether he survived. Independent research shows that he didn't, and that the accident happened during a public ceremony opening a new railroad line.

All this is not to deny that *Melbourne* possesses considerable merits, which doubtless account for its modest but persistent place in the bestseller lists. After the usual scholarly biography, written in barbarous academese and presenting large hunks of raw data untouched by human thought, it is a relief to come on something that has form and style. Cecil is at home with the language in a way that many English and few American writers are today. Describing the Prince of Wales, he can modulate from the colloquial ("He expected his friends to take part in every chop and change of his endless quarrels") to the Johnsonian ("the kaleidoscopic effusions of his preposterous egotism"), and both, I think, are effective. The book is, furthermore, an artistic whole, consistent and harmonious within the author's scope.

Unfortunately, the scope is limited and the artistry is secondrate. *Melbourne* is an inside job—the author's mother was the greatgrandniece of the subject—and it is cramped by the author's upper-class point of view. The intricacies of party politics and the personal relations of leaders are adequately presented, but only muffled echoes of the industrial revolution, amidst whose brutalities Melbourne made his career, reach these well-bred pages. To get any real idea of the suffering and degradation of the common people while Melbourne and his fellow Whigs and Tories were ruling them, one must turn to such books as the Hammonds' life of Lord Shaftesbury, the factory-law reformer, and Engels' *The Condition of the Working Class in England in 1844*. It is a somber background to Melbourne's charming personality, and one to which he was distressingly insensible.

The prologue, a justly celebrated bit of bravura impressionism depicting the world of the great Whig families, shows Cecil at his best and worst. It is done *con amore*, with the rich detail of a romantic snob—and it conveys no historical meaning whatever. We learn that "red Foreign Office boxes strewed the library tables" of the Whig magnates, but not what was in them. We are fully informed about their conversations, country houses, balls and bastards, but told so little of their politics that it is not even clear how they differed from the Tories. There is more icing than cake.

Nor is the icing of the best quality. Considering the high literary gloss our author tries for, he is remarkably prone to cliché. Reaction is blind, hope gnaws, emotions are pent up until they pour forth, increase is by leaps and bounds, ordeals are protracted, mobs are roused to frenzy, candles gutter pale in the light of the dawn, stony hearts are melted, and patience reaps its reward. Climaxes are too often in the forcible-feeble style; the first half of the book ends, "Smiling, indolent, and inscrutable he lay, a pawn in the hands of fortune." The picture of the Whig world concludes, "The whole social life of the period shines down the perspective of history like some masterpiece of natural art—a prize bloom, nurtured in shelter and sunshine and the richest soil, the result of generations of breeding and blending, that spreads itself to the open sky in strength and beauty." Eloquent but overblown. Lytton Strachey, whom Cecil has acknowledged as his master, did this sort of thing better, with more wit and less schmalz.

—*The New Yorker*, March 12, 1955

The
Mills Method

In *White Collar: the American Middle Classes* (Oxford, 1951) C. Wright Mills' theme is the rise of the "new" American middle class: office workers, executives, government employees, salaried professionals, salesgirls, and other service workers. The "old" middle class are independent free-enterprisers, exploiting either their own property (farmers and businessmen who own their own farms and businesses) or their own talents on a free-lance basis (self-employed lawyers, engineers, writers, doctors, etc.). The "new" work, for wages or salary, for somebody else; it might be called a salariat and is more significant today in this country than is Marx's concept of a proletariat. Mills estimates that between 1870 and 1940 the "new" has increased from 15 percent to 56 percent of the total middle classes, while the "old" has sunk from 95 percent to 44 percent. Since both the fact of this shift and its general implications have long been familiar, the point of Mills' book must lie elsewhere.

He might have given us a good description of the "new" middle class, the sort of thing the Lynds did in *Middletown*. Or, following Veblen, an aesthetic impression and a moral evaluation. Or, as Marx did in the first volume of *Capital*, both of these within the frame of a new historical interpretation. Indeed, he has attempted all three, but with an unexpected lack of success. Unexpected because he has written some excellent things in the past, has done a lot of sociological field work, is well versed in theory, and, himself, is a lively, intelligent, irreverent, omnivorous fellow, the least academic professor I know. Yet I must confess I found his book boring to the point of unreadability. Of course this may be my fault. But it may also be his.

As a descriptive sociologist, Mills fails because he is forever getting in the way of his data, like an M.C. who talks through the acts. *Middletown* was interesting not because of any literary talent or power of generalization, but simply because the authors respected their material: they let it speak for itself, giving it in great crude unrefined hunks. But Mills pokes and pulls and prods his data, "processing" it so relentlessly that its intrinsic quality is vitiated. I'm told that in preparing the book, he and his wife collected a number of long and interesting "depth interviews" with typical middle-class people and that at one point he thought of giving a lot of space to these. I wish he had. Here we get only *membra disjecta*, a few sentences here and there, plucked out to illustrate a special point. It is Professor Mills lecturing, with exhibits; it is the radio M.C. who gives the contestant fifteen seconds to tell why he got married.

However, the author is at least democratic: he treats his peers with an equal lack of respect. Just about "everybody" is quoted, usually once: Péguy and Proudhon, Kafka and Kautsky and Kierkegaard, Reich (W., on repression) and Rahv (P., on alienation). As an attempt to broaden the usual academic bounds, this is praiseworthy. But many of the quotes seem rather dragged-in, as if to adorn the argument with the plumes of the culturally chic, and most are mere snippets, a sentence or even a phrase or two tailored to fit the author's needs of the moment. Nor does he give any references, so one cannot tell where or when these truncated remarks were uttered, thus stripping them of their identity and reducing them to bricks in *his* wall.

Like Veblen, Mills mixes moral judgments and aesthetic impressions into his sociology, an old-fashioned custom it's good to see revived. He makes it clear he thinks ill of the culture and the style of life of the middle classes, and he prophesies ruin and disaster. He is right, though the gloom is overdone in the heavy Marxist-apocalyptic style. But he fails to plant these legitimate points in the reader's imagination because he lacks the special talents for the job, talents which Veblen so abundantly had: a sensibility that can select the essential details, and an expressive prose style. His book is cluttered with miscellaneous information, with facts and references that just get in each other's way and trip each other up; one reason he doesn't give, as noted above, enough space to any one thing to let it make its own authentic impression is that he can't because he touches briefly on so many things. Perhaps the chief trouble with the book, certainly what makes it hard to read, is the style, which is inexpressive and monotonous in a vigorous way. It seems almost deliberately designed to keep the writer at a distance from both his material and his readers.

For one thing, it is horribly abstract. I can take a certain number of abstract words in a sentence and still keep my bearings, but when they multiply without being anchored to some concrete word, then my attention wanders. Thus I find the following sentence impenetrable, not because of any subtlety or complexity of thought but simply because I get lost in the terminology: "To the economic facts of abundance, the rise in real standards of living, and the upward mobility, there was added a relatively fluid system of deference in a rising status market." And when the abstract is wedded to the self-obvious, then one is not only baffled but also irritated. Viz.: "Political consciousness is most immediately determined by politically available means and symbols." It is not *just* a question of abstract terminology: Veblen used plenty, as does Marx, without ceasing to communicate pleasurably. But their styles express their own personalities, and a person is not abstract but concrete and thus comprehensible, since the reader is also a person. But Mills' personality, which as a matter of fact is quite pungent, comes through not at all in his writing, at least in this book; here he wears the drab uniform of the academic sociologist, and expresses, or rather suppresses, himself as conventionally as his colleagues do. He does make fitful efforts to be literary and "brilliant," but these are just changes of uniform: sociologese is replaced by journalese. And not very good journalese, because he hasn't a good ear. "In the main drift of this structure"—but a structure doesn't drift, it stands still. "The mass media hold a monopoly of the ideologically dead: they spin records of political emptiness"—the parts just don't fit together, verbally.

Mills says a little about a great many things, so little and about so many that one's curiosity is never really satisfied. Instead of developing—or, sometimes, even defining—his leading concepts, he plays with them, he, so to speak, "refers" to them, arranging and rearranging them but neither giving an adequate description of the reality which these concepts are, after all, just a shorthand way of talking about, nor working out logically the relations of these concepts among themselves.

Thus he makes great play with the term "bureaucracy," and yet, though he himself has written much about it in the past and though it is so much used, and abused, today that one cannot be sure what it means to any writer unless he tells one explicitly, the nearest he comes to defining it is a couple of sentences on page 78 which raise more questions than they answer. So too, with "prestige," another of his key concepts. Here, true, he leads off with a definition—but what a definition!

> Prestige involves at least two persons: one to claim it and another to honor the claim. The bases on which various people raise prestige claims, and the reasons others honor these claims, include property and birth, occupation and education, income and power—in fact, almost anything that may invidiously distinguish one person from another. In the status system of a society, these claims are organized as rules and expectations which regulate who successfully claims prestige, from whom, in what ways, and on what basis. The level of self-esteem enjoyed by given individuals is more or less set by this status system.

My dictionary does the job better in six words: "ascendancy based on recognition of power." This kind of thing is academic leaf-raking; its chief utility is that it gives employment to sociologists. It is a substitute for thinking. So is its "opposite number," the melodramatic journalese the author uses when he tries to flee the groves of academe (but vigor of statement cannot make up for lassitude of thought).

In this book, Mills is a propagandist rather than a thinker. A certain *disinterestedness* is necessary if one is to think about, or describe, reality. Oddly enough, I think one finds this in Marx: he wanted to fit things into his theoretical framework, true, but there is also always present an intellectual fascination with finding out how reality "works"; this, I think, has produced the lasting elements in Marx's thinking. One feels little of this here. Propaganda rather than reflection is the note—as, the chapter headings, punchy as an ad man could dream up ("The Managerial Demiurge," "Brains, Inc.," "The Great Salesroom," "The Enormous File"), which, like advertising slogans, are so much more fascinating than the products they announce. Like the middle-class salaried brainworkers whose life-style he deplores—there is a curious subterranean bond between the author and the people he so indignantly writes about—Mills is too busy, in too much of a hurry to get much thinking "done."

But even as special pleading, the book fails because the author doesn't make clear what he is propagandizing for, who his client is. I think this is because he doesn't himself know, because he is himself drifting, confused, and, above all, indifferent. The only pages which seemed alive to me were 324–332, on the general political indifference that has become so widespread in this country since 1940. I think, or at least suspect, they are alive because here Mills for once is talking about himself and his own problems.

The masses today are indifferent for the same reason so many of us intellectuals are: you can't work up much interest in a process you feel you can't affect. Almost everybody, masses and intellectuals alike, feel ineffectual in politics (which is why half the eligible voters don't vote even in presidential elections), but we intellectuals suffer a further frustration: can we understand politics and history any more, can we fit them into any conceptual frame, can we still believe that we can find the theoretical key that will lay bare the real forces that shape history—indeed, can we believe there *is* such a key at all? The liberals and the Marxists, as Mills points out, had their keys, but they didn't fit the lock. Mills recognizes this, but he has no alternative theory or explanation of why things are as they are. I suspect he feels modern society is just not understandable, that he feels helpless and confused, as, for that matter, I do myself. Only Mills won't admit it. So he writes a book in which he tries to disguise his indifference, and therefore his lack of ideas or even of interest, by energetic manipulation of impressive abstract words, by interrupting both his interviewees and his quotees before they can say anything, and indeed by constantly interrupting *himself* before he can say anything either, or rather before he can give away the fact he hasn't anything to say. I wish he hadn't done it.

—*Partisan Review*, January–February, 1952

Afterword

White Collar was the last C. Wright Mills book to which adjectives like "drifting" or "confused" or "indifferent" could be applied. He soon began to make up his mind, "to get his head together," and his stuff became rather *too* clear, and one-sided, for my taste: i.e., he judged capitalist America with a severity he didn't apply to socialist competitors like Castro's Cuba. The double standard is as unattractive in politics as in sex. His premature death in 1962 at forty-six was specially unfortunate because it came before the Republic began to self-destruct under the consulates of Johnson and Nixon. Had Mills survived into these evil days, his intemperate blasts at the U.S.A. would have been useful and (at last) justified. You might call him a premature anti-American.

The above review ended a friendship. I first met Mills in 1943, a few years after he had broken out of his native Texan corral, like a maverick bull, to seek greener intellectual pastures up north. Our common interest was an antiwar monthly I was planning that materialized the next year as *Politics*—a perfect name that was his suggestion; all I could think of were leaden clichés like *The Radical Monthly* and, actually, *New Left Review*. We took to each other partly because we were isolated radicals in a wartime period and misery loves company but mostly because of a temperamental affinity: we were both congenital rebels, passionately contemptuous of every received idea and established institution and not at all inarticulate about it—he could argue about practically anything even longer and louder than I could. Also we had in common a peculiar (and incompatible, really—but there it was) mixture of innocence and cynicism, optimism and skepticism. We were ever hopeful, ever disillusioned. He wrote for *Politics* and gave me encouragement and stimulation. Also advice which I sometimes accepted—after lengthy argumentation.

Mills took my review of *White Collar* personally. When Norman Thomas asked him to take part in a panel discussion (I've forgotten the topic) and mentioned I was to be a member, Mills replied he wouldn't share a public platform—"public" in the Old Left sense, we hoped for a hundred listeners—with a frivolous and irresponsible political dilettante like me. Or words to that effect—the noun may have been "lightweight." Later I made overtures—Nothing personal intended and why can't we still be friends even if I didn't like his book?—to which he responded grumpily but more in sorrow than anger. (He couldn't hold a grudge, another thing I liked about him.) But it was never the same again and we drifted apart in the fifties, he intensifying and expanding his radicalism, I losing hope, and therefore interest, in mine. . . . On rereading this piece in galleys, I can see why Wright took it "personally." Whatever my intentions, its effect is to demonstrate that *White Collar* fails on all fronts: stylistic, sociological, intellectual, and political. It caught him in the helpless chrysalis stage between academic caterpillar and radical butterfly. Less egotistical pundits than Wright would have resented such exposure.

Mr. Schlesinger's
Realpolitik

Of the twenty essays here,* written between 1949 and 1960 for a spectrum ranging from *Partisan Review* down to the *Saturday Evening Post*, six seemed to me excellent, nine poor, and five so-so.

Quality was in inverse ratio to length and ambitiousness. Of the good ones, two are reportage: "Varieties of Communist Experience," about a month's trip in Russia, Poland, and Yugoslavia, and "Invasion of Europe, Family Style," a *feuilleton* carried off with style in a mere six pages. Four are polemics: "The Causes of the Civil War"; "The Statistical Soldier," a debunking of "social science" via a review of a two-volume work he describes as "a ponderous demonstration in Newspeak of such facts as these: new recruits do not like noncoms; front-line troops resent rear-echelon troops; married privates are more likely than single privates to worry about their families back home"; "The Politics of Nostalgia," the best brief exposé I know of the pretensions of the Buckley-Kirk "new conservatives" to either the noun or the adjective; and a fine deflation of John Osborne's *Look Back in Anger* as social criticism—and as drama. The five so-so pieces make up section III ("Men and Ideas") and deal with Reinhold Niebuhr, Walter Lippmann, Bernard De Voto, Whittaker Chambers,

---

* *The Politics of Hope*, Houghton Mifflin, 1963.

and J. Robert Oppenheimer. They are long—half the book—and disappointing; much intelligent comment but neither the Men nor the Ideas are made very interesting.

When he is not confronted with a polemical subject that tightens up his style and forces him to think (which he can do when he has to), Schlesinger likes to slip into something more comfortable. His judgments tend to become official and reverential and to be expressed in the orotundities of the hardened public speaker. The conclusion of his essay on Niebuhr, for instance:

> If his searching realism gave new strength to American liberal democracy, or, rather renewed sources of strength which had been too often neglected in the generations since the American Revolution, his own life and example have shown in compelling terms the possibilities of human contrition and human creativity within the tragedy of history.

The intonations of the fashionable preacher blend into those of the ideological con man—"human contrition" and "the tragedy of history" indeed! The last paragraph of the long piece on De Voto (and why such labors over that middlebrow?) also makes me queasy:

> This was, as DeVoto saw it, the meaning of democracy. And fighting such a battle, DeVoto might have added, vindicates democracy by producing men of compassion, of courage and of faith. These men justify the battle and renew the strength and decency of a civilization. Bernard DeVoto was such a man.

That dying fall! That cant! These qualities are even more pronounced in the remaining essays, which are mostly political. Here the author's yea-saying, true-believer aspect emerges most clearly.

Schlesinger made his reputation with *The Age of Jackson*, which I thought at the time turgidly written and structurally confused. But the time was 1946 and the liberals—having just lost Roosevelt and gotten Truman—were understandably worried. *The Age of Jackson* reassured them: it gave a rosy picture of Jacksonian democracy (myself, I see it as the first big turning point downward away from our political golden age—the Jefferson-Madison period) and, more important, implied a parallel with the New Deal. The results were a Pulitzer Prize and Schlesinger's emergence as the scholarly (Professor of History at Harvard) spokesman for what he was later to call, flatteringly, the Vital Center—or, more prosaically, the liberal-Northern wing of the Democratic Party. He became its Virgil —all the more speedily because he was a facile and copious journalist —but a Virgil whose Augustus was in exile. He was active, as speech-writer and adviser, in the 1952 and 1956 Stevenson campaigns, and he wrote his *Aeneid*: the three-volume *The Age of Roosevelt*, which provided for future Democratic administrations a historical-mytholog-ical underpinning. As the *Encyclopaedia Britannica* puts it: "The problem [confronting Virgil] was to compose a work of art which should represent a great action of the heroic age and should also embody the most vital ideas and sentiments of the hour."

After his two disappointments with Stevenson, Schlesinger shifted his allegiance to Kennedy some time before the 1960 convention. (I imply no censure: Stevenson was politically dead after 1956 and rightly so: he had trimmed his sails but had capsized anyway.) And so at last, after a decade of frustration, Schlesinger became a special assistant, in the White House, to an American president. The present book is mainly interesting for the clues it gives to his political thinking.

The title comes from Emerson who, in one of those capsule Gems of Thought he specialized in, saw "mankind" as divided be-tween the party of conservatism-past-memory and the party of inno-vation-future-hope. If I had to choose between these Procrustean simplicities, I would choose the former. But I don't have to and so I don't. Neither does Schlesinger, but he does. His Introduction, which for some reason is *not* dated "The White House, 1962," is the triumphal chant of the prophet who, after seven-plus lean years, sees his people liberated from the Egyptian bondage of the Eisenhower administrations:

> We no longer seem an old nation, tired, complacent and self-righteous. We no longer suppose that our national salvation depends on stopping history in its tracks and freezing the world in its present mold. Our national leadership is young, vigorous, intelligent, civilized and experimental. . . . We are Sons of Liberty once again. . . . We have awakened as from a trance. . . . The peculiarities of the fifties have almost the air of a forgotten nightmare.

He ends with an Emersonian Gem: "Freedom is inseparable from struggle; it is a process, not a conclusion."

The first two essays are "On Heroic Leadership and the Dilemma of Strong Men and Weak Peoples" (1960) and "The Decline of Greatness" (1958). The mere titles reveal a yearning which is a bit surprising in such a dedicated liberal and democrat, a desire which one assumes by now has been satiated by the President and his attorney general who are Heroic Leaders if ever there have been such, willing nay eager to assume "the Promethean responsibility to affirm human freedom against the supposed inevitabilities of history" and to "combat the infection of fatalism which might otherwise paralyze mass democracy." My view is that "mass democracy" is as much a contradiction in terms as was Hitler's "national socialism," but let it pass as an anarchist vagary.* I cannot let pass, however, a sentence on page 17: "While the Executive should wield all his powers under the Constitution with energy, he should not be able to abrogate the Constitution except in face of war, revolution or economic chaos." True that the sainted Lincoln did suspend *habeas corpus* and when the chief justice of the United States freed a Southern sympathizer on the ground he had been illegally arrested, kept the prisoner in jail nonetheless, observing, "Justice Tawney has made his ruling. Now let him enforce it"—an aside all too reminiscent of Stalin's famous query as to how many divisions the Pope commanded. Also true that Wilson and Franklin Roosevelt cut a few corners in wartime—and why is it always the great liberal presidents who do these things? Maybe because they have good consciences, supplied by intellectuals like Mr. Schlesinger.

But even a liberal Democrat might be given pause by the above formulation. He might think these wartime abrogations of the Constitution were shameful and against his principles; he might remember that, except for Lincoln, no president, even in wartime, has openly "abrogated the constitution," although our author takes it as a matter of course. And he might remember that no president so far has abrogated the Constitution on the plea of "economic chaos," and won-

---

* (1973) And my present feeling is that the more "mass democracy" is paralyzed the better. Those landslide votes for Johnson in 1964 and Nixon in 1972!

der why Schlesinger should give away in advance, nay actually suggest, such an invasion of our Constitutional rights. In fact, he might have disturbing thoughts about Heroic Leadership and about the part played by liberalistic ideologues like Arthur Schlesinger, Jr., in justifying such illiberal, not to say unconstitutional, tactics even before the Heroic Leaders themselves have attempted them.

In "*Time* and the Intellectuals," Schlesinger sneers at Henry Luce for demanding from writers positive and noncritical attitudes toward American institutions: "Those intellectuals who have faith in *Time*'s America and are ready to denounce their colleagues for criticising it are, in *Time*'s valuable phrase, Men of Affirmation. The Men of Protest are a disgruntled collection of snobs, grouches and expatriates, grumbling and griping in the outer darkness." He goes on to speak in eloquent and convincing terms of "the historical role of American intellectuals" as essentially one of protest. He was writing in 1956, when Eisenhower was in the White House, but now we have a different occupant and our author sings a different tune. "We need more people who don't give a damn and can awaken responses in us," Schlesinger wrote in 1956. But the basic quality needed to be a Special Assistant to the President is that one does give a damn. I wish my friend Arthur Schlesinger, Jr., who is a witty, clever, sensible, and decent fellow, had never gotten involved with high politics.

—*The New York Review of Books*, #1 (Special Issue) 1963.

Afterword

The following exchange appeared in the next issue of the *Review*:

To the Editors:

Perhaps it might be well to point out to your readers that the sentence in *The Politics of Hope* which led Dwight Macdonald to a long paragraph of lamentation over my moral and political condition was nothing more than a gloss on the quotation from Thomas Jefferson which immediately preceded it:

> To lose our country by a scrupulous adherence to written law, would be to lose the law itself, with life, liberty, property and all those who are enjoying them with us; thus absurdly sacrificing the end to the means. . . . The line of discrimination between cases may be difficult; but the good officer is bound to draw it at his own peril, and throw himself on the justice of his country and the rectitude of his motives.

Now there are no doubt those who dismiss Jefferson and join with Macdonald in saying that it is more important to save the letter of the law than to save the nation. But it seems a little extreme to suggest that those who disagree with Macdonald and agree with Jefferson on this matter are necessarily, as old Dwight implies, wicked, un-American or even illiberal.

If Macdonald is going to continue to write about American history, I wish someone would tell him that the remark "he made his law; now let him enforce it," if ever said at all, was said by Jackson about Marshall, not by Lincoln about Taney (whose name, both Mr. Macdonald and the editors of the *New York Review* might note is *not* spelled "Tawney").

Arthur Schlesinger, Jr.
Washington, D. C.

Dwight Macdonald replies:

That's quite a gloss that Mr. Schlesinger (young Arthur) has glossed on Jefferson's truism. Let me write a nation's glosses and I care not who writes its laws—assuming any are left. I agree with Jefferson (old Tom) that "to lose our country by a scrupulous adherence to written law" would be folly, and I disagree with the formulations that young Arthur has glossed into my mouth: "It is more important to save the letter of the law than to save the nation." Of course it isn't. The political—as against the debating—point is not whether one would choose to sacrifice the law in order to preserve the republic of which the law is an expression, but rather what are the grounds on which one decides such a choice has become necessary. "The line of discrimination between cases may be difficult," Jefferson writes, but Mr. Schlesinger makes it sound as easy as falling off a log called the Constitution. In my declining years, I have come to have a great respect for that ancient document for somewhat the same reason the frogs came to prefer King Log to King Stork: it may not be very dynamic but it does, occasionally, protect us against the storkish aggressions of an authoritarian executive and a majoritarian Congress.

The Schlesinger gloss on Jefferson, by the way, to which I objected was: "The Executive . . . should not be able to abrogate the Constitution except in the face of war, revolution or economic chaos."

Let me thank Mr. Schlesinger for correcting me on the spelling of Chief Justice Taney's name and also on the attribution of that damaging quote to Lincoln. It was sporting of him to substitute his own very first Heroic Leader, whose respect for our Constitution was even more moderate than Lincoln's. I was writing from unprofessional memory and should have looked it up. However, I shall "continue to write about American history" as long as Mr. Schlesinger continues to write about movies.*

---

* (1970) He's still doing it. So am I.

Hannah Arendt
and the
Jewish Establishment

When the front page of the *New York Times Book Review* a year ago carried a "review" of Hannah Arendt's *Eichmann in Jerusalem* which described it as defending the Nazis, the Gestapo, Himmler, and Eichmann (while slandering their Jewish victims) I shrugged and thought, well, Musmanno, and well, the Sunday *Times*. (Whose editors echoed their reviewer's demagogy with the heavy-ironic headline: "MAN WITH AN UN-SPOTTED CONSCIENCE.") For I had read the book and found it a masterpiece of historical journalism that explained the real horror of Nazi genocide, as against the clichés of forensic indignation mobilized by Judge Musmanno.

My shrug was premature. The *Times* review proved to be merely an early gun in a barrage that was already being laid down in the Jewish press while the book was being serialized in *The New Yorker*. The headline in the *Intermountain Jewish News* (April 12, 1963) was a little blunt: "SELF-HATING JEWESS WRITES PRO-EICHMANN SERIES"—haven't seen "Jewess" in print since those fascist sheets in the thirties. But it indicated an approach that came to include magazines I read, respect, and even write for. Their strictures were more moderate and sophisticated, but they followed the Musmanno line: the book was soft on Eichmann, hard on the Jews. And the closest to Musmanno in spirit was Lionel Abel's, I'm sorry to say, since I've been associated with *Partisan Review*, as editor and contributor, for a long time. I thought Mary McCarthy's "Hue and Cry" brilliantly (and sensibly) dealt with Mr. Abel—settled his hash you might say— and I shall try not to re-hash too much.

The moral crux of Abel's indictment is that "He [Eichmann] comes off so much better in her book than do his victims." Because, he claims, the author takes a heartless aesthetic approach to the whole ghastly business:

> If a man holds a gun at the head of another and forces him to kill his friend, the man with a gun will be aesthetically less ugly than the one who out of fear of death has killed his friend. . . . And if we turn to the extermination of approx- imately five million people, does it seem proper that the executioner and his host of victims should be judged in aesthetic rather than in moral and political terms?

Miss McCarthy has shown the logical and moral fallacy in the first sentence, which is so gross as to raise doubts about Abel's competence in both departments. As to the second, I would answer with the rhetorically expected no, adding that it also would seem to me "im- proper," to say the least, to present Eichmann as "better" than his victims. If I thought this were the tendency of the book, I should not defend it, nor should I have the respect and affection for Hannah Arendt that I do. In fact, I don't see how I could bear to be in the same room with her. I have known both Mr. Abel and Miss Arendt for many years, and I must confess that the notion of the former giving lessons in morality to the latter strikes me as comic.

I must admit, however, that Abel's line of attack has been taken by others, in print and in talk. Less crudely and with less personal malice—I remember an extraordinary article by Abel in *New Politics* which contemptuously dismissed Miss Arendt as a philosopher (in- deed, as the most modestly endowed of rational creatures)—but with the same content. A distinguished Jewish man of letters—an old friend of Miss Arendt's who had defended her against intemperate attacks like Abel's—said to me recently: "Yes, a brilliant book, but I wish she hadn't blamed the victims more than the executioners." This (to me) startling judgment was echoed in *Dissent* by Marie Syrkin: "The only one who comes out better than when he came in is the defendant. The victim comes out worst." And in *Commentary* by Norman Podhoretz: "In place of the monstrous Nazi, she gives us the 'banal' Nazi; in place of the Jew as virtuous martyr, she gives us the Jew as accomplice in evil; and in place of the confrontation of guilt and innocence, she gives us the 'collaboration' of criminal and victim." To "cultural lag" we must now add a new concept: "cultural throwback." One would think Mr. Podhoretz had never read any of the literature on the Nazi concentration camps, whose rationale was carried over into the wartime death camps. As described by Rousset, Kogon, Bettelheim, and other survivors, this rationale was precisely what Mr. Podhoretz calls, with an air of incredulity, "the 'collaboration' of criminal and victim."*

"I have it on the authority of Dr. Jacob Robinson, special assistant to Justice Jackson at the Nuremberg Trials and to Prosecutor Hausner in the preparation of the case against Eichmann," Abel writes impressively, "that there are some eight monographs in Yiddish and in Hebrew on the discussions of the Jewish Council's leaders with left-wing Zionists and Socialists." He continues less impressively: "I have not been able to examine these monographs myself; they are yet to be translated. But I have it again on the authority of Dr. Robinson that in these discussions outright defiance of the Nazis was proposed. . . . What arguments were given by the Councils' leaders one would like to know. . . . Now I, for one, am not at all sure that the arguments for collaboration might not have been more logical. . . ."

Abel takes the word of an interested party for the contents of "some eight monographs" he hasn't seen and couldn't have read if he had. He "would like to know" the arguments for collaboration—one would think he and Dr. Robinson could have found an hour or two for some oral translation—and then proceeds to demonstrate just what the arguments must have been. How enviable, such a mind! Miss Arendt's is comparatively pedestrian: to reach conclusions, it must labor through court records and other boring data. Abel's needs only one datum: itself. It is a perpetual-motion machine, self-powered and

---

* (1973) His quotes around "collaboration" may be rhetorical bad faith—or innocent ignorance. In either case, they are not justified by the most superficial reading of the copious literature on the Nazi camps.

frictionless, since it has freed itself from outside data (whose introduction into the mind invariably causes friction since they are not identical with it). The only trouble is that those eight monographs turn out to be irrelevant to Abel's argument. For Miss Arendt, far from demanding "outright defiance," is at pains to show it would have been useless and suicidal. Her objection is simply to the Councils' *existence*; she thinks that Jewish leaders should not have cooperated with the Nazis to form them: "There was no possibility of resistance, but there existed the possibility of *doing nothing*." The distinction between passive evasion and "outright defiance" may be a nuance too subtle for Abel's intellectual machinery, which has lately produced a remarkable statistic. "Miss Arendt's book was anything but truthful," he writes in a letter in the *New Republic* of April 4, 1964. "It contains no less than 600 distortions of fact, a record, I believe, for a book of 256 pages." Not 587 distortions of fact, not 608, but exactly 600. Dr. Mortimer J. Adler, whose mind has something in common with Abel's, has counted the Great Ideas of the Western World, but he ended up with an untidy 102.

Miss Arendt's subtitle, "The Banality of Evil," has been objected to. In *Encounter* (January, 1964) Gershon Sholem calls it "a catchword" that is not "the product of profound analysis,"* unlike her earlier concept of "radical evil." She agrees she has changed her mind since *The Origins of Totalitarianism*: "It is my opinion now that evil is never 'radical,' that it is only extreme, and that it possesses neither depth nor any demonic dimension. . . . Only the good has depth and can be radical." I see nothing shocking here: the discrepancy between the personal mediocrity of Stalin and Hitler, the banality of their ideas, and the vastness of the evils they inflicted—is she really the first to notice this? "She claims that Eichmann was commonplace and mediocre," writes Abel. "But by the power of the totalitarian state, he was able to exterminate a whole people." I don't understand that "but." I wonder if Abel thinks Lee Oswald became less "commonplace and mediocre" after he had killed President

---

* (1973) In the fifteen years since Ms. Arendt coined the phrase, it has been widely and continually quoted in all kinds of contexts. Profound or not, "the banality of evil" is a concept our time seems to need.

Kennedy—Oswald's mother has told reporters they'd better take her and her son more seriously "because we're in the history books now."

Dostoevsky would not have found "the banality of evil" a catchword. When Satan visits Ivan Karamazov, he proves to be a shabby-genteel "hanger-on of the better class." "You flunky!" cries Ivan, threatening to kick him. "You are stupid and vulgar." This devil sounds very much like Arendt's Eichmann: "My friend, above all things I want to be a gentleman and recognized as such. . . . It's generally accepted in society that I am a fallen angel. By God, I can't conceive how I could ever have been an angel. . . . I prize only my reputation as a well-bred gentleman." Like Eichmann, he has pretensions to big ideas. "Don't talk philosophy, you ass!" Ivan exclaims. But the devil's final speech is a shrewd thrust: "I repeat, moderate your expectations. . . . You are really angry with me for not having appeared to you in a red glow, with thunder and lightning, with scorched wings, and for showing myself in such a modest guise. You are wounded, in the first place, in your aesthetic feelings, and secondly, in your pride." That five million Jews could have been slaughtered by contemptible mediocrities like Eichmann must be hard for the survivors to accept; it trivializes the horror, robs it of meaning. It must be especially hard to take the fact that Eichmann wasn't even a serious anti-Semite—in fact, wasn't a serious anything.

Miss McCarthy's claim that reviews by Gentiles were favorable and those by Jews unfavorable was not convincing to me. Seven exceptions were too many, especially when the four Jewish exceptions were such weighty names as Alvarez, Bell, Lichtheim, and Bettelheim—the last's article in the *New Republic* was the best treatment I've seen. However, the hostile reviews I've read do seem motivated less by rationality than by Jewish patriotism—goys like Crossman and Musmanno might be called Honorary Semites. And I think Miss McCarthy's broader claim is accurate: that reactions *in general* divide along Jewish and non-Jewish lines, and that this "is even more pronounced in private conversation." I've had the same experience of feeling "like a child with a reading defect in a class of normal readers" when discussing the book with Jewish friends. We often disagree even on what the book is *about*: Eichmann and Nazism, I'd thought, but they talk, and write, as if it was equally about the Jewish Councils. Yet out of 256 pages, less than fifteen are devoted to this question. Abel devotes half his space to this one-eighteenth of the book, nor is this ratio exceptional. So I conclude they are writing more as Jews than as critics.

And as peculiarly organization-minded Jews at that. These fifteen pages criticize not, as the critics imply, the Jewish *masses* but the Jewish *leadership*. "If the Jewish people had really been unorganized and leaderless, there would have been chaos and plenty of misery, but the total number of victims would hardly have been between 4,500,000 and 6,000,000 people." Why is this sentence so universally shocking? That more Jews would have escaped if their leaders, thinking they could bargain with the Nazis, had not formed Jewish Councils to organize them for transport to the death camps— this seems a reasonable speculation, if only because a leaderless flock is harder to round up. (Also it's hard to see how the catastrophe could have been *greater*.) Miss Arendt also makes a moral criticism of the Jewish leadership: she says they should have refused to do the Nazis' dirty work for them and that there is no moral arithmetic by which X lives can be sacrificed to save Y lives, because nobody has the right to decide who should be saved at the expense of whom. I agree but even if I didn't, I would think this a perfectly respectable, and familiar, position. Unless, of course, I thought it wrong, per se, to criticize Jews. Although some of Miss Arendt's most violent denouncers cut their eyeteeth on Marxist theory, they in this case identify the Jewish masses with their leaders, writing as though European Jewry were a classless utopian community. They actually seem to have forgotten more Marxism than I have.

I object to some of Miss Arendt's generalizations about the Germans —but this doesn't make me reject the whole book. She states that "many Germans . . . probably an overwhelming majority . . . knew, of course," about the death camps. I've been following this question since 1945, when I wrote "The Responsibility of Peoples" (reprinted in *Politics Past*; see esp. pp. 42–43), and the "of course" seems to me to run the other way: the Nazis did everything possible to keep the 1942–1944 Jewish death camps secret—in contrast with the publicity they gave, for reasons of political terrorization, to the earlier concentration camps. I also object to her calling the German people *en masse* "accomplices," since even those who did know would have had to be heroes to do anything about it; and, as she herself has observed, it is inhuman to demand more than a few heroes from any population—German, Russian, Jewish, or American. And I further object to her statement that the July, 1944, conspirators against Hitler were "not inspired by a crisis of conscience or by what they knew other people had been made to suffer; they were motivated exclusively' by their conviction of the coming defeat and ruin of Germany." Allen Dulles's *Germany's Underground* states of the Kreisau Circle, led by Count von Moltke and Count von Wartenburg, which prepared the 1944 plot: "Its economic and political program was one of Christian Socialism," with which William L. Shirer's *Rise and Fall of the Third Reich* agrees. Shirer writes of Count von Stauffenberg, who planted the bomb: "The anti-Jewish pogroms of 1938 first cast doubts in his mind about Hitler," while Dulles quotes an exchange from Wartenburg's testimony before the Nazi court that condemned him:

> Prosecutor Freisler: But concisely, you declare on the question of the Jews that you disagreed with their extermination?
> Wartenburg: The decisive factor which brings together all these questions is the totalitarian claim of the state on the individual which forces him to renounce his moral and religious obligations to God.

I also find unsatisfying her rationale for hanging Eichmann: "... We find that no one, that is, no member of the human race, can be expected to want to share the earth with you. This is the reason, and the only reason, you must hang." But in fact many people still exist who are quite willing to share the earth with an Eichmann: fascists, Nazis, anti-Semitic fanatics like our own George Lincoln Rockwell, and I don't see how they can be deprived of their human status—it's not like citizenship, after all—unless by circular reasoning: if you want to share the earth with an Eichmann, you are not human.

But these errors, if such they be, don't seem to me to importantly affect the book, nor do I feel it necessary to explain them by imputing to the author callousness, perversity, distorting of facts, or other moral defects. True, I'm not German. Also I'm not Jewish, granted. But if I were either, I'd hope my response to Miss Arendt's

book would be less clannish, to use my native idiom, than the
Semiticist reflex it provoked in too many Jewish intellectuals.

A Jewish friend complained that Miss McCarthy had "raised the
Jewish issue," another puzzlement, since I had thought that was
precisely what critics like Podhoretz and Abel had done, and that she
was objecting to this tactic. I find it depressing to have to talk about
"Jewish friends" and "Jewish critics" after all those years when I'd
thought we'd gotten beyond such labels in serious discussion, but I
can see no other explanation for the virulence with which *Eichmann
in Jerusalem* has been attacked. A hitherto respected political thinker
is treated like a suspect in a police court. She uses irony, for instance, a dangerous device if the reader, from stupidity or calculation, insists on reading it straight. (In this case, I'd call it calculated
stupidity.) "Should any one be blamed for raising an eyebrow to
the suggestion that Eichmann loved the Jews?" Judge Musmanno
inquires. Mr. Podhoretz paraphrases Miss Arendt: "It even called for
a certain idealism to do what Eichmann and his cohorts did," though
on pages 37–38 she explains just what she means by Eichmann's
"idealism." "Miss Arendt in this connection," he continues, "quotes
the famous remark attributed to Himmler," which he then tran-
scribes dead-pan; one gets the impression she drew on Himmler for a
definition of idealism. Mr. Abel is solemnly foolish, as usual: "Now
Miss Arendt's effort to present Eichmann as a convinced adherent of
the Zionist ideology is, as Marie Syrkin has shown, completely unconvincing. For quite obviously a man in charge of the extermination
of all European Jewry could hardly have been committed 'forever'
to the Zionist ideology." Obviously. One might expect even Miss
Arendt to see *that*.

It is often implied, in these reviews, that to say the Jewish
leadership shouldn't have cooperated with the Nazis is to say they are
equally guilty, much as certain Catholics complain that Hochhuth's
The Deputy displaces the guilt for the death camps from the Nazis
onto the Pope. This is such nonsense, logically, that I can't but see
prejudice: to critize people for not speaking out against a crime (the
Pope) or for mistakenly trying to moderate it by assuming some of
the control (the Jewish Councils) is not to minimize the responsibility of those who actually commit the crime. The fault of the Pope

and the Councils was that they compromised with an evil that was as close to being absolute as anything is in this imperfect world. But it was the Nazis alone who killed the Jews.

It is an interesting, and depressing, historical exercise to imagine what the reactions would have been to a book like this in the thirties, when all of us, from Miss McCarthy to Mr. Abel, despised national and racial feelings and were hot for truth, justice, and other universals. The suggestion that certain people and institutions should be exempt from criticism would have embarrassed everybody (except the Stalinists). But the death camps have cast their shadow. Even Daniel Bell concludes on what seemed to me a false note: "Many of Miss Arendt's strictures are correct, if one can live by a universalistic standard." "In this situation," he continues, "one's identity as a Jew, as well as a *philosophe*, is relevant. The agony of Miss Arendt's book is precisely that she takes her stand so unyieldingly on the side of disinterested justice, and that she judges both Nazi and Jew. But abstract justice, as the Talmudic wisdom knew, is sometimes too 'strong' a yardstick to judge the world." And in his *Encounter* letter, Gershon Sholem makes the same complaint: "In the Jewish tradition, there is a concept . . . we know as *Ahabath Israel*: 'Love of the Jewish people.' In you, dear Hannah, as in so many intellectuals who came from the German Left, I find little trace of this."

I think Mr. Bell and Mr. Sholem have made explicit, because their intention was understanding rather than polemics, the concealed, perhaps often unconscious, assumption that explains the violence of the Jewish attacks on Miss Arendt's book. Both reproach her because she lacks a special feeling in favor of her fellow Jews. But such a prejudice would have made it impossible for her to speculate on how the catastrophe might have been less complete had the Jewish leadership followed different policies, or to attempt a realistic interpretation of the Nazi horror as the work of men (who can be understood) and not of "monsters" and demons (who cannot). That is, she tried to learn something from history, an enterprise in which I don't think either the Talmud or *Ahabath Israel* would have been useful.*

---

* One might expect the editor of our most intelligent Jewish magazine to see that Miss Arendt's criticisms, however tactless, of the policies that at least

I don't agree with Daniel Bell, the most moderate and reasonable of Miss Arendt's Jewish critics—he has an instinct for the center, vital or dead according to one's political temperament, of a dispute—that "in this situation, one's identity as a Jew . . . is relevant." I.e., that a special yardstick must be used to measure this particular historical case because that of "abstract justice" is "too strong." That Mr. Bell should retreat to this marshy ground when Miss Arendt asked some awkward questions about the Jewish catastrophe—and tried to suggest answers with some awkward speculations and, worse, data—this seems to me a cop-out for a generally tough-minded social historian. I conclude he found himself an interested (as against a disinterested) observer and so was pushed off his normal centrist balance. Otherwise he would have realized that a yardstick which varies depending on the measurer's gut reaction to the phenomenon being measured isn't very useful. And that justice isn't justice unless it is "abstract," that is, "universalistic"—to use another adjective he uses here in a pejorative sense. I'm old-fashioned enough, my political education going all the way back to the thirties, like Mr. Bell's, to find any exceptional category morally suspect and intellectually confusing. So I take heart in a book like *Eichmann in Jerusalem.*

didn't *prevent* the 1942–1944 catastrophe might hold lessons for the future. But Mr. Podhoretz ends his article plaintively: "The Nazis destroyed a third of the Jewish people. In the name of all that is humane, will the remnant never let up on itself?" Letting up on one's self may be humane—there are other adjectives—but it doesn't make for understanding, or survival.

1917 from Below:
"It Was All
Very Interesting"

"Tuesday, February 21, 1917: I was sitting in my office [in the Ministry of Agriculture]. Behind a partition, two typists were gossiping about food difficulties, rows in shopping queues, unrest among the women, an attempt to smash into some warehouse. 'D'you know,' suddenly declared one of these young ladies, 'it's the beginning of the revolution!' . . . These philistine girls whose tongues and typewriters were rattling away didn't know what a revolution was. I believed neither them, nor the inflexible facts, nor my own judgment. . . . Revolution!—everyone knew this was only a dream, a dream of generations and of long, laborious decades. Without believing the girls, I repeated after them mechanically: 'Yes, the beginning of the revolution.'" A week later, the revolution was well under way, and the diarist in question, who, after a hard day's work helping it along, had gone to sleep in the chamber in which the Duma had up till then functioned, was awakened by "strange noises." "I got up," he writes, "and saw two soldiers, their bayonets hooked into the canvas of Repin's portrait of Nicholas II, rhythmically tugging it down. A minute later, over the chairman's seat there was an empty frame."

So begin N. N. Sukhanov's memoirs, which have recently been translated and abridged (to a mere six hundred and sixty-five pages!) by Joel Carmichael and published by the Oxford Press as *The Rus-*

sian Revolution 1917. Mr. Carmichael's Introduction is a fine piece of historical exposition and his translation is lively and readable. I can't judge his abridging skill since I don't read Russian, but if he omitted very much material superior to what he gives us, Sukhanov must be an even more remarkable diarist than he here appears. For his memoirs are not only personally frank, politically intelligent and exciting as a historical narrative, full of scenes observed with a novelistic eye for detail—one keeps coming across vignettes that Eisenstein and Pudovkin have translated into cinema—but also the most important original source on the 1917 revolution. They are, notes Mr. Carmichael, "the sole full-length eye-witness account of the entire revolutionary period," from the leaderless, spontaneous "March Days" that overthrew the Czar in a fit of absent-mindedness to the not at all absent-minded Bolshevik *putsch* in October that ended the revolutionary chaos with a new order about which Sukhanov had mixed feelings. In writing his *History of the Russian Revolution*, a work as tendentiously structured as Sukhanov's is not, Trotsky drew heavily on Sukhanov, citing him almost a hundred times; only three names get more space in the index: Miliukov, Kerensky, Lenin.

Trotsky's is a bird's-eye view—a revolutionary eagle soaring on the wings of Marx and History—but Sukhanov gives us a series of close-ups, hopping about St. Petersburg like an earth-bound sparrow—curious, intimate, sharp-eyed. *His* history has a small "h." Not that he was a mere gossip, though he doesn't despise a good story or an irreverent glimpse of the underpinnings of Historical Figures. He was a leading revolutionary journalist (under his *nom de plume et de guerre*, Sukhanov—his real name was Himmer), and he analyzes, often more realistically than the History-intoxicated Trotsky, each turn of the eight months' drama. It was a drama in which he himself figured importantly as a member of the Executive Committee of the Petersburg Soviet, which shared "dual power" with the successive governments until the Bolsheviks made their *putsch* with the slogan "All Power to the Soviets!" Once in control, they revised it slightly to read "All Power to the Bolshevik members of the Soviets," which definitely did not include Comrade Sukhanov.

Like Trotsky, Sukhanov was one of those brilliant, cultivated, passionately intellectual Russian radicals who prepared the revolution that was to erase their type and replace it with the stolid primitives of the Stalin era. Herzen, Bielinsky, Chernyshevsky, Plekhanov, Martov, Bukharin, Serge, Radek, Gorky, Ryazanov. Between such men and a Zhdanov, a Molotov, or a Fadayev yawns a millennial cultural gap. Evolution has been running in reverse in the Soviet Union.

As a historian, Sukhanov has qualities lacking in Trotsky, who was too much the ideologue and the man of action, determined to make History come out right. Sukhanov is detached, critical about his own miscalculations and prejudices. His temperament is that of the observer, the spectator, indeed at times the tourist. Asked to go to the Peter and Paul Fortress, for generations the most dreaded *oubliette* of the czars, to prevent a threatened massacre of deposed officials held prisoner there, he jumps at the chance. "The excursion upset my plans," he writes, "but nevertheless I needed no lengthy urging. I had never yet set foot in the famous Fortress. I was tempted by the opportunity of visiting it." (To give him credit, he consistently and courageously opposed all forms of lynch law, even in the sacred name of Saving the Revolution.) His mission succeeded, but he was "quite disappointed" in the prison. "There was absolutely nothing either menacing, frightening, or gloomy in the broad grass-covered square or the surrounding buildings. Led by the commandant past some tumbledown carts, rusty kettles, and other prosaic objects, we came to the crude and unimpressive gate of the Trubetskoy Bastion. The sentry let us through quite indifferently. . . . We were taken to an office which looked not merely unprisonlike, but even unofficial, with its shabby, almost homelike furnishings." In short, the excursion was a touristic flop.

Sukhanov seems not to have been aware of the predominance in his nature of the observer over the activist. "Having left my office between twelve and one o'clock, I went out into the streets to watch the people's revolution being accomplished," he writes on the first day of the March uprising.

Military detachments were going past, no one knew where to, some with red banners and some without, mingling and fraternizing with the crowd, stopping for conversation, and breaking up into argumentative groups. Faces were burning with excitement. . . . It was clear to me that I must make my way at once toward the center, to the Tauride Palace [where the Provisional Government had set up headquarters]. But what I should find there was not clear at all, nor what I should do. My dejection at being in the miserable position of an observer of great events reached its lowest depths. I would do anything at all, so long as it was active.

And he did do a lot, but without ever becoming a man of action for all that. Lenin would have known exactly what he had to do when he reached Tauride Palace. When someone proposed that the Executive Committee of the Petersburg Soviet review the troops, Sukhanov laughed at the idea of himself on horseback. Trotsky would not have laughed—the eyeglassed intellectual, fresh from playing chess and writing Marxist theory in the cafés of Vienna, rode a horse many times as commander-in-chief of the Red Army without causing anybody, including himself, to think him at all ridiculous. Not of such stuff was Sukhanov. His favorite word of praise is "interesting." The word crops up repeatedly in his famous report on Lenin's return from exile. This is how he describes the reception at the Finland Station:

Lenin . . . stood there [listening to the speech of welcome by the Menshevik Chkheidze, representing the Executive Committee of the Petersburg Soviet] as though nothing taking place had the slightest connection with him—looking about him, examining the persons around him and even the ceiling of the imperial waiting room, adjusting his bouquet (rather out of tune with his whole appearance), and then, turning away from the Executive Committee delegation altogether, he made this "reply": "Dear Comrades, soldiers, sailors, and workers! I am happy to greet in your persons the victorious Russian revolution . . . the vanguard of the worldwide proletarian army. . . . The piratical imperialist war is the beginning of civil war throughout Europe. . . . Long live the worldwide Socialist revolution!" . . . Suddenly, before the eyes of all of us, completely swallowed up by the routine drudgery of the revolution, there was presented a bright, blinding, exotic beacon . . . a note that was novel, harsh, and somewhat deafening. . . . It was all *very* interesting.

A few hours later, Sukhanov has wangled his way into Bolshevik headquarters to see how Lenin and his followers, so long separated, are getting along. "Lenin, excited and lively, greeted me very affably: 'Ah! Himmer-Sukhanov—very happy indeed! You and I have had a lot of disputes on the agrarian question. Why, I followed the way you and your SRs [Social Revolutionaries] got into a fight. And then you became an internationalist. I got your pamphlets. . . .' Lenin smiled, screwing up his merry eyes, and, wagging his untidy head, took me into the dining room." Sukhanov found the orations with which the Bolsheviks greeted their leader monotonous and tiresome. (Trotsky writes that "Lenin endured the flood of eulogistic speeches like an impatient pedestrian waiting in a doorway for the rain to stop.") The rain finally stopped, and "the celebrated master of the order himself" rose to reply. "I shall never forget that thunderlike speech, which startled and amazed not only me, a heretic who had accidentally dropped in, but all the true believers," Sukhanov continues. "I am certain that no one expected anything of the sort. It seemed as though all the elements had risen from their abodes, and the spirit of universal destruction, knowing neither barriers nor doubts, neither human difficulties nor human calculations, was hovering . . . above the heads of the bewitched disciples."

What shocked both Sukhanov and Lenin's own Bolsheviks, every one of them a veteran Marxist accustomed to sober consideration of historical and economic factors, was Lenin's brushing aside all the majestic paraphernalia of Marxism—his speech, the author complains, "had no analysis of 'objective premises' [or] of the socioeconomic conditions for Socialism in Russia"—and presenting "a purely anarchist schema" of All Power to the Soviets; that is, no state power beyond the direct action of the workers and peasants, who had been organized in soviets that were barely past the embryonic stage. They just couldn't understand, and they were right intellectually; when Lenin did take power, he paid little attention to the soviets and simply made his party into the state. But *he* was right practically; it was his Bakuninistic *élan*—plus his own specialty: a ruthless use of organized force—that made History. Whether it *should* have been made that way poor Sukhanov was never quite able to decide. All he knew, from the first, was that Lenin's way was not for him. "I went out into the street," he says. "I felt as though I had been beaten about the head with flails. Only one thing was clear: Lenin and a 'wild' [i.e., independent] one like myself could not be travelling companions."

But it was all *very* interesting. The Menshevik leader, Tsereteli, reads out publicly a list of the ministers in Kerensky's new cabinet and cannot keep back the embarrassed smile of a schoolboy who has distinguished himself when he says, "Minister of the Interior—Tsereteli."

A peasant delegation is received by Kerensky and his ministers:

> A gray little peasant began urgently and almost tearfully asking the Ministers for a law to preserve land resources. He was impatiently interrupted by the pale and agitated Kerensky. "Yes, yes, that will be done. The Provisional Government is already taking steps. Tell them there is nothing to worry about. The Government and myself will do our duty."
>
> One of the deputation . . . tried to put in the remark that the law had been promised long since but that nothing was happening. By now Kerensky was furious and began a thorough tongue-lashing, practically stamping his foot: "I said it would be done, that means it will! And there is no need to look at me so suspiciously!"

The common people are described in as intimate detail as are their "leaders" (the Bolsheviks took off the quotes in October):

> Near the entrance to the *Letopis* offices [Sukhanov was a chief contributor to this Socialist magazine, which was edited by Maxim Gorky], at the gates of the neighboring factory, I met a small group of civilians, workers by the look of them. "What do they want?" said one grim-looking fellow. "They want bread, peace with the Germans, and equality for the Yids." "Right in the bull's eye," I thought, delighted with this brilliant formulation of the programme of the great revolution.

That was in the first days. A few weeks later, Sukhanov is describing the soldiers and peasants who rose in the soviet assembly hall and "uttered their stormy, heroic hymns to the revolution, although they were incapable of saying what revolution meant and barely able to pronounce the word itself."

Their speeches were not always clear, they had no core nor any real content. But everyone listened excitedly and everyone understood. . . . I remember one fellow in a brown peasant's overcoat, with his hair cropped all round, broad-shouldered, red-faced, snub-nosed, a typical, primeval shepherd and not a bad model for a Russian Simple Simon. Speaking quickly in a thin voice, calling us "brethren" and "dears," he uttered or cried out his elemental lyrical improvisation. God knows what unendurable oppression the revolution had lifted from this barbarian—if he had been snatched from the talons of some savage noble landlord or ferocious officer and was rapturously drinking in his new freedom like a desert stallion. The chairman didn't interrupt him. The "conscious" politicians, the scientific Socialists, with burning eyes and fixed smiles, breathing hard and devouring every word—all listened to Simple Simon.

Peasants often climbed up on to the platform of the White Hall with their bundles on their backs. Once there came a soldier from the trenches, dragging after him a dirty sack. . . . Quietly, with no wasted words, he began talking about his comrades who had sent him to salute the vanguard fighters, teachers, and brothers. . . . In the trenches they didn't know what they could do for the revolution. . . . "So we decided to bring you the most precious thing we had. . . . In this sack are all the decorations we won with our blood; no one kept anything for himself. Here are the St. George's Crosses and Medals. I've been sent to give them to you. . . ."*

The eye rested with satisfaction on the rare figures of sailors with their bronzed faces, charming childish jackets, and naïve little ribbons on their caps. "From the Black Sea Fleet—greetings!"

The Russian revolution differed from the French and American ones as an earthquake differs from erosion. It took the Americans from 1776 to Yorktown, in 1781, to free themselves from King George III—and another six years to decide on a constitution. The Estates-General met in 1789, but Louis XVI was not dethroned until 1792. The slow tempo provided time for the new heirs of power to create new social forms and institutions. But the first great street

---

* (1971) Cf. our own Vietnam veterans last spring throwing away their medals on the Capitol lawn.

demonstrations in Petersburg took place on February twenty-fifth of 1917, and the czars fell, forever, on March second.*

Thus the workers and peasants who made the Russian Revolution had days, instead of years, to develop a new social order. Furthermore, unlike the American colonists and the French bourgeoisie, they were an almost totally submerged class, economically as well as politically, without any experience in government. Power was "lying in the streets," in Trotsky's phrase; it "could be seized in bare hands," in Sukhanov's. The whole vast glittering edifice of czarism, with its brazen crowns, double-headed eagles, and Corinthian façades, simply collapsed into rubble overnight under the dumb, inexorable, leaderless pressure of the masses, and a scratch crew of bourgeois and Socialist politicians was left in full command of the ruins, to put together a new social order as best it could. Improvisation was the order of the day. Some time after the revolutionary government had taken power—or, rather, picked it up—Sukhanov suddenly remembered a slight omission:

> I reminded Kerensky of Secret Police headquarters. It appeared that it hadn't been taken, and Kerensky proposed that I undertake to seize it and secure all its archives. He spoke as though there were a detachment and some transport for this, but I saw this was not so. In any case, as a deep-dyed civilian, I refused this enterprise, since I was more attracted to politics than strategy.

No doubt some less civilian character finally got around to taking over the secret police. A few days later, Sukhanov was writing the constitution:

> Steklov had vanished somewhere and I was left alone with Miliukov [the bourgeois Premier of the first revolutionary government] to complete the Constitution. I remember that the irregular scrap of paper on which the proclamation was

---

* This period is generally called the March Days; the old Julian calendar, which Sukhanov uses, runs almost two weeks behind the revised Gregorian calendar, which has been used in the West—except Russia—for centuries. For the same reason, the Bolshevik coup in October, 1917, is often called the November Revolution. Lenin introduced the Gregorian calendar, along with a few other things, into Russia.

written passed into my hands, and with Miliukov's help I wrote at the top of it: "In its activities the Government will be guided by the following principles."

Now—how should the document be headed?

"From the Provisional Committee of the Duma," Miliukov suggested to me. But I was not satisfied. "Why the Duma?" "To preserve the succession of authority," Miliukov replied. "After all, Rodzianko [president of the Duma and a right winger, like Miliukov] ought to sign this document." I didn't like any of this. I preferred to dispense with the succession, and with Rodzianko. I insisted that the document be headed "From the Provisional Government." . . .

The Constitution was prepared and transcribed. I gave one copy to a comrade, a messenger, for emergency printing, having written on it the appropriate directives ("on one sheet of paper, in thick type, to be pasted up in the streets in the morning").

Things were rather different around Independence Hall, Philadelphia, in 1787.

Among Sukhanov's other odd jobs during the first week of the revolution were reopening the banks and deciding whether the Grand Duke Michael should have a special train from his country seat to Petersburg, to consult with his brother the Czar. He resolved the latter problem by ruling that "Citizen Romanov can go to the railroad station [and] buy a ticket." The first problem was more complicated:

The phone rang at my side. "Soviet of Workers' and Soldiers' Deputies? . . . I'm speaking for the Council of Representatives of the Petersburg banks. We want permission to open the banks at once. . . ."

Without relinquishing the receiver, I called over a nearby Executive Committee member, consulted with him for two minutes ("pro" and "con") and asked "What's the attitude of the higher and lower employees toward opening the banks?"

"All the employees are ready to start working right now and are only waiting for your permission." . . .

"Very well, you have it. If it's needed in written form, then make it up yourselves on an ordinary sheet of paper and send it to the Tauride Palace, Room 13, to be signed and stamped."

The heroes of the first four-fifths of Sukhanov's memoirs are not the political leaders, not Kerensky or Trotsky or Lenin, and certainly not Stalin. There are only eight references to Stalin. Six of them just mention him in passing as one of the lesser Bolshevik chieftains; the seventh mentions his having favored in June an attempt to overthrow the Kerensky government, a move Lenin declared was premature (this was the only time Stalin played a role of his own); the eighth is the celebrated "gray blur" description:

> At this time Stalin appeared in the Executive Committee [of the Petersburg Soviet] for the Bolsheviks, in addition to Kamenev. This man was one of the central figures of the Bolshevik Party and perhaps one of the few individuals who held (and hold to this day [1922]) the fate of the revolution and the State in their hands. Why this is so I shall not undertake to say; "influence" in these exalted and irresponsible spheres, remote from the people and alien to publicity, is so capricious. But at any rate Stalin's rôle is bound to be perplexing. The Bolshevik Party . . . had a whole series of most massive figures and able leaders among its generals. Stalin, however, during his modest activity in the Executive Committee produced—and not only on me—the impression of a gray blur, looming up now and then dimly and not leaving any trace. There is really nothing more to be said about him.

Nor was there, then. It took years for Stalin's sinister genius to find the right conditions for expansion; only after the impetus of the revolution had been completely dissipated did his talent for intrigue and boss politics come into play. Another old-style intellectual, Trotsky, was also bewildered by Stalin; he could never understand how "that gray mediocrity" could so easily dispose of him and the Party's other "massive figures." No, the heroes of all but the last month of the eight months' revolution that Sukhanov has chronicled were the Russian people—the workers, peasants, and soldiers, whose "self-organization was progressing not hourly but by the minute" and who were symbolized by the regiment Sukhanov encountered one evening on the Suvorovsky Prospekt:

> This was not in the least a mob; it was a highly organized troop formation. But I didn't see a single officer. I have a lively memory of the feeling of great triumph and tenderness that

came over me. In these stern, fatigued, and concentrated columns no one could have seen any sign of elemental passions, of abuse of liberty, or of disintegration. . . . No one had brought them to Petersburg; they had come themselves. Why? Doubtless not one of them could have given a clear explanation. . . . They were going to Okhta for the night. They weren't on quite the right road to Okhta; they evidently didn't have anyone with them who knew the capital, and I suppose they were marching more or less haphazard.

Yes, all was well; everything was going as marvellously as one might have dreamed but hardly expected in reality.

All was not well, however. Our author puts it in a sentence: "The proletariat of backward, petty-bourgeois Russia leaped up and soared to an unheard-of height, then faltered, grew confused, collapsed, and fell in an unequal struggle beyond its strength." And when that happened, the receivers were ready to take over the bankrupt revolution—a small, well-disciplined, single-minded group of "professional revolutionaries" who knew why they had come to Petersburg, who knew the right road to Okhta and many other things. Led by the two geniuses who were pushed to the top by the events of 1917—Lenin, the "mechanic of revolution," and Trotsky, the orator, pamphleteer, and organizer of the Red Army—the Bolsheviks rushed into the power vacuum created by the sudden collapse of czarist authority before any alternative form of political power had developed. Once in, they stayed. If they didn't know how to use power to bring about Socialism, they did know how to keep it.

Sukhanov's own tragedy was that he could never quite make up his mind about the Bolsheviks. His temperament had something to do with this. "Trotsky spoke last and briefly; everything was clear for him," he writes, with scorn—or is it envy? But his dilemma had deeper roots, for while he was attracted by the Bolsheviks' program, he was repelled by their methods. He, too, rejected the successive governments that preceded the Bolshevik coup in October, because they were tied to the bourgeoisie and because they continued the war; he, too, was for the immediate establishment of a workers' and peasants' state along socialist lines. But he deeply distrusted Lenin's methods: "We were divided from the Bolsheviks not so much by theory as by practice . . . not so much by slogans as by a profoundly different conception of their inner meaning. The Bolsheviks reserved that meaning for the use of the leadership and didn't carry it to the masses." He saw, as well, that Lenin's exclusion of the other left-wing parties from power, after October, was not the way to build socialism in Russia, simply because it was such a vast and backward country that one party could not possibly provide adequate leadership. When Lenin returns to his party's headquarters at the Smolny Institute (a girls' school in czarist times) after the October *putsch*, Sukhanov, of course, is there, with all his doubts and enthusiasms coming to a discordant climax:

> The whole Præsidium, headed by Lenin, was standing up and singing, with excited, exalted faces and blazing eyes. . . . Applause, hurrahs, caps flung up in the air. . . . But I didn't believe in the victory, the success, the "rightfulness," or the historic mission of a Bolshevik régime. Sitting in the back seats, I watched this celebration with a heavy heart. How I longed to join in, and merge with this mass and its leaders in a single feeling! But I couldn't.*

—*The New Yorker*, February 18, 1956

---

* (1970) This is the closing scene in Eisenstein's *Ten Days that Shook the World*, released in 1927 to celebrate the tenth anniversary of the Bolshevik *coup d'état*, sometimes misnamed the October Revolution. (Stalin was already powerful enough to compel Eisenstein to cut out all shots of its chief organizer, Trotsky.) When I first saw it in the early thirties, I responded as wholeheartedly as the director of this greatest of all propaganda films intended me to. But when I've re-viewed the film in recent decades, I shared Sukhanov's heavy heart: "How I longed to join in and merge with the mass and its leaders in a single feeling! But I couldn't." My feelings about some recent New Left manifestations are similarly divided. As a political animal, I'm of the herbivorous *genus Sukhanov*, not of the Lenin-Trotsky-Stalin carnivores.

Trotsky, Orwell,
and Socialism

In the mid-thirties, two very different political thinkers wrote two very different books. During 1935, when he was in exile in France and then in Norway, Leon Trotsky kept a diary, which has now been published by the Harvard University Press. At about the same time, George Orwell wrote *The Road to Wigan Pier*, which has now been republished by Harcourt, Brace. Orwell and Trotsky were antithetical political types—the British empiricist versus the Russian-Jewish ideologue. Trotsky applied a consistent and taken-for-granted doctrine to each new situation, showing the greatest ingenuity in each application but never modifying the basic dogma. Orwell, a trueborn Englishman, had no talent for systematic thinking and, indeed, tended to regard over-all ideologies as either absurd or harmful, or both; he was always ready to abandon his most cherished beliefs if he came to the conclusion that they no longer "worked." Both were political moralists, but how differently! Orwell's code was a simple one, based on truth and "decency"; he was important—and original—because he insisted on applying that code to his own socialist comrades as well as to the class enemy. Trotsky's code was also simple, but the reverse of Orwell's; his was a class morality (more accurately, a party morality —the tendency to confuse one's own party with the proletariat seems to be endemic in Marxism), and truth and decency were relative terms, depending on the class-party interests involved. The left-wing

politics of our time have been played out between the extremes
represented by Trotsky and Orwell.

Trotsky's diary is brief (158 pages, plus 38 pages of editorial notes)
and perfunctory. It can't be compared for biographical interest to his
My Life, unfortunately long out of print. The first entry suggests
what's wrong:

> *February 7, 1935:* The diary is not a literary form I am
> especially fond of. . . . Lassalle wrote once that he would
> gladly leave unwritten what he *knew* if only he could ac-
> complish at least a part of what he felt able to *do*. Any
> revolutionary would feel the same way. But one has to take the
> situation as it is. For the very reason that it fell to my lot to
> take part in greater events, my past now cuts me off from
> chances for action. I am reduced to interpreting events and
> trying to foresee their future course. At least this occupation
> is more satisfying than mere passive reading.

The crude contrast between knowing and doing, the notion of
being "reduced" to interpreting events, the reference to "mere passive
reading"—such is not the temper of the successful diarist. Still, the
book is revealing. I was not prepared for the depth of Trotsky's
feeling for his wife, Natalia—the love, gratitude, and admiration he
expresses again and again. I was prepared for the rigidity of mind.
Not that there aren't some very good things—after all, it's Trotsky.
Such as his comment on the Norwegian socialists: "The war and the
October Revolution, the upheavals of Fascism, have passed them by
without a trace. . . . For them the future holds hot and cold showers."
(Though, come to think of it, the Norwegians showed very different
stuff once they *were* involved with war and fascism a few years
later.) Or a lapidary note: "The radio reminds one how broad and
varied life is and at the same time gives an extremely economical
and compact expression to this variety. In short, it is an instrument
perfectly suited to a prison." There are a few glints of self-awareness,
such as his realization that his diary had taken a political-literary
rather than a personal form. "And could it actually be otherwise?
For politics and literature constitute in essence the content of my
personal life. I need only take pen in hand and my thoughts of

their own accord arrange themselves for *public* exposition. . . . You can't alter this, especially at fifty-five years of age."

But such flashes are rare. For all its vigor, Trotsky's mind was strait-jacketed by Marxism. "There is no creature more disgusting than a petty-bourgeois engaged in primary accumulation," he complains, apropos of his neighbors in provincial France. "I have never had the opportunity to observe this type as closely as I do now." Yet he feels no need to add any details; it is enough to classify the specimen in the Marxian catalogue. Nor is the political analysis any more perceptive. Is there a psychosociological law that once a man has tasted supreme power, he is doomed never to doubt his ideas again? Like Napoleon on St. Helena, Trotsky in exile was sure he still knew all the answers:

> I imagine an old doctor, devoid of neither education nor experience, who day after day has to watch quacks and charlatans doctor to death a person dear to him, knowing that this person could be certainly cured if only the elementary rules of medicine were observed. That would approximately be the way I feel as I watch the criminal work of the "leaders" of the French proletariat. Conceit? No, a deep and indestructible conviction.

But the trouble was precisely that his conviction *was* indestructible. One might think that after six years of reflection in exile he could have had doubts. He might have realized, for example, that his own prophecy, long before the October Revolution, about the totalitarian drift of Lenin's organizational methods had been fulfilled by Stalin, wherefore his own attempt to compete with Stalin as a pure Bolshevik, between 1924 and 1928, had been a mistake; after all, Stalin controlled the Party bureaucracy. And he might have realized that he and Lenin should have compromised with the Kronstadt sailors in 1921 instead of crushing them with troops led by Trotsky. Or that the dispersal by force of the Constituent Assembly, the reduction of the popular soviets to impotence, the outlawing of Shliapnikov's Workers' Opposition faction in the Party, and other such policies of Lenin and himself had taken power from the people and given it to the Party bureaucracy, and so had prepared the road for Stalin. Or, finally, that his whole estimate of

Stalin had been wrong—he had seen Stalin as a man of the right and had worried about his restoring capitalism, but the danger lay in just the other direction. Once Stalin had sent Trotsky into foreign exile in 1929, he adopted Trotsky's own "Left" program of industrialization and agricultural collectivization, which was just what he needed to get the workers and the peasants under totalitarian control.

However, Trotsky resisted all such heretical thoughts; his Leninist convictions remained, to the end, "deep and indestructible." In twelve years of exile, he only once, as far as I recall, recognized even the possibility that Leninist Marxism might have to be revised—in his "The U.S.S.R. in War," in *The New International* for November, 1939. He used his enforced leisure, instead, in a desperate effort to fit an increasingly recalcitrant reality into his outworn formulae. He defended all the major actions of himself and Lenin from 1917 to 1923, including Kronstadt; he reached no more brilliant conclusion about Stalin's Russia than that it was "a degenerated workers' state" and therefore must be "supported," and he even justified the Russian invasion of Finland in 1939 on the ground that the Red Army was still a revolutionary force (slightly degenerated, chipped, and shopworn) that was liberating the Finnish masses from their bourgeois exploiters. (One of the many awkwardnesses of this position was that the Finnish masses, to a man, woman, and dog, fled from their liberators back into territory still held by Baron Mannerheim and their class enemies, leaving nobody to be freed from the shackles of capitalism.) He was quite willing to split the most important group of his adherents, the American Trotskyites, on this issue, and he denounced us with all the old papal fervor as "petty-bourgeois capitulators" when we couldn't see any difference in principle between Stalin's Russia invading Finland and Hitler's Germany invading Poland.

Trotsky's career poses an enigma. How, on the one hand, could the man of action who had important roles in both the 1905 and the 1917 Russian revolutions and who organized and led to victory the Red Army, the man who was a world-historical figure, be so easily deposed by the unknown Stalin? And, on the other hand, how explain the sterility and timidity of thought, after 1928, of the daring intellectual who, except for Lenin, was the only major leader to see that power could be taken and held by the Bolsheviks in 1917? Trotsky was a dazzling combination of the intellectual and the man of action, but he was not a genius; he was enormously able but he was not inspired, and the situations, practical or ideological, that he had to meet after Lenin's death were so novel and so extreme that they could be mastered only by a genius; that is, someone who was willing to violate all the rules and theories and principles. Stalin and Hitler were such, for all their mediocrity of character and intellect compared to the superlative Trotsky. I think it is also possible that Trotsky's unusual combination of talents was often a disadvantage. His intellectuality sometimes interfered with his effectiveness in action, as when he tried to fight Stalin, of all people, on principles (and mistaken principles, at that), while his practicality was too narrowly practical (intellectuals tend to go to extremes), so that he tried to solve political problems by administrative measures. A curious instance of the latter failure was his proposal for dealing with low productivity in the early years of the revolution by organizing "labor battalions" under quasi-military discipline—a solution that Lenin, a genius of the practical, rejected not on any principled grounds but simply because he saw it was politically impossible.*

"The depth and strength of a human character are defined by its moral *reserves*," Trotsky wrote in his diary on April 5, 1935. "People reveal themselves completely only when they are thrown out of the customary conditions of their life, for only then do they have to fall back on their reserves. N. and I have been together for almost thirty-three years (a third of a century!), and in tragic hours I am always amazed at the reserves of her character." Exile revealed in him plenty of certain kinds of moral reserves—courage, pride, faith— but also a startling deficiency in intellectual reserves and an almost complete lack of a quality that is partly moral and partly intellectual; namely, objectivity. He maintains a double standard throughout his

---

* (1971) The close reader may have noted that in the preceding review of Sukhanov's memoirs, I called Trotsky "one of the two indisputable geniuses who were pushed to the top by the events of 1917." Let me herewith recant. Though not as to the other one, Lenin—if only he had *not* been a genius!

diary, using one set of values for his side and another for the enemy. He makes great sport of bourgeois politicians for their fine phrases, yet he writes sentences like "In the blood of wars and revolts a new generation will rise, worthy of the epoch and its tasks." On page 24 he says, "In view of the prolonged decline in the international revolution, the victory of the bureaucracy—and consequently of Stalin —was foreordained." But eight pages later he refuses this alibi to Léon Blum, dismissing his excuse for not bringing about a revolution ("conditions were not yet ripe for socialization") as a "mechanistic, fatalistic conception." He points out that the October Revolution, after all, did take place, adding contemptuously, "Those parliamentary dilettantes have learned *nothing*." (Blum might have retorted that the degeneration of the October Revolution proved that conditions in Russia were not ripe for socialism.)

But the most extraordinary instance of double-standard thinking (and feeling) in the diary is implicit in the long entry of April ninth on the execution of the Czar and his family at Ekaterinburg. Trotsky reveals that the massacre was ordered by Lenin from Moscow. He notes that certain liberals had tried to exculpate Lenin by claiming that the executions were carried out by the local Bolsheviks on their own. Similarly, the present regime in Russia recently took pains to deny the story that Lenin had spared the life of Dora Kaplan, the young Social Revolutionary who had seriously wounded him in 1918. Mercy is a bourgeois weakness, it would seem, and Lenin was a sound Bolshevik.

Therefore, Trotsky not only takes the trouble to record Lenin's complicity in Ekaterinburg but also goes on to justify it: "The decision was not only expedient but necessary. The severity of this summary justice showed the world that we would continue to fight on mercilessly, stopping at nothing. The execution of the Czar's family was needed not only in order to frighten, horrify, and dishearten the enemy, but also in order to shake up our own ranks, to show them that there was no turning back, that ahead lay either complete victory or complete ruin." (So Hitler used Buchenwald and Dachau to frighten the enemy and to involve the Germans in blood guilt—"there was no turning back.") This entry is sandwiched in between many entries revealing Trotsky's anxiety about the fate of his son Seryozha, a nonpolitical engineer who had just been arrested by Stalin simply because Trotsky was his father. Trotsky thinks this is barbarous, which it was, and refers to Seryozha as "an innocent bystander," which he was, but it doesn't occur to him that the late Czar might have considered his fourteen-year-old son another innocent bystander, not to mention his four young daughters and the family servants. Trotsky would undoubtedly have been horrified if Stalin had justified Seryozha's imprisonment—and execution a year later—with the same *raison d'état* he thinks justified Ekaterinburg.* The next day he explains why Lenin had decided to shoot the Czar and his family without trial: "Under judicial procedures, of course, execution of the family would have been impossible." So, naturally, there was no alternative (except not to shoot them). Immediately after this, he writes, "No news about Seryozha." The unconsciousness of all this is amazing. One suspects that it never occurred to the diarist that the reason he thought about the fate of the Czar's family just then was his anxiety about his own son. For if he had been conscious of this, he would have been a different, and bigger, person, and he might not have been so addicted to the double standard.

The first half of George Orwell's *The Road to Wigan Pier* describes the life of the miners and the unemployed in Lancashire and Yorkshire in the mid-thirties. It is the best sociological reporting I know. The trouble with most such works—I am thinking of classics like Engels' *The Condition of the Working Classes in England in 1844*, Mayhew's volumes on the London poor, the Russell Sage Foundation's *Pittsburgh Survey*, of 1909, and the Lynds' *Middletown* books—is that the writers are at a distance from their subjects in two ways. They exclude their own reactions, because of a mistaken idea of scientific objectivity—mistaken because the study of human behavior cannot, by its very nature, be scientific. And they maintain a psychological distance; they conscientiously spend much time in "the field," but it is always "the field." George Orwell, however, lived the life of the people he wrote about. When the Left Book Club commissioned him to do the volume, he simply went to Wigan and took a room in a cheap lodging house. He was no neophyte. He had

---

* (1971) Which was that if the Romanov, or the Trotsky, blood line was not completely extirpated down to infants, "pretenders" might arise later. (Cf. *Macbeth*.) But the servants were hardly a dynastic threat.

already lived at the bottom—and not as a sociological "observer" but as a participant, a penniless tramp who survived on bread and tea between dishwashing jobs—and had written a remarkable book about it, *Down and Out in Paris and London*. What is even more notable about Orwell's safaris into lower-class life is that, while immersing himself in the most concrete, physical way, he never ceased to judge it by his own personal standards. The romanticism of poverty is a luxury idea, possible only to slummers from above, like Rousseau's concept of the noble savage; the poor are too busy keeping alive to feel romantic or, except occasionally, to realize fully the horror of their lives. Rarely does an observer come along who is neither a tourist nor a detached sociologist and who is able to submerge himself in the actual existence on the bottom without losing his bearings. Such was Jack London when he wrote *The People of the Abyss*, after living among the London poor at the turn of the century. Such was Simone Weil, who in the thirties worked for two years in the Renault and other factories in Paris and who has left us some explicit and disturbing commentaries in two of her books: *The Need for Roots* and *Factory Work*. And such was Orwell.

Perhaps the chief virtue of his reporting is that he combines indignation with specificity, as in his description of the boarding-house table:

> I never saw this table completely uncovered, but I saw its various wrappings at different times. At the bottom there was a layer of old newspapers stained by Worcester sauce; above that a sheet of sticky white oilcloth; above that a green serge cloth; above that a coarse linen cloth, never changed and seldom taken off. Generally the crumbs from breakfast were still on the table at supper. I used to get to know individual crumbs by sight and watch their progress up and down the table from day to day.

Or the vignettes of two subscription-agents who were fellow lodgers:

> The newspapers engage poor desperate wretches, out-of-work clerks and commercial travellers and the like, who for a while make frantic efforts and keep their sales up to the minimum; then as the deadly work wears them down they are sacked

and fresh men are taken on. I got to know two who were employed by one of the more notorious weeklies. [What sociologist could permit himself the luxury of that "notorious," so
emotional, so unscientific, so inspiriting!] Both of them were
middle-aged men with families to support, and one of them
was a grandfather. They were on their feet ten hours a day,
"working" their appointed streets, and then busy late into the
night filling in blank forms. . . . The fat one, the grandfather,
used to fall asleep with his head on a pile of forms for some
swindle their paper was running. . . . Neither of them could
afford the pound a week which the Brookers charged for full
board. They used to pay a small sum for their beds and make
shamefaced meals in a corner of the kitchen off bacon and
bread-and-margarine which they stored in their suitcases.

This kind of emotional identification with the people he lives
among sometimes reaches an intensity that lights up the horror and
injustice of a class society. Consider this glimpse as his train slowly
trundles by "row after row of little grey slum houses":

At the back of one of the houses a young woman was kneeling
on the stones, poking a stick up the leaden wastepipe which
ran from the sink inside and which I suppose was blocked. I
had time to see everything about her—her sacking apron, her
clumsy clogs, her arms reddened by the cold. She looked up
as the train passed, and I was almost near enough to catch her
eye. She had a round pale face, the usual exhausted face of
the slum girl who is twenty-five and looks forty, thanks to
miscarriages and drudgery; and it wore, for the second in which
I saw it, the most desolate, hopeless expression I have ever seen.
It struck me then that we are mistaken when we say that "It
isn't the same for them as it would be for us," and that people
bred in the slums can imagine nothing but the slums. For what
I saw in her face was not the ignorant suffering of an animal.
She knew well enough what was happening to her—understood
as well as I did how dreadful a destiny it was to be kneeling
there in the bitter cold, on the slimy stones of a slum backyard, poking a stick up a foul drainpipe.

There is a curiously similar passage in Trotsky's diary for April
27. Walking with Natalia "in a drizzling rain," he meets a young
working-class woman, "in the very last stages of pregnancy," strug-

gling along with a baby in her arms, pulling a goat with a kid, and trying to control a girl of two or three. The goat keeps trying to browse, the kid keeps getting tangled in the underbrush, and the little girl "would lag behind or run ahead." When he and Natalia turn back, they meet the group again: "They were slowly continuing their advance toward the village. In the still fresh face of the woman there was submission and patience. She was probably Spanish or Italian, perhaps even Polish—there are quite a few foreign working-class families here." Trotsky is not insensitive to the young mother's plight— this is one of the few glimpses his diary gives us of everyday life— but it doesn't occur to him to talk with her ("She was probably Spanish or Italian"). Unlike Orwell, who felt a compulsion that was almost neurotic (please note the "almost") to share the life of the masses, Trotsky approached the masses from above, with the abstract, generalizing view of the intellectual or with the utilitarian purpose of the man of action. When he actually ran into one of them on a country road, he was at a loss, for all his ideological sympathy. There may be some significance in the contrasting descriptions of the two young women's expressions—Orwell saw a consciousness of degradation, Trotsky merely "submission and patience."

Perhaps each saw what he was looking for. Trotsky, though he looked at the masses from above with the most benevolent intentions, still looked from above; the Marxian revolutionary and the social worker are not so far apart. But Orwell, looking up from below, in his second chapter makes it clear just how unbelievably difficult work in a mine is by no more esoteric a device than describing the effect on his own muscles of simply getting to the working face. He notes that when a miner leaves the elevator that takes him down into the mine, he must go through one to three miles of twisting corridors, nearly always stooping and sometimes crawling. He notes that the miner is not paid for this journey, which may take an hour each way, the fiction being that it is the same as the office worker's journey to work on the bus. (Portal-to-portal pay has been won by our own United Mine Workers, although the socialized mines of England have not got around to giving it.) This concern for the trivia of working-class life, which aren't so trivial if you are a worker, distinguishes Orwell's reporting. Thus, it does not escape him that old miners don't get their pension checks in the mail but must report once a week to the

colliery office, waiting in line for hours and wasting an afternoon—
not to mention the sixpence for bus fare, a trifling sum unless one
measures one's income in sixpences.

> It is very different for a member of the bourgeoisie, even such
> a dawn-at-heel member as I am. Even when I am on the verge
> of starvation I have certain rights attaching to my bourgeois
> status. I do not earn much more than a miner earns, but I do at
> least get it paid into my bank in a gentlemanly manner. . . .
> This business of petty inconvenience and indignity, of being
> kept waiting about, of having to do everything at other people's
> convenience, is inherent in working-class life. A thousand in-
> fluences constantly press a working man down into a *passive*
> rôle. He does not act, he is acted upon. He feels himself the
> slave of mysterious authority and has a firm conviction that
> "they" will never allow him to do this, that, and the other.

The second half of *The Road to Wigan Pier* is a general discussion
of socialism that, at first glance, seems to have nothing to do with the
first half but that, on second glance, is related to it by the sensitivity
to class revealed in the foregoing quotation. Orwell begins this half,
characteristically, with a painfully honest sociobiography that might
be titled *Up from Snobbery*. He spares himself nothing. "Here you
come to the real secret of class distinctions in the West," he writes,
"the real reason why a European of bourgeois upbringing, even when
he calls himself a Communist, cannot without a hard effort think of a
working man as his equal. It is summed up in four frightful words
which people nowadays are chary of uttering, but which were ban-
died about quite freely in my childhood. The words were: 'The
lower classes smell.' " Frightful words, certainly, and brave words for
a socialist, but perhaps they tell us more about Orwell than about class
distinctions. The point is not whether the lower classes smell—after
all, everybody smells, according to our advertising—but why this is so
important to him. (Orwell concludes, with his usual quiet reason-
ableness, that they don't smell intrinsically but do extrinsically, because they have less access to baths and laundering; all this should
be put in the past tense now, considering the equalizing of living
standards that has taken place in the last twenty years here and in
England, and perhaps the very term "the lower classes" is happily
obsolescent.) An interesting monograph could be written on "Ol-

factory Perceptions in the Writings of George Orwell," or, for the Luce papers, "Orwell & Smell." This is the most primitive and un-answerable of the senses—one can say "You sounded (or looked) bad" but not "You smelled bad"—and references to it are curiously frequent in Orwell's writings, as in his famous phrase about "the smelly little orthodoxies of the Left." I hazard that these references are merely the most obvious expression of a penchant for the painful, the demeaning, and the repulsive that runs through his work, from the crimson birthmark that disfigures the face of the protagonist of *Burmese Days* to the intimate dwelling on torture at the end of *1984*. In short, there is something masochistic about Orwell's per-sonality, for all the moral courage and the penetration of his politi-cal thought, and there's no use blinking it (as he himself might have written). For he, too, had a double standard, though just the reverse of Trotsky's—he was tougher on himself and his own side than he was on the class enemy.

A good deal of this second half is devoted to an attempt to explain why socialism had not made more progress among the British masses. He blames the situation mostly on the socialists, whom he sees as health cranks, epicene pacifists, and, in general, "mingy little beasts." The rhetoric of abuse with which he overwhelms his com-rades is more exuberant than anything he says about the bourgeoisie: "Socialism, *in the form in which it is now presented*, appeals chiefly to unsatisfactory or even inhuman types . . . that dreary tribe of high-minded women and sandal-wearers and bearded fruit-juice drinkers who come flocking toward the smell of 'progress' like blue-bottles to a dead cat . . . the intellectual, tract-writing type of Social-ist, with his pullover, his fuzzy hair, and his Marxian quotation. . . . The worst advertisement for Socialism is its adherents." Even to one who, like myself, no longer agrees that "Socialism is such elementary common sense," and even granting that Orwell, who had actually lived with the lower classes, had some right to be impatient with the middle-class romantics who preached socialism to "the masses" they knew nothing about, the abuse seems overdone.

However, it is better to turn the double standard against one's own side than against one's enemies, if the choice must be made, since it leads to more understanding. It is true that Orwell, like al-most all political writers in the thirties, when Marxism permeated the air with illusions of omniscience, was often too quick on the draw with a prediction, as when he writes, "Of course it is obvious now that the upper middle class is done for." (In modern English prose, one puts in "of course" and "obvious" when the matter is not at all obvious, just as "undoubtedly" indicates doubt.) Or: "Under the capitalist system, in order that England may live in comparative comfort, a hundred million Indians must live on the verge of starvation —an evil state of affairs, but you acquiesce in it every time you step into a taxi or eat a plate of strawberries and cream." The British upper middle class is still very much with us, and although India has been freed, the British standard of living is higher than before,* and there are still lots of taxis and strawberries around. But while Trotsky was, so to speak, systematically wrong, much of Orwell is still fresh and to the point: his criticism of the socialist romanticism about industrial progress, for example, and his still disregarded advice that it is the exploited middle classes the socialists should try to recruit, and his debunking of the "liblab" (Liberal-Labour) cant idealizing the working class and the parallel cant of the proletarian intellectual, from the communists to D. H. Lawrence with his mystique of the potent gamekeeper and the eunuch landlord. He is also still to the point when he objects that modern socialists, bemused by Marx's historical materialism and by Stalin's Five-Year Plans, have forgotten the great moral goals, like Justice and Liberty, that have historically inspired their movement, and when he insists, with a side glance at the Communists, that "the real Socialist is one who wishes . . . to see tyranny overthrown."

Somebody at Harcourt, Brace had the happy idea of reprinting Victor Gollancz's Foreword to the original edition in 1937. "This Foreword is addressed to members of the Left Book Club (to whom *The Road to Wigan Pier* is being sent as the March Choice), and to them alone," it begins. "Members of the general public are asked to ignore it." Poor Mr. Gollancz, who had founded the Club earlier that year—with John Strachey and the late Harold Laski—was in a tough spot. The Club had commissioned Orwell to do a study of the unem-

---

* (1974) Written in 1959, the good old days before the Tory-Labor stalemate became a mutual and national suicide pact.

ployed in the North of England. He had done a masterly job, exactly what the Club had hoped for, but then, after exposing the horrors of capitalism, he had characteristically insisted on exposing the horrors of socialism. To their credit, the Messrs. Gollancz, Strachey, and Laski, although then (in those long-ago days) ardent Popular Fronters and sympathizers with the Soviet Union, printed the book as Orwell wrote it. (The British sense of fair play and open discussion has rarely been more agreeably demonstrated; one cannot imagine their American opposite numbers at the time acting so.) But the 38,000 members of the Left Book Club, hungry (and trusting) sheep looking up to be fed, had at least to be warned. British fair play is, after all, a human virtue, not an angelic one. So Mr. Gollancz, in the most reasonable and friendly style, defuses as many of Orwell's booby traps as he can. Sometimes he is acute ("Mr. Orwell calls himself a 'half-intellectual,' but the truth is that he is at one and the same time an extreme intellectual and a violent anti-intellectual"), sometimes he is persuasive (his defense of vegetarians, pacifists, and feminists), and sometimes he is absurd, as when he complains that "He even commits the curious indiscretion of referring to Russian commissars as 'half-gramophones, half-gangsters.'" But, given his dilemma, he didn't do badly. And he did produce what is now a most interesting historical document.

Another interesting, if depressing, document is *Voices of Dissent* (Grove Press, 1959), an anthology of pieces from *Dissent*, which has been appearing quarterly since 1954. *Dissent* is undoubtedly (see preceding gloss on this word) the best left-wing political magazine we have, which makes it all the more depressing. (Perhaps I should note that "left wing" includes among its meanings "anticommunist," our Communists having been for many years, *pace* the late Senator McCarthy, neither socialists nor revolutionaries.) Irving Howe, who, with Lewis Coser, has been the mainspring of the editorial board, defines *Dissent*'s purpose as providing of "a forum for the discussion of the ideals and problems of democratic socialism." If this formula sounds a little dusty, so do most of the articles here reprinted. Not that *Dissent* has been doctrinaire. It has tried to live up to its name, and has printed a great variety of socialist thinkers, and even a few nonsocialists. The difficulty seems to be that the very idea of socialism is no longer interesting; it is at once banal and ambiguous. It would take another Marx, God forbid, to redefine in the light of modern experience either "socialism" or "democracy." Meanwhile, *Dissent* keeps the franchise open, and perhaps this isn't a bad thing. But why is there such a lack of the individual accent in these articles, why do Orwell and Trotsky sound like men, while so many of these articles sound like the product of thinking machines? Is it because socialism is no longer, pro or con, connected with our actual life? There is a mandarin quality about this book: the writers are serious, they are in admirable revolt against our society, but they somehow deal with things at a distance; they are professors of revolution, members of the socialist academy. The few sharper, more direct articles merely emphasize the gray tone of the collection. Howe's "Stevenson and the Intellectuals" is incisive political criticism. Norman Mailer's whirling, breathless, earnest "The White Negro" is cockeyed but imaginative. He subtitles it "Superficial Reflections on the Hipster," but they aren't at all superficial; they are much too deep. William L. Neumann's "Historians in an Age of Acquiescence" is good old-fashioned cultural muckraking. And Czelaw Milosz's open letter to Picasso, though it is only three pages, makes an impact because it is *felt*; one has the impression he is saying something that makes a real difference to him as a writer, and not just holding up the by now rather tattered banner of Socialism. There are three or four other nonmandarin pieces—those by Nicola Chiaromonte, Paul Goodman, and Harvey Swados come to mind—but the general tone is definitely gray. And there are far too many sentences like "Folded in the center of capitalist dynamics Marx detected a stasis in which completed being embodied itself continually."*

—*The New Yorker*, March 28, 1959

---

* (*1973*) This is still about the state of expectation in which I approach reading (or postponing reading) *Dissent*, to which I have been a fickle subscriber for years.

A Heroine
of Our Time

The most extraordinary and, for
once in these depressing times, inspiriting news of the month is the
Petition to the Presidium of the Twenty-third Congress of the Soviet
Communist Party signed by sixty-three Soviet writers, including Ilya
Ehrenburg, protesting against the sentencing, nine months ago, of
two well-known literary figures, Andrei Sinyavsky and Yuli Daniel,
to terms of seven and five years, respectively, at hard labor in a work
camp for having published satiric fantasies which the court considered "anti-Soviet." The group asked that Sinyavsky and Daniel,
who are middle-aged, not robust, and reported to be suffering physical
hardship under the rigorous camp regime, be released, offering to
"stand surety" for them. The petition reads, in part:

> Although we do not approve the means by which these
> writers published their works abroad,* we cannot accept the

---

* They sent their writings abroad—through friends, not by Western diplomatic
or espionage channels—because they couldn't publish them in their own
country. Sinyavsky (who recently edited an edition of Pasternak's poems and
is a prominent Soviet literary scholar) used the name "Abram Tertz." *The
Trial Begins, On Socialist Realism, The Makepeace Experiment* and other
productions have made "Tertz" one of the most admired Soviet writers in
the West. Daniel used the name "Nikolai Arzak," *Moscow Calling* being his
best-known work abroad. The reproof about "the means by which these
writers published their works abroad" would seem to be a tactical concession
rather than a serious point since among the many awkwardnesses the prosecution had to surmount to get a conviction were the facts that in Soviet law
neither sending manuscripts abroad nor using pseudonyms is a crime.

view that their motives were in any way anti-Soviet, which alone could have justified the severity of the sentence. . . . The condemnation of writers for the writing of satirical works creates an extremely dangerous precedent and threatens to hold up the progress of Soviet culture. Neither learning nor art can exist if neither paradoxical ideas can be expressed nor hyperbolic images be used as an artistic device. In our complex situation today, we need more freedom for artistic experiment. . . . The trial of Sinyavsky and Daniel has already caused us more harm than did any of their mistakes.

A rather cautious and overqualified protest, in Western terms, but extraordinary in Soviet terms. In fact unique. There have been instances of highly placed individuals intervening with the Kremlin to protect writers and artists, as Maxim Gorky often did with Stalin, sometimes successfully, but I can recall no instance in the whole history of Soviet culture since 1917 of a group of writers addressing a public protest to the authorities on behalf of colleagues tried and condemned on political grounds. It is inspiriting that so many writers had the courage to do so—all the more since the group has only one big "name," Ehrenburg. And it is also inspiriting, to slightly shift the angle, that while it took courage, it didn't take heroism—that is, there was a risk but a reasonable one, not the kind there would have been under Stalin. Heroes are rare and I cannot believe in 63 of them showing up all at once. So I deduce, inspiritedly, that the political-cultural climate in Russia today is more clement than it appeared to be last year when Sinyavsky and Daniel, despite widespread protests and pleas from intellectuals in Western countries, including many Communists, were tried on such flimsy charges and condemned to such barbarous sentences. Indeed, the opposition inside Russia is broader than the above petition, which is quoted from the *New York Times* of November 19, 1966; other reports state that 95 Soviet intellectuals have expressed themselves publicly in one way or another, and that a total of 381 letters, petitions, and depositions have come out of Russia about the case, which would seem to be becoming a national scandal, a Soviet Dreyfus Affair.

There was, however, at least one hero, or rather heroine, among the sixty-three signers of the Petition: Lidiya Chukovskaya, identified by the *Times* as "critic" and also as the daughter of Kornei I. Chukovsky, whose name comes first in the list of signers. Miss Chukovskaya wrote a letter of her own which is about four times as long and eight times as heroic as the Petition she signed, along with the other sixty-two writers. I don't mean to belittle them; they were brave men and women, responsible to their calling, and their collective Petition was, as I've noted, unique and inspiring in Soviet cultural history. However, Lidiya Chukovskaya is a heroine. Her letter is moving, eloquent, and beautifully direct. It is addressed to Mikhail Sholokhov, with copies to eight literary groups, including the Board of the Union of Writers of the Union of the Soviet Socialist Republics and the editors of *Pravda, Izvestia,* and *Literaturnaya Gazeta.* Mr. Sholokhov won a Nobel Prize with a novel of some forty years ago, *And Quiet Flows the Don.* When Pasternak was forced by the Khrushchev regime to give up the Nobel Prize awarded him for *Doctor Zhivago,* Sholokhov sided with the Kremlin, denouncing the novel as unpatriotic and insisting he was the only Soviet writer who had ever really won the Nobel Prize, since Bunin was a geographical exile and Pasternak a spiritual one. Then came the Sinyavsky-Daniel case.

"When you spoke at the Twenty-third Party Congress, Mikhail Alexandrovich," she begins,

you went to the rostrum not as a private person but as "a spokesman for Soviet literature." You thereby made it legitimate for every writer, including me, to pass judgment about the things you said supposedly in the name of us all. Your speech really can be called "historical." In the whole history of Russian culture I know of no other case of a writer publicly expressing regret not at the harshness of a sentence but at its leniency.

Furthermore, you were upset not only by the sentences— you also did not like actual court proceedings [which] you found too pedantic, too legalistic. You would have liked it better if the court had tried these two Soviet citizens un-hampered by the legal code, if it had been guided not by the law but by its "sense of rough justice." I was staggered by this suggestion and I have good reason to believe that I was not alone in this. Stalin's contempt for the law cost our people millions of innocent victims. Persistent attempts to return to the rule of law . . . constitute the most precious achievement of our country during the last ten years. . . .

For a long time now, Mikhail Alexandrovich, you have been in the habit . . . of talking about writers with scorn and crude mockery. . . .

Here are your actual words: "If these fellows with their black consciences had been caught in the memorable Twenties, when people were tried not on the basis of closely defined articles of the criminal code but 'in accordance with the revolutionary sense of justice' . . . they would have got something quite different, these turncoats! And then, if you please, people talk about the sentence's being too harsh."

You said in your speech that you were ashamed for those who tried to get a pardon for them. . . . But, quite frankly, I am ashamed not for them, or for myself, but for you. They were following the fine tradition of Soviet and pre-Soviet Russian literature, whereas you, by your speech, have cut yourself off from this tradition. It was in the "memorable Twenties" . . . that Maxim Gorky brought all the weight of his authority . . . to save [writers] from prison and deportation. . . . The greatest of our poets, Alexander Pushkin, prided himself that "for mercy on the fallen I have called!" . . .

By reducing complex propositions to simple ones, by bandying around the word "treason" . . . you have once again, Mikhail Alexandrovich, been false to the writer's duty of constantly explaining and bringing home to everybody the complexity and contradictory nature of the literary and historical process. . . .

I protest against the sentence pronounced by the court. Why? Because the trial was in itself illegal. Because . . . a work of literature—whether good or bad, talented or untalented, truthful or untruthful—cannot be tried in any court . . . except the court of literature. A writer, like any Soviet citizen, can and should be tried by a criminal court for any misdemeanor he may have committed, but not for his books. . . . Ideas should be fought with ideas, not with camps and prisons.

This is what you should have said if you had really gone to the rostrum as a spokesman for Soviet literature.

But you spoke as a renegade. Your shameful speech will not be forgotten by history.

And literature will take its own vengeance. . . . It has

condemned you to the worst sentence to which an artist can be condemned—to creative sterility. And neither honors nor money nor prizes can turn this judgment from your head.

—Lidiya Chukovskaya

This letter, so free and passionate and yet so scrupulous—she attacks Sholokhov violently but never in ideological abstractions, always in terms of his function as a writer and his being as a man—reminds me of Herzen, Bielinsky, and other radical Russian intellectuals of the last century. She addresses him, note, not as "Comrade Sholokhov," the conventional bureaucratic hypocrisy, but as "Mikhail Alexandrovich," the old patronymic style, formal yet personal, that assumes a human connection. Despite the 1917 chasm and the Stalinist abyss, the Russian intellectual tradition persists. Their cultural continuity has not been destroyed so long as individuals like Lidiya Chukovskaya continue to exist, and to speak out.

Coming across her letter is like finding a plant still alive and growing after the glacier has moved on.

—*Esquire*, February, 1967

Afterword

More recent stubbornly growing plants are the courageous Medvedev brothers, Roy and Zhores, the former a historian, the latter a biochemist. "Sons of the Marxist philosopher, Alexander Romanovitch Medvedev, who was executed in the 1938 purges," Harrison Salisbury writes in the December 26, 1971, *New York Times Book Review*, "they are the authors of four major works on Stalinism and the contemporary Soviet era, none published in the Soviet Union except in *samizdat* [underground circulation in mimeographed copies, an evasion of the censorship that has become widespread of late years— D.M.]. These are, by Zhores, *The Rise and Fall of T. D. Lysenko* [a charlatan who rejected modern biological theory, from Mendel on, as "bourgeois defeatist" and insisted, as a good "Marxist," that acquired characteristics could be genetically inherited; Stalin gave him complete control over Soviet biology with disastrous results to both theory (and many eminent theoreticians) and agricultural practice—D.M.] and *The Medvedev Papers*, analyzing the Soviet censorship system and controls over intellectual life. And, by both Zhores and Roy, *A Case of Madness*, dealing with the efforts of the Soviet authorities last year to concoct a psychiatric case against Zhores and forcibly confine him in an asylum. [A tactic devised by Czar Nicholas I in 1836 to discredit and discipline Chaadayev, a critic of too high a status to be disposed of by more direct methods—see Alexander Herzen's *My Past and Thoughts* (Knopf, 1968, pp. 516–521); Nicholas's invention, a political practical joke so to speak, has been much plagiarized by his current successors; the logic is that only a madman would speak out against such overwhelming power.— D.M.] The fourth is the present monumental study by Roy of the whole Stalin epoch [*The Origins and Consequences of Stalinism*, Knopf, 1972, 566 pp.], the first known to have been undertaken within the Soviet Union.

"That the Medvedev brothers have not yet been imprisoned is due in large measure to the powerful and vocal support they have been given by important elements in the Soviet intellectual community, including that of world-famous physicists like Kapitsa and Sakharov, major literary figures like Solzhenitsyn and Tvardovsky, and certain unnamed influential members of the Soviet Government who must have included at least one member of the Politburo itself."*

The post-Stalin situation in Russia has some interesting similarities to the post-Nicholas situation a century earlier. Nicholas died in 1855, Stalin in 1953. Nicholas's successor, Alexander II, was (relatively) liberal—he abolished serfdom, formally, about the same time Lincoln freed the slaves, formally—who represented, as Khrushchev did, a less extreme kind of bureaucratic control, a relaxation into a more human style in which experimental compromise was more the note than absolute certainty.

It is significant that the critical, muckraking paper Herzen

---

* (1973) Now should be added Zhores's book about the Solzhenitsyn case, *Ten Years After Ivan Denisovich* (Knopf, 1973).

edited in London, *The Bell*, had its apogee of underground influence inside Russia between 1857 and 1862, when it was read by "everybody" including all levels of the bureaucracy right up to the Czar himself. Partly anxious curiosity—*The Bell* was always *au courant* about the latest Russian scandal, from willing, and well-informed, correspondents—but mostly, I think, from bad conscience on the part of many czarist bureaucrats. The same uncertainty and guilt, according to Salisbury, infects some sectors of the post-Stalin bureaucracy.

André Malraux observed, during the later Stalin period, that the most ominous historical difference between the East and the West was that the postwar ruling classes in the West had a bad conscience about their political crimes while those in the East perpetrated their infamies with a good conscience. So the former drew back from freely exercising their power (who can feel solid ground underfoot, after Marx, in bourgeois capitalism?) and the latter pressed ahead in firm moral conviction (who cannot feel confident, after Marx, in the communist faith?). Perhaps this faith is eroding now inside the Soviet Union—it's our, and their, one hope.

Addendum

The sturdiest plant of all to miraculously survive the Soviet glacier has just surfaced: Solzhenitzyn's *The Gulag Archipelago, 1918–1956*, massively researched and passionately written. Judging from the lengthy excerpts printed in the *New York Times* of December 29, 30, and 31, 1973, this is by far the most detailed and extensive *exposé* that has ever come out of Soviet Russia, drawn from over two hundred interviews with survivors of the secret-police "Gulag" prison and camp system, plus his own nine years as a Gulag convict. Also the most politically drastic: Solzhenitzyn compares Stalin (unfavorably) to Hitler and accuses Lenin directly as the historical accomplice and progenitor of Stalin's crimes.

Today's *Times* (January 10, 1974) reports: "The Moscow Writers Union [yesterday] expelled Lidiya K. Chukovskaya, a prominent novelist, for having come to the defense of the dissident atomic physicist, Andrei Sakharov, when he was under attack last fall. . . . She was charged with having 'slipped into an anti-Soviet swamp.' Mr. Sakharov immediately issued a statement calling her essay in his behalf last fall 'a continuation of the best Russian humanistic traditions,' adding: 'She dares to say what many others, with reputations and honors to protect them, prefer to remain silent about.' . . . Miss Chukovskaya, who is nearly blind and has a weak heart . . . is the daughter of one of the Soviet Union's best-loved children's writers, Kornei Chukovsky, and is known abroad for a number of works including *The Deserted House*, a semiautobiographical account of a woman's life during the Stalinist purges." Asked by one of the literary commissars of the Writers Union, when she insisted dissident writers were persecuted, "Why does all this happen around you and nothing like that happens around me?," Chukovskaya replied: "I don't know. Maybe you are living on an island. Perhaps you make a special effort not to see."

4

A POLITICAL CHRONICLE
1938-1974

Kronstadt Revisited

Dear Comrades:

Trotsky's article on Kronstadt in your April [1938] issue was disappointing and embarrassing. Disappointing because I had hoped for a frank and reasonably objective explanation of the Kronstadt affair. Embarrassing because I admire Trotsky and accept many of his theories. An article like this—essentially a piece of special pleading, however brilliant—makes it harder to defend Trotsky from the often-made accusation that his thinking is sectarian and inflexible.

For those who believe, as I do, that the proletarian revolution is the only road to socialism, the question of the day is: how can we avoid the sort of degeneration that has taken place in the U.S.S.R.? Specifically, to what extent must Bolshevist theory bear the responsibility for the rise of Stalinism? In *The Revolution Betrayed*, Trotsky demonstrates that Stalinism is primarily a reflection of the low level of productivity and economic development of Russia. But even if one accepts this analysis, as I do, an important contributory cause may still be found in certain weaknesses of Bolshevist political theory. Is it not the duty of Marxists today relentlessly to search out these weaknesses, to reconsider the entire Bolshevist line with scientific detachment? My impression is that Trotsky has shown little interest in any such basic reconsideration. He seems to be more interested in defending Leninism than in learning from its mistakes.

The article on Kronstadt is a good example of what I mean. It is impassioned, eloquent, and—unconvincing. Trotsky may be correct in all his contentions. But he approaches the subject in such a way as to make it impossible for the detached observer to form an intelligent opinion. I have neither the time nor the knowledge—and *The New International* certainly hasn't the space—to argue the Kronstadt question here. But I would like to indicate a few misgivings about the *tone* of Trotsky's article. In general, it seems to me that Trotsky takes a polemical approach to a question that should be considered dispassionately, with some respect for the other side. The very title is contemptuous: "Hue and Cry Over Kronstadt." The opposition is characterized in police-court terms—"this variegated fraternity," "this truly charlatan campaign." To justify such abuse, Trotsky must bring forward much stronger evidence to offset the statements of Serge, Thomas, Berkman, and Souvarine than he has up to now.

Trotsky begins his article with an amalgam worthy of Vyshinsky: "Participating in the campaign . . . are anarchists, Russian Mensheviks, left social-democrats . . . individual blunderers, Miliukov's paper, and, on occasion, the big capitalist press. A 'People's Front' of its own kind!" The only category which seems to fit me is "individual blunderer." Trotsky seems unable to imagine anyone criticizing Kronstadt unless he has a political ax to grind or is a dupe, just as the Stalinists catalogue all critics of the Moscow Trials as Trotskyists, fascists, assassins, and—my own label—Trotskyist stooges. I can't see as much difference as I would like to see between Trotsky's insistence that, because the enemies of the revolution have used the Kronstadt affair to discredit Bolshevism, therefore all who express doubts about Kronstadt are ("objectively" considered) allies of counterrevolution and Vyshinsky's insistence that the Fourth International and the Gestapo are comrades-in-arms because both oppose the Stalinist regime. This exclusion of subjective motivation as irrelevant, this refusal to consider aims, programs, theories, anything except the objective fact of opposition—this cast of mind seems to me dangerous and unrealistic. I insist it is possible to have doubts about Kronstadt without being either a knave or a fool.

Having created his amalgam, Trotsky defines its lowest common denominator—and very low it is. "How can the Kronstadt uprising cause such heartburn to anarchists, Mensheviks, and 'liberal' counter-revolutionists, all at the same time?" he asks. "The answer is simple: all these groupings are interested in compromising the only genuinely revolutionary current which has never repudiated its banner. . . ."

The answer is perhaps a bit too simple—another thing that bothers me, by the way, about Trotsky's answers. So far as I am conscious, I am not interested in "compromising" Bolshevism; on the contrary, I wish I were able to accept it 100 percent. But I unfortunately have certain doubts, objections, criticisms. Is it impossible to express them without being accused of counterrevolution and herded into an amalgam of anarchists, Mensheviks, and capitalist journalists?

Most of Trotsky's article attempts to show that the social base of the Kronstadt uprising was petty bourgeois. He makes one major point: that the Kronstadt sailors of 1921 were quite a different group from the revolutionary heroes of 1917. But the rest of his lengthy argument boils down to an identification of all the elements which opposed the Bolsheviks as "petty bourgeois." He advances little evidence to support this labeling, beyond the indisputable fact that they were all anti-Bolshevik. His reasoning seems to be: only the Bolshevist policy could save the revolution; the Makhno bands, the Greens, the Social Revolutionaries, the Kronstadters, etc., were against the Bolsheviks; therefore, objectively, they were counterrevolutionary; therefore, they were, objectively, working for the bourgeoisie. This reasoning begs the whole question. But even if the initial assumption be accepted, it is still a dangerous intellectual process. It rationalizes an unpleasant administrative necessity—the suppression of political opponents who also are acting for what they conceive to be the best interests of the masses—into a struggle between Good and Evil. A police measure becomes a moral crusade, by simply refusing to distinguish between the subjective and the objective categories—as if a bank robber should be indicted for trying to overthrow capitalism! Stalin has learned the trick all too well.

Trotsky has very little to say about the way the Bolsheviks handled the Kronstadt affair itself. He presents no defense for the mass executions which, according to Victor Serge, took place for months after the rebels had been crushed. In fact, he doesn't mention this aspect at all. Nor does he pay much attention to the crucial question: how seriously did the Bolshevists try to reach a peaceful settlement before they brought up the field guns? He dismisses this: "Or perhaps it would have been sufficient to inform the Kronstadt sailors of the N.E.P. decrees to pacify them? Illusion! The insurgents did not have a conscious program and they could not have one because of the very nature of the petty bourgeoisie." Here Trotsky admits, by implication, what Souvarine states: that Lenin was putting the finishing touches on the NEP during the Tenth Party Congress, which broke up to allow the delegates to take part in the attack on Kronstadt. It was a serious decision Lenin and Trotsky took: to withhold public announcement of NEP until after the rebellion, which asked for some of the very concessions which the NEP granted, had been drowned in blood. How could they be so sure it would have been impossible to compromise with the Kronstadters on the basis of the NEP? A few sentences earlier, Trotsky admits that "the introduction of the N.E.P. one year earlier would have averted the Kronstadt uprising." But the Kronstadters, writes Trotsky, being petty bourgeois, didn't have any "conscious program" and so couldn't have been appealed to by programmatic concessions. Petty bourgeois or not, the Kronstadters *did* have a program. Souvarine, for one, gives it in his life of Stalin as "Free elections to the Soviets; free speech and a free press for workers and peasants, left-wing socialists, anarchists and syndicalists; the release of workers and peasants held as political prisoners; the abolition of the privileges of the Communist party; equal rations for all workers; the right of peasants and self-employing artisans to dispose of the product of their work." Perhaps Trotsky uses the term "conscious program" in a special sense.

To me the most interesting statement in the article is: "It is true . . . that I had already proposed the transition to N.E.P. in 1920. . . . When I met opposition from the leaders of the party, I did not appeal to the ranks, in order to avoid mobilizing the petty bourgeoisie against the workers." As Trotsky points out, Lenin admitted that the policy of "War Communism" was adhered to longer than it should have been. Was this simply a mistake in judgment, as Trotsky implies, or was it a mistake which springs from the very nature of Bolshevist political organization, which concentrates power in the hands of a small group of politicians so well insulated (by a hierarchic, bureaucratic party apparatus) against pressure from the masses that they don't respond to the needs of the masses—until too late? Even when one of the leaders is able correctly to judge the needs of the masses, he can only try to persuade his colleagues of the correctness of his views. If they can't be persuaded, he is inhibited by his political philosophy from appealing to the rank and file for support. It is true, as Trotsky writes, that the bourgeoisie would have sought to profit by any division in the ranks of the Bolsheviks. But are not the dangers of an air-tight dictatorship, insulated against mass pressure, even greater? Are not episodes like Kronstadt inevitable under such conditions? And would a Stalinist clique be able so easily to usurp control of a party which allowed greater participation to the masses and greater freedom to left-wing opposition, both inside and outside the dominant party?

These are the questions which Kronstadt raises. Trotsky does not answer them when he summarizes: "In essence, the gentlemen critics are opponents of the dictatorship of the proletariat and by that token are opponents of the revolution. In this lies the whole secret." The secret is more complicated than this formulation. Rosa Luxemburg all her life opposed Lenin's conception of the dictatorship of the proletariat. But the Guard officers who assassinated her in 1919 knew very well what her attitude was towards the 1917 revolution.

—*The New International*, July, 1938

Afterword

The above, together with the first installment of a topical column entitled, "Reading from Right to Left," marked my debut in the Trotskyist press, to which I contributed copiously for the next four years. That I should begin my Trotskyist period with a polemic, and on a specially sore point, against the grand master of the order himself was either high-minded or arrogant or naive or just plain schitzy, maybe a bit of each. It was also characteristic.

It's to the credit of the editors of *The New International* that they printed not only my letter but also an equally long protest by Victor Serge against Trotsky's curious attempt to gloss over Kronstadt after so many years. Serge's critique carried weight because he had been active in Leningrad in 1921 as a member of the Workers' Opposition faction of the Bolsheviks and had gone through the whole traumatic experience. See his *Memoirs of a Revolutionary* (London,

1963); and for a recent scholarly work Paul Avrich's excellent *Kronstadt 1921* (Princeton University Press, 1970), a judicious reconstruction, from original sources, of what really happened, and why.

I call Trotsky's 1938 stonewalling on Kronstadt "curious" because I would expect him by then to have realized that the Kronstadt sailors had raised, however crudely, a legitimate protest against his and Lenin's continuation of "War Communism" long after the White armies had been defeated—a protest they implicitly recognized, *after* their bloody repression of the Kronstadt rebels, by relaxing economic controls with the New Economic Policy (NEP). Also to have been able to admit, after seventeen years' reflection, that their reliance on force, as against political bargaining. and compromise, had been the same kind of bureaucratic reflex he was later to criticize in Stalin. And if such a public admission of error is too much to expect from a Marxist ideologue—they don't go in for *mea culpas*—and if one assumes he was a tough-minded *realpolitiker* like Lenin, then one would expect him to understand, by 1938, that his chief political capital was his moral crusade against Stalinism, that Kronstadt was marshy ground for a firm stand, and that a tactical (and hypocritical) concession on this academic issue from the long-dead past was indicated. Instead he met the Kronstadt critics—who weren't limited to Serge and myself among his sympathizers—in a head-on collision. The Old (Bolshevik) Guard dies but it never surrenders! Whence I conclude that my onetime leader was not serious as a revolutionary in either the *realpolitik* or the idealistic sense of that term. He was neither a practical Lenin nor a principled Luxemburg and so he never knew, as they did, just where to draw the line (at rather different meridians) between theory and practice, the ideal and the real. He tried to straddle both antinomies because, as I now see him, he was, psychologically, more a bureaucrat than a radical.

The
Willkievelt Campaign

The 1940 presidential campaign has taken place in the midst of the supreme historical crisis of world capitalism, an era of upheaval unprecedented since Napoleonic times. Since the campaign began, Germany has established its political and military control of the European continent, the British Empire has entered into a life-and-death struggle with the Axis powers, Japan has joined the Axis to establish a new "world order," warning the United States that any direct participation in the war in either the Atlantic or the Pacific will mean war in *both* oceans. These events have stimulated the Roosevelt administration to bold countermoves which are changing the face of American politics.

The internal development of capitalist democracy, under the tremendous pressure of the overseas crisis, has greatly speeded up in the last few months. Economically, the drift towards state capitalism proceeds faster than ever. . . . Politically, parliamentary democracy has received severe blows: the President's consummation of the destroyer deal with Britain without consulting Congress; the swift passage of the peacetime conscription legislation in the face of widespread popular opposition. . . .

This is the great dum-dee campaign in American history, the campaign in which the electorate are offered a choice between Tweedledum and Tweedledee. There are no issues not because the country is united behind the policies of the Roosevelt administration

—a large section of the population is antiwar and anticonscription—
but because the ruling class is united and because the crisis is much
too severe to permit the luxury of a democratic discussion of the
issues. Roosevelt and Willkie, the only candidates with a chance of
election, stand shoulder to shoulder on all the important issues because the bourgeois interests which use them indifferently as mouthpieces are similarly indivisible today.

One of the reasons for the unreality of the campaign is that one of
the contestants, Roosevelt, has refused to campaign. With a cynicism
which contrasts ironically with his fervent speeches about "democracy," Roosevelt has refused to carry out the minimum responsibility
of a candidate seeking election: to present his view of the issues to the
voters. He has taken full advantage of his position as president to
identify his official acts with his candidacy, to make Willkie's criticisms seem to be traitorous attacks on the president's office, even to
raid the political camp of his opponent for his secretaries of navy
and war.

   A cursory review of Willkie's speeches reveals that he is definitely
FOR the following (1) democracy; (2) profits; (3) "national defense";
(4) business ("There are, including farmers, over 10,000,000 private
businesses in the United States."); (5) more aid for the farmers; (6)
more aid for labor; (7) more aid for business; (8) more aid for all
other groups and subdivisions of the population not included under
the three aforementioned heads; (9) common sense; (10) Roosevelt's
foreign policy; (11) Roosevelt's domestic policy (except it should be
more efficient); (12) prosperity; (13) peace (unless it is necessary to
go to war); (14) the Declaration of Independence, the Constitution,
and Abraham Lincoln. On the other hand, Willkie has taken a firm
stand AGAINST the following: (1) red tape; (2) inefficiency; (3)
high taxes on business; (4) Hitler; (5) an unbalanced budget; (6)
unemployment (his remedy: more jobs); (7) the Roosevelt administration (except for its foreign and domestic policies).

*There are two major issues in the campaign, on both of which the
candidates are in agreement: (1) foreign policy—the attitude of the
United States towards the rise of Germany and the decline of the
British Empire; (2) domestic policy: the devolution of bourgeois*

democracy into Bonapartism through extension of the executive power and the undermining of the authority of Congress. The two are, of course, closely connected, the bourgeoisie finding that, because of the terrible speed and pressure of the crisis, it can protect its interests only by short-circuiting the processes of democracy. Hence Willkie, agreeing on foreign policy, has been unable to capitalize politically on the domestic issues.

Willkie got the Republican nomination partly because he had some of the political "it" which Roosevelt has, partly because he aroused a real crusading enthusiasm among stockbrokers and Park Avenue matrons ("the Bryan of the rich," in Alice Longworth's phrase), but chiefly because Hitler was winning his *Blitzkrieg* against France and Belgium in appallingly little time. All through the winter, when the war was in its "quiet" stage, the leading contenders for the Republican nomination played, like their party in general, a demagogic "antiwar" game designed to make political capital out of the powerful isolationist sentiment of the masses. Taft, Vandenburg, and, after considerable fence-sitting, Dewey—all took this line. As a principled and conscious Wall Streeter, however, Willkie had from the beginning lined up with Roosevelt on foreign policy. When the *Blitzkrieg* came, the business community suddenly realized that Roosevelt had been a far-sighted imperialist, and that the threat to American imperialism from the Nazi war machine had become *the* all-important issue. At the Republican convention, a curious conflict took place between the professional politicians who wanted a more stable and amenable candidate and who were also willing to play around with the war issue in order to keep as many isolationist votes as possible, and their big business backers, who insisted on putting the war issue first. The business forces won out and Willkie was nominated.

The same conflict—with the same results—has cropped up now and then in the campaign, between political bosses who want first of all to win the election, and Willkie, who wants first of all to save American imperialism. Heroically refusing to make "a political football" out of so sacred a matter, Willkie is losing the election for the same reason he won the nomination: because he supports in every detail the Roosevelt foreign policies. With a fidelity to principle worthy of a better cause, he has thrown issue after issue away. Despite the widespread unpopularity of peacetime conscription, he came out for it even before Roosevelt did. He refused to make even minor concessions: although 140 Republican congressmen voted to delay the draft until an attempt had been made to raise enough men by voluntary enlistment, Willkie, "disregarding strong pressure from members of the Republican organization," came out flatly for immediate conscription. He had no criticisms to make of the administration's South American commitments at the Havana Conference. He endorsed the most audacious strokes of Roosevelt foreign policy—the military alliance with Canada and the trade of destroyers for British naval bases. With the basic elements in Roosevelt's defense policy—control by businessmen, "encouragement" of private industry through liberal amortization and war-profits tax provisions—Willkie naturally had no quarrel. And even such a development as the Rome-Berlin-Tokyo alignment against the United States has found Willkie with nothing much to say because Roosevelt's "forward" policy in the Pacific is precisely the one which he, and his Wall Street friends, have long favored.

Thus on the crucial issues of war and conscription our political system provides no channel for the expression of the opposition to the Roosevelt policies of a large section of the electorate.

—*The New International*, October, 1940

The Crisis of the Word

"Greeks! We shall now prove
whether we are worthy of our ancestors and the liberty which our
forefathers secured for us. . . . The time has come for all Greeks to
fight to the death for all they hold dear." Such was the Periclean
appeal made by Premier Metaxas on the day the Italians began to
invade Greece. The spectacle of the quasi-fascist dictator, Metaxas,
calling on the Greek masses to fight to the death for the liberties he
himself extinguished five years ago, this is the latest and not the last
irony in the world struggle between fascism and "democracy." As
the war spreads like a fungus over the globe—the last "world war"
was a provincial backyard affair compared to this one—from Danzig
to Vyborg to Trondheim to Louvain to Dunkirk to Dakar to Dong
Dang to Sidi Barrani to Bahrein to Thailand to Athens, the question
becomes ever more urgent and ever more obscure: What is a
"democracy"?

A rough empirical definition seems to be: any country that
comes into opposition to the Axis powers. The American press
stands ready to confer a brevet rank in the army of Democracy on
any leader—from Baron Mannerheim to General de Gaulle—or any
nation—from feudal Poland to semifascist Greece—which, for whatever reasons or however reluctantly, finds itself on the side of the
angels. The Latin American dictatorships have lately been found to
be "democracies," and the *New York Times* has a form editorial
standing ready in type, lamenting in pathetic tones the extinction of

one more heroic little "democracy," which is printed whenever the Axis invades a new nation. On Greece, the *Times* found it strategic to say more about Pericles than about Metaxas. And doubtless when and if the Reichswehr moves into the Ukraine, the *Times* will see the violation of the Soviet border as one more breach in the citadel of Democracy.

The point is, of course, that just as fascism takes power internally only after bourgeois democracy has strangled in its own economic and social contradictions, so on the international scene the Axis armies overthrow governments already compromised and enfeebled, democratic in form only—or not even in form. The war is constantly exposing the meaninglessness of the concept "democracy" in the modern capitalist world. So is it, also, with the other terms in the lexicon of bourgeois idealism. Think of the millions of noble words which were reduced to so much baled newsprint by the French debacle! *"Be faithful and united. Your sacrifice will not be in vain"* (Weygand to his troops, on assuming command during the Battle of France). *"France enters this war with a pure conscience, which for her is not a word. The world will perhaps soon know that moral forces are also forces"* (Reynaud, on Italy's declaration of war). *"We shall defend every stone, every clod of earth, every lamp-post and every building. We would rather have Paris razed than fall into German hands"* (the French "official spokesman," the day before the Germans entered Paris—unopposed).

The difference between such words and the reality that came to pass must either rouse a people to revolutionary passion or stun it into apathy and cynicism. The latter seems to have resulted in France, whence the survival of the Vichy "government"—a frail shell empty of all social content, which the first stirrings of the French masses will shatter. The quintessence of Vichy is the official report on the recent meeting between Pétain and Hitler: "The Marshal was received with the honors due his rank." One recalls Pétain's comment on the armistice: "The terms are severe, but our honor is safe." We may be sure that the French people are thinking less in Pétain's than in Falstaff's terms about this concept: "Honor pricks me on. Yea, but how if honor pricks me off when I come on? How then? Can honor set a leg? No. Or an arm? No. Or take away the grief of a wound? No. Honor hath no skill in surgery then? No. What is honor? A word. What is that word honor? Air. A trim reckoning!"

The almost daily reminders that the fine words of bourgeois ideology, whether in the mouth of a Roosevelt or a Pétain, are so much air have naturally had an effect on popular consciousness. The process began long before the war; it has been going on, in fact, since the Great French Revolution, and with unparalleled intensity abroad since 1914 and in this country since 1929. By now, bourgeois democracy has broken down so completely as a social and economic system that increasingly large sections of the population have lost all faith in it. They just don't believe the words any more.

From the viewpoint of the bourgeoisie, this is a very serious matter. "The characteristic of the attitude of the younger generation which most disturbs their elders," said Archibald MacLeish in his famous Association for Adult Education speech last summer, "is their distrust not only of all slogans and tags, but even of all words, their distrust, that is to say, of all statements of principle and conviction, all declarations of moral purpose." MacLeish, who as the Librarian of Congress and the confidant of President Roosevelt is himself not the least securely entrenched of these "elders," is quite properly concerned over the impotence today in America of what he calls "The Word." This mystic entity, which he capitalizes throughout, MacLeish seems to conceive of, much as Hitler does, as a sort of medicine man's charm which can *of itself*, regardless of its relationship to reality, sway men to action. To reject The Word as the young men of America are now doing, is "to stand disarmed and helpless before an aggressor whose strength consists precisely in destroying respect for the law, respect for morality and respect for The Word."

Now, of course, Hitler, far from destroying respect for The Word, has exploited it more successfully than any demagogue in history. What MacLeish is really complaining about is that Hitler's Word has shown itself so much more potent than *his* Word as to destroy "respect" for the latter. Hitler has won the youth of Germany, as is well known, by persuading them that fascism offers them what they want from life, that it is worth fighting and dying for. (If respect for The Word is the mark of a healthy society, as MacLeish implies, then Nazi Germany is the high point of civilization.) This is a lie, but it is believed. MacLeish's complaint seems to be that *his* —and Roosevelt's—lies are *not* believed.

—*Partisan Review*, January–February, 1941

Those
Mad Germans

One way of looking at fascism is as the *systematization* of the brutalities, contradictions, and lunacies of monopoly capitalism. (That in the process of systematizing them, the fascists destroy the capitalist system itself—this is another story.)*
Several years ago, for example, a Nazi economist proposed *planned* depressions: "If there must be crises, then let us have planned and limited crises." He suggested that the disorderly old-fashioned "business cycle" be replaced by "a planned upswing epoch of say thirty years," to be followed by a "sacrificial year" of collapse and ruin. This *annus terribilis* "should be announced at least ten years in advance, to give every one time to prepare for it." His proposal was stillborn, since obviously if the State has enough control over economic forces to *plan* depressions, it can also *prevent* them, which is what seems to have happened in Germany since 1933.

It is significant, however, that such a proposal should have been seriously made. The Nazis are true Germans in this remorseless application of system to the irrational as well as to the rational. Before Hitler and Goebbels went to work, who would have thought that anti-Semitism, most primitive of cultural hangovers from the Middle Ages, could become the State doctrine of the most advanced industrial nation of Europe? There is a touch of the paranoiac, with his

---

* (1973) See my article in the May–June, 1941, *Partisan Review*: "The End of Capitalism in Germany."

systematized delusions, in this, and it is not surprising that the unsystematic Anglo-Saxon nations have long regarded the Germans as not wholly sane. When the liberal weeklies depict Hitler as a madman, they are carrying on a long tradition. Disraeli denounced "the fifty mad professors at Frankfurt," Palmerston called Bismarck "the crazy minister at Berlin," and Lord Salisbury was sure that Wilhelm II "must be a little off his head." Actually, the lunacy lies deep in the economic and social system of modern monopoly capitalism, and the Germans are guilty merely of doing consciously and systematically what other imperialist nations do under cover of a smokescreen of hypocrisy. But of course everyone is shocked when the fig leaf is dropped.

In their military tactics, also, the Germans, with that method and thoroughness and lack of all taste and proportion which is the maddening thing about them, have simply dared to carry out the logic of imperialist warfare.* The object of warfare, they reasoned in their earnest Teutonic way, is to demoralize and destroy the enemy. Therefore, in addition to the usual technology, the Nazi general staff devised such refinements as air bombs with terrifying sirens attached to them, the use of refugees as an instrument of war (forcing or decoying them onto the roads so as to block enemy troop movements, and often, to ensure traffic jams, later machine-gunning them from the air), parachute troops who landed dressed as peasants, motorists, enemy officers, even priests and nuns, and the whole fantastic "fifth column" technique of spreading confusion and despair behind the enemy lines.

Such methods were used in the most deliberate, purposeful way. These were no hordes of Mongols, lusting for destruction, but rather the highly trained employees of the firm of A. Hitler & Co., specialists in war. It is significant that there are no atrocity stories in this

---

* Lest I be accused of overemphasizing racial traits, I hasten to add that the Nazi military triumph is due also to the fact that the Germans had to face the unworkability of democratic capitalism much sooner than did other nations. The Allied democracies won the last war and had vast resources and colonial empires to draw upon, but the Germans had to grapple with problems of class struggle, of huge productive capacity and inadequate markets of extreme economic instability. Adversity is a great disciplinarian and teacher. Nations, like individuals, do more thinking in hard times than in prosperity.

war, no tales of rape and looting. On the contrary, all reports stress the extraordinarily "correct" behavior of the German soldiery. When the Nazi troops entered Paris, they strolled about the city gaping at the sights, guide book in hand, like so many quiet, sober workmen on a cultural holiday. The "Strength Through Joy" organization was ready with maps of Paris and sightseeing tours. Descriptions of the organization and methods of the Reichswehr read like the articles *Fortune* prints on manufacturing technique. Destruction has been rationalized, and the business is gone about with the orderly precision of any large-scale industrial process.

This is especially notable in the air force, where destruction is turned on and off like a water tap. Nazi bombers developed such skill that they were able to destroy every building around the cathedral of Rouen without seriously damaging that historic structure—a feat which there are photographs to prove. It was a commonplace of their bombing technique in the Low Countries to bomb not roads and streets, thus impeding the advance of their own troops later on, but rather objects alongside the roads, so that whole towns would be leveled to dust without a single bomb crater in the streets.

But the showpiece of the Luftwaffe was the destruction, between the hours of 12:00 and 2:30 on the afternoon of May 14, of the central district of Rotterdam. The Luftwaffe demonstrated its virtuosity by localizing all the destruction in a sharply defined area of two and a half square miles. In presenting pictures of the results, *Life* (September 9) states: "By 2:30 some 26,000 buildings were in ruins. The sewer pipes, the water mains, the canal machinery had been smashed. The falling wreckage had trapped great masses of citizens in their bomb shelters. Either they were drowned by the water or they were roasted alive by the fires set by incendiary bombs. The Germans estimated that only 300 Rotterdammers had been killed. The Dutch knew that more than 25,000 were killed. For seven days they kept finding an average of 1800 bodies a day, after the streets had been cleared of dead. . . . The stink of embers, stagnant water and dead flesh hung over the city for a month." No military purpose was served by the destruction, which took place after the Dutch army had surrendered. It was strictly a demonstration of craftsmanship, planned and executed to impress the citizens of Paris . . . and London.

—*Partisan Review*, January–February, 1941

The
Absent-Minded
Professor

An example of a rare, almost extinct, species of *homo sapiens* has been found in Finland: a man who speaks his mind openly under circumstances which any sensible progressive could have told him were completely hopeless. His name is A. I. Virtanen, and he is a professor at the University of Helsinki and a Nobel Prize winner. Last December Dr. Virtanen took a trip to Sweden to talk to some of his colleagues in his field, which is agricultural research. A press conference was held in Stockholm for the distinguished visitor. A local Communist reporter asked him what he thought of recent Russian discoveries in agricultural science, and whether he thought the Russians would use his methods. No doubt the unfortunate journalist anticipated a pleasant tribute to the scientific achievements of Finland's mighty neighbor. Instead, one of the really great moments of recent history took place. Terming it "an idiotic question," Dr. Virtanen went on to formulate his feelings about Russia in the following precise terms: "I must say that I am very critically minded so far as the Soviet Union is concerned. As long as the Russians think it is right to conquer a neighbor's territory, such as Karelia, but do not permit Germany to make conquests, I cannot collaborate with them. One cannot treat the matter as if nothing has happened and I'll have nothing to do with the Soviet Union."

One can imagine the hush that fell over the press conference after that. Also the "scandal and great uproar" in Finland and Sweden that followed the next day. "It is regrettable," editorialized one Swedish paper, shocked to its marrow, "It is regrettable that a man with Professor Virtanen's prominence makes such a careless statement at an open press conference." As for Dr. Virtanen, he declared "he could not understand why newspapers should be interested in his personal opinion of the Soviet Union." The professor is either very innocent or very the reverse. In either case, it is inspiriting to know that a few such sensible fools still exist.*

—*Politics*, October, 1946

---

* (1973) Dr. Sakharov, the Soviet Union's most eminent physicist, is a current example.

Why Destroy
Draft Cards?

NOTE BY D.M.: On February 12, 1947, some four or five hundred Americans either publicly destroyed their draft cards or mailed them in to President Truman. The demonstrations signaled these individuals' decision to refuse further cooperation with military conscription. (See page 31, Politics, January, 1947, for a full statement of their position.) In New York City, a meeting was held at which Bayard Rustin was chairman; speakers were James Blish, David Dellinger, A. J. Muste, and myself; 63 persons destroyed their draft cards in the presence of reporters, cops, FBI agents and an audience of about 250. The following is what I said there.

This demonstration has two purposes: (1) to take a public stand against military conscription; (2) to protest against the preparations of the U.S. Government for World War III. Or, in general terms: civil disobedience and pacifism.

As to the civil disobedience: we have decided to attack conscription by the simplest and most direct way possible: that is, by refusing, as individuals, to recognize the authority of the State in this matter. I cannot speak for the motives of my comrades in this action. But for myself, I say that I am willing to compromise with the State on all sorts of issues which don't conflict too oppressively with my own values and interests. I pay taxes, I submit to the postal and legal regulations, which are not very burdensome, about publish-

373

ing a magazine. These commands of the State appear to me to affect my life only in minor, unimportant ways. But when the State—or rather, the individuals who speak in its name, for there is no such thing as the State—tells me that I must "defend" it against foreign enemies—that is, must be prepared to kill people who have done me no injury in defense of a social system which has done me considerable injury—then I say that I cannot go along. I deny altogether the competence—let alone the right—of anyone else, whether they speak in the name of the State or not, to decide for me a question as important as this. If it be argued that I am an American citizen and so have an obligation to "defend my country," I would note that my being born on American soil was quite involuntary and that I have not since signed any social contract. In such a serious matter as going to war, each individual must decide for himself; and this means civil disobedience to the State power that presumes to decide for one.

Many people think of pacifism as simply a withdrawal from conflict, a passive refusal to go along with the warmaking State. This sort of pacifism is better than assenting to the coercion of the State, but it does not go far enough, in my opinion. Pacifism to me is primarily a way of actively struggling against injustice and inhumanity; I want not only to keep my own ethical code but also to influence others to adopt it. My kind of pacifism may be called "nonviolent resistance," or, even better, "friendly resistance." Let me illustrate. Pacifists are often asked: what would you have advised the Jews of Europe to have done after Hitler had conquered the continent—to submit peacefully to the Nazis, to go along quietly to the gas chambers? The odd thing about this question is that those who ask it have forgotten that this is pretty much what most of the Jews of Europe did in reality, not because they were pacifists, for they weren't, but because they, like most people today, had become accustomed to obeying the authority of the State: that is, essentially, because they recognized the authority of force. Suppose the Jews had been pacifists—or rather, "friendly resisters." They would not have resisted the Nazis with guns, it is true. But they would have resisted them with every kind of civil disobedience—they would have made it difficult, and probably impossible, for the Nazis to have herded them by the millions into the death camps. They would have done this by going underground in the big cities, ignoring the orders of the German authorities to report at a certain time and place, falsifying papers, establishing contacts with anti-Nazi groups and families in the local population and hiding out with them, taking to the forests and hills in country districts. Techniques of sabotage and evasion can always be worked out, provided one has developed the will to resist and has thought about the problem. But if one thinks in terms of law and order, of being part of an established society, there is no hope.* So we get the paradox that those who accept force as a means to social ends are likely to act in a passive—though not pacifist—way when the force is on the side of their enemies. While those who reject force are free to resist it in an active way.

The most common argument against pacifism is: what would you do if you saw a man torturing a child? Wouldn't you use force to stop him? I don't know what I would do; I know that I would try to prevent such an act, and I rather imagine that, if nonviolent methods didn't work, I should attempt violence. To this extent, I suppose I am not a complete pacifist. But those who pose this problem do so only in order to make an analogy: if you would use force to prevent the torture of a child, why wouldn't you use force to prevent, say, the Nazis from killing and torturing thousands of children? The analogy seems to me defective. If I use violence myself in a concrete limited situation such as the one just outlined, then I can know to some extent what will be the results. Even if I have to kill the man in order to prevent him from killing the child, it can still be argued that my action is a just one, since, if one or the other must die, it is better the man die. But in a war against Nazism—or Stalinism—those who suffer on *both* sides are mostly as helpless and innocent as the child. Nor can we see what the results will be—or rather we can see all too clearly. The means that must be employed are morally so repugnant as to poison the whole culture of the victor. How does it punish the Nazis for massacring helpless Jews and Poles to massacre ourselves helpless Germans in saturation bombing? But if we use the

---

* (1971) Hannah Arendt's later researches into this question—why and how six million Jews let themselves be rounded up for the death camps with so little resistance—led her to much the same conclusions. See her *Eichmann in Jerusalem* and pp. 308–317 above.

instrumentality of the State and organized warfare, the only way we can prevent massacre and atrocities is to commit them ourselves— first.* And justice is done for the innocent not by executing their murderers but by ourselves killing hundreds of thousands of "enemy" innocents. This is a kind of bookkeeping which I don't accept.

To return a moment to the problem of the man who tortures the child: Tolstoy once remarked that people were always bringing this hypothetical monster up to him—the argument is not a new one—but that, in a long lifetime full of the most varied experiences in war and peace, he had never yet encountered this brute. On the other hand, he *had* encountered, every day at every step, innumerable real men who hurt and killed other real men in the name of some creed or social institution. He had frequently met, in the flesh, judges and government officials and army officers who habitually used violence toward the weak, who forcibly exploited the great mass of their fellow human beings. So he concluded, reasonably enough, that the problem of what to do about some hypothetical individual brute whom he had never personally encountered was not so important as the problem of what to do about the numerous real users of violence whom he was constantly meeting face to face. And he further concluded that it was the real and widespread use of violence that he was against, its use in war and in the defense of an unjust social system, and that pacifism was the only way to counter *that* violence.

Finally, let me admit that the method we have chosen to implement our protest against military conscription is open to many practical objections. How effective it will be I don't know. But I have adopted it because it is the only action I can think of which directly expresses my opposition to conscription. A beginning must be made somewhere. We can only hope that others will think of more effective ways to arouse people against the violence and killing which have become the most prominent features of the age we live in.

—*Politics*, March–April, 1947

---

* (1971) "Prevent" is obviously wrong—my rhetoric got out of hand. The Anglo-American massive bombings of German cities did not save a single Jew or Pole, and were not intended to. They did slaughter 300,000 German civilians, however.

A Note on
"Common Man"
Politics

Henry Agard Wallace is often compared to an earlier word-intoxicated demagogue from the prairies: William Jennings Bryan. The parallels are striking. The populist crusade against "Wall Street" which Bryan led from 1896 to 1908 has found its chief modern leader in Wallace. The Great Commoner becomes the prophet of the Common Man. Both teetotalers, both religious, both addicted to biblical imagery, both rhetoricians rather than thinkers or doers, both hated by the rich and ridiculed by the sophisticated, both even sharing the rare distinction of being accused of violating the Logan Act (Bryan was thus attacked during his 1917 peace campaign).

The comparison, however, is unfair to Bryan, who had serious convictions about the interests of the "common people" with whose cause he identified himself, and who was willing to make sacrifices for those convictions. Unlike Wallace, who has never voluntarily relinquished a post of power except to gain a higher one, Bryan resigned, on an issue of principle, the secretaryship of state. Even that grotesque coda to his long career, the Scopes Trial, has a certain dignity about it. Bryan took his backwoods revivalism seriously: he was willing to defend a fundamentalist position on Darwinism against the formidable Clarence Darrow (who might be said to have

377

made a monkey out of him). Wallace hedges, trying to combine revivalism with scientific enlightenment. Bryan was absurd in his attempt to prove that the Bible is literally and completely true, but one respects his moral courage—and even his intellectual consistency. But how can one respect a man who wants to have *both* God and Darwin on his side?

Bryan's superiority is specially marked on the issues of war and imperialism. Wallace was an uncritical propagandist for World War II, Bryan a consistent opponent of World War I; Wallace has draped imperialism—first American, now Russian—in "common man" rhetoric; Bryan struggled against the imperialism of his day. For all his religiosity, Wallace has never shown any interest in the peace movement, and his only expressed reaction to it, so far as I can discover, is the recent sneer at "namby-pamby pacifism." Bryan was proud to call himself a pacifist, however. In 1903 he visited Tolstoy at Yasnaya Polyana and was deeply impressed.* There was often, as with Henry Wallace, a startling gap between ideology and action. Thus although he opposed the Spanish-American war while it was brewing, once it was declared Bryan volunteered to lead a regiment. And in his early years as Wilson's secretary of state, he dealt with Latin Americans on the usual armed-force basis, sending the navy to occupy Vera Cruz and imposing on Nicaragua the treaty which later became the basis for landing the marines. But in the supreme test of World War I, Bryan was the most realistic and level-headed member of the cabinet. He was able to see through the pro-British propaganda which deceived Wilson and Colonel House. He saw the danger in loans to belligerents, for example, and officially declared—for the first time in history—that such loans were inconsistent with the spirit of neutrality. He tried unsuccessfully to get Wilson to protest as strongly against the British blockade as against German submarine warfare, and to warn American citizens

---

* Tolstoy's account of his discussion with "the remarkably clever and progressive American, Bryan" is interesting. It was in this interview that he gave his classic answer to the classic what-would-you-do-if-you-saw-a-man-torturing-a-child? question still ritually asked of pacifists: that he'd never met this hypothetical monster but had met many real men who justified killing other real men for some future gain that might or might not come about; the only thing we can be sure of in such projective, preventive killings is that many real men will die. (See Merle Curti's excellent monograph, "Bryan and World Peace," *Smith College Studies in History*, April–July, 1931.)

off ships carrying munitions. Finally, in the spring of 1915, Bryan reached the reluctant conclusion that Wilson's policy was pro-British and not neutral and that it was leading to war; he resigned the only high position he had ever held in his long and frustrated political career.* It is true that when war was declared, Bryan climbed down from this moral elevation, offering to enlist as a private and even favoring the suppression of free speech and CO's. And that when he died, he was given a military funeral and buried in Arlington—both at his request. All this shows that, like Wallace, Bryan was an unstable and naive personality—and also, at bottom, a good patriotic citizen, who could not understand individual resistance to the State because he believed the State was simply the voice of the people. It makes it all the more significant that the earlier populist demagogue should have, in the First World War, shown up better in action than the later one in the second.

Bryan's moral superiority to Wallace was, I think, due to historical rather than personal factors. At the turn of the century populism corresponded to real mass interests and emotions; hence its prophet behaved with some consistency. Populism today is a shell which can be filled with any content, even Stalinism, and hence offers its prophet no guide to behavior. Compare Bryan's and Wallace's audiences. Bryan's favorite platform was the Chatauqua lecture: when he was secretary of state, he was criticized for continuing to appear on the Chatauqua circuit along with Swiss bell ringers and "Sears, the Taffy Man." The Chatauqua audience was composed of religious-minded, agrarian provincials who hated "Wall Street" and detested the sophisticated, irreligious culture of the eastern seaboard. But Wallace's audience is drawn from liberals who are well-off and sophisticated. For them, populism is, culturally, a phony way of making a connection with the inarticulate masses (like Josh White's songs).† And, politically, a style for engaging in world power politics under moralistic slogans. I didn't like Henry's pitch

---

* (1972) Bryan is the only American cabinet member in this century—including Wallace and McNamara—who resigned on an issue of principle. . . . (1973) Add Elliot Richardson.

† (1971) I'd now add Pete Seeger, reluctantly, for his simple strophes hymn all the right Causes from getting out of Vietnam to getting into ecology. But they're folkery-fakery for all that. (Country Joe McDonald is a better kettle of Fish.)

when he rhapsodically predicted a glorious "People's Century" when and if the right side (U.S. or us) won the hot war.* Nor were his later cold-war attempts to gloss over Stalin's kind of imperialism—you might call it "people's imperialism"—with a *volkisch* veneer much to my taste, either.

It is significant that Bryan's medium was the spoken word, while Wallace's is the written word, and that Bryan was a practical politician, while Wallace is a government administrator who, in politics, is a helpless figurehead manipulated by practical politicians. The orator and the political boss (Bryan controlled the Democratic Party for most of the 1896–1912 period) are types thrown up by the masses and skilled in dealing with them. Bryan's first big speech was an oration delivered on the spur of the moment, filling in for a speaker who didn't show up. ("Mary, I have had a strange experience," he told his wife the next morning. "Last night, I found I had power over the audience. I could move them as I chose.") Wallace's first big speech was his "People's Century" or "Free World" address in 1942, a written editorial which he *read* to an audience of New York City upper-middle-class liberals. It became famous not because of any spontaneous response from the listeners (Wallace was as depressing an orator as Bryan was exhilarating) but because Ralph Ingersoll, the publisher of a local Stalinoid-*cum*-populist daily called *P.M.*, read it late that night, realized this was the kind of inspirational "positive" statement of war aims his readers had been thirsting for and hadn't been getting from Roosevelt (for obvious reasons), tore up the first three pages of *P.M.*—his editors, like those on the other dailies, had considered Wallace's speech a lot of guff and had played it down—and printed the complete text in large type. Ingersoll was right about the level of his liberal readership: they ate it up—at last an idealistic rationale for the war: "This is a fight between a free world and a slave world. . . . I say that the century on which we are entering—the century that will come out of this war—can and must be the century of the common man."

Henry Wallace is the spokesman *for*, the friend *of* The Common

* See "The (American) People's Century" (*Partisan Review*, July–August, 1942) in which I made an "amalgam"—still think it was valid—between the postwar scenarios of the two Henrys, Luce and Wallace.

Man, separated from the lower-case common man as a lawyer is separated from his client. But Bryan was "The Great Commoner"— i.e., a common man himself.*

—*Politics*, May–June, 1947

---

* (*1971*) As was Huey Long, the most effective populist demagogue of my time. If that obsessed young doctor had not cut his career short in 1936 just as it was peaking nationally, we might not be enjoying even the present attenuated forms of our traditional liberties. Huey had brains, daring, flair, and ruthlessness—qualities in which Wallace was strikingly deficient—and he knew how to appeal to the passions, and the interests, of the actual American common man, a considerably less attractive human type than the decent little-man-what-now? lay figure, leaking sawdust at every pore, Henry Wallace and his upper-class liberal followers had constructed out of sentimental condescension—plus a hard-headed instinct *they* could control *him*. They denounced Long as an incipient fascist, and so he was. But there was more to it. Huey got through to the nonmythological common man because he was one himself and never forgot it. His political style was as low down as Henry's was elevated. He was bursting with underdog resentment against the Establishment and all its works, including the electoral (and, on occasion, other) laws, right up to the Constitution itself. He ran Louisiana with the same cynical perversion of legality—and disregard of it when necessary—with which Hitler was then running Germany, his state police providing the same *ultima ratio* of force the Nazi storm troopers did, less drastically only because the historical situation was less extreme over here. But that might have changed, with some help from Huey.

Most threatening of all, he attacked the New Deal *from the left*. His "share-the-wealth" agitation, proposing a $4,000-a-year minimum family income (at least double that in 1971 dollars) to be guaranteed by the federal treasury really shocked Roosevelt and the liberals, as did his abrasively impudent— indeed, downright vulgar—manners during the two years he played a hillbilly Catiline in the Senate. His muckraking of the income tax (which he wanted to pervert into a means of "soaking the rich") plus "Wall Street" plus even the sacrosanct Federal Reserve Board—these forays appalled the New Dealers as crude and irresponsible anachronisms from a simpler age, as in fact they were. Huey's chief supporters in Washington, significantly, were a few old-line liberal-populist senators like Norris, Borah, and LaFollette (Jr.). Like Senator Robert Taft and other respectable conservatives later when Senator Joseph McCarthy, another populist demagogue, was riding high, they didn't like Huey's methods but they approved of what he was trying to do. They were more justified logically: the Louisiana Kingfish's social program was in their style, while Tail-Gunner Joe's tactics in his sham battle with communism were radically subversive of the law-and-order his conservative admirers believed in. But politically Norris was less justified, and rasher, than Taft: Long was a real tiger who exploited real issues of social injustice, and had not young Dr. Weiss gunned him down—for once, one of our assassinations was historically beneficial—he might have broken out of his Southern cage onto the national scene with results of which one can predict only they wouldn't have been good.

Deponent
Sayeth Not

On January 21, 1950, Alger Hiss was convicted, by a jury in New York, of perjury on two counts: (1) that he had lied when he told a previous grand jury that he had not turned over any government documents in 1937–1938 to a Soviet spy named Whittaker Chambers; and (2) that he had lied when he said he had not seen Chambers after January 1, 1937. Thus ended, after a year and a half during which it was seldom off the front pages, the celebrated Hiss Case.

The antagonists were important in themselves—Hiss was then the $20,000-a-year president of the Carnegie Endowment for International Peace, whose board chairman was a corporation lawyer named John Foster Dulles, while Chambers was a $30,000-a-year senior editor of *Time*—and even more so as symbols. Alger Hiss, with his Ivy League good looks and his earnestness, seemed to many liberals to stand for the New Deal; he had been secretary to the revered Justice Oliver Wendell Holmes, had served under Henry Wallace, and had occupied high posts in the State Department from 1936 to 1947, accompanying Roosevelt to Yalta and figuring prominently in the founding of the United Nations. Chambers, on the other hand—graceless, secretive, fat in a sinister rather than a jolly way—was an outsider for all his $30,000 a year, the very type of Communist turncoat who now embraced patriotism and religion as grossly as he once had embraced their antitheses. It was, therefore, a shock to many when, through eighteen months of testimony, the dubious Mr. Chambers more and more emerged as an honest witness and the distinguished Mr. Hiss more and more as a liar.

Now Alger Hiss, having served his prison sentence, has written *In the Court of Public Opinion*, a book that indicates another startling reversal of roles. During the trials, it was always Chambers', not Hiss's, mental balance that was in question; two eminent psychiatrists, testifying for the defense, even attempted the heroic operation of psychoanalyzing Chambers right in the courtroom. But *In the Court of Public Opinion* suggests it was Hiss's mind that needed looking into and provides a clue, I think, to one of the most baffling aspects of the case: the pertinacity with which, in the face of overwhelming evidence, Hiss continued to deny everything—not just that he didn't give the documents to Chambers, but also that he didn't know him as a Communist, and, indeed, had never had anything at all to do with Communism or Communists.

The contrast to Chambers' book is extreme. *Witness* is in many ways a repulsive book—melodramatic, cheaply sentimental, coarse-grained, egotistical in a malformed, unhealthy way—but it is fascinating reading because a personality, a human being, is speaking, and one feels that Chambers is able to be conscious of himself and to come to some kind of terms with his actions. But in the present book there is no self-revelation, no facing up to moral or intellectual problems, no human voice, only the drone of a legal machine geared to special pleading.

His book indicates that in Hiss the legalistic, bureaucratic mentality is developed to a point approaching madness. Lunatics are generally considered interesting; in fact, they are often bores because their view of reality is one-sided and hence both false and predictable. So with the present book, which is a dreary, jumbled, pettifogging rehash of the already familiar record, in which every point, no matter how trivial, that can be turned to the author's advantage is gone into at length, while the awkward (and often crucial) points on the other side are evaded or lightly blurred over. I have compared the book and the original testimony on a few items— such as how Hiss's old car got into Communist hands—and the cuttlefish can take lessons from our author on how to obscure an issue.

The only new, and interesting, material in the book is the last chapter, which presents the two briefs submitted by Hiss's appeal lawyer, Chester T. Lane. These present the novel and startling theory of "forgery by typewriter"—that Chambers had a machine built whose typing exactly duplicated that produced by the original Woodstock machine owned by the Hisses in 1937–1938, on which the incriminating documents were typed. The appeals court, and the Supreme Court, refused a new trial, and I think they were justified. Mr. Lane did in fact have a machine built which he claims, with supporting testimony from experts, produced typing that cannot be distinguished from that of the trial documents. But even granting his experts are right, the theory demands too much luck and cleverness on Chambers' part. For instance, how did Chambers "plant" the forged machine with the owner who had it in 1948, when Hiss's lawyers tracked it down by following a ten-year chain of ownership? Deponent sayeth not.

The bureaucratic side of Hiss's mind shows in his reaction to the "moment of truth"—Chambers' unexpected production of the "Pumpkin Papers," the actual documents he alleged Hiss gave him in 1938: "When on the next day my attorneys showed me photostats of the typewritten pages, I immediately directed that the papers be turned over to the Department of Justice, as it was evident that they were copies and summaries of State Department documents which warranted inquiry as to how they came into Chambers' possession." That is, the criminal confronted with the stolen goods calls for . . . the police. Also note the "I directed," as if Hiss were still a government functionary. It is clearly impossible for him to believe that any responsible, respectable citizen could question an action of his, since he, as an official, is by definition responsible and respectable. He accuses Nixon and other Republicans of making "prejudicial statements" about him, as indeed they did, just as he makes prejudicial statements about *them*; it seems not to occur to him that even a Republican politician has a right to attack even him. He thinks it improper that one juror expressed pleasure after the guilty verdict in the second trial, but quite in order that another showed "signs of tears."

But the most psychologically revealing thing about this book is that public opinion is nowhere appealed to (since for the bureaucrat such opinion is a bother, a presumptuous intrusion into holy and

arcane matters). He gives no account of his own political development, says not a word as to what he now thinks or what he ever
thought or felt about communism, and shows hardly any indignation at the monstrous injustice he claims has been done to him. On
the last page, apparently sensing that perhaps something has been
omitted, he adds what he calls "a personal comment":

> The ordeal of fighting false charges has disrupted my life
> and has brought pain to myself and my family. But nothing can
> take away the satisfaction of having had a part in government
> programs in which I strongly believed. I feel deep satisfaction
> that I took part in the creative efforts of the New Deal and
> in the formation of the United Nations.
>
> The democratic ideals which motivated me in government
> service continue to shape my outlook in life.

One wonders which to be most amazed at—the mind that can limit
its political exposition, in a book on a case whose roots are wholly
political, to these perfunctory, ceremonial phrases; or the heart that
can see this as "a personal comment."

—*The Observer* (London), June 2, 1957*

---

* (1973) For a lucid and detailed analysis of the failure of *In the Court of
Public Opinion* to refute, or indeed to confront, Chambers' most damaging
testimony (*re.* the rug, the car, the typewriter, etc.) see the four-page review
by Professor Paul R. Hays of the Columbia Law School which appeared in the
New Leader about the same time (May 27, 1957) as my review above.

A Confession

Sirs:

In your Spring issue Richard Rovere charges that I don't regard the history of my own time as *contemporary* history, that I seem to have had no direct contact with it and to have been dependent entirely on the *New York Times* as a source. This is a very serious accusation to make against a political journalist. Unfortunately, it's true.

When I lived in London last winter, I noticed that I actually met trade union leaders and members of Parliament at parties and that intellectuals were part of the political life. Over here, in this too large and too specialized society, it's just as Rovere says—except for left-wing politics (a world small enough for one to cope with). A New York intellectual even in the politicalized thirties and forties had no contact with Congressmen or government officials or businessmen or labor leaders, and really did see current events mostly through the *New York Times*.

—Letter to *Columbia University Forum*, Fall, 1958

"A Good American"

To the Editor of *The Twentieth Century,*
Sir:

In your editorial preceding my "America! America!" you write: "We would not publish Mr. Dwight Macdonald's spirited and witty comment on American life were not Mr. Macdonald himself a good American." I must object to this on both factual and logical grounds.

Factual: How do you know I *am* "a good American"? I do have a purely personal affection for some aspects of my native land (and a purely personal dislike for others), but patriotism has never been my strong point, and I don't know as I'd call myself A Good American. I'm certainly A Critical American, and I prefer your country, morally and culturally, to my own.

Logical: You confuse the source of criticism with its validity. A Bad American, cynical and traitorous, might still make perfectly sound criticisms of his country. And if they were sound, it would be your editorial duty to print them. It's in that other place to the East that civic virtue is the indispensable passport to print.

Dwight Macdonald
—*The Twentieth Century* (London), December, 1958

"America's
Conscience"

I have come to appreciate and admire Norman Thomas.

When I was a revolutionary-socialist several centuries ago, I didn't think much of him. In fact, I wrote a polemical article in the October, 1944, issue of my then personal organ, *Politics*, entitled "Thomas for President?" (the question mark was rhetorical-negative). I have just reread this and find I was right (as far as I went). "My objection," I wrote, "is that he is a liberal, not a socialist, that is one who has taken the first simple step of breaking with present-day bourgeois society." ("Simple"!!!) I then showed in detail that Thomas had illusions about "our" side in the war, that he insisted on believing, against the mounting evidence, that the United States and its allies were motivated by high democratic-humanitarian principles in their war against Nazi Germany and that he was therefore constantly asking, in the plaintive tones of *The Nation* and the *New Republic* when confronted with the latest reactionary twist in Roosevelt's war policy, "Why, Mr. President . . .?" I think I was right about his line on the war and also about his not being a socialist. But of late years socialism, whether reformist or revolutionary, has become an academic question, and I think both Mr. Thomas and I have been right to cease taking much interest in it.

I now see Norman Thomas as indeed a liberal, but as a real, old-fashioned, unreconstructed liberal who believes in freedom and justice for everybody. (Like Oswald Garrison Villard and not like his successor at *The Nation,* Freda Kirchwey.)

I have come to admire Norman Thomas because he really *is* "America's Conscience," a phrase I'm afraid I sneered at in 1944. He has been devoted, and—what is perhaps rarer—energetic in defense of what I now think is our greatest national heritage, the Bill of Rights. (The Constitution to which it's attached isn't so bad either.) Thomas has been the one prominent personage who could be relied on to give his name, to write letters, to raise money, and in general to interest himself actively in individual cases of injustice, whether the victim was a pacifist, an anarchist, an ex-Communist threatened with deportation, or a Trotskyist threatened with the opposite, namely denial of a passport. I had a few dealings with Norman Thomas in such matters in the last ten years, and I must say it is a relief to find a liberal "name" who is positively eager to stick his neck out and who gets actually and personally indignant at injustice.

There will be a lot of official hoopla about Norman Thomas's seventy-fifth birthday. I daresay the *New York Times* will run an editorial and I'm sure that all kinds of "liberals"—the quotes are intentional—will salute him at ceremonial dinners. But, as one who knows the absurd lengths to which this near-octogenarian, the last of our old-style liberals no quotes, will go when he is appealed to on a matter of principle, I should like to echo the last words that Nick Carraway shouted across that Long Island lawn to Gatsby: "They're a rotten crowd. You're worth the whole damn bunch of them put together."

—*Jewish Newsletter,* November 16, 1959

A Note
on Style

Editors, Dissent:

Irving Howe claims that if Christ gave his Sermon on the Mount next week, among other routine reactions would be that "Dwight Macdonald would write that while 'Mr. Christ makes some telling points' they suffer from syntactical confusion and 'a woolly pretentious style.' "

This is singularly inept buffoonery, since the Sermon on the Mount is notably clear and simple, at least as rendered in the King James Version, to which I have paid public homage on several occasions. But there is this much point to it, which some of your contributors might ponder: that *were* the Sermon woolly and pretentious in style, that would indeed be my reaction, and I should be right, since in that case the Sermon would not be the great moral message it is but a botch, and not only in style. Great ideas can only be expressed in a great style. There is no such thing as a clear message delivered in a confused style; the message is the style and the style is the message. Selah!

Speaking of style, I note that Mr. Howe has been converted to Christianity, since he refers to Christ as "He." (To me, he's "he.") This shows what discoveries can be made if one pays attention to style. And, on Mr. Howe's part, what an admirably subtle way of breaking the news!

Dwight Macdonald
January 5, 1960

After the
Assassination

Of the three political assassinations in my time that have most appalled me, that of President Kennedy was in some ways the most horrible. Gandhi and Trotsky were old men who had played out their historical roles: India was free, Russia was Communist. They were also disillusioned old men: the communal massacres, the rise of Stalin showed the solutions they had devoted their lives to realizing were at best superficial—"You are late," were Gandhi's last words, addressed to his murderer. But Kennedy was a young man who had just begun to assume his role on the great stage, whose work was still undone. A handsome, vigorous young man with a great deal of style.

Whatever his virtues may prove to be, however faithfully he carries out Kennedy's program, the new president will bring the White House back to what an earlier president called "normalcy." Kennedy was an aristocrat—we speed up the process over here—Johnson is a . . . politician. "One could not imagine President Kennedy ending a speech with the chorus of *America, the Beautiful,*" Anthony Lewis wrote in the *Times* apropos of Johnson's address to Congress. "For President Johnson, this homely and emotional touch was entirely natural. . . . He took 27 minutes to read a speech that would have taken Mr. Kennedy not more than 15, pausing often and ringing changes in his voice for dramatic emphasis. He was applauded 32 times. Delivering the same speech, one observer said, President Kennedy would have left gaps for applause only four or five times."

But style is not everything—perhaps, in American politics, not

much. My guess is that Johnson will do about what Kennedy would
have done. Ours is a mass democracy, which is a contradiction in
terms since the masses are too big and unwieldy to express themselves democratically. All the varied interests and aspirations of a
hundred million voters (or rather citizens eligible to vote—almost half
of them don't take the trouble in most elections, which is perhaps
the most significant single fact about "American democracy") must
be squeezed flat into two package deals labeled Rep. and Dem. So
the president does what he must, not what he would. There are
today, for example, three major domestic problems, complexly inter-
related: racial equality, economic stagnation, and poverty. Of these
only the first is also a political issue, and this not because of anything Kennedy did but because the Negroes have admirably insisted
on making it one. On none of the three did the Kennedy administration show much leadership, on none of them did Kennedy himself
(aside from two fine speeches—the one at Yale on deficit financing
and the one last spring [1963] on racial equality) make any systematic
attempt to educate the public. Instead he relied on "realistic" power
politics, i.e., deals with the Republican-*cum*-Southern Democrat bloc
in Congress, deals which rarely paid off since the reactionaries had
the congressional votes and the President didn't. (An essay, a book
could be written on the unrealism of liberal *realpolitik* in America.)
While Johnson is not a "liberal," whatever that tired term means by
now, neither was Kennedy until he became president. And if it
continues to be a matter of horse-trading with Congress, I would
expect Johnson to be more adept at this dirty business than were
Kennedy and his bright young men. He has had more experience.

—*New York Review of Books*, December 26, 1963

Afterword

This was written for a symposium on "The Fate of the Union—
Kennedy and After." In general the above obviously wasn't one of my
higher prophetic flights. I foresaw that LBJ would be more "adept"
at getting liberal legislation enacted than JFK had been—no great

boast—since he was more experienced in congressional maneuver and had far more of a following in both houses; also that his administration would lack JFK's high style. "The new president will bring the White House back to 'normalcy,' " I wrote, on style, adding, on content: "My guess is that Johnson will do about what Kennedy would have done." But whatever the atmosphere of LBJ's White House, it wasn't normal, and his military interventions in the Dominican Republic and Vietnam went far beyond the relatively pragmatic JFK canon: I think Johnson would have sent in the air cover at the Bay of Pigs, nor can I imagine him later admitting publicly that the whole affair had been a miscalculation. I mistook Johnson for another limited provincial like Harding, Coolidge, or Truman, but he proved to be both more and less: a monster, not a mediocrity.*

My fellow symposiasts included Hannah Arendt, Richard Hofstadter, Irving Howe, Hans J. Morgenthau, David Riesman, Richard Rovere, and C. Vann Woodward. They didn't distinguish themselves in the Cassandra line either: they too were better at extrapolating from past data than forecasting the future. "At this moment," Arendt wrote, "when we have been reassured of the continuity of American policy both on the domestic and the international plane, it appears that the country, far from entering a new era, is falling back into its old fold. . . . It has been stressed that everything will go on just as before—except that it will be done in a different *style*." She apparently accepts this view since the bulk of her contribution is an analysis, brilliant and subtle, of JFK's style.

Morgenthau, who fifteen months later would become one of the most effective critics of Johnson's Vietnam escalation, here presented a capsule theory of presidential impotence: "The conditions of modern life impose narrow limits upon the initiative of statesmen. [!] . . . An American President . . . cannot radically alter the course of events. [!!] . . . In foreign policy, it is difficult to see what initiatives a Johnson Administration would take that a Kennedy Administration did not take. [!!!]" Or as I put it then: "The President does what he must, not what he would." By the spring of 1965, we were both singing a different tune.

---

* I made the same mistake about Nixon. I thought he'd be another do-nothing Eisenhower conservative. He turned out to be an active subverter and corruptor of our institutions: a Weatherman Mafioso. But at least I didn't vote for him.

Two of the symposiasts did prophesy that Johnson might make a difference in more than style, but their forebodings were beside what turned out to be the historical point, indeed in some ways diametrically opposed ot it.

Howe worried lest Goldwaterism would infect the new administration: "The issue is [still] between a firm decision to pull away from modernity and social responsibility, and the inclination to move (more often, stumble) towards an enlarged welfare state." He also wondered how firmly Johnson would reject Goldwaterism in foreign policy, resisting its "nostalgic impulse to shake off the complexities—which, in the absence of a coherent liberal leadership, have a way of emerging as the confusions—of world politics." His worries about Johnson drawing back from "an enlarged welfare state" were, of course, needless—the new president in his first year and a half didn't "stumble," he positively leaped, in that direction. The danger lay precisely in the "coherent liberal leadership" Johnson did provide all too firmly in world politics, which I find it hard to see as less "nostalgically confusing" than Goldwater's conservatism would have been. But Howe and his neo-Marxian colleagues on *Dissent* never did seem to react very strongly, in action terms, to Vietnam, as compared to less politicized types like Spock and Chomsky. Of course it's hard to fit Vietnam into Marxist—or any rational—categories.

"Vice-presidents have not been fortunate as fulfillers of the plans of stricken Presidents," C. Vann Woodward begins, citing the first Johnson, but he thinks the second may do even better than "the outstanding exception to the rule so far," Truman: "Now we wait with misgivings, but with larger confidence." He goes on to suggest a darker future than did the rest of us Panglosses. "The political crisis to be resolved in 1964" he defines as an "ominous," "ugly," and "paranoid" split that is developing between the metropolis and the provinces, and he even remarks: "The spirit of violence has spilled over into foreign relations and given both our allies and our enemies reasons for grave apprehensions. The metropolis has taught us to expect the worst from the provinces. . . ." Aha! But then, instantly, not aha! ". . . and the metropolis breeds its own conspiratorial theories," he unexpectedly concludes the sentence. And when he writes "The new President is pre-eminently a man of the provinces" and may therefore be able to heal the paranoiac split and bring us back to nonviolent civic sanity, one's flesh creeps at this unconscious stroke of dramatic irony, the audience today knowing what Mr. Woodward didn't then: what the future actions of this "man of the provinces" were to be. Hindsight of course, and I speak as an admittedly urban type, but if "the metropolis has been taught to expect the worst from the provinces," I now would judge this a sensible lesson and not paranoia, after seven years of first Mr. Johnson from Johnson City, Texas, and then Mr. Nixon from Whittier, California.

So we were all wrong, not a Cassandra in a carload. Granted we were intellectuals and so habituated, at least formally, to thinking in rational categories and therefore ill equipped to deal with our presidents' Indochinese policies which haven't fitted into them as noted. But might we not have had forebodings had we been more sensitive to Johnson's *style?* Many of us were sensitive to Kennedy's, but we didn't worry about Johnson's, though already, as one learns from later biographies like the Evans-Novak book, he had demonstrated, on the domestic scene, the same kind of bull-it-through, duplicitous, mentally and morally crude power politics that brought him, and us, to ruin when applied on a world scale. Although we talked much about the contrast between his and Kennedy's styles; maybe we didn't take style seriously enough as a historical factor.

We should have remembered Lenin's final awakening to the real danger from Stalin—an awakening that came too late, but that it came at all to a doctrinaire like Lenin shows he was a genius as well as a Marxist. Lenin's worry wasn't Stalin's ideology, since he had none, but his character, which Lenin came to realize was "too brutal" and too primitive (Georgia was then the Texas of Russia, or one of them). "Comrade Stalin, having become General Secretary, has concentrated an enormous power in his hands; and I am not sure he always knows how to use that power with sufficient caution," Lenin wrote in his deathbed "testament" to the Party, in words that apply also to our last two presidents. He later added, apropos of what he called "Stalin's Great-Russian Nationalistic Campaign" against minority republics (including his native Georgia), warnings against Stalin's "hastiness and administrative impulsiveness . . . also his spitefulness—spite in general plays the worst possible role in politics." Finally (January 4, 1923) he dictates a P.S. to the testament,

"Stalin is too rude and this fault . . . becomes quite intolerable in the office of the General Secretary. Therefore I propose that the comrades find a way to relieve Stalin from that position. . . . This may seem an insignificant trifle . . . but it is such a trifle as may acquire a decisive significance." As it did, more and more, historically, right up to 1953 when Stalin finally, mercifully, died. Or as Trotsky reports Lenin, in his last days, predicting: "This cook will prepare peppery dishes." I do think *one* of us symposiasts might have had some slight foretaste of the pepper our new president was shortly to add to our political soup.

"Fears in
Solitude"

Looking through Coleridge the
other day, I came on a poem, *Fears in Solitude*, which struck me
as an "ancestral voice prophesying war"—and Vietnam. We are now
in much the same moral situation, and for much the same reasons,
as the poem describes. The subtitle is: "Written in April, 1798,
During the Alarm of an Invasion." The invasion Coleridge feared
was by the French revolutionary armies commanded by General
Bonaparte.

England's situation then was curiously similar to ours now,
geographically and politically. Snug, and smug, behind the English
Channel—as we are protected by two oceans—the English had enjoyed "peace long preserved by fleets and perilous seas." They had
not been invaded for seven centuries, not since the Norman Con-
quest; we have not for two centuries—you can't call English raids
during the 1812 war invasions even if a lucky expedition did burn
down the White House. In world politics, the England of Pitt
played the role that is now played by postwar America: the last
great bastion of democratic freedom against revolutionary tyranny.
(I use both nouns, and both adjectives, rather loosely, Pitt's England and Johnson's America being about as democratic as Napoleon's France and Ho Chi Minh's "Republic" of North Vietnam
were revolutionary.)

The prospect of a French invasion horrified Coleridge both

politically, as a conservative, and existentially, as an Englishman. His poem begins and ends with deeply felt, and moving, celebrations of the pastoral beauties of the English countryside that was threatened with rapine and destruction. But at the same time, perhaps because he was an old-style conservative and so had a sense of justice even when it was inconvenient to his side, he was able to see the invasion as retribution for his beloved country's oppression of weaker peoples throughout the world. England had used its power unjustly, had become insensitive to the sufferings of alien peoples on whom they had forcibly imposed their self-righteous ideas. Just as we are doing in Vietnam.

The relevant passages are:

> We have offended, Oh! My countrymen!
> We have offended very grievously,
> And been most tyrannous. From east to west
> A groan of accusation pierces Heaven!
> The wretched plead against us; multitudes
> Countless and vehement, the sons of God,
> Our brethren! Like a cloud that travels on,
> Steamed up from Cairo's swamps of pestilence,
> Even so, my countrymen! have we gone forth
> And borne to distant tribes slavery and pangs
> And, deadlier far, our vices. . . .
> . . . Meanwhile, at home,
> All individual dignity and power
> Engulfed in Courts, Committees, Institutions,
> Associations and Societies,
> A vain, speech-mouthing, speech-reporting Guild,
> One Benefit-Club for mutual flattery,
> We have drunk up, demure as at a grace,
> Pollutions from the brimming cup of wealth.
>
> Thankless too for peace
> (Peace long preserved by fleets and perilous seas)
> Secure from actual warfare, we have loved
> To swell the war-whoop, passionate for war!
> . . . and forth
> (Stuffed out with big preamble, holy names,
> And adjurations of the God in Heaven)
> We send our mandates for the certain death

Of thousands and ten thousands! Boys and girls,
And women, that would groan to see a child
Pull off an insect's leg, all read of war,
The best amusement for our morning meal!
The poor wretch, who has learnt his only prayers
From curses, who knows scarcely words enough
To ask a blessing from his Heavenly Father,
Becomes a fluent phraseman, absolute
And technical in victories and defeats,
And all our dainty terms for fratricide;
Terms which we trundle smoothly o'er our tongues
Like mere abstractions, empty sounds to which
We join no feeling and attach no form!
As if the soldier died without a wound.

Therefore, evil days
Are coming on us, O my countrymen!
And what if an all-avenging Providence,
Strong and retributive, should make us know
The meaning of our words, force us to feel
The desolation and the agony
Of our fierce doings?

It is all there: the brutalization of our feelings as what Dean Rusk has called "that dirty little war" goes on and on ("all our dainty terms for fratricide"); the national smugness ("One Benefit-Club for mutual flattery"); the infliction of our vast military power on two nations that are so far away, and small, as to be invisible to our feelings ("We send our mandates for the certain death/Of thousands and ten thousands!"). When will we "know/The meaning of our words"? When will we be forced to feel "The desolation and the agony/Of our fierce doings"?

—*Esquire*, January, 1967

Norman Thomas
at the Garden

The 1966 SANE rally in Madison Square Garden had a good turnout, some eighteen thousand, and some good speakers, but, like most Worthy Cause meetings, it rambled on far too long, more than four hours. Hitler could hold a mass audience that long, with the aid of Goebbels' showmanship— banners, uniforms, drills, music, ritual, all precisely timed and choreographed. But liberal meetings in this country are strictly amateur night.

There were two memorable talks: Gunnar Myrdal's thoughtful, scholarly, and despairing lecture, "The Vietnam War, and the Political and Moral Isolation of America," and Norman Thomas's speech. Unfortunately, both came at the very end, after some three hours of oratory that was, like most oratory, stronger on quantity than quality. By the time Dr. Myrdal was done, it was getting on toward midnight and there were vast deserts of empty seats, and a few oases populated by several thousand diehards who, like the present writer, had stuck it out because we had a special feeling about Norman Thomas. It was a pleasure to see him still alive and kicking in 1966, a glorious anachronism, long out of fashion but apparently indestructible.

Norman Thomas was the member of the board of the American Civil Liberties Union who proposed a resolution after Pearl Harbor protesting what, months later when the issue was academic (and safe), the Union dared to call "the worst single violation of civil rights in American history": President Roosevelt's executive order permitting the army to remove from their homes and confine in government camps in the interior the entire Japanese-American population of the West Coast, some 115,000 persons, two-thirds of whom were American citizens for all the good it did them. The army's only, criterion was race: there were no hearings, no chance for individuals to appeal or try to prove their loyalty, no inquiry into pro-Japanese sympathies or acts by the 115,000 persons who were accused, condemned, transported, and imprisoned. (In fact, as in Hawaii at the time of Pearl Harbor, the Japanese-Americans were overwhelmingly, almost embarrassingly considering our treatment of them, loyal.) Thomas was voted down by his colleagues on the Union's board, including the founder and long-time chairman, his old friend, Roger Baldwin, who agreed with the majority that "the first and essential consideration," taking precedence over the defense of civil liberties for which, as young men, Baldwin and Thomas had founded the Union, was the protection of "the West Coast area." There was much talk about "military necessity" and when Thomas, "difficult" and stubborn as always, at the next meeting again suggested that the imprisonment without trial of American citizens because they belonged to the wrong race might properly concern an organization that called itself the American Civil Liberties Union, he was again voted down. Still, he had saved a little of the Union's honor—not much but some.

"The Conscience of America" would be mawkish-pompous applied to anyone else, but as a summary of Norman Thomas today it is so accurate as to verge on the prosaic.

So now he is eighty-two and he has to be helped to the speaker's stand, but once there, in the old familiar stance, facing the crowd— they are on their feet, applauding, smiling, calling out to him—he takes a firm grip on the rostrum, throws his head back, and begins to talk in a voice that is quavering (as it has been for many years) but also strong and resonant, easily reaching the highest galleries. For ten minutes he baits the President, modulating from irony to polemic to indignation to humor to fact to reasoning, speaking in a rapid businesslike way without rhetorical effects. At his first pause there is the usual automatic clapping, which he waves away impatiently with both hands, he's too old for such nonsense: "It's late. You probably want to get home and I certainly do, so if you must applaud, please do it after I'm finished." As the high-pitched, rasping, virile voice throws out unanswerable questions with a kind of contemptuous sympathy for the President, it occurs to me he is an old hand at talking to presidents, though I'd be surprised if he'd been invited around recently.

He winds up briskly, with professional *brio*, as how many times, how many many times? We get to our feet again to clap, to cheer timidly, to smile at one another as members of the same family do when a beloved elder acquits himself well in public. The old man endures the applause politely for a reasonable time, then begins to make his way back to his seat, slowly, uncertainly—he has been practically blind for years—inclining his patrician gray head and smiling his bony smile, more of a grin, as his peers on the speaker's platform pay their respects. He looks tired, and a little bored. Eighty-two years is a long time.

—*Esquire*, March, 1967

A General View
of the Ruins

I can't get away from it, and I can't get used to it. What do we think we're doing over there, don't we know what we're doing? (Or should it be "they"? In the last two years, for the first time in my life, I'm ashamed to be an American. But I am one, so let it stand "we.") How can we use the world's biggest air force to bomb into submission a tiny country, dropping a greater tonnage of explosives on it last year than our air force expended on the whole Pacific theater in the last war?* How come four hundred thousand American soldiers are fighting in a civil war in a small Asiatic nation—more precisely, in half of a small Asiatic nation—of minimal strategic or other importance to our interests? What right have we to decide they shall have one form of government (ours) rather than another? Who asked us to protect them against Communism, destroying their land and people and culture in the process, that is, who besides a twelve-year series of quisling puppets, from Diem to Ky,† who couldn't maintain themselves in power without our military support? Who do we think we are? Jesus Christ at the Second Coming—or maybe, considering those B-52 heavy bombers, God at the Last Judgment?

---

* (1970) It's now equal to the bomb tonnage dropped in Europe *and* Asia—or is it double?

† (1970) And Thieu.

A Quaker merchant was a passenger on a ship that was boarded by pirates. True to his principles, he stood by with folded arms as the battle raged around him, until the pirate captain, slashing and stabbing, came within his reach. Seizing him from behind, the Quaker carried the captain to the rail and, remarking, "Friend, thou hast no business here," dropped him overboard. But that is just a story.

"In what way were we trapped? where, our mistake? what, where, how, when, what way, might all these things have been different, if only we had done otherwise? if only we might have known. Where lost that bright health of love that knew so surely it would stay; how, how did it sink away, beyond help, beyond hope, beyond desire, beyond remembrance. . . . How, how did all this sink so swift away. . . . How are these things? . . . How did we get caught? Why is it things always seem to go against us? . . . How were we caught? What, what is it has happened?" So muse, in their troubled sleep, the Southern poor whites in James Agee's *Let Us Now Praise Famous Men.* How has it now happened to all of us, so that ours has become in a scant two years a nation hated and feared (and despised) in the way Hitler's Germany and Stalin's Russia were? In what way were we trapped? Where, our mistake? How might all these things have been different if only we had done otherwise, if only we had known? How, how did all this sink so swift away?

Well, it began on February 7, 1965, when President Johnson ordered his (our?) planes to bomb North Vietnam. He announced that it was in retaliation for a successfully lethal Vietcong attack on an American air base—his weightier, less public object was to buck up the sagging morale of the South Vietnamese generals. Similarly, his excuse in August, 1964, for demanding from the Senate the Tonkin Gulf Resolution that gave him a free hand in North Vietnam without a formal declaration of war (which would have required the Senate's approval) was that an American destroyer had been attacked by North Vietnamese torpedo boats, total damage one headlight.* That in war troops and destroyers may expect to be·

---

* (1970) Later hearings before the Fulbright Committee have suggested maybe there was no attack at all, just a misreading of the radar screen. A matter of blips, not ships.

attacked by the enemy forces is usually assumed, but not in this case, where it was considered uncalled-for and downright impudent. So the President got his Resolution from the Senate and he retaliated with his bombers, and has kept retaliating ever since.

More important, whether he intended it or not, the bombing of North Vietnam solved his greatest problem: how to change the Vietnamese conflict from a civil war, in which the U.S. had no business intervening, into a conventional war against another state, and one whose army was invading South Vietnam as the North Koreans had tried to invade South Korea. When the bombing of North Vietnam began, there were, according to Defense Secretary McNamara, less than five hundred of its regular army troops fighting in South Vietnam, not enough for even a Johnsonian *casus belli*. But escalation stimulated escalation on the other side, so that by now there are fifty thousand North Vietnamese regulars in the South. The war is, or can be made to appear, not a civil war but the more respectable kind of conflict between nations.

Best of all, President Johnson can now reply to President Ho Chi Minh's reasonable insistence that a cessation of the American bombing of his country is the first condition for peace negotiations—that this is asking us to give up something for nothing; he can therefore demand, as a *quid pro quo*, that North Vietnam stop sending troops and supplies into South Vietnam. This is not an equal arrangement since we could stop the bombing of the North and continue to bomb the South and to supply our troops there, while their forces in the South, and those of the allied Vietcong, would be more and more crippled if supplies and reinforcements from the North were cut off. But it can be made to appear to be equal—plausibility is all that LBJ has ever required, he's a realist—and so the war can be prolonged until the American superiority in manpower and materiel brings about not "unconditional negotiations" but unconditional surrender.

One of Hawthorne's last letters, written during the Civil War, contains the Delphic warning: "You will live to see the Americans another people than they have hitherto been." In his cool way, conservative to the point of cynicism, Hawthorne understood the war's historical meaning more realistically than optimistic ideologues like Emerson and Whitman. For Hawthorne was right: that war did change Americans, and not for the better. What can be expected, then, from our present burlesque in Vietnam, which lacks both political rationality and moral justification? Defective in both as the Civil War may seem to us now as we look back on its causes and its consequences, at that time many Americans, and those not the worst or the least, believed in them. Almost no one seriously believes in this war, including many who feel obliged to support it in public—this war which is not even a war, legally, but an end run around the Constitution, a shady maneuver by a flim-flam artist who conned the Senate, on false grounds of "national emergency" into surrendering to him, via the Tonkin Gulf Resolution, war-making powers he is making more than the most of.

The Civil War was a tragedy. The Vietnam nonwar is an accident that has turned into a disaster. Were it not so increasingly destructive of lives, and many other human things, such as the national identity Hawthorne worried about, it would be slapstick comedy. Like slipping on a banana peel, if one can imagine a whole nation taking a pratfall.

The morning paper has seldom been a bearer of glad tidings to me in my adult lifetime, which began with the 1929 Depression and the rise of Stalin and Hitler. But I used to get a wry satisfaction out of having it confirm my worst expectations—what fools these mortals be!—and, besides, most of the news made some kind of sense. Now my darkest suspicions about Johnson's Vietnam policy constantly lag behind the even darker reality, while as to making any political sense out of it. . . . And so I've come to dread each morning's encounter with the familiar, conscientious old *New York Times*: the daily box score of how the game is going, so many of Them killed versus so many of Us; the latest widening of the "credibility gap"; the newest turn of the escalation screw; or a description of some recent "advance" in our military technology.* As if that mad

---

* When Martin Luther King recently compared the use of new American weapons on the Vietnamese peasantry with the Nazis' testing of "new medicines and new tortures in the concentration camps," I thought he exaggerated. Then I read in Lee Lockwood's fair and informative photographic essay in the April 7, 1967, *Life* on his recent four weeks in North Vietnam: "Much of the outrage against U.S. bombing is directed at the use of anti-

rifleman in the tower at the University of Texas had held out for two years instead of two hours—was still holding out, shooting down people at random—and one had to read of his latest kills every day on the front page. Only this is a different Texan, our president, the one we (and I) elected, not a maniac, though he has his quirks, but a leader for whom all of us have some responsibility. It won't do to exonerate "the American people," as Ho Chi Minh does for tactical-ideological reasons and some of our New Leftists do for sentimental ones, and blame it all on the White House and the Pentagon. Granted their occupants exhibit symptoms of mental disease in dealing with Vietnam, also that they have the power and the masses don't, still it is of some significance that in the Gallup and Harris polls—where the masses are presented with free choices if not with power—they have backed Johnson's escalation policies by about two to one, the precise ratio depending on how vigorously he has been escalating at the time of the poll, i.e., the more vigorously, the larger his majority.

Two front-page stories on successive days in the *Times*:
    "Washington, April 19—The United States proposed today that each side in Vietnam pull back its military forces ten miles from the demilitarized border zone as a first step toward peace talks."

---

personnel bombs—particularly the C.B.U.'s (Cluster Bomb Units), canisters which burst in the air, each scattering 300 baseball-sized explosives which detonate on impact, each spraying hundreds of pea-sized steel pellets at high velocity over a wide area. The pellets are coated with napalm and stick when they hit. . . . One eighteen-year-old girl had taken a pellet through her left arm, one in her intestine, one through her finger and lower lip and one, which I could feel with my fingers, embedded in the heel of her hand." I still think Dr. King's comparison is exaggerated but not as much as I did before reading about our CBU. Some actual person must have dreamed it up, patiently "ironed out" all the "bugs," probably with the aid of a devoted research team of brother scientists, and made it at last practical and, so to speak, useful. I hope to meet him some day, partly to satisfy a morbid curiosity but mostly to ask him how he ever thought—indeed could think—of the ultimate touch of coating the pellets with napalm so they will stick to flesh better. There was a great public outcry when one side, I forget which, used dumdum bullets in the Boer War—those were the good old days! There were even some Englishmen who thought it was unfair of their big nation to subdue by arms such a small one as the Boer Republic (whose guerrilla fighters gave the British as bad a time as the Vietcong is giving the Americans).

"Saigon, April 20—United States planes struck targets in Haiphong today for the first time."

The "credibility gap" is a splendid euphemism invented during the consulship of LBJ by some politicosemantic genius unknown to me who understood that when official lying chronically exceeds even the broad latitude normally granted to governments, some less direct term must be devised if the confidence of the citizens in their republic is to survive. One of its results is a distressing nongap, amounting to a collision, between words of peace and deeds of war. *Si vis pacem, para bellum* was the Roman tag. Our consul from the Pedernales has given it a slight wrench: if you want war, prepare for peace. The above twenty-four-hour sequence is the most extreme example of the incredibility nongap to date: almost before Ho Chi Minh had time to find his glasses and read our president's proposal for a "first step" toward peace, American jets were blasting power plants in his chief port city, Haiphong. A senior American official in Saigon who, understandably, preferred to remain anonymous called the strike "a tremendously important intensification—escalation if you will—of the air war," adding that it was, in the *Times'* paraphrase, "part of a series of steps ordered by the White House to penalize North Vietnam for refusing to agree to negotiations." Or more accurately, penalizing it in advance of the refusal, which President Ho, evidently a prompt correspondent, did manage to get off the day after the raid.

It is probably true that, as the Pentagon claims, the raid on Haiphong had been prepared for several weeks and was made on that particular day only because it was the first time the monsoon had let up enough for clear bombing weather—the monsoon season is ending and so the front-page headlines will become more and more depressing. But the President could have stopped the strike had he wanted to; he has tight control over military decisions, and is said to insist on approving, personally, every new escalation, however minor (and this was the most important in many months). The planes took off from the carriers *Ticonderoga* and *Kitty Hawk*— such a debasement of good American names!—which steamed north from what is known as "Yankee Station" in the Gulf of Tonkin. The gulf will probably be renamed Lyndon Bay soon. We do make ourselves at home over there.

Johnson's "peace offer" also had some curious aspects. It amounted to requesting Hanoi to kindly make it easier for us to keep their troops and supplies out of South Vietnam. Not that Hanoi took that line in its official note which rejected the proposal as "a maneuver aimed at masking the whole of America's policy of aggression and the creation of a broad no-man's-land designed to divide Vietnam for a long time"; the note also accused the U.S. of having "sabotaged" the demilitarized zone by conducting military operations there. All true enough, but the real reason for Hanoi's turning down the proposal, and Washington's making it, was that it would have widened the demilitarized zone between North and South Vietnam from its present six miles to twenty-six miles, making it harder for Northern troops and supplies to get through it without detection. (An April 23 item from Saigon estimated there were then 35,000 North Vietnamese troops "in and around" the zone.) Hanoi couldn't say this, though, because it has its own lies, one of which is that none of its regular army is fighting in the South. Officially, that is.

Sometimes Johnson uses peace talk to mask future war action, as described above. And sometimes he reverses the process, using escalation to sabotage peace moves by others. Secretary-General U Thant of the UN has been the victim of this kind of Johnsonian booby trap, as has the Pope, as well as the late Adlai Stevenson and Premier Kosygin of Russia. (See Theodore Draper's article in the May 4, 1967, *New York Review of Books* for details.) Whichever way the trick is worked, only Hubert Humphrey—and Jack Valenti—can still believe the President has the slightest desire to end the war by negotiations. He is obviously aiming at a military victory, which he thinks we can win—and we probably* can. Such a triumph, however, may give historians an up-to-date cliché to replace "a Pyrrhic victory." For then the real problems will begin, the political ones which military force can suppress for a time but cannot ever solve. The American tragicomedy as a world power is that we are very good at force and very bad at politics.

At the Guam Conference last March, General Ky solemnly

---

* (*1970*) Revise to "improbably." . . . (*1973*) Revise to "definitely cannot."

handed to President Johnson a copy, handsomely bound in red leather, of the new constitution of the Republic of South Vietnam which had just been passed by the Constituent Assembly of the Republic of South Vietnam and accepted, under considerable American pressure, by General Ky and his military colleagues.

"I looked at it just as proudly as I looked at Lynda, my first baby," Johnson said later, with his flair for the very common touch. Maybe he should have read it too. The constitution does provide for elections and it gives civilians a chance to compete with generals as the future leaders of the Republic, but, as Clayton Fritchey noted in his March 31, 1967, column in the New York *Post*—a magisterial debunking of the hopes and pretensions of the much-publicized "pacification" or rural reform program—the civilians who wrote the constitution were as reactionary on social-economic issues as the generals: "When Dr. Phan Quang Dan urged that the new Constitution guarantee every peasant the right to own the land he tilled, the proposal got just three out of one hundred seventeen votes." He also quotes an American expert's summary of the results to date of all the reform programs: "The fundamental problem is that, after thirteen years of American sponsorship, virtually every major social problem in South Vietnam remains unsolved. And until they are solved, there can be no hope for a non-Communist South." Short of perpetual American military occupation—which may be just what is in the back of the President's mind, a place that's all right for a visit but I wouldn't want to live there—the National Liberation Front will probably take over after the war, if only because politics abhors a vacuum. The curious and depressing thing is not only that the Communists, and North Vietnam, are more than likely to win politically in the South once the fighting stops, but also that it won't make much difference whether peace is achieved through an American military victory or around Johnson's famous "negotiating table." In fact, a negotiated "peace without victory" might make it harder for the Communists since it would mean some concessions, while Johnson's Texas-style solution by brute force would leave the country so ruined and chaotic that the disciplined cadres of the NLF would meet with little opposition.*

---

* (1971) "The new radicals, seeking a neutralist-nationalist solution for South Vietnam, would find themselves in trouble in the event of a Communist vic-

At the risk of sounding reasonable, I must state that some of the assumptions common among the New Left opponents of Johnson's war are, in my opinion, unfounded.

(a) The Americans are not the only brutalitarians in what used to be called "a nasty little war" and now has become a nasty big war. It is a cruel and barbarous affair on both sides, though in different ways. Our heavy bombers and big guns—some admirals want to reactivate one or two of the old battleships with sixteen-inchers to give coastal areas a *real* working over*—deal out terror and death indiscriminately. The Vietcong, lacking our advanced technology, must be more selective in their terrorism, which is hand-tailored to the individual victim and which uses intimate weapons like knives and pistols. "The Vietcong aren't fighting with snowballs," wrote the late Bernard Fall, one of the most rigorous and well-informed critics of Johnson's policies in Vietnam, and his own recent death from a VC booby-trap mine tragically proved his point. According to the U.S. Mission in Saigon (Associated Press dispatch of March 18), "Vietcong terrorists have killed 11,967 civilians and kid-

---

tory. Caught, as they and other opposition elements are, between the repressive methods of Thieu and the even harsher ones of the Communists, the radicals are in a difficult position. They are fully aware of this, and much of their anti-Americanism arises from their conviction that by backing Thieu so strongly we have made life more dangerous for them. And it can hardly be disputed that by having involved ourselves both so deeply and so ineffectively in Vietnam we have helped polarize the political forces throughout the country—that if we have prevented or delayed a Communist victory, we also have inhibited the natural development of revolutionary movements that might have survived independently or made their own accommodation with the Communists from a stronger position."—Robert Shaplen in *The New Yorker*, November 13, 1971. Nixon's Indochinese strategy of withdrawing American combat troops—there was one week recently when *no* American battle deaths were recorded—and increasing the bombing, also extending it massively in Laos, Cambodia, and North Vietnam, is popular with the American people and, doubtless, with President Thieu, but it is of course even more destructive to the native populations than Johnson's was—and to any hope of viable postwar non-Communist governments—not that our president has any intention of getting trapped in a postwar situation over there. For that would mean politics and while Mr. Nixon, like Mr. Johnson, is an enthusiastic practitioner of the art at home—really hooked, you might say—like him, he prefers simpler methods, like B-52s, in Indochina. Our quisling-comprador regimes in Laos and Cambodia are losing ground to the Communists but that just makes larger areas for the bombers to work over. *Realpolitik* is for advanced societies, *bombpolitik* is good enough for the colonies.

* (1970) The *New Jersey* is now doing exactly this.

napped 40,988 in the last nine years." Granted: (1) not the most
objective source; (2) given the obvious impossibility of any definite
count, those definite, not-rounded-off figures inspire suspicion rather
than confidence; (3) that four times as many victims of the VC ter-
rorist squads were kidnapped than were killed suggests both that
one's chances are better with the VC—our victims stay killed or
wounded, no kidnapping—and also the great attention paid by the
VC to political indoctrination, presumably the reason for the kidnap-
pings; (4) a civilian might be as legitimate a target as a soldier in
South Vietnam. How many of the killed, for instance, were bureaucrats Diem sent into thousands of villages to supersede their own
elected chiefs because he knew he could rely on his appointees to
carry out his repressive policies? Such Diem men were legitimate—
and, with the villagers, doubtless popular—targets for the VC. . . .
Still, the VC *has* used terror: widely, horribly (disembowelments,
mutilations, often with the family forced to look on) and, in the past,
sometimes indiscriminately, as in those bombings of Saigon streets
and bars and restaurants.*

(b) North Vietnam is a totalitarian dictatorship and not, as Tom
Hayden and Staughton Lynd appear to believe, judging from their
recent political travelogue, an agrarian democracy—though I'm willing to grant it is a "people's republic," just like in Albania and
Bulgaria. Stalin would be more at home there than Jefferson.
The Vietcong–North Vietnamese resistance to the American "presence" in their country is a colonial struggle against foreign imperialism, but it is not a war of national or any other kind of
liberation (except from us—not enough). It is not comparable to
Garibaldi's or Gandhi's campaigns of liberation. Nor, in our own
brief but squalid history as a colonialist empire (to which Mr. Johnson is adding not the least squalid chapter), to resistance movements
like Aguinaldo's in the Philippines after the Spanish-American war

---

* (1970) The massacre of some three thousand civilian captives by the Vietcong in Hué during the 1968 Tet offensive (which I take to have been confirmed beyond any reasonable doubt, like the Stalin regime's slaughter of
captured Polish officers in the Katyn forest early in World War II) is a more
recent example. Also cf. the escalation of rural terrorism by the Communists
—Southern guerrillas and/or Northern troops—this year. In at least one instance,
a whole village was wiped out, deliberately, over a period of three or four
hours, old and young, women and infants, with satchel bombs thrown into
underground shelters to finish them off. Barbarous. Atrocious. Just like My Lai.

or Sandino's in Nicaragua in the twenties. Ho Chi Minh is an old, experienced, indurated Marxist politician, trained and educated in Europe, more sophisticated and of an older vintage as a leader than Mao Tse-tung. That is, a doctrinaire who believes not in "freedom" or "democracy," terms that to him must have a deplorably bourgeois ring, but in State control of every aspect of human existence (in the name of "Marxian Socialism," of course, and in the interests of the Toiling Peasants and Workers, also of course). Until our president began to escalate, few of us thought of Comrade Ho as the George Washington of his country, for the reasons noted above, out of which I won't be bullied by any amount of escalation.*

(c) The American air force is indeed bombing, defoliating, napalming, and CBUing the Vietnamese people on a hideous scale. This is not because Americans are genocidally minded, I think, but simply because we have the machinery for such an operation and the trained personnel to run it. The Vietcong and their Hanoi allies are not retaliating in kind because they don't have the resources to do so. No moral distinction between us and them follows from the above, in short, any more than it does from the fact that Hitler's Luftwaffe limited itself mostly to "tactical" bombing—i.e., in direct support of ground troops in the field—while the Anglo-American air forces went in mostly for "strategic" bombing—i.e. general destruction (it's also called "area" or "saturation" bombing) directed against cities and calculated to cause, as it did, enormous civilian casualties. Tactical bombing is obviously more civilized than strategic, but the Nazis' preference for it reflected not a superior ethical code but merely the fact that, after the United States got into the war, their enemies had the huge industrial resources needed for area bombing and they didn't. They had shown what they would have continued to do, had their supply of planes and bombs and

---

* (1970) I still don't see the late Ho Chi Minh as a Washington or North Vietnam as a democracy but I must confess I've been bullied into a more tolerant attitude by three more years of our government's lethal intrusion into Vietnamese affairs—or should it now be "Indochinese," after Nixon's Cambodian caper? Even my flag reflexes are going. At the 1967 Pentagon march, I deplored the North Vietnamese flags and wasn't offended by our own ill-designed but homey stars and stripes. But last year, at the November peace march in the same city, I couldn't work up any hostility to those red-green-yellow cloth squares; they aroused in me the same apathy as the red-white-blue ones.

crews continued to be as superior to their enemies' as it was in the early part of the war, when they massacred some ten thousand civilians in one brief, unannounced raid on the center of Rotterdam, and in the 1940–1941 raids on London, Coventry, and other English cities. That we had dropped on German cities by the end of the war ten times the tonnage of bombs the Luftwaffe had dropped on England—with Hiroshima and Nagasaki thrown in for good measure, plus our "fire bombings" of Tokyo that killed millions—merely showed that we had the stuff to do it. Also, to reverse my field a bit, that our ethics, while superior to the Nazis', no great boast, were not as superior as they might or should have been.*

(d) I have not been a pacifist since 1950 and so it's not the Vietnamese war in itself I object to—I was enthusiastically for the Berlin airlift, despite its threat of war, and I saw the necessity, less enthusiastically as it ground on and on, for Truman's making a stand in Korea. Nor are the civilian casualties what bother me— some are inevitable—but rather the nature of this war, which has produced an excessive number of them. Partly because it's hard for American troops to distinguish between "enemies" and "friends" among Vietnamese peasants, all dressed alike and all looking alike to the unsophisticated Western eye.† But mostly because of the immoderate way we have applied our technological power in Vietnam: a

---

* Like most ethical questions, it's all in Lewis Carroll. After Tweedledee has recited his poem about the Walrus and the Carpenter and the too-trustful little oysters, another stage of Alice's education begins: "I like the Walrus best," said Alice, "because he was a *little* sorry for the poor oysters." "He ate more than the Carpenter, though," said Tweedledee. "You see he held his handkerchief in front, so that the Carpenter couldn't count how many he took: contrariwise." [The Walrus is in the grand style of LBJ or Mao Tse-tung, a real showboater, while the Carpenter is more in the Coolidge-Eisenhower style, his remarks limited to such practicalities as "The butter's spread too thick!"] "That was mean!" Alice said indignantly. "Then I like the Carpenter best—if he didn't eat so many as the Walrus." "But he ate as many as he could get," said Tweedledum. This was a puzzler. After a pause, Alice began, "Well! They were *both* very unpleasant characters—" Which will do well enough for the Luftwaffe pilots who bombed Rotterdam and the American pilots who atomized Hiroshima and Nagasaki, plus the late Robert Oppenheimer and his team of distinguished scientists who brought to practical success the compact little horror the crew of the *Enola Gay* delivered so efficiently to the right address.

† Indignation is usually centered on the bombing of North Vietnam. But I think our bombing of the South is more disgusting, and certainly more illog-

"strike" by a squadron of B-52s excreting over several square miles their five-hundred-pound bombs simply can't help obliterating everything alive, friend or foe, in the area. Also accidents will happen in the best-regulated air forces, as they did on two days recently—those were the only ones acknowledged—when a hundred or so "friendly" villagers were wiped out by mistake. (Sorry about that.) On the other hand, I don't agree with the New Left ultras that Johnson or McNamara are deliberately out to massacre the Vietnamese people. I'm even willing to believe that our pilots have strict instructions to avoid killing civilians as much as possible, though what "possible" is is sometimes a metaphysical question. (Also there is napalm and the CBU and other practical jokes our military scientists have devised. Also we have no business dropping bombs there, or being there, in the first place.) What we are doing in and to Vietnam is sometimes called "genocide," but I think this too free a use of the word, which means the deliberate killing of entire peoples and was invented in our time to describe the indescribable: Auschwitz, Bergen-Belsen, and the other Nazi "death camps." These camps, or factories, were a more extreme "rationalization," in Max Weber's sense, and a more direct application of terror and death than even our bombings of German and Japanese cities—which were, so to speak, second-degree genocide. At first glance the word doesn't seem to apply at all to what our boys are doing in Vietnam, their object being not to kill civilians but quite the contrary: the White House is very sensitive about that kind of thing, such bad press notices, so damaging to the national image. A second glance shows that, given the power and abundance of our weapons and the extravagance with which we are using them to shoot up the place, a great many of its inhabitants can't escape getting wounded and killed, regardless of our intentions. I suggest a compromise: as the Republicans used to call the New Deal "creeping socialism," what is happening in Vietnam might be called "creeping genocide." Inadvertent, absent-minded genocide, didn't-know-it-was-loaded genocide, sorry-about-that genocide. It is significant that "Sorry about that" has become the most popular slang phrase used by our troops in Vietnam—ironical, cynical, a little shamefaced.

---

ical, since our leaders affect to be defending the South against the communistical designs of the North. Some defense!

Whatever it is called, Vietnam is a senseless atrocity, the least excusable war in our history, including that 1846–1848 one with Mexico which gave us . . . Texas. One of its peculiar, and inadvertent, horrors is quantitative. The sheer physical bulk and spread of "the American presence" is slowly macerating the cities, villages, land, culture, and people of Vietnam, North and South. (Not so slowly of late.) Since 1954, when the French were forced out, a large, powerful, "advanced" Western people has been trying to impose its values, and prejudices, on a small, weak, "backward" Asiatic people under the pretext of preserving their liberty. *You* there, you be free, you hear me, boy?

"Vietnam is a nightmare from which President Johnson cannot awake," I wrote here several months ago. The formulation was inadequate: a nightmare is a human experience which can therefore be understood, as Freud showed, by human intelligence. But our intervention in Vietnam has ceased to be intelligible. It has become a mindless, impersonal process that keeps grinding on and on at an accelerating tempo like a machine out of control, a blind extension of mass-industrial civilization into the life of a people who can only be damaged and corrupted by it: they are not strong enough to resist it and yet are unable to accept it because it is so foreign to their own history, culture, and traditions. Mary McCarthy's superb reportage series on South Vietnam in the *New York Review of Books* (April 20, May 4, and 18, 1967) shows exactly how this process is working. She didn't see any fighting and she doesn't go in for political analysis but concentrates on the effect of the American presence on the South Vietnamese. The picture she gives, in scrupulous detail, is unrelievedly depressing, and all the more so because the American officials she interviewed were often so sincere—and so obtuse. They had the best intentions—we always do—and were quite unconscious of the ruin their simply being there is inflicting on the South Vietnamese, a ruin caused by our civilian as well as our military presence. "Friend, thou hast no business here."

—*Esquire*, July, 1967

"Why Do Men
Have to Die?"

On April 15, 1967, several hundred thousand Americans marched in New York City and in San Francisco to protest the Vietnam "war." It was a varied, representative gathering, I can testify as a participant, a cross section that included the old and the young, the sedate and the kooky, bourgeois families with neckties, basic black dresses, and infants in strollers—also pale adolescent girls with designs painted on their faces clinging to pale adolescent boys with long hair and assertive beards. Naturally the press and TV coverage concentrated on the beatnik types—*Time* even got in a few sneers at some American Indians who headed the march. (If they don't like it here why don't they go back where they came from?) But it was in fact a sober, relaxed family party, pushing forty rather than thirty—there aren't 200,000 beatniks in the city, after all. It was also the biggest peace demonstration in our history.

Three days later, President Johnson ordered his bombers to strike for the first time inside the city limits of Haiphong and Hanoi. A week later, he brought back General Westmoreland to address a joint session of Congress. For the first time a commander had been recalled from active duty in the field to explain to the legislators the political justification of a war they had not ordered him to undertake. The assembled legislators gave the general's simple rhetoric an enthusiastic reception; the general responded with some snappy salutes, and later Senator Fulbright, who had been restrained in his applause, shook hands with the general for the TV cameras, forcing a gentlemanly smile, to show he understood the general Had a Job to Do and they were both good Americans and there were no hard feelings, personally.*

To moral protests and practical criticisms directed against his private, undeclared (who could it be declared *against*, exactly? the Vietcong is not a country, we don't recognize the *de jure* existence of North Vietnam, and it would take an ingenious lawyer to define a *casus belli* against either from the standpoint of injury to our national interests) and illegal war (we *did* sign the UN covenant), to all such flak our President reacts with characteristic evasive maneuvers. Lyndon's got style, too, just like Jack, only it's a different kind of style, a sort of antistyle, like negative space. In quick succession, he produces like a cuttlefish an instant redi-mix of pacific sentiments, martial deeds plus a cement of lies, or "the credibility gap." When he returned from Germany on April 26 after attending Adenauer's funeral, he found increasing congressional uneasiness about Vietnam even among Republicans and conservative Democrats. He was scheduled to address the American Physical Society that evening and he poured out his big generous Texan id to them. "Every day, good people, wise people say to me, why can't we have a political settlement? Why can't we understand our fellow human beings? Why can't we negotiate? Why do men have to die? I ask myself that every morning and reflect on that every night. I want to negotiate. I want a political settlement. I want more than any human being in the world to see the killing stopped. Maybe somewhere, somehow, some day, someone will sit down to talk instead of

---

* I wish there had been hard feelings, personally. I wish the Senator had not made a point of patriotic solidarity with the general. I've always admired Dean Acheson because, when he was greeted, in a Capitol elevator, by the late Senator Joe McCarthy, with a cheery "Hi, Dean!" he turned slowly red but did not say a word until he escaped at his floor. Without making any invidious comparison between McCarthy and Westmoreland (who seems to be a splendid fellow, physically) I'd say there are times when the impersonal should become personal—and that Senator Fulbright was not as acute as Dean Acheson in sensing one of those times.

kill. If they do, I'll be the first one at the table."* Now what can a political critic do with *that*? Any comment would be overkill.

But there is worse; there is the "my little monks" story the President has been telling since the middle of 1966, it seems, but which only was printed on May 12 after Secretary-General U Thant wondered out loud if we are not "witnessing today the initial phase of World War III." The news peg was irresistible and the *Washington Post* ran the story at last, on the women's page, with the rather striking lead: "President Johnson told his daughter, Luci, last June: 'Your daddy may go down in history as having started World War III.'" As summarized by Max Frankel in the *Times*, late on the night of June 29, 1966, Luci "found her father looking tired and deeply worried and asked him what was wrong. He replied this was to be the night for the first bombing raids close to the heart of Hanoi and Haiphong. . . . He was worried that something would go wrong, that many civilians would be hurt, that a Soviet ship might be damaged and that . . . he may have precipitated World War III. He felt he had no alternative. [I can think of one.] . . . He had taken all possible precautions to limit the effects, but there was reason to worry. . . . Mrs. Nugent said that whenever she felt blue and worried, she visited with 'my little monks' at a Roman Catholic Church. . . . And so Mr. Johnson . . . near midnight went with his daughter to her church. They knelt and prayed for some time." Lyndon B. Lincoln, the Man of Sorrows—"Take a letter to Mrs. Bixby"—bearing the lonely burden of power, agonizing in the night lest the bombs (including those ingenious practical jokes I described

---

* The President means that famous "negotiating table" he has been trying to persuade Ho Chi Minh to approach for so long with every wile in his arsenal —and what an arsenal! He's tried bombing Comrade Ho's steelworks, power plants, air fields, oil refineries, cities, and bridges. No go. He's napalmed Comrade Ho's troops and, if they aren't nimble, his people, even throwing in a few CBUs to make his friendly intentions clear. No response. He has ordered a battleship reactivated so it can steam up and down the coast firing a few salvos from its sixteen-inch guns more or less at random, just to keep in touch. Yet they still think Johnson is not friendly and they will not come to that table. We all hope it won't be necessary to use nuclear weapons to convince Comrade Ho of our president's goodwill—all he wants to do is develop the Mekong Delta on the lines of TVA and no one regrets more than our president the necessity for destroying it first—and that Comrade Ho will come to the negotiating table while he is still in one piece.

last month, the CBUs) may hurt somebody. Trouble is those bombs are awfully *big*, but what can he do, he's the commander-in-chief and war is, after all, war. It's enough to make a crocodile weep. Enough to bring a sob, a politely muffled sob, to the editors of the *New York Times* who, under the heading, "A Troubled President," wrote not long ago: "The impotence of power was never more somberly in evidence than in President Johnson's news conference yesterday. . . . One saw, heard and had to believe that this was a man who had prayed and pondered and who longed with all his heart to find an honorable way out of that faraway war—but had failed." Why the editors "had to believe" this isn't clear—aside from their being gentlemen—since they go on to suggest, as they had often before—and after—that "a bombing pause in North Vietnam is worth trying." Not such an original, or drastic suggestion, but one which Our Troubled President's prayers and ponderings have not led him to adopt. Could those little monks be agents of . . . The Opposition?

The American people are behind their President. The same split as in the McCarthy period* is appearing between the intelligentsia and the rest of the country. While the more informed, articulate, and politically concerned part of the nation is increasingly appalled by Johnson's escalation of the war, it seems to have actually increased his popularity with the majority. The cautious Bobby Kennedy has recently lost ground vis-à-vis Johnson because he has criticized him on Vietnam, cautiously but apparently not cautiously enough. A Gallup poll released on May 14 reported that 59 percent of the respondents "believed in the moral justification" of the war, 26 percent did not, and 15 percent had no opinion; also that "one of four American adults favors the use of atomic weapons to gain a military victory in Vietnam." A Harris poll at the same time reported: "The war is producing a decisive impact upon voters and is enhancing President Johnson's prospects for reelection." The poll also found, for the first time, a majority in favor of "a total military victory" (45 percent) as against a withdrawal under UN super-

---

* (1970) The first McCarthy, Joe. This was written before Gene surfaced, for a while.

vision (41 percent). Last November 57 percent were for a UN supervised withdrawal and 31 percent for "total military victory" (whatever that means—we're getting pretty total already without much victory in sight).

Granting that the polls can measure only passive replies to their questions and so are misleading on subjects a minority feels strongly about and so is more active and so carries more political weight pro rata; also granting that Vietnam is such a subject—at least twice as many people marched against the Vietnam war in New York on April 15 as marched for it a month later, to take a primitive index; and also granted that any administration in any war has an edge over the opposition in mass support. Granting all this, the fact is that Johnson's recent escalations which seem manic and senseless to me seem to the majority of my fellow Americans sensible. The President is "giving the people what they want" and it won't do to pretend, like the Marxists, that he is "betraying" the masses. He is only betraying the best of our country's history and traditions as exemplified in the Declaration of Independence and the Constitution. What political leaders we had then! And how we minded our own business! We liberated ourselves and that was enough.

—*Esquire*, August, 1967

My Kind of
Anticommunism

Forenote: The following questionnaire was sent me by
Commentary *in the spring of 1967:*

"Liberal Anti-Communism Revisited"

*1. It has recently been charged that the anti-Communism of
the Left was in some measure responsible for, or helped to
create a climate of opinion favorable to, the war in Vietnam.
What justification, if any, do you find in that charge? As someone whose name has been associated with the anti-Communist
Left, do you feel in any way responsible for American policies
in Vietnam?*

*2. Would you call yourself an anti-Communist today? If so,
are you still willing to support a policy of containing the
spread of Communism? If not, why have you changed?
Assuming that you once supported containment because you
were opposed on moral rather than narrowly political grounds
to the spread of a totalitarian system, why do you think it
wrong to apply the same principle to Vietnam?*

*3. Do the recent revelations concerning covert CIA backing of
projects, some of which you probably sympathized with, or may
perhaps have been involved in yourself, prove that liberal
anti-Communism has been a dupe of, or a slave to, the darker
impulses of American foreign policy?*

The most interesting and difficult of your questions is (2) "Would
you call yourself an anti-Communist today?" My answer is Yes,
Maybe, and No.

YES: if you mean not the ideas of Marx and Engels but their post-1917 exploitation, under the name "Communism," with varying degrees of faithfulness to the original, as a technique of action and propaganda for gaining power and holding it. This kind of communism seems to me a regression even from the modest standards of freedom, democracy, and equality before the law the bourgeois West has achieved after centuries of political struggle. A regression that sometimes, as with Mao's Red Guards and their anticultural Cultural Revolution, becomes a mirror-image reversal, Left becoming Right, of Marx's vision of communism as "a society in which the full and free development of every individual becomes the ruling principle." In Mao's China, the ruling principle seems to be rather the full and free repression of every individual. Even the more bourgeoisified Communist countries lean more toward the Maoist than the Marxist line on the individual. In this sense, then, I am anticommunist. I think the toiling masses need liberation from their liberators, and I believe that Western capitalism now offers them a better life, morally and materialistically, than communism does.

MAYBE: When the Moscow Trials awakened me to what had actually been going on in Russia since 1929, Communism was a geographical and political monolith. The U.S.S.R. was not only the sole Communist country but it was also big ("One-Sixth of the Globe"), rich ("Moscow Gold" was not a Hearst fantasy), and totalitarian (the Stalin bureaucrats demanded the same instant service from the comrades abroad they had become used to at home). Therefore the Third International followed the Moscow line with a tropistic automatism the Kremlin's present occupants must recall with nostalgia as the caviar and vodka go round. After the war the monolith began to fragment with Tito's break in 1948. Stalin's death in 1953 was followed by the great "thaw" in Russia itself, a trend toward a more humane, liberal, bourgeois system which, after twelve years, seems clearly not a tactic, like Stalin's alternation of "hard" and "soft" periods, but a long-range strategy. The bases of totalitarian control remain, but the more extreme barbarities of the 1929–1953 period have been abolished and seem unlikely to return. The 1956 revolts in Poland, East Germany, and Hungary, provoked by Khrushchev's "thaw," were put down by Khrushchev's troops, but the East European satellites have been revolving in orbits ever more erratic, and independent, in relation to the Soviet planet. The taking of power by Communist regimes since the war in countries as diverse as Cuba, Algeria, Ghana, North Vietnam and China—by leaders as varied, in doctrine and in personality, as Castro, Boumédiene, Nkrumah, Ho, and Mao—all this has caused such extensive further fragmentations of the monolith as to suggest that the only reasonable definition of "a communist" today, as of "a Jew," is somebody who calls himself that. As a universal menace, "communism," *tout court*, has become a dead horse useful only for ritual floggings by our less sophisticated and/or more cynical politicians.

NO: if you mean the kind of crusades mounted *in nomine* anti-communism, domestically by the late Senator McCarthy and abroad by our present President. They do little, if any, damage to the Communists and a great deal to us. The latter point hardly needs laboring here beyond noting that the evil McCarthy did has been interred with his bones while the evil Johnson is doing to "the American image" globally and, more important, to our own image of ourselves and our traditions, seem likely to leave permanent scars. "Tail-Gunner Joe" had no armies at his command and so his power for mischief was limited, despite the worst possible intentions. But now another demagogue with the same ignorance, or shall we say lack of curiosity, about communism and the same weakness for lies, or shall we say "credibility gap," is by historical accident actually in the White House, and he does have armies.

The chief reason I'm not "anticommunist" in the McCarthy or Johnson sense is that I'm against real communism. The principal results of the Senator's search-and-destroy commando raids were to give publicity to an expiring CPUSA, down to its last twenty thousand members including FBI agents, and, by the absurdity and unfairness of his accusations, to gain sympathy for communism. Our present president's genocidal crusade in Vietnam makes the enemy look good, relatively. If I were a South Vietnamese, I'd vote for the Vietcong over Ky and Westmoreland—if such a vote were miraculously permitted. As an old commie fighter, I rate Johnson about as, I imagine, old Indian-fighters rated General Custer: rash, hot-headed, vain and alarmingly ignorant of the nature of the enemy. Ho Chi Minh may go down in history as LBJ's Sitting Bull—or, if the war continues to be catastrophic for us, perhaps LBJ will get a footnote as Ho's Custer.

To answer your other questions, briefly:

(1) No, I don't feel personally responsible for Vietnam since I've done what I could to oppose Johnson's escalation by speaking, writing, and signing those ads. I even signed an *ur*-ad against Kennedy's meddling there—which I don't think was on the same level, morally, as Johnson's escalation, nor do I think the latter was a necessary consequence of the Vietnam tactics of his two predecessors. Kennedy didn't send the air cover at the Bay of Pigs and he later admitted the invasion was a mistake; Johnson would have sent in the planes, he never admits mistakes, especially serious ones, and had he been in charge we would still be blasting away in the Sierra Maestra, with disappointing results despite the leveling of Havana and Santiago. Eisenhower never did much of anything in Vietnam or anywhere else, a presidential quality we can appreciate now we have a man of action in the White House.

I suppose "the anticommunism of the Left" did help create a favorable climate of opinion for Johnson's war, but I don't see how this could have been avoided unless we had shut up, which would have made us accomplices of the other side.*

But there is another kind of responsibility, the kind one feels as a citizen whose government commits atrocities one knows about but cannot prevent (Vietnam, Hitler's prewar concentration camps, Stalin's forced-labor camps) or doesn't even know about until afterward (the development of the atomic bomb and its use on Hiroshima and Nagasaki; Hitler's wartime "death camps"). The guilt one feels about such atrocities is not personal but national: my country did these things. I am part of it, I have helped shape it, and have been shaped by it. In Vietnam we see the darker side of our technological productivity and our mass industrial society—a sinister extension of "the American way of life."

(3) I was indeed "involved" in the secret financing of *Encounter* by the CIA during the year I was a special editor, unwittingly and

---

* (1973) "The other side" too equal—should have been "the greater evil."

"unwittily" as they say, and I think I was played for a sucker and I'm still sore about it. I see no justification for secret subsidies of any kind for cultural activities. I don't know what you mean by "the darker impulses of American foreign policy," since this implies there are some lighter ones.

—*Commentary*, September, 1967

Some Reflections
on Our Boys
in Vietnam

One's horror at what our armies
are doing in Vietnam tends to make one forget that while the
Vietnamese civilian populations, North and South, are the principal sufferers from Mr. Johnson's private war, the combat troops
who are fighting it are victims as well as executioners, in the phrase
of Albert Camus. A poignant illustration is Pierre Schoendoerffer's
"The Anderson Platoon," a documentary he made in Vietnam last
year for French television. It has been shown several times on the
CBS network.

For six weeks M. Schoendoerffer and his camera crew lived
with an American combat platoon commanded by Lieutenant (now
Captain) Joseph B. Anderson, a West Pointer and, like some of his
men, a Negro. The result is a quiet triumph of art and perception:
the prose of war, no heroics, no editorializing, the camera, which is
businesslike, and the commentary, which is dryly factual, confined
strictly to the thirty-three infantrymen led by Lieutenant Anderson.
They are shown not as soldiers or Americans but as individuals,
each of them somehow emerging as a person under the big, clumsy,
webbed helmets, inside the bulky battle dress (more like a garage-
man's overalls than a uniform) and apart from the grenades fes-
tooning their bodies and the heavy automatic weapons they lug

along like an awkward fifth limb. They are introduced and rein-
troduced by name each time and with closeups of television's most
interesting landscape, the human face, as they trudge along a forest
path in single file, as they sprawl exhausted during a halt, as they eat
their rations hastily, warily, in the speckled shadows of a clearing, as
they fool around at mail call or bathe, with splashing horseplay, in a
jungle stream. One gets to know the soberly competent Negro ser-
geant; the cocky "Bronx beatnik" (later killed in action); the kid
from South Carolina on his leave in Saigon, trying to live it up with
the pretty, strange B girls, bewildered but determined, investing his
last cash in a guitar which he insists on giving one of them—she
tries, politely, to refuse—explaining, in a last desperate stab at communication: "So now you have a *gee*tar an' you can make some
money singing."

A gentle, sad film, like the soldiers' faces in it, which are often
touched with beauty. Living with death is the kind of serious experience few Americans today are exposed to, and it shows in their
faces. As in Sherwood Anderson's stories, one sees here the refine-
ment, the wonder and strangeness and nobility of the ordinary, commonplace person—"I crown myself a man" one of his characters
says. The faces are also for the most part unexpectedly, touchingly
young. No trace in their tense, worried expressions of Kipling's
"white-man's-burden" empire-building exaltation, nor of Hemingway's tough-guy martial romanticism, nor even, except for the lieutenant and his noncoms, of the brisk workmanlike assurance of the
professional soldier. These are civilians, very young civilians, who by
ill luck have been conscripted to fight in a remote country a war
whose purpose is obscure to them, as to me. To fight against the
odds: one was killed while the film was being made, four more have
died in action since then, not good military odds, leaving aside the
platoon's "wounded," on which I have no data, a category that can
mean anything from a scratch to a foot (or two) blown off by a
booby-trap mine—they all get the Purple Heart, good for morale,
and the Pentagon statisticians don't, understandably, discriminate.
Reverting to Kipling: "We're poor little lambs who've lost our way/
Baa! Baa! Baa!" Or calves: Veal for Vietnam.

Not that the Anderson platoon, on the cinematic evidence,
wasn't Doing The Job. On the contrary. One of the most striking,

and curious, aspects of Mr. Johnson's war is how well his (our?) troops are fighting with so little motivation. They aren't defending their homeland, like the Israelis, nor is there any larger, more abstract interest visible to the naked eye. Their anticommunist convictions are, I'd suppose, as nebulous as the antifascist convictions of their GI predecessors in World War II, who also fought well. Their morale seems to have no grander foundations than a bourgeois sense of craftsmanship and duty, a pride in Doing The Job which the Egyptian and the Congolese armies, for example, don't seem to share. And, more important, a loyalty not to their country but rather to their group: the buddies they live with and fight beside and depend on for survival, a fraternity they are sealed to for the duration. Not grand but enough for practical purposes.

In one way it is admirable that men should fight bravely in a cause they don't care much about or understand very clearly. But in a larger sense, it's depressing: a stoic endurance with no greater aim than—to endure. I kept wondering why the kids in the Anderson platoon had let themselves be drafted, as perhaps they did too after they got over there and found themselves both victims *and* executioners. Why they hadn't become what the press calls "draft dodgers," though "draft colliders" is usually more accurate. I would advise any young reader to have a look at the next rerun of "The Anderson Platoon" to see what he's letting himself in for.

If he is worried in more idealistic terms about what his adding one to the half million Americans already there will mean, concretely, for the people of South Vietnam he will be defending, abstractly, against "communism"—for this kind of orientation he should consult Jonathan Schell's "The Village of Ben Suc" in the July 15, 1967, *New Yorker*. Mr. Schell—a very young journalist, a Harvard graduate student; this is his first professional writing—deals with the destructive effects of "the American presence." Not the military horrors, the napalm and the CBU fragmentation bombs, the B-52 "saturation bombings," the "search and destroy" raids à la John Wayne, the "free kill" zones à la Alfred Hitchcock. But rather the noncombat destruction, intimately connected with the other kind but different and, in some ways, worse, certainly more permanent:

the crushing of a traditional way of life, a whole culture by the sheer mass, weight, and technological power of our alien "presence." With, of course, the best intentions.* Mr. Schell narrows his focus to one prosperous but, unfortunately, pro-Vietcong (or supposed to be so) village whose 3,500 inhabitants we transported to a "resettlement camp" after which our bulldozers crushed back into the soil their houses and their ancestral tombs, with some help from our bombing planes, "as though," he concludes, "having once decided to destroy it, we were now bent on annihilating every possible indication that the village of Ben Suc had ever existed." The article is beautifully conceived, the observation is subtle, the style is admirably objective and unemphatic. I will allow myself one more quote, from his description of the arrival of the first thousand deportees at the camp: "When they climbed slowly down from the backs of the trucks, they had lost their appearance of healthy villagers and had taken on the passive, dull-eyed, waiting expression of the uprooted. It was impossible to tell whether deadness and discouragement had actually replaced a spark of sullen pride in their expression and bearing or whether it was just that any crowd of people removed from the dignified context of their homes and places of labor, learning and worship, and dropped, tired and coated with dust, in a bare field would appear broken-spirited to an outsider."

Another aspect of the Vietnam war suggested to me by "The Anderson Platoon" was explored by the New York Times' military expert, Hanson W. Baldwin, in the August 13, 1967, issue. "TROOP LOSSES LAID TO INEXPERIENCE—Pentagon Sources Link Rise in Vietnam Casualty Rate to Rapid Turnover" was the front-page headline. His lengthy, authoritative, and unreadable article makes two rather sensational points, which it does its best to conceal: (1) our

---

* " 'Two days wrong!' sighed the Hatter (looking at his watch). 'I told you butter wouldn't suit the works!' he added, looking angrily at the March Hare. 'It was the best butter,' the March Hare meekly replied." Cabinet meetings on Vietnam must be rather in this style, a mad tea party where time stands still and nothing works. I don't know who Alice is, maybe Mr. McNamara, but I know who the Mad Hatter is, and Dean Rusk, of course, is the Dormouse. " 'The Dormouse is asleep again,' said the Hatter, and he poured a little hot tea on its nose."

casualties have risen enormously since the start of 1967; and (2) this is because, while the first combat units were "thoroughly professional and well-trained," they are now being replaced—because of the one-year limit on combat duty in Vietnam—by less-experienced troops (like the Anderson platoon). The statistical results, when one digs them out of Mr. Baldwin's clotted prose, would be incredible if they were not official.

The total American battle casualties in Vietnam from 1961 through 1966 were 6,644 dead and 37,738 wounded. *This six-year total—which includes the first two years of Johnsonian escalation—is almost matched by the first seven months of this year: from January 1 to July 29, 1967, American casualties were 5,625 dead and 37,080 wounded.* Mr. Baldwin comments: "During the first half of this year, heavy casualties have been inflicted upon many U.S. units. . . . Some platoons and companies have been almost wiped out. . . . Ambushes did not occur in 1965 and 1966 to as large units, or with the frequency that has marked 1967. Some officers believe that American troops have become less experienced, less professional and that enemy forces—the North Vietnamese in particular—have become more so." The problem is escalating even faster than the war: "During this fiscal year, between 550,000 and 600,000 servicemen will complete their tour of duty in Vietnam and must be replaced—considerably more than one hundred percent turnover." We may, therefore, expect casualties to climb even more steeply from now on as relatively green troops replace the veterans. There is no way out of this dilemma since the one-year limitation on Vietnam duty is necessary "for morale purposes"—a sidelight, by the way, on the nature of this war. Our soldiers will do their duty but they mustn't be pushed too far. There isn't any one-year limit on the enemy's tour of duty, but they have something to fight for.

There is one interesting military statistic that hasn't been released and probably hasn't been compiled. As is well known, a modern American army is unevenly divided between those who do the fighting, like the Anderson platoon, and those who help them fight from a safe distance, by supplying them with shoes, ammunition, cigarettes, ice cream, movies, Bob Hope shows, and other military essentials including those printed forms without which up-to-date warfare is unthinkable. The most recent Pentagon figure is 125,000 combat troops to 335,000 noncombat. Thus two out of three of our soldiers in Vietnam function in what the *Times* calls "a variety of relatively safe combat support and logistics roles." The story adds, without comment: "All get combat pay." (Could this be true?)*

My question is: What is the ratio of career professionals to conscripted amateurs (a) in combat units and (b) in noncombat units? I have seen no Pentagon figures on this delicate point. Unless the army is unlike other bureaucracies, I suspect more than a few experienced veterans are entrenched in "relatively safe roles" who could with advantage be pried loose for more arduous duties; also that it is precisely their greater experience, or seniority, that has enabled them to latch on to the best, i.e., safest, jobs and leave the dirty work to the amateur newcomers. "The old army game" it's called. In pro baseball and football, the veterans carry the brunt and the rookies are sent in only after the contest is in the bag. The contest in Vietnam is far from in the bag. One would like to assume that our Pentagon managers are running their show as astutely as our sports managers run theirs, and that boys aren't being sent in to do a man's job while men are still warming the bench in Saigon. But it would be interesting to have the figures, especially interesting to young civilians.

Perhaps the maverick, abrasive Secretary McNamara, unique among our war leaders for his pragmatic curiosity, will look into the matter.† (He must be a great trial to the Joint Chiefs of Staff, as if the College of Cardinals found themselves with an atheist Pope.) He might also consider, if he wants to beef up our ground forces in Vietnam with real pros, giving cops an automatic 1-A draft rating —an idea I owe, in a way, to Governor Rockefeller who has proposed that policemen and firemen be exempted so they can fight the war at home more effectively. I'm for exempting the latter, but the former seem to me just the kind of seasoned experts in violence we need over there and I recommend their drafting *en masse* to Secretary McNamara on practical grounds, which I'm sure will appeal to him. The President might also consider the proposal on the political

---

* (1970) Yes, it could. See Afterword.
† (1970) He didn't.

grounds that interest *him*. He needs popular campaign slogans (among other things) and I can think of few with a wider appeal than: "Cops to the Front!"

—*Esquire*, November, 1967

Afterword

I. F. Stone's Bi-Weekly for July 27 and September 7, 1970, quotes some authoritative sources which—at last—give some information on the ratio of draftees to professionals in combat and noncombat roles in Vietnam:

"Army draftees were killed in Vietnam last year at nearly double the rate of non-draftee enlisted men. [31 draftees killed per thousand vs. 17 nondraftees; 234 draftees killed or wounded, vs. 137 nondraftees] *Draftees comprised 88 percent of infantry riflemen in Vietnam last year, first-term Regular Army men 10 percent and career Army men 2 percent.* [My emphasis.—D.M.]

"Previously unavailable statistics reveal that [in the period 1965–1969] draftee casualties have run 130 per thousand per year and non-draftee casualties 84 per thousand. The Army General Staff prepared the study."

> —Article from the *National Journal* put into the *Congressional Record* of August 21, 1970, by Senator Proxmire, who has an amendment pending to forbid sending draftees to Southeast Asia.

A CBS broadcast by Morley Safer, on July 17, 1970, gives a glimpse of the old army game:

"This is Long Binh Army Post, 16 miles from Saigon . . . a city of 26,000 men. . . . You can spend your year in Vietnam here with very little feeling of a war going on. . . . These are the air-conditioned soldiers. . . .

"Many of the combat companies in Vietnam are 40 men under

strength. At Long Binh Post there are units 400 men over strength. Of more than 400,000 Americans in Vietnam, only 75,000 are considered to be combat troops [though all get combat pay]. *In the rifle companies, eight out of ten men are draftees.* [My emphasis.—D.M.] Long Binh has a disproportionate number of career officers and NCO's."

"It is almost exactly five years since I first arrived in Vietnam. In 1965, the troops seemed to be mostly paratroopers and Marines. . . . Now it looks like a different army. Half the troops in the field seem to be wearing peace symbols around their necks and everywhere they greet each other with the V-for-peace sign. . . .

"The force now in Vietnam—especially in the combat units—is overwhelmingly draftee rather than regular army. . . . And the draftees complain that the regulars and veterans by now have pretty well managed to get assigned to safe and comfortable rear area jobs."

—Raymond Coffey writing from Saigon in the
Washington *Star*, July 12, 1970.

Down the Drain

At the present writing, according to usually well-informed sources, the world is going to hell. All of it, everywhere, impartially, and without regard to race, creed, or previous condition of servitude. It's all going down the drain. The young are as passionately prejudiced as their elders, and less well-informed. The "left," new or old, is as alarmingly abstract in its political thinking as the "right." The decisions of those in control are as catastrophic as the reactions of those on the outside. The Black Power demagogues are giving the White Power demagogues a run for their (honky) money, track slow and muddy. Dictatorship calleth unto dictatorship, Athens to Prague, Cuba to Bolivia, Saigon to Hanoi, South Korea to North Korea, and the "left" fancies one and the "right" fancies the other and it's all very confusing.*

Things used to be clearer in the old days way back when the Old Left wasn't old (but wasn't young either), when men were men and Ypsels (Young Peoples' Socialist League) knew their place and we didn't trust anybody under forty, the days when principles were principles and revolutions were revolutions. In those days, one of the

---

* About the only major peak of agreement, looming majestically above the clouds of ideological controversy, the one common focus of universal criticism, is our obsessed President—he is, you might say, Vietnamized, like being lobotomized.

political problems we used to worry about was that of when, if ever, to choose "the lesser evil," a problem involving calculations of ethics, rationality, and other old-fashioned factors. But now there seem to be only greater evils. The choices were all invented by somebody named Hobson.

Mao or Ky? Nasser or Ben-Gurion? Tshombe or Boumédiene? Governor Wallace or H. Rap Brown? Johnson or Nixon? Hanging or shooting? Check the ballot for the so-and-so of your choice. And what is *your* view, sir, on Vietnam, should we escalate or negotiate? Pull out or push in? Use The Bomb or make a survey of land tenure? Hope for the best? Fear the worst? Is the President handling it badly, well, fairly well, fairly badly, don't know? And, dear sir or madam, the ghetto riots, what of them? Yes? No? Don't know? And what do they portend, would you say, in confidence, the dawn of hope (Andrew Kopkind in the *New York Review of Books*), the twilight of disaster (Dwight Macdonald in *Esquire*), or Don't Know (Governor Romney in the Michigan statehouse)? The Gallup Poll will protect your anonymity to the death—and, sir or madam, what might be your views on that perennial problem: afterlife? no afterlife? heaven and no hell? hell and no heaven? both? neither? *nada*? maybe? don't know? Check one, please. Indeed, the Gallup Poll will not only respect your anonymity as one blank unit in our great multiblank democracy, but will absolutely insist on it. So what is your free, democratic, anonymous opinion about the late disturbances (a) sociologically, (b) ecologically, (c) logically? Check the box of your choice, like what turns you on, are you a burn-baby-burn cat or do you favor urban renewal and the Great Society?

It's all going down the drain. A political commentator, this one anyway, is overstimulated, like a switchboard with too many calls coming in, or a badly programed computer asked too many contradictory questions too fast, or a Pavlovian mouse in a maze whose terminals deliver only shocks or frustration.

"U.S. JETS FLATTEN BUILDINGS IN RAID ON CENTER OF HANOI" . . . "18 U.S. FLIERS LOST IN THREE DAYS' RAIDING" . . . "VIETCONG ATTACKS KILL OR WOUND 355/Most Victims Are Civilians" . . . "VIETCONG MORTAR ATTACK KILLS FIFTY CIVILIANS IN DELTA" . . .

"KY PUTS WAR NEED AT 600,000 G.I.'s" . . . "CONGRESS CHIDED BY KY ON ELECTION." The U.S. Congress, that is, some of whose members had expressed doubts about the complete democracy of the coming South Vietnam presidential elections. "Since the American and Vietnamese nations are together defending freedom," Premier Ky observed, "and are consenting to tremendous sacrifices, I deem it my duty to affirm again the principles which command the conduct of national affairs by my Government." Now what can one say to that? And is it different when American bombs kill North Vietnamese civilians and when Vietcong terrorists slaughter South Vietnamese civilians?

"RED GUARDS SACK BRITISH CHANCELLERY AND ATTACK STAFF/Envoy to Peking Beaten as He Rejects Ultimatum and Refuses to Bow Head" . . . "500 TIBETANS FLEE FROM RED GUARDS/Refugees Housed in Camps in India." The latter story continues: "The refugees said that with the formation of the Red Guards, meetings have been called in villages, monasteries have been razed and ancient lamaist scriptures have been burned." Some will find these easy items to deal with: the British consul and his staff are imperialists, the lamas are re-actionary. I find it more complicated.

"JOHNSON AT TEXAS MASS HEARS SERMON BACKING VIETNAM AIMS: . . . The Most Reverend Robert E. Lucey, the seventy-five-year-old Archbishop of San Antonio and a long-time friend of the President . . . invoked the writings of the late Pope Pius XII to support his thesis that 'apathetic neutrality' is harmful to world peace. . . . Referring to American intervention in Vietnam, the Archbishop said: 'Unjust aggression must be halted by the nation as a whole. Such intervention is not merely allowed and lawful. It is a sad and heavy obligation imposed by the mandate of love.' " Well, *that's* clear enough. But oh for more apathetic neutrality! And a little less love.

"ISRAELIS ARE FIRM ON REFUGEE LIMIT/Reject Jordan's Request to Extend August 31 Deadline." According to the figures of the International Red Cross, there are 170,000 Jordanians who crossed the river, fleeing before the Israeli armies, who have asked permission to return to their homes; if the Israeli government holds to its August 31st deadline, only 40,000 of them will be able to be repatriated. And it may well do so. After the 1948 war that established Israel, some 700,000 Arabs who had fled Palestine during the fighting were not allowed to return. I protested this inhumanity at the time, as did a few eminent Israelis, such as Martin Buber and Judah Magnes, who proposed not a Jewish state but an Arab-Jewish state, for which they were denounced as unpatriotic at best and "Jewish anti-Semites" at worst. I was considered by some of my Jewish friends here just the straight kind of anti-Semite, especially when I asked why the American Jewish community, so generous with its money in support of the war, didn't raise funds to help the Arab refugees. Now it's all happening again, the Israeli government is again treating the new refugees not as victims but as enemies and potential fifth columnists, is again preparing to rob them of their homes and property, and American Jewry, which raised in two weeks, according to the August, 1967, *Commentary*, over $100,000,000 for the defense of Israel, is far from its first half million for the new Arab refugees. This callousness is distressing in a people who throughout history have been themselves victims and refugees. I was delighted when the Israeli army heroically and effectively resisted the Arab threat to "push them into the sea," as noted in this column, but I think this treatment of the refugees caused by their war is disgraceful and let my anti-anti-Semitic Jewish friends make the most of it. I'm once more an anti-anti-anti-Semite, if you follow me, or did I miscount? Oh, What a Lovely War! And Oh, What a Lousy Peace!

"S.N.C.C. CHARGES ISRAEL ATROCITIES/Black Power Group Attacks Zionism as Conquering the Arabs by 'Massacre.' " The story quotes from the latest Snick *Newsletter*: "Do you know . . . that the Zionists conquered the Arab homes and land through terror, force and massacre; that . . . Zionists lined up Arab victims and shot them in the back in cold blood. This is the Gaza Strip, Palestine, not Dachau, Germany. . . . [Do you know] that the famous European Jews, the Rothschilds, who have long controlled the wealth of many European nations, were involved in the original conspiracy with the

British to create the 'state of Israel' and are still among Israel's chief supporters . . . [and] that the Rothschilds control much of Africa's mineral wealth?" Well no, I didn't know any of these things: the American press, doubtless controlled by the Rothschilds along with "much of Africa's mineral wealth," or perhaps by the Elders of Zion in their underground cavern two miles directly down from the Bank of England, reported no massacres by the Israeli armies. Criticizing Snick these days is like taking candy from a baby, but sometimes a baby needs a little spanking when it behaves as nastily as these callow *luftmenschen*—you'll excuse the Yiddish expression—who think they're *übermenschen*—no apologies needed for the German. Such malice—and such ignorance! The editors of the Snick *Newsletter* must have gotten their information about the present importance of the Rothschilds from that George Arliss film on the Late Show, failing to notice that Arliss and the cast were dressed up in funny old costumes. Instead of making the one effective and reasonable criticism—of the postwar treatment of the Arab refugees—they blew it with wild Goebbels-Streicher stuff. God help us, and them, if they ever get hold of the Protocols of the Elders of Zion! But they probably won't—they're not strong on library work.

"S.N.C.C. HEAD ADVISES NEGROES IN WASHINGTON TO GET GUNS/Burning Capital Urged, If Needed/Brown Denounces Johnson and Racial Leaders Who Asked End to Violence." H. Rap Brown, that is. The story concludes: " 'How do you spell Rap?' a white reporter asked. 'Spell it R-A-P, honky,' was the answer." I just can't seem to work up much affection for Mr. Brown and Mr. Carmichael and Mr. Featherstone (of the *Newsletter*) and the rest of the Black Power boys, for some reason, maybe skin trouble—I'm definitely, hopelessly white. Or maybe it's something deeper. I couldn't even thrill to Mr. Carmichael's clarion call from Havana: "The United States is going to fall. I only hope to live to see the day." I'm not against the fall of empires, Roman or American or Russian or Chinese, but I'd like to know what comes after, and, as of now, I hope I don't live to see the fall of the United States if the Snick boys and their "colonial revolution" are what comes after.

The deterioration of Snick has been appallingly rapid even for these speedy times: racial hatred, a neurotic delight in violence, corny melodrama, ignorant fanaticism—how did all that dedication and idealism sour so rankly in two or three years? To think I gave them $25 once! This honky wants a refund, blackey.*

—*Esquire*, November, 1967

---

* (*1971*) I got it. Last spring I was lunching in the faculty club at U. Mass.–Amherst when two youngish blacks came over to our table—a Mr. Thelwell of the history department, and Julius Lester. Thelwell handed me his personal check for $25, said it was a refund from Snick and, refusing our invitation to sit down, left before I'd grasped the situation. Later I went over and thanked him for an amusing ploy, but he didn't smile—though Lester was amiable enough to ask me if I'd go on his TV talk show some time. I said yes—it's a good show. I thought of giving the check to the Angela Davis defense fund but decided this would be interpreted as white race guilt, so I gave it to the War Resisters League, which I preferred anyway.

Civil Disobedience:
Theory and Practice

---

(1) Theory

Civil disobedience means, to me, the deliberate, public, and non-violent breaking of a law because to obey it would be to betray a higher morality. Examples in our past were the widespread sabotage in the North of the Fugitive Slave Law before the Civil War and the celebrated refusal of Henry David Thoreau to pay his local taxes as a protest against the Mexican war. "What are you doing in there, Henry?" his neighbor and friend, Emerson, asked him through the bars of the Concord jail. "What are you doing out there, Waldo?" he replied. An apocryphal story, I'm told, but the essence of civil disobedience, tactically and morally, is there—as its theory is in Thoreau's essay on the subject.

I think civil disobedience is justified when one has come to believe that (1) in enforcing a specific law, the authorities are themselves violating the spirit of the lawful order in general; (2) protests within the limits of legality are no longer tactically effective, have become inadequate as a response to the situation, and (3) the actions of the government have become so obnoxious to one's own personal ethics that one would feel oneself a coward and a hypocrite in continuing to submit to a law which enforces these actions.

Some time last summer I concluded—as did others who, like myself, had not hitherto gone beyond the legal limits in opposing the Vietnam war—that all three conditions had been fulfilled.

(1) The war has become senseless and destructive to a point where a reasonable case can be made that the government waging it is violating the spirit—and also, indeed, the letter—of our Constitution. (2) When the President responded to the massive April peace marches by escalating the bombing of North Vietnam and setting an ominous precedent by recalling General Westmoreland from the field to justify the war, in full-dress uniform, before the Congress that had not been consulted about its escalation, then it became evident to me that two years of writing, speaking, and demonstrating against the war had not got through to our president, and that we objectors must do a little escalating ourselves. And (3) I, personally, couldn't go along with the horror any more, I had to put myself outside the limits of the legality that justified it.

Specifically, I have conspired with such coevals as Spock, Goodman, Lowell, Mailer, Chomsky, and Coffin to give aid and comfort, publicly, to the young men of draft age who are, also publicly, refusing to be conscripted for Mr. Johnson's war. (Our action is called "Resist," theirs "The Resistance.") This is a violation of the draft act and is punishable by the same penalties they are subjected to. It will, we hope, be awkward for the authorities if they punish them and spare us.

The limits of civil disobedience? By definition, they stop short of violence, since it is an illegal tactic within the framework of, if not legality, at least the *civis*, an attempt to demonstrate to our fellow citizens that our common interests demand such a repudiation of the letter in order to preserve the spirit. Nor is it posited, for me, on any affection for the other side: I don't consider Ho Chi Minh (or the late Che Guevara) my guy any more than Thoreau did Santa Anna in the Mexican war. I didn't like the two Vietcong flags carried by a small contingent of my fellow marchers on the Pentagon, and still less their (fortunately abortive) attempt to mix it up with the MPs there.

The march on the Pentagon was needed to dramatize our protest and—though one would hardly gather it from the press and TV coverage, including that of the *New York Times*, alas—it was a remarkably sober, prosaic, and peaceful assemblage. The hippies and kooks and violentists got the coverage, of course, for technical mass-media reasons as well as political ones, but what struck me was the nonviolent steadfastness of the great majority of the demonstrators. The violent minority believed, I assume, that our institutions are so corrupt that only revolutionary action on the barricades was adequate to deal with the problem. Leaving aside the fact that the American masses don't share this feeling—hence violence is a political error, a social *gaffe*, so to speak—I myself don't feel this alienation. I don't believe our traditions lead up, or down, to Lyndon B. Johnson. I think he is not representative of our country. And so I conclude that civil disobedience, as defined above, is the necessary next step of opposition to the Vietnam war, in the present historical context: neither too little nor too much.

—New York Times Magazine, November 26, 1967

(2) Practice

Author's Note: In his column of December 5, 1967, in the New York Post, *under the headline, "A Challenge," William F. Buckley, Jr., wrote:*

The morning's news brings yet another defi from the lawbreakers, couched this time in language most provocative. The idea is to "close down" an induction center in Manhattan by physically interfering with anyone who seeks to enter the building. It all began, as ever, with a press conference, Dr. Benjamin Spock, the baby doctor, and Mr. Dwight Macdonald, the critic, presiding.

These gentlemen, who even now will swoon with dismay at the mere recollection of Senator McCarthy's "methods," are in fact not particularly interested in testing the validity of certain Congressional statutes authorizing the draft and prohibiting seditious resistance to the draft. They are interested in any method of interfering with the prosecution of a particular war, the war in Vietnam.

Nevertheless, they find it rhetorically convenient to frame their case against these laws in generic language. . . . Accordingly, Dr. Spock talks as though the law against counseling young men to refuse to register were unconstitutional (that law was upheld unanimously in 1917 by the Supreme Court and, indirectly, as recently as in 1956). "The government," said Dr. Spock, "is not likely to prosecute us. Its bankruptcy in the moral sense is proved by its refusal to move against those of us who have placed ourselves between the young people and the draft."

A reporter fished around for the meaning of that statement and then asked the gentlemen whether they didn't in fact suspect that the Justice Dept. was avoiding prosecution because it feared to take steps that might be interpreted as suppressing dissent? "No," Mr. Macdonald answered unequivocally. "What we're doing is not just dissent, it's a deliberate violation of the law."

That would appear to remove such doubts as might have existed concerning defendants' knowledge as a mitigating factor. Mr. Macdonald is being as plain as any man can be. He appears to desire to break the law. And Dr. Spock, egging on the Justice Dept., dares it to defend such laws as, in their sovereign wisdom, he and Dwight Macdonald choose to break.

So I called the U.S. Attorney, Mr. Robert Morgenthau, and asked him. Has Washington instructed him not to prosecute?

No, he replied.

Well then, would you feel free to prosecute on your own initiative, or would you refer such a matter as this to Washington?

In such a case as this, with national implications, he would probably consult Washington.

Well, do you intend to prosecute, or to ask Washington whether to prosecute?

The U.S. Attorney's Office does not, as a matter of policy, hand out advisory judgments.

I reached a gentleman with full working knowledge of how these things go, and he advises me that the heroic lawbreakers are for the most part a foxy lot who are engaged in psychological rather than legal gambits. They call their press conferences and make their speeches. But they keep a subtle ace up their sleeve.

The draft card turns out not really to be a draft card, but a facsimile. Take them to the grand jury and all of a sudden, in the privacy of the chamber, they will plead the Fifth Amendment, and the government will not have a prosecutor's case. Most of the lawbreaking you read about in this field, my informant advised me, is mock-lawbreaking.

One wonders whether Dr. Spock and Mr. Macdonald are, on top of everything else, breaking the rules of lawbreaking. Surely it would be worthwhile finding out just who is funking what under laboratory conditions. I therefore cordially invite Mr. Dwight Macdonald to violate the law, at 3 p.m. on Thursday, the 4th of January, at my offices at 150 E. 35th St., New York 10016.

He is invited there and then, in the presence of witnesses and a television camera, to counsel young men to refuse to register and serve in the armed forces. Young men will be provided. A representative of the Justice Dept. will be invited upon receipt of a written acceptance to this invitation. We shall see who is lacking the moral courage Dr. Spock refers to.

Author's Note: At Mr. Buckley's invitation, I wrote a reply to the above "Challenge" which he printed, with extensive cuts (which I've restored, in brackets, below) in his column in the December 16, 1967 New York Post, prefacing it with "I have a reply from the aspirant lawbreaker, Mr. Dwight Macdonald, the literary critic" and following it with five inches of Buckleyesquerie (my letter was six inches, cut) which repeated, in a shriller key, his original unsound arguments and really don't seem worth reprinting here.

Mr. Buckley challenges me to put up or shut up about civil disobedience and lawbreaking. He proposes a *High Noon* shoot-out in the offices of his magazine on January fourth at exactly 3:00 P.M. (tick, tock, tick, tock) and he offers to provide young men for me to attempt to subvert into refusing conscription for the Vietnam war, in the presence of TV cameras, a representative of the Department of Justice and, of course, himself. I must regretfully decline the gambit, for several reasons. How does he get into the act, in the first place? Who appointed *him* sheriff? Assuming the government needs more evidence of my lawbreaking than I've given in writing and verbally (twice with TV cameras in action), why should I provide it in the offices of the *National Review* [a magazine for which, as Mr. Buckley knows, my admiration is not excessive]?*

* (1973) See my lengthy critique of the first eleven numbers of that magazine in the April, 1956, *Commentary* (reprinted in *Politics Past*, pp. 331–343). The issues I've caught, or been caught by, since then have not changed my

Martyrdom, if it comes to that, can be staged under more dignified conditions than a publicity stunt [for my friendly enemy, or inimical friend, Bill Buckley, and his mag, or rag].

But I deny his assumption that the Department of Justice needs any more evidence than Dr. Spock and myself have copiously, tediously provided, including what Mr. Buckley quotes from our remarks at the press conference that set him off. [He chides us, indeed, for issuing a brazen *"défi"* to The Law. He quotes my statement, "What we're doing is not just dissent, it's a deliberate violation of the law" and remarks: "Mr. Macdonald is being as plain as any man can be." But not plain enough for him, it seems, since a few inches further on, in one of those dizzying trapeze leaps of illogic that make his writing so charming, he finds we are "a foxy lot" with "a subtle ace up their sleeve," namely: "The draft card turns out not really to be a draft card, but a facsimile. Take them to the grand jury and all of a sudden, in the privacy of the chamber, they will plead the Fifth Amendment, and the Government will not have a prosecutor's case."]

[My draft card, and Dr. Spock's and those of our two thousand coevals who have by now signed a "Call to Resist Illegitimate Authority" which notifies the authorities that we are illegally conspiring to support and encourage young men to resist the draft—our cards are not even facsimiles. They are nonexistent. I burned mine, for instance, in 1948 during a demonstration against peacetime conscription.]

As for "taking the Fifth," we would be as illogical as Mr. Buckley if we did so since it would negate the two purposes we have in mind by taking a stand of civil disobedience: to make it awkward for the authorities to continue to prosecute young draft refusers without also prosecuting their elders who are breaking the

---

judgment ("amateur night," "even duller than the liberal weeklies," "neither good nor conservative," "the voice of the *lumpen-bourgeoisie*") though I must admit the *National Review* has survived for nearly twenty years. Or perhaps "therefore" would be a more accurate conjunction than "though." Norman Cousins' *Saturday Review* is going strong as ever (under a new alias) after twice that life-span. My laborious exposures of such midbrow journalistic enterprises always seem to boomerang, survival-wise. The kiss of life. Maybe I overestimate our reading public.

same law, and to bring about a demonstration trial, which the press would not ignore, in which the immorality, and the illegality, of the Vietnam war could be thoroughly, dramatically explored by the defense. I agree with Dr. Spock that the authorities have no ardent wish for such a trial. If they decide to risk it, there will be no need of *High Noon* melodramatics presided over by Sheriff Bill [to give them evidence for indictment. Nor will there have to be a rendezvous at the *National Review* if they want to arrest us. I'm in the Manhattan phone book and Dr. Spock can be found on the nearest picket line.]

Afterword

Three weeks after the above exchange, Johnson's Department of Justice—headed, alas, by Ramsey Clark—moved to indict in Boston Dr. Spock, the Reverend William Sloane Coffin, then (and now) chaplain of Yale, and three others for conspiracy to violate the draft act. Seven of us (including Paul Goodman, Dave McReynolds of the War Resisters League, Muriel Rukeyser, and me) staged in support of "the Boston Five" the sacrificial ritual for which Buckley had offered me his magazine's (bad) offices. We preferred the neutral turf of the Overseas Press Club. Two young men gave us their draft cards to mail to Attorney General Clark along with their written refusal "to serve in the U.S. armed forces at this time." Our covering letter stated that we supported and encouraged their illegal act.

The next morning (January 12, 1968) the *Times* ran a twelve-inch story: "GROUP BACKS TWO IN DRAFT PROTEST/Critic [me] and Author [Paul] Support Registration Card Return." When Dave asked me to "say a few words" at this meeting, I of course agreed but with a heavy heart. I'd said and written so many words on Vietnam for so long and nobody except us seemed to be listening and I was mentally bored and morally depressed by the subject. So I came and read a minimal statement: three short sentences. They seemed to go over better than my longer efforts—I'm no orator, maybe less is more with me—and the *Times* enshrined two of them as its Quotation of the Day: "I have reluctantly decided that civil disobedience is the only answer to the immorality of our times. This is the first time in my life that I have ever felt obliged to violate the law.*—Dwight Macdonald, the literary critic, supporting a draft protest." Great! But on second glance, it looked a little blurred: they'd left out the last sentence, "Nothing less seems adequate."—doubtless for space—and "the immorality of our times" sounded more like Max Lerner than me. I looked up my written text and found I'd said not "the immorality of our times" but "the illegality and immorality of our Government's action in Vietnam." So I wrote the *Times* noting that although their reporter's (one Douglas Robinson) rephrasing had "a fine gnomic ring and philosophical sweep," what I actually had said was "less cosmic but clearer." They didn't print the correction but I did get a specially typed letter from one George Palmer, "Assistant to the Managing Editor," explaining: "Our reporter, who we assure you had no intention of misquoting you, felt sure that he had quoted you correctly." So *that* was cleared up.

At the end of 1968 I got a note from Leonard Boudin, Dr. Spock's lawyer, enclosing a Xerox of pages 85–88 of the Government's brief. They made it more obscure than ever why the Boston Five was not the Boston Fifteen including me: "There was ample evidence that the individuals—not named as co-conspirators—whose statements were introduced over objection at the trial, were members of the same conspiracy of which appellants were found to be members. Throughout the late summer and fall of 1967, Dwight MacDonald, Ashley Montague, Arthur Waskow, Noam Chomsky, Robert Lowell and Paul Goodman became intimately involved in the effort to assist 'resistance' to the Vietnam war by draft-age young men. A tract entitled 'A Call to Resist Illegitimate Authority' was circulated within the professional community together with a letter signed by Spock, Coffin, MacDonald and Chomsky which urged others to join in their effort (19 App. 3336)." Some two thousand co-conspirators did sign, as I recall. Boston Fifteen, hell—Boston Fifteen Hundred! Modesty forbids me to quote the other three and a half pages or to

---

* (1973) Actually it wasn't. I forgot my arrest in 1942 for picketing the Soviet consulate after the GPU murder of Trotsky.

note that "MacDonald" pops up in them nearly as often as Dave McReynolds (a ringer, after all) including "a prominent role in the planning leading up to the Whitehall Street induction station sit-in" of which I was unaware; in fact, I got there late, couldn't find Dave or anybody in charge and was lost hopelessly in the crowd. I even failed to get arrested—as usual.

An Exchange
on the
Columbia Student
Strike of 1968

I

To the Editors:

This is a personal, and urgent, appeal for money. The SDS—Students for a Democratic Society—which played a major part in the recent and, in my opinion, beneficial disturbances on the campus of Columbia University, is about to be evicted from its New York headquarters. It needs $3,400 for the down payment on larger, cheaper offices in a friendly cooperative building. This will be a permanent solution for at least one of its problems. I hope you will contribute.

"In the last ten months," writes Anita Simpson of the SDS regional staff,

> the New York office has been evicted from three locations. The charges against us have always been vague—"bearded and unkempt people in the corridors," "other tenants request your relocation"—but the message is always emphatic: 30 days to get out, lease not withstanding. As long as our organization is kept in packing cases, it is dead. Our printing equipment is sitting idle, its installation frustrated. To end this nonsense, we would like to locate in a co-op building. We have an option

450

on a loft in such a building on Prince Street. Its cost is $3,400
down and a monthly charge of under $100. This is less than
half of our present rent. Please don't let the voice of SDS be
stifled . . . Hail Columbia!

It's always hard to write a "begging letter" and this one is
especially hard for me because, as a member of the Old Left, I've
long had, and still do, mixed feelings about the New Left, especially
about the SDS, or, as they disarmingly style themselves, the Students for a Democratic Society. Their political line—if one can use
so definite a term, an attractive aspect of the SDS being that its
organization is open, democratic, indeed anarchistically porous—
has often seemed to me alienated to the point of nihilism, while
their methods have sometimes been both deplorable, from a libertarian viewpoint, and, from that of making friends and influencing
people, counterproductive. The only justification for such ideology
and such tactics would be that there is a revolutionary situation in
this country, which there obviously is not, in general. But on two
particular, and major issues today, Vietnam and race-*cum*-poverty,
there is such a situation, I think. The follies and the injustices of
the Establishment, in these two cases, are so extreme and so indurated as to make necessary the use of extralegal pressures. Like, for
example, the occupation—or, more accurately, the "liberation," as
the phrase was—of certain buildings on the Columbia campus to
which the students had a moral right, from concrete use and interest, that they successfully asserted against the abstract ownership of
the trustees; for a while, anyway. The other condition, also met by
the Columbia sit-ins, for revolutionary, extralegal tactics is that there
will be a broad response to the minority action from the majority
directly involved—in this case the Columbia undergraduates—a general recognition that such actions, while unlawful and even, at first,
statistically undemocratic, are the only ones adequate to the historical situation: the kind of outrageous defiance of the Establishment
which can shove it off its dead-center stasis toward basic reform.
Like what the Sorbonne students are doing; they may not topple
de Gaulle, or they may, but the old place won't be the same again.
Nor will Columbia.

So, on balance, I'm for SDS and I think the Establishment

needs its shoving and I hope you'll help SDS to survive—and to keep shoving.

Dwight Macdonald

P.S. Please make checks payable to "Students for a Democratic Society" and send them to: Students for a Democratic Society, c/o Macdonald, 56 East 87th Street, New York, N.Y. 10028.

—*New York Review of Books*, June 20, 1968

II

An Open Letter to Dwight Macdonald

Dear Dwight,

Thank you for your letter asking me to contribute to the SDS. My instinctive sympathies tend to be on the side of protesters, demonstrators, and dissenters. They are the yeast of society. (For eight years I have been working for Amnesty International, and our group has secured the release of political prisoners in many parts of the world; this again would put me on the side of people, like the SDS students at Columbia, who are asking for amnesty.)

But I fear I can have little sympathy with the leaders of the recent demonstrations who, impatient with slower and more boring methods of (as you put it) "shoving society," decided to resort to violence. I could go on *ad nauseam* explaining the events of the past months at Columbia that have led me to this conclusion. But I think it is all epitomized in a recent news story that you must have read: during one of the "liberations" of Hamilton Hall the results of a decade of historical research (on the French Revolution, as it happens) by Professor Orest Ranum were deliberately destroyed by demonstrators who regarded him as antagonistic to their cause.

Please try to imagine what you would feel if one of your masterpieces, on which you had spent ten years of work, were to be destroyed by people because they happened to disagree with your political or other views. And let me add that it could easily happen. If you justify violence of this kind, there is no guarantee that it will be practiced exclusively by people on your side of the fence.

Intellectuals, especially those of the Left (Old and New), will be the natural underdogs in the United States if violence is ever allowed to take over. Surely they should be the last people to condone it now.

Ivan Morris
Columbia University

Dwight Macdonald replies:

I'm grateful to Ivan Morris for an opportunity to explain why I concluded, after visiting the campus to see for myself, that the Columbia students strike was a beneficial disturbance. My fund-raising letter for the New York chapter of SDS which stimulated his Open Letter to me was undertaken mostly because I admired the Columbia SDS for the spirit and the courage with which they gave the initial stimulus to the strike. (The amount needed has now been raised, I'm glad to report, and the new SDS headquarters are a reality.)

But first let me deal with Professor Morris's specific accusations —or, more accurately, assumptions. He accuses "the leaders of the demonstrations" of a "resort to violence," including arson, and me of justifying "violence of this kind." But so far as I saw in my five visits over six weeks to the campus, or read in the not overly sympathetic (to the strikers) *New York Times*, there was remarkably little violence: scuffles between "jocks" and strike sympathizers around Low Memorial (black eyes, bloody noses total damages, and the jocks weren't exactly pacifists), vulgar taunting of the police and some throwing of pop bottles at them when they invaded the campus those two frightening nights—I deplore the taunts and the missiles but much more so the invasion—and minimum resistance when the police cleared the occupied buildings, unless Professor Morris considers, as the cops do, that going limp and refusing to move when ordered by a policeman are categories of "violence." No, that commodity was monopolized by New York's Finest, as they used to be called, and they used it freely, sending a dean and a university chaplain to the hospital along with many students and some faculty members. Or perhaps by "violence," he means the immobilization of Dean Coleman in his office? I don't justify that—I'm even against restricting the freedom of movement of Dow recruiters, or, indeed, anybody, but it seems not a crucial charge: the dean could have freed himself by a phone call to the campus cops; that he didn't was a tactical decision: he and his three fellow immobilizees were not threatened, were well fed and treated by their own account, and they emerged from their ordeal unruffled, unstruck, and unindignant; anticlimax.

Or by "violence" does Professor Morris mean the occupation of the buildings (which I do justify)? If so, he confuses illegality with violence. I oppose the latter, on tactical as well as principled grounds, and I've criticized in my *Esquire* column the romantic exhortations of certain New Left and Black Power leaders for a scorched-earth violentist policy aimed at bringing on a "revolutionary" catastrophe. I can see a catastrophe resulting from such tactics, but it will be a counterrevolutionary one. In the last year, however, as a founder of Resist and a Vietnam tax refuser, I've lost some of my bourgeois inhibitions about illegality. In certain circumstances— as when an administration, of a nation or a university, chronically ignores lawful protests against its destructive policies—it seems to me more moral to break a law with Dr. Spock than to obey it with President Johnson, or President Kirk. (This is also, by the way, a bourgeois reaction.)

As for the burning of Professor Ranum's manuscript, must I explain to my old friendly acquaintance Ivan Morris that I think it base and disgusting, and that far from "justifying" it, I should have had had nothing to do with a group that used or tolerated such acts. But how does he link that act with my letter, which was written a week before it happened, or, more important, with the demonstrators he assumes were responsible for it? Is he not aware that the fire broke out after all the demonstrators had been removed by the cops from Hamilton Hall and were safely on their way to jail? I don't know who set it—hope he is arrested and given the maximum—or the four or five other small, so to speak symbolic, quickly extinguished fires that broke out in other buildings around the same time that night. Perhaps some nut fanatics among the students, perhaps ditto from outside the campus, perhaps police provocateurs. The *Times* reported at least one police spy—disguised as a hippy—who was up to no good on the campus. There is also testimony from eyewitnesses who saw the police, at the time of the first "bust," breaking up furniture and otherwise vandalizing the occupied buildings during or after the removal of the demonstrators —destructive acts which are often blamed on the students.

Whoever the arsonists, to assume, as Professor Morris does— also some others who have troubled to write me, usually *molto vivace* if not *agitando*, explaining just why they wouldn't be caught dead giving a nickel to SDS, really unusual to hear from people who *won't* contribute—as I was saying, whoever the arsonists, it seems to me absurd, logically, to assume they were encouraged by the strike leaders, SDS or others (for there were others, one shouldn't forget). To believe this one must also believe they lacked all tactical sense, indeed all common sense. For one would not have to be a genius of maneuver to foresee that arson—and arson escalated to such vindictive meanness as burning the papers of a faculty member who had prominently opposed the strike, thus adding an instant solution to one detective problem: motive—that this was admirably calculated to alienate all the sympathizers so hardly won and patiently wooed. Fortunately, not many of us jumped to the soggy conclusion Ivan Morris has bogged down in. In my case, leaving aside the fact that no evidence has yet been produced as to who did it,* I cannot believe that the student leaders who for six weeks out-maneuvered President Kirk—perhaps no great feat—and, more impressive, accumulated increasing support on the campus until the original "tiny minority" had won the sympathy of the majority of Columbia undergraduates for its six demands, I cannot believe that such leaders could have calculated that burning Professor Ranum's papers would help their cause. And if it is argued that the atmosphere of "violence" and illegality, no quotes, created by the strike leaders may have stimulated some of their less stable followers to set the fires, I would have to agree, adding that such are the risks of any rebellious effort to shatter an undesirable *status quo*, and the question is are the probable gains greater than the probable risks? (Note that I have refrained, with some difficulty, from saying you can't make omelettes without breaking eggs. To think I should come to this in my sunset years!)

---

* (1973) The crime is still unsolved.

I've written so much that I haven't space for much detail on my own reasons for backing the strike. When I first read about it in the press, I was against it on general principles: I don't approve of "direct action" that interferes with the freedom of others, nor could I see the justification for a minority occupying college buildings and closing down a great university—or even a small, mediocre university. That was in general. But, as has often happened in my life, the general yielded to the pressure of the particular. On Friday I went up to Columbia to see for myself. I was egged on by my wife, who was sympathetic to the strike, on *her* general principles, and stimulated by Fred Dupee who, when I phoned him to ask what in the world was going on, said: "You must come up right away, Dwight. It's a revolution! You may never get another chance to see one." I came up and he was right. I've never been in or even near a revolution before. I guess I like them. There was an atmosphere of exhilaration, excitement—pleasant, friendly, almost joyous excite- ment. Neither then nor on any of my four later trips to the campus did I have any sense of that violence that Ivan Morris sees as a leading characteristic of the six weeks. Everybody was talking to everybody those days, one sign of a revolution; Hyde Parks suddenly materialized and as abruptly dispersed, all over the place; even the jocks were arguing. It was as if a Victorian heavy father had been removed from his family's bosom (or neck)—later I got a load of President Kirk on TV and I realized my simile was accurate—and the children were exulting in their freedom to figure out things for themselves. A fervid rationality was the note, a spirit of daring and experiment, the kind of expansive mood of liberation from an op- pressive and, worse, boring tyranny that Stendhal describes in the Milanese populace after Napoleon's revolutionary army had driven out the Austrians. The SDS *putsch* became a revolution overnight: like the Milanese, the Columbians had realized with a start how dull and mediocre their existence had been under the Kirk administra- tion.

But what really changed my mind about the sit-ins was my own observation of two of the "communes," as the occupied buildings were ringingly called: Mathematics Hall, which I was let into— after a vote, everything was put to a vote in the communes—on Friday and Fayerweather Hall, into which I was allowed to climb—

all access was by window—on the Monday afternoon before the Tuesday morning police raid. Mathematics was the Smolny Institute of the revolution, the ultraleft SDS stronghold (said to have been liberated by a task force led by Tom Hayden in person) while Fayerweather was the Menshevik center—the "Fayerweather Formula" was an attempt on Monday to reach a compromise with the administration, but Dr. Kirk was as firmly opposed to it, doubtless on principle, as was Mark Rudd of the SDS. The two communes, nevertheless, seemed to me very much alike in their temper and their domestic arrangements. Rather to my surprise (as a reader of the *New York Times*), the atmosphere in both was calm, resolute, serious, and orderly; I saw no signs of vandalism, many efforts to keep the place clean and the communal life disciplined. I sat in on a meeting at Mathematics—the communes were forever having meetings, must have become as deadly as a nonstop political caucus, but at least it was, or seemed to be, participatory democracy—which discussed the tactics to be used if the jocks tried to put them out as against those suitable for resisting the police. Everybody had his say as far as I could tell—had same impression at the Hamilton Hall sit-in before the second police raid—and the conclusion arrived at was sensible: resist the jocks because their armament was muscular only, hence the fighting would be on equal terms; don't resist the police because they had superior force—clubs, guns, tear gas—and also were trained in violence (this proved a true prophecy). One communard added that fighting was not the only possible strategy with the jocks; they could also be talked to, perhaps even persuaded because, unlike the cops, "they're like us"; I thought this a shrewd point. In general, what struck me about the two communes I visited was the resourcefulness and energy with which the students were meeting problems they had never had to think about before, such as getting in and distributing food supplies, arranging for medical first aid, drawing up rules for living together in an isolated society (for, as it turned out, six days) with some decorum and harmony, electing leaders, working out a line in democratic discussion that had to keep changing to meet the latest development in the complicated interaction between the white communards, the blacks in Hamilton Hall, the sympathizers and the opponents of the strike on the campus, the administration, the trustees, and the various faculty groups, plus the "community" in Harlem and in the immediate neighborhood. My impression is that the communards met these problems rather well, showing that intellectuals can be practical when they have to be. Also that they got a lot of education, not paid for by their parents, out of those six days, and that so did the thousands of students who milled around on the campus arguing tirelessly the questions raised in the first place by the SDS zealots. I'm told that one of the jocks admitted, under pressure of debate, that while he still didn't think a Tiny Minority had any Right, etc., he had learned more in those six weeks than in four years of classes.

—*New York Review of Books*, July 11, 1968

III

To the Editors:

The nub of Dwight Macdonald's reply [*NYR*, July 11], if I follow the drift correctly, is that I confuse violence with illegality. With all respect I suggest that the confusion is in the mind of my eminent friend. Violence and illegality overlap, but are far from being identical. Violence, as we know all too well, can often be legal; and certainly illegal action takes many nonviolent forms. Mr. Macdonald grants that the act of holding Dean Coleman hostage was unjustified (though, somewhat cavalierly, he adds that since the dean could have freed himself by a simple telephone call, this is "not a crucial charge"); but the occupation of university buildings, though illegal, was not in his view an act of violence. Indeed the only people he believes committed real violence were the police who were summoned to remove the trespassers.

Surely the time has come to specify what violence means before we get hopelessly enmeshed in quibbles. I propose the following homemade definition: violence is the use of force on the body or mind or property of another person or group against the wishes of that person or group and to the detriment of that person's or group's well-being or rights or both. Thus, if I decided for the most sincere and idealistic of motives to break into Mr. Macdonald's apartment and to barricade the door so that he could not gain access, if I then rifled Mr. Macdonald's desk to discover what I regarded as incriminating papers and, if finally I threw open the window and used a megaphone to broadcast my loathing of Mr. Macdonald's views to all passersby, I should be committing acts of violence just as much as if I tweaked Mr. Macdonald's beard or struck him with my umbrella or bombarded him with spitballs; and, however noble my aims might be, he would have every right to ask the police to remove me by force. The same would apply, *mutatis mutandi*, if I organized an occupation of the new SDS headquarters that he has helped to finance. And the same applies to the students who forcibly occupied the Columbia buildings and disrupted the work of our university.

Can such violence ever be justified? Mr. Macdonald declares that he is opposed to violence on principle but that he has lost some of his "bourgeois inhibitions about illegality." Here I would actually go further than him and suggest that in certain conditions even violence, repugnant as it must invariably be, is justifiable. If a person or group lives in a society where his or other people's fundamental rights are intolerably curtailed for a protracted period of time and in which the infliction of such violence is the only remaining method that may effectively remedy the situation, then the infliction of the least necessary amount of violence is, in my view, warranted. But the insurgent students at Columbia, "dull and mediocre" as Mr. Macdonald believes their existence to have been until this spring, were definitely not justified in using violence according to this or any other reasonable criterion.

Finally I must return to the destruction of Professor Ranum's manuscripts, a violent act that I take to be of particular symbolic importance. Mr. Macdonald says that "not many of us jumped to the soggy conclusion" that the students were responsible. I have no idea who "us" may be; but I do know that I was constantly at Columbia during the disturbances and that I never met one person, even among those most sympathetic to the demonstrators, who doubted that it was their doing. According to Mr. Macdonald, the student leaders had too much common sense to commit such an act, and he suggests that the culprits may have been "police provocateurs." If he actually believes that, he can believe anything.

Whoever may have been responsible for the destruction, Mr. Macdonald evidently regards it as "one of the risks of any rebellious effort to shatter an undesirable *status quo*" or, to revert to the cozy old image, one of the eggs that must be broken to make an omelette. I take it that the right to make omelettes in this fashion is restricted to people whose objectives Mr. Macdonald happens to support.

Ivan Morris
Department of East Asian Languages and Cultures
Columbia University, New York City

Dwight Macdonald replies:

Ivan Morris now proposes a "homemade definition" of "violence" that fits his argument like a glove. But if controversialists bully words in this Humpty-Dumpty style, discussions won't get far. "The question is who is to be master," Mr. Dumpty explained to Alice, adding that he paid extra when he made his words work hard, as when "glory" had to mean "a nice knockdown argument." I'd rather not think how much overtime Professor Morris had to pay "violence." So let's try a real, manufactured definition, one in a dictionary. The two on my desk give: "Proceeding from or marked by great physical force or roughness; overwhelmingly forceful" (Funk & Wagnalls) and "Acting with or characterized by uncontrolled, strong, rough force" (Random House). I think my eminent friend would have to agree that these don't describe the tactics of the student strikers and do describe those of the police when they were called onto the campus, twice, by Dr. Kirk and Dean Truman to help them run their university.

The analogy between the taking over of President Kirk's office and a hypothetical occupation by Professor Morris of my apartment fudges over the difference between the personal and the professional spheres—making distinctions isn't his forte. It takes a heap o' living to make an office a home, and although from Dr. Kirk's laments about the brutalization of his office—he was so shook up that he forgot to express similar regrets about the brutalization of his students by the cops he called in—one realized that to an inured bureaucrat his office *is* his home, still, in the real, or nonbureaucratic, world, the students took over an office, a more legitimate object of occupation because of its public, professional function. If my friend and his cronies hijacked my office, I'd temporize, partly because I'd be curious to see what their "rifling" of my disordered correspondence files turned up and partly because I would recognize an obligation to negotiate, really negotiate, not just in form.

On the burning of Dr. Ranum's research papers: I gave three possibilities: "perhaps some nut fanatics from among the students, perhaps ditto from outside the campus, perhaps police provocateurs." I did judge it unlikely—giving reasons—that the strike leaders had anything to do with this disgusting, and counterproductive, act of petty revenge. Now Professor Morris omits the first two categories and implies the cops were my chief suspects, adding he's never met anyone "even among those most sympathetic to the demonstrators, who doubted it was their doing." But *whose* doing? The responsive leaders, or some irresponsible followers? It makes quite a difference— as noted, distinctions aren't his strongest point—and until our police, who seem better at cracking skulls than at sleuthing, on the Columbia campus at least, solve the crime, he knows just what to do about it, which is nothing.

And why does my friend assume he's won the argument when he triumphantly concludes: "I take it that the right to make omelettes in this particular fashion is restricted to people whose objectives Mr. Macdonald happens to support."? Oh dear, more distinctions. As a supporter, and former board member, of the New York Civil Liberties Union, let me state the obvious: (1) There is no general moral "right" to break the law as the student strikers did when they occupied the buildings (or as the 1936 sit-down strikers did when they occupied the Detroit automobile plants). (2) Whether one supports such actions or not depends on (a) whether one agrees with the aims of the law-breakers; (b) whether one thinks the actions, the means are congruent with the ends and so won't corrupt or subvert them, and (c) whether one believes that lawful means have been tried and have failed. I've recently conspired with Dr. Spock, Chaplain Coffin, and many others I know as well as I do them, which is hardly at all, to give support and encouragement to young men who violate the Selective Service Act; I'm also refusing to pay 25 percent of my federal income tax; both illegal actions that seem to me—as those of the Columbia strikers did—to satisfy requirements (a), (b), and (c) given above. (3) Therefore, if the jocks or the Birchers take over Hamilton Hall and refuse to leave until the trustees agree to begin building again that unfortunate gym in Morningside Park (this time on a lily-white basis, no place for the black community at all, top or bottom, segregated or not), when they appeal to me for support, enclosing a marked copy of my friend's letter, I'll have to say sorry, all a misunderstanding, you're on your own, baby, as far as I'm concerned.

Finally, Professor Morris's letters do raise, in however muzzy a form, a serious problem. I tried to meet it in some of my remarks at a para-Commencement mounted by the strikers on the campus last spring while the official one was going on at the Cathedral of St. John the Divine:*

> While I find your strike and your sit-ins productive, I don't think these tactics can be used indefinitely without doing more damage than good to the university. It would be a pity if Columbia became another Latin American type of university in which education is impossible because student strikes and political disruptions have become chronic. Nor do I think that our universities should be degraded to service as entering wedges to pry open our society for the benefit of social revolution. I'm for such a revolution but I don't think it is a historical possibility in the foreseeable future in this country, and premature efforts to force it will merely damage or destroy such positive, progressive institutions as we have. Their only effect—if any— will be to stimulate a counterrevolution which will have far more chances of success.
>
> An example of this kind of tactics—one can hardly call it thinking—is a recent manifesto by Tom Hayden in the June 15 issue of *Ramparts*.† "The goal written on the university walls," he begins, "was, 'Create two, three, many Columbias' [a reference to the late Che Guevara's "Create two, three, many Vietnams in Latin America"—one is enough for me, and also Che's effort didn't turn out a very solid enterprise, speaking in terms of history, not rhetoric]. It meant expand the strike so that the US must change or send its troops to occupy American campuses. . . . Not only are these [Columbia] tactics already

---

* (1973) For details see the *New York Times*, June 4, 1968, pages 1 and 32.

† (1973) At this point, some of the audience—including Mr. Hayden who was in the foreground, next to my wife—began hissing and groaning in a polite way.

being duplicated on other campuses, but they are sure to be surpassed by even more militant tactics. In the future it is conceivable that students will threaten destruction of buildings as a last deterrent to police attack. Many of the tactics learned can also be applied in smaller hit-and-run operations between strikes: raids on the offices of professors doing weapons research could win substantial support among students while making the university more blatantly repressive. . . . The Columbia students . . . did not even want to be included in the decision-making circles of the military-industrial complex that runs Columbia. . . . They want a new and independent university standing against the mainstream of American society, or they want no university at all. They are, in Fidel Castro's words, 'guerrillas in the field of culture.' ' "

This program might be called "Building Socialism in One University" and it would have the same effects on the campus as Stalin's "Building Socialism in One Country" did on the Soviet Union; as in that case, the means would vitiate the ends and the result of Hayden's "hit-and-run operations," raids on professors' offices and chronic guerrilla warfare would be not socialism, and certainly not culture, but a Hobbesian chaos of mindlessly reflexive "confrontations"—how he gloats over provoking the academic authorities into becoming "more blatantly repressive"!—about which a safe prediction is that it would undoubtedly be nasty, brutish—and short. An even safer prediction is that the campuses won't be Haydenized. A lot of capital has gone into our universities, and the bourgeois trustees and state legislators who control them are not about to turn over these plants to Mr. Hayden's, and my, revolution. He talks grandly of "the students" throughout his article, but this is as undiscriminating as Professor Morris's references to "the demonstrators." A majority of Columbia students responded to the SDS initiative because the demands were limited and reasonable—a brighter administration would have granted them before things got ugly, and "the military-industrial complex" wouldn't have been even dented—but, in a recent (June 6) poll by Columbia's Bureau of Applied Social Research (C. Wright Mills was its cofounder) only 19 percent of the student respondents favored (as Mr. Hayden and I did) the tactics of the demonstrators, while 68 percent were against them. The actual occupation of the buildings was carried out by a large group—about seven hundred, many of them Barnard girls—but it was still very much a minority, and even among these activists there was dissent from some of the more "militant" and uncompromising tactics of the SDS leadership, as in the big Fayerweather Hall "commune."

The para-Commencement at which I spoke, for example, was organized not by the SDS but by the Students for a Restructured University, who had split from the SDS-dominated strike committee because they had the same objections to Building Socialism in One University that I expressed above. (The SDS was dubious up to the last day, worried lest even a mock imitation of the real thing was not too great a concession to bourgeoisdom, since parody implies some parallelism.) The other speakers were two university chaplains, Jewish and Protestant, Dr. Ehrlich of the Economics Department, Harold Taylor, and Erich Fromm, and it was a beautiful occasion, spirited and friendly and dignified, with an audience of some four thousand, including three hundred members of the graduating class in their caps and gowns.

When Columbia reopens this fall, I hope there will be no more *High Noon* showdowns between the Kirk administration and the SDS revolutionaries, and that both will compromise their principles for the sake of Columbia—and of sanity. The SRU has received a grant of $10,000 from the Ford Foundation to study and formulate proposals for reform, and something may come of this.* Before Ivan Morris writes a third letter asking why I raised funds for the SDS instead of the SRU, let me explain that the former asked me and the latter didn't, perhaps because it wasn't in existence at the time; also that SDS is broader, and looser, than its Haydenesque and Ruddite infantile ultraleftists (and I even like *their* spirit); and finally that the strike was needed and that the SDS lit the fuse. "If we succeed in reforming Columbia," John Thoms of the SRU is quoted

---

* (1973) Nothing much did, aside from reports, surveys, resolutions, etc. Asked by a campus little Peterkin today, "But what good came of it at last?" I'd have to reply with old Kaspar: " 'Why that I cannot tell,' " said he./"But 'twas a famous victory.' " What we used to call in college sports during the twenties, "a psychological victory."

in the June 10 *Times*, "it will be because of the radicals." I agree with him.

The threat to Columbia this fall will come not from the SDS but from the petty, vindictive and inept policies of the Kirk-Truman administration. By refusing to drop criminal trespass charges against hundreds of demonstrators and by supplementing them with suspensions, President Kirk and the trustees are sailing their ship into the minefield that blew it up last spring, setting the stage for a second round of student protest, police violence, and general uproar (this time, it won't be so creative, I think, and much more unpleasant). If Columbia is ever Guevaraized, the credit will go to Dr. Kirk more than to Tom Hayden. The new undergraduate dean, Carl Hovde, wants the criminal charges dropped but is against academic amnesty for the strikers. Most of the faculty (78 percent) and even the students (70 percent) agree with him. The usual argument is that if you violate the rules, or the law, as a demonstration of principle, it is not logical to ask to be let off paying the penalty. Maybe not logical but standard procedure in the other kind of strike: the first union demand is always that strikers shall be rehired without discrimination and that illegal acts of pickets shall not be prosecuted by the company. The 1936 Detroit sit-in strikers occupied far more valuable properties than five college buildings and for a much longer time, causing losses of hundreds of millions to the automobile companies, but the settlement of the strike provided no punishment for them. Of course, they won. And the demonstrators so far have not won. But let's be clear: the denial of amnesty is for that reason, not because of any moralistic nonsense about paying the price, etc. The Columbia bureaucrats think they can operate without settling the strike, i.e., granting amnesty. I don't. We'll soon see which view is right.

—*New York Review of Books*, August 22, 1968

Afterword

We didn't see, soon or later. The Columbia University bureaucrats didn't press charges, on the one hand, and they admitted students and faculty to some degree of formal participation in running the university. On the other, when the SDS tried to hot up confrontational tactics that fall, they got scant response from the students, who apparently concluded—in my view correctly—that the strike demands had been won and that they wanted to get on with an education rather than with a Haydenesque scorched-earth policy: One Columbia had been enough for them. Later, there were efforts by Guevara-type ultras at first Harvard, then Cornell, and finally Buffalo to create Two, Three, Four Columbias—with escalating violence and diminishing rationality—but they didn't "take" either. They were minority *putsches* rather than majority revolutions—also, unlike the October, 1917, Bolshevik *putsch*, they didn't work. The campuses have gone from rebellion to lethargy in the short timespan that seems our youths' norm: as a visiting professor of English at SUNY—Buffalo in 1973, I find it hard to realize it was barely two years since the "time of the troubles," so thickly has the healing grass grown over that battle-scarred campus. Too thickly indeed—my impression is that political extremism has been replaced by its religious opposite number, equally nutty but at least nonviolent. "Hare Krishna!" I find more agreeable as a slogan than "Burn It Down!" or "Off the Pigs!" But I agree with the complaint of Professor George Wald of MIT, after a campus appearance last spring, that our students are now much too politically apathetic for his—and my—taste.